RESEARCH IN PERSONNEL AND HUMAN RESOURCES MANAGEMENT

RESEARCH IN PERSONNEL AND HUMAN RESOURCES MANAGEMENT

Series Editors: M. Ronald Buckley, Jonathon R. B. Halbesleben, and Anthony R. Wheeler

Recent Volumes:

RESEARCH IN PERSONNEL AND HUMAN RESOURCES
MANAGEMENT   VOLUME 34

RESEARCH IN PERSONNEL AND HUMAN RESOURCES MANAGEMENT

EDITED BY

M. RONALD BUCKLEY
University of Oklahoma, Norman, OK, USA

JONATHON R. B. HALBESLEBEN
The University of Alabama, Tuscaloosa, AL, USA

ANTHONY R. WHEELER
Bryant University, Smithfield, RI, USA

Emerald

United Kingdom − North America − Japan
India − Malaysia − China

Emerald Group Publishing Limited
Howard House, Wagon Lane, Bingley BD16 1WA, UK

First edition 2016

Copyright © 2016 Emerald Group Publishing Limited

Reprints and permissions service
Contact: permissions@emeraldinsight.com

British Library Cataloguing in Publication Data
A catalogue record for this book is available from the British Library

ISBN: 978-1-78635-264-4
ISSN: 0742-7301 (Series)

Printed and bound by CPI Group (UK) Ltd, Croydon, CR0 4YY

ISOQAR certified
Management System,
awarded to Emerald
for adherence to
Environmental
standard
ISO 14001:2004.

Certificate Number 1985
ISO 14001

INVESTOR IN PEOPLE

CONTENTS

LIST OF CONTRIBUTORS

P. Matthijs Bal	School of Management, University of Bath, Bath, UK
Ho Kwan Cheung	Department of Psychology, George Mason University, Fairfax, VA, USA
Gerald R. Ferris	Department of Management, Florida State University, Tallahassee, FL, USA
Paul G. W. Jansen	Department of Management & Organization, VU University Amsterdam, Amsterdam, the Netherlands
Molly Kilcullen	Department of Psychology, George Mason University, Fairfax, VA, USA
Eden King	Department of Psychology, George Mason University, Fairfax, VA, USA
Donald H. Kluemper	Department of Managerial Studies, University of Illinois at Chicago, Chicago, IL, USA
Alex Lindsey	Department of Psychology, George Mason University, Fairfax, VA, USA
Graham H. Lowman	Department of Management, Culverhouse College of Commerce, University of Alabama, Tuscaloosa, AL, USA
Louis D. Marino	Department of Management, Culverhouse College of Commerce, University of Alabama, Tuscaloosa, AL, USA
Hannah M. Markell	Department of Psychology, George Mason University, Fairfax, VA, USA

Charn P. McAllister   Department of Management, Florida State
                          University, Tallahassee, FL, USA

Ashley Membere   Department of Psychology, George Mason
                          University, Fairfax, VA, USA

Arjun Mitra   Department of Managerial Studies,
                          University of Illinois at Chicago, Chicago,
                          IL, USA

Eddy S. Ng   Rowe School of Business, Dalhousie
                          University, Halifax, NS, Canada

Emma Parry   Cranfield School of Management,
                          Cranfield, Bedfordshire, UK

Reginald L. Tucker   Department of Management, Culverhouse
                          College of Commerce, University of
                          Alabama, Tuscaloosa, AL, USA

Siting Wang   Department of Managerial Studies,
                          University of Illinois at Chicago, Chicago,
                          IL, USA

MULTIGENERATIONAL RESEARCH IN HUMAN RESOURCE MANAGEMENT

Eddy S. Ng and Emma Parry

ABSTRACT

Interest in generational research has garnered a lot of attention, as the workplace is seeing multiple generations (i.e., the Silent Generation, Baby Boomers, Gen Xers, and Millennials) working side-by-side for the first time. However, it is unclear how multiple generations of workers interact with each other and affect the workplace. Although there is extant litera-ture on generational differences, some scholars have argued that the effect sizes are small and the differences are not meaningful. The focal aim of this chapter is to present the current state of literature on generational research. We present the relevant conceptualizations and theoretical frameworks that establish generational research. We then review evidence from existing research studies to establish the areas of differences that may exist among the different generations. In our review, we identify the issues arising from generational differences that are relevant to human resource management (HRM) practices, including new workforce entrants, aging workers, the changing nature of work and organizations, and leadership development. We conclude with several directions for future research on modernizing workplace policies and practices, ensuring sustainability in current

Research in Personnel and Human Resources Management, Volume 34, 1–41
ISSN: 0742-7301/doi:10.1108/S0742-730120160000034008

employment models, facilitating future empirical research, and integrating the effects of globalization in generational research.

Keywords: generational differences; human resource management; recruitment and retention; work/life balance; leadership; changing nature of work and organizations

INTRODUCTION

Interest in generational research has garnered a lot of attention, as the workplace is seeing multiple generations working side-by-side for the first time (Dries, Pepermans, & De Kerpel, 2008; Lieber, 2010; Lyons, Schweitzer, & Ng, 2015). However, much of the attention has been cast on the Millennials (those born after 1980), as they represent the largest and most recent entrants into the labor market (cf. Ng & McGinnis Johnson, 2015). Millennials now make up over 53 million or a third of the U.S. workforce, surpassing Gen Xers and Baby Boomers, as the latter begin to exit the labor market in large numbers (Fry, 2015). This demographic shift is also evident in other parts of the world. For example, the Millennial generation also makes up 27 percent of the population in Canada and Europe (Statistics Canada, 2011; Stokes, 2015), 31 percent in China (Duggan, 2015), and 30 percent in India (Nielsen, 2014).

As the Millennials, who are children of Baby Boomers, enter adulthood and the workplace, the focus — particularly in popular media — has been on the stereotypes that persist among the Millennial generation. The literature has been quick to report that Millennials have been raised with unprecedented levels of self-esteem, entitlement, and narcissism (Stein, 2013), leading commentators to caution that the Millennial generation will present challenges to organizations and employers (Culpin, Millar, & Peters, 2015; Thompson & Gregory, 2012; Twenge & Campbell, 2008). Indeed, research studies have shown that Millennials have high expectations of themselves, their careers, and prospective employers (Hill, 2002; Ng, Schweitzer, & Lyons, 2010; Westerman, Bergman, Bergman, & Daly, 2011) raising concerns over how best to attract and retain the Millennial generation. However, it is unclear if the Millennials are indeed different from previous generations, and if so, how are they different, and what are the issues that arise out of generational differences in the workplace? The purpose of the chapter is to review the current state of literature on generational research and to identify potential human resource management (HRM) issues that will impact workplace and organizational performance.

It is important to understand how multiple generations at work affect the workplace because:

1. Existing HRM policies are created by the Baby Boomers for themselves, and many existing practices may not reflect contemporary organizations (Burke & Ng, 2006). As a result, a comparison of generational differences in terms of work values, attitudes, and career expectations would be helpful in informing current HRM policies and practices to benefit future generations of workers (Crumpacker & Crumpacker, 2007; Culpin et al., 2015). Furthermore, a shortage of skilled workers will require employers to find the right combination of tools to attract young workers and retain older workers at the same time.

2. Given the purported differences in work values and career priorities among the different generations (Dencker, Joshi, & Martocchio, 2007; Rudolph & Zacher, 2015), intergenerational conflict can arise and disrupt individual, team, and organizational performance (Lancaster & Stillman, 2009; Pritchard & Whiting, 2014). In this regard, it is important to manage these differences to ensure that intergenerational conflicts are minimized and the different generations can work well together. Furthermore, different generations of workers working side-by-side each other may require different management and leadership styles (Ahn & Ettner, 2014; Gentry, Griggs, Deal, Mondore, & Cox, 2011).

3. As the Baby Boomers exit the workforce in large numbers, it is also critical for organizations to ensure successful knowledge transfer from the older generation to the younger generation (Bennett, Pitt, & Price, 2012; Burke & Ng, 2006). Younger workers lack experience and institutional memory could be lost when older workers retire. Compounding this problem, generational biases toward each other may impede the transfer of knowledge (Arnold & Yue, 2012; Liebowitz, Ayyavoo, Nguyen, Carran, & Simien, 2007), although there has been a suggestion that Gen Xers may be the bridge between Baby Boomers and Millennials in facilitating knowledge transfer (McNichols, 2010). At the same time, older workers can also learn from younger workers to help them acquire new skills, as younger workers are much more knowledgeable about and comfortable with using new technology and social media (Murphy, 2012; Ng & Law, 2014; Piktialis & Greenes, 2008).

Although there is extant literature on generational differences (Campbell, Campbell, Siedor, & Twenge, 2015; Cogin, 2012; Hansen & Leuty, 2012; Lester, Standifer, Schultz, & Windsor, 2012; Lyons, Ng, Schweitzer, & Kuron, 2012; Twenge & Campbell, 2008, 2012), some scholars argue that the effect sizes are small and the differences are not meaningful (Becton, Walker, & Jones-Farmer, 2014; Benson & Brown, 2011; Costanza, Badger, Fraser, Severt, & Gade, 2012; Costanza & Finkelstein, 2015; Kowske, Rasch, & Wiley, 2010; Mencl & Lester, 2014; Wong, Gardiner, Lang, & Coulon, 2008). This chapter will review evidence from existing research studies to establish the areas of differences that may exist among the different generations. First, we present the relevant conceptualizations and theoretical frameworks that establish generational research. We then review existing research studies and document differences that exist among the different generations, with a particular emphasis on the Millennial generation. Following this, we identify the pressing issues arising from generational differences that are relevant to HRM practice. Finally, we conclude with directions for future research. Before proceeding, we first provide an overview of the generations that currently exist in the workforce.

GENERATIONS IN THE WORKPLACE

The literature generally refers to the four generations as the "Silent Generation," "Baby Boomers," "Generation X" ("Gen Xers"), and "Generation Y" ("Millennials") (Howe & Strauss, 2009; Hansen & Leuty, 2012; Mencl & Lester, 2014). The Silent Generation (also referred to as the "Matures" or "Traditionalists" in some literature) are those born prior to 1946 or the end of the second world war; Baby Boomers are those born between 1946 and 1960 as children of post-war survivors; Gen Xers are those born between 1960 and 1980; and Millennials are born between 1980 and 1995 as children of Baby Boomers (Foot & Stoffman, 1998; also see Reeves & Oh, 2008). In reality, the workplace is composed primarily of Baby Boomers, Gen Xers, and Millennials as most members of the Silent Generation are aged 70 or older at time of writing, and most would have retired from the workforce. At the same time, children of Gen Xers (those born after 1995, and tentatively labeled "Generation Z" or "Gen Z") (Reeves & Oh, 2008; also see Gibson, 2015) are still pursuing their education, and their representation in the workforce is relatively small. We note that the exact boundaries (i.e., years) demarcating a generation are less important than shared historical events and experiences arising from social changes (cf. Lyons & Kuron, 2014; Parry & Urwin, 2011).

THEORIES OF GENERATION

A useful definition of generations is provided by Becker (1992, p. 23) as "a clustering of birth cohorts that are marked by a specific historic location, common traits at an individual level (life courses, value orientations, and behavioral patterns) and at a system level (size and composition, generational culture and generational organizations)." This definition builds on the work of Mannheim (1952) who is commonly seen as the source of generational theory. Mannheim described generation as a "social location" similar to that of social class, in that it does not involve physical location or proximity. Mannheim explained that the creation of generational groups is a result of the emergence of new participants and disappearance of former participants in the cultural process, so that members of a generation are limited in their participation in the historical process leading to a continuous transition between generations. Individuals who share a common year of birth have a common location in the historical process, and consequently, they are limited to a particular range of experience thus predisposing them to a certain mode of thought and experience. However, sharing a common birth year is not sufficient for individuals to also share a generation. As well as "generational position" (period an individual was born and raised), Mannheim (1952) identified two other aspects that are important for the formation of generations: "generational context" or the connections among individuals created by the shared experiencing of a common destiny and major societal events and "generational unit," the organizations or informal cooperations that crystallize and reflect the style of the generation involved. For example, the Millennial generation grew up in a time of 33 expanding possibilities offered by the Internet and social media, which has had a profound impact on this generation in relation to communication 35 and connecting with others, and perceptions of power and hierarchy in organizations (Eisner, 2005). This means that members of a generation must also be in the position to share common experiences in order to develop a concrete bond between them so that they share not only a common historical location but also a "distinct consciousness of that historical position ... shaped by the events and experiences of that time" (Gilleard, 2004, p. 108).

This stipulation has been operationalized in later research as collective memories (Halbwachs, 1980). Generational theory suggests that events and changes experienced during one's adolescence or youth are particularly memorable, and are thus retained by individuals and become imprinted on a generation to affect their values, attitudes, and preferences (Schuman & Scott, 1989). However, the literature on collective memories also emphasizes the fact that people obtain and recall their memories in a social and cultural setting, meaning collective memories will also be shaped by conversations and the media so that not everyone's memories of a particular event are the same (Kligler-Vilenchik, Tsfati, & Meyers, 2014). Despite this, research has provided significant evidence that critical events are remembered by those who experienced them during adolescence and youth (see, e.g., Schuman & Corning, 2012). Generational theory builds on this evidence to suggest that an age cohort who experienced, and thus remembers similar events in a similar way will develop similar values, attitudes and expectations as a result of this.

More recently, theorists have suggested that the focus on historical events in Mannheim's work is too narrow and suggested that individual values are also affected by the availability of resources and cultural elements such as the music and fashion that they experience during this formative period. For example, Eyerman and Turner (1998) suggested that a generational cohort maintains its cultural identity by excluding others access to shared resources and develops its values via the development of a collective memory of its struggle for resources. In addition, building on Pierre Boudieu, Turner and colleagues defined a generation as "a cohort of persons passing through time who come to share a common habitus and lifestyle" (Turner, 1998, p. 302); the idea being that members of a generation develop a shared cultural field and a set of embodied practices (including aspects such as sports and music preferences) (Eyerman & Turner, 1998). Drawing on the idea of collective memories, scholars have suggested that individuals are socialized in relation to aspects such as music, clothes, and film stars (Holdbrook & Schindler, 1989, 1994), and therefore share cultural symbols such as music, fashion, and technology (Bryant, 2005; McMullin, Comeau, & Jovic, 2007).

Generation as an Identity

The conceptualization of a generation as a collective identity has received a lot of attention in recent years (see Joshi, Dencker, Franz, & Martocchio,

2010, e.g., Roberto & Biggan, 2014; Urick & Hollensbe, 2014). Joshi et al. (2010, p. 393) integrated ideas of identity and social identity with generational theory in order to define "generational identity" as "an individual's knowledge that he or she belongs to a generational group/role, together with some emotional and value significance to him or her of this group/role membership." This approach therefore relies on self-definition of membership (Urick & Hollensbe, 2014). This conceptualization also draws on self-categorization theory (Ashforth, Harrison, & Corley, 2008) and social identity theory (Tajfel, 1978). Urick and Hollensbe (2014) explained that generational identities can be based on the fact that membership of a certain generation is consistent with their views of who they are (age-based generation identity); relationships with those who preceded or succeeded them in a particular role (genealogy-based generation identity), or a set of shared organizational experiences and outcomes (life-stage-based generation identity). This approach to conceptualizing generations is a departure away from the idea of generational diversity being based purely on year of birth and expands the concept of "social space" (Mannheim, 1952).

Critique of the Generational Literature

Despite the popularity of the notion of generational differences, several authors have expressed their concerns about the quality of the evidence on which this idea is based (see, e.g., Costanza & Finklestein, 2015; Giancola, 2006; Parry & Urwin, 2011). Despite these analyses, the evidence base remains questionable and wrought with a number of problems. First, most research about generational differences relies on cross-sectional studies which are problematic in their failure to distinguish between cohort (generational), age (maturation), and period (the time in which the research was conducted) effects (Parry & Urwin, 2011; Rhodes, 1983). Rhodes explained that if differences in work-related attitudes were age effects, then we would expect younger adults to become more like older adults as they age. If, however, differences were due to cohort effects, we would expect these attitudes and the differences between age cohorts to remain relatively stable. Cross-sectional designs can identify differences between age groups, but cannot establish whether these are due to age or cohort effects, and might actually ignore the true effects of age (Rudolph, 2015). What this means is that, despite the significant amount of work done to identify the characteristics of generational groups, not only are these findings mixed (Parry & Urwin, 2011), but we cannot be sure that any differences can actually be ascribed to generational effects. Some recent studies have used longitudinal research in order to overcome these problems (Smola & Sutton, 2002; Twenge, Campbell, Hoffman, & Lance, 2010; Urwin, Buscha, & Parry, 2014), but the fact remains that most work in this area is still based on cross-sectional research designs. Some researchers have used cross-temporal meta-analyses (CTMA) which relied on time-lagged data to help untangle the age and period effects to ascertain true changes that occur within a generation (Gentile, Twenge, & Campbell, 2010; Twenge, 2013; Twenge & Campbell, 2001; Twenge, Konrath, Foster, Campbell, & Bushman, 2008). Suffice to say, more research using longitudinal designs that can truly distinguish between age, generation, and period effects is therefore needed.

Second, the approach to identifying generations commonly adopted in practice, and also by many scholars in their research does not allow for a true definition of a generation, as conceptualized by Mannheim (1952), but only provides a description of different age cohorts. As discussed above, a true definition of a generation should consider characteristics of "social space" other than birth year, such as geographical location or gender (Parry, 2014). Indeed, previous studies have found heterogeneity within generational groups based on factors such as gender or race (Eskilson & Wiley, 1999; Parker & Chusmir, 1990). More research that looks at heterogeneity within generations is therefore needed. In addition, research that starts from the point of clustering generations and then looks at the demographic factors that might drive these clusters (rather than starting with the demographic characteristics of birth year) would also be an important step forward in this field (Urwin et al., 2014).

Third, a number of scholars have suggested that the four generations described above are not valid outside of the western world (e.g., see Hui-Chun & Miller, 2003, 2005; Parry, Unite, Chudzikowski, Briscoe, & Shen, 2014). Indeed, most of the research on generational differences has been conducted in Western contexts (mostly the United States), leading to a tendency for both scholars and practitioners to adopt the American definitions of generations as though they are globally applicable. However, as suggested above, generational theory (Mannheim, 1952) emphasizes the need for individuals to experience historical events in the same way in order to comprise a generation, suggesting that generations should be conceptualized as being within a particular national context. Some research has examined generational characteristics in non-Western countries. For example, qualitative work from Parry et al. (2014) across several countries suggested that generational characteristics differ according to national context. Egri and Ralston (2004) found clear differences between Chinese and US generational characteristics. Similarly, Whiteoak, Crawford, and Mapstone

(2006) found differences in values between older and younger UAE nationals. These studies provide support for the notion that generational groups will differ not only within cultures, but also across cultures. It is clear therefore that future research needs to move away from the simplistic application of the North American categorizations of generations to examine differences between national contexts in relation to collective memories and the resulting values and attitudes.

It is also important to note that, in relation to the North American generational categories, a new generation will soon be entering the workforce − Generation Z ("Gen Z") − who are said to be born after 1995 (Holderman & Walls, 2008; Robertson, 2009). Much less is known about Gen Z compared to other generations as they are not yet adults and have not entered in the workforce in sufficiently large numbers. Commentators have noted that Gen Z is seen as the first truly digital and global generation. Having grown during times of great economic insecurity, more than any generation since the Great Depression, Gen Z craves both financial and workplace security (Half, n.d.). Their parents marry later in life, and authors have noted that Gen Z is the new conservative generation embracing traditional beliefs and highly valuing the family unit. They are also said to be more responsible (Williams & Page, 2011). Gen Z is a global and diverse generation, who grew up in a wider mix of backgrounds than other generations (Labi, 2008). They are confident, very optimistic, imaginative, and think more laterally than other generations (Matthews, 2008). Undoubtedly, interest in this group will rise as its members reach adulthood and rigorous research to examine their collective memories, values, and attitudes will be needed.

HUMAN RESOURCE MANAGEMENT STUDIES ON GENERATIONAL DIFFERENCES

Given the interest in Millennials, many of the studies were concerned with how the Millennials were different from previous generations. This interest − particularly among management scholars − is sparked in part by a study by Smola and Sutton (2002). Based on the large number of studies that are focused on the Millennials, our review will also have the same emphasis, although we will highlight how the Millennials are different from previous generations when appropriate data are available.

Smola and Sutton (2002) compared a number of work values between workers in 1974 and those in 1999. They were interested in whether the work values among the different generations were different from each other, whether they were different in 1999 (year survey was carried out) than they were 25 years ago, and whether work values change as workers age. The authors found significant differences between the work values of Gen Xers and Baby Boomers (with Gen Xers reporting less loyalty, scoring lower on work centrality, and desiring more rapid promotions). Even between workers in the same life span (aged 27–40 years), those in 1999 expressed lower work centrality. Furthermore, as workers aged (comparing younger workers in 1974 with older workers in 1999), the older workers were also more likely to express work as being an important part of their lives. The Smola and Sutton (2002) study points to three important points: work values change as individuals age (maturation effect), values espoused by one generation are different to those of a different generation (generational effect), and values change with changing times (period effect). Although the study is limited to a comparison of Baby Boomers and Gen Xers, it nonetheless establishes a recent first in empirically comparing generational differences in the study of work values.

Jean Twenge, a social psychologist, has also documented differences in work values, attitudes, and personality across different generations. Twenge (2000, p. 1008), examining anxiety levels across college students and children in a meta-analysis, noted that personality traits among individuals remained relatively stable as they aged, but in cross-sectional studies, large effects were observed in personality shifts arising from age differences. She concluded that birth cohort, which is a proxy for sociocultural environment, may explain the contextual influence on personality shifts over time. In other words, cohort effects exist in the differences observed in anxiety levels, which she then attributed to environmental threat, economic conditions, and social connectedness. Twenge's study lends support to Mannheim's (1952) conceptualization of shared experiences in shaping shared (work) values, attitudes, and beliefs. These differences among the different cohorts, in turn, affect individual behaviors and workplace dynamics.

GENERATIONAL DIFFERENCES IN WORK VALUES, ATTITUDES, AND BEHAVIORS

Since the Smola and Sutton study, and Twenge's early work, a large number of studies have sought to document a multitude of generational differences across different dimensions in personalities, work values, and attitudes. In the next section, we will highlight and summarize key research studies on how the generations may differ on various psychological traits, with implications for employers and organizations.

Personalities

Early work on generational differences focused on the Big 5 personality traits (openness to experience, conscientiousness, extraversion, agreeableness, and neuroticism) (see Twenge & Campbell, 2012 for a review). Although personality traits are largely stable across an individual's life span (single generation), they can shift over time (across successive generations), in response to changes in the external environment. For example, peers, culture, media, and the education system impact character development and adaptation, which is formed during adolescence and carried into adulthood (McCrae et al., 2000, 2002; also see Westerman et al., 2011). The digital age, for example, contributes significantly to an increasingly impatient generation and a greater dependency on technology (Leung, 2004; Parker-Pope, 2010). As a consequence, a shift in personality traits, for example, in extraversion, may result in a rise in other traits such as assertiveness, self-esteem, and narcissism (Twenge, 2000; Twenge & Campbell, 2012). Therefore, it is no surprise for recent literature to draw attention to the Millennials who display high degrees of self-esteem and narcissism (Twenge & Campbell, 2008), leading to popular stereotypes that characterize Millennials as lazy, spoilt, and entitled (Alsop, 2008; Howe & Strauss, 2009).

Indeed, Twenge and colleagues have generated a large body of literature that documents how self-esteem is on the rise among students from 1930s to the 2000s, with self-esteem scores peaking with Millennial students (Gentile et al., 2010; Twenge & Campbell, 2001, 2008). Gentile et al. (2010), in three meta-analyses, found increasing self-esteem among high school and college students between 1988 and 2008. Eighteen percent of the respondents in 2008 also had perfect self-esteem scores. Twenge and Campbell (2001) also reported similar patterns of rising levels of self-esteem among students in elementary school through to college from earlier periods (1968–1994). The rise in self-esteem occurs as the students age, particularly during high school and college years. Of note, narcissism levels are rising alongside self-esteem scores, with the Millennial generation scoring at unprecedented levels. Self-esteem is a belief that one is as good as everyone else, while narcissism is a belief that one is better than everybody else (Twenge & Campbell, 2009). This level of narcissism has raised concerns that that the Millennials are overconfident and they react with anger easily (Twenge & Campbell, 2008, 2012). Twenge and Campbell (2012) also noted that narcissists are motivated to achieve individual victories over group goals, and they tend to blame others for their failures (i.e., having high external locus of control). Commentators have attributed this to a high-involvement parenting style (cf. Ng & McGinnis Johnson, 2015; also see Brummelman et al., 2015) where there are encouraged to develop strong self-esteem and a belief that they can achieve whatever they want. As a result, Millennials are much more likely to exhibit signs of individualism and to think highly of themselves, as compared to previous generations (Foster, Campbell, & Twenge, 2003; Twenge, 2013).

It should be noted that the rising levels of self-esteem and narcissism in successive generations have not been accompanied by greater level of competence or performance. For example, Twenge, Campbell, and Gentile (2012) reported that college students rated themselves highly (above average) on academic abilities, leadership abilities, motivation, and public speaking, although such self-assessments have not been accompanied by high SAT scores (i.e., more objective academic assessments). In another study, Twenge and Campbell (2008) observed that students in 2006 (Millennials) also thought of themselves as "very good" spouses, parents, and workers, which are more positive self-views than students in 1976, but they scored lower on two self-competence measures. These studies point to a disconnect between ability and performance. According to Hill (2002), Millennials have been told to focus on effort over performance, where successes and failures are less important than doing one's best. Hill coined the term "ability-performance nexus problem" to describe Millennials' tendency to equate effort with performance, which has led to a constant need for feedback and positive reinforcement (i.e., praise). For example, students often bemoan receiving a "B" grade after having spent the entire weekend sacrificing leisure time to work on their term papers.

The combination of high self-esteem, narcissism, and strong individualism has translated into a sense of entitlement among the younger generation of workers that has been the focus of the media (Stein, 2013). Therefore, it should come as no surprise for the Millennials to form high career expectations of themselves and prospective employers. Ng et al. (2010) surveyed the Millennial generation in Canada about their careers and reported inflated expectations in terms of pay and promotion. Two-thirds of the Millennials indicated they expected a first promotion in 15 months after starting their first career. They also expected an average of

63 percent increase in pay over a five-year period. Perhaps not surprisingly, the study found no relationship between Millennials' career expectations and their academic performance, suggesting an entitlement that has no relation to actual achievement, corroborating with Hill's (2002) ability-performance nexus. In another study comprising of business students in the United States, Westerman et al. (2011) found that high levels of narcissism were also related to an entitlement to jobs, salary, and promotion. Students with high narcissistic scores expected greater career success, even after controlling for GPA. Both studies suggest a general pattern that demonstrates how successive generations are more individualistic and have higher levels of self-esteem and narcissism than the Baby Boomers, with a corresponding upward shift in school and workplace expectations.

Work Values

Work values are generalized beliefs about desirable aspects of work (Lyons, Higgins, & Duxbury, 2010). While personality and psychological traits are predictive of workplace behaviors, work values, in turn, are predictive of the career preferences and types of work individuals prefer (cf. Lyons, Duxbury, & Higgins, 2006; Ng & McGinnis Johnson, 2015; Zytowski, 1970). There are six basic work values that are widely studied: extrinsic, intrinsic, social, altruistic, prestige, and leisure (Elizur, 1984; Lyons et al., 2006; Ng & Sears, 2010; Ros, Schwartz, & Surkiss, 1999; Twenge et al., 2010). Extrinsic work values encompass material aspects of work, such as pay, benefits, and job security. Intrinsic work values include psychological satisfactions, such as interesting work, challenge, and intellectual stimulation. Social values are concerned with relations with coworkers, supervisors, and other organizational members. Prestige values are related to self-enhancement such as being proud of the company you work for, influence in the organization, and influence at work (Ros et al., 1999). Altruistic values are related to a concern for others, such as social justice and fairness (Lyons et al., 2006; Ng & Sears, 2010; Twenge, Campbell, & Freeman, 2012). Finally, leisure values refer to a willingness to accommodate work for family and personal lives, such as a preference for work/life balance (Twenge et al., 2010).

A number of studies have documented small differences in work values across the different generations. Hansen and Leuty (2012) examined work value differences across three generations (Silent Generation, Baby Boomers, Gen Xers) using a sample of vocational assessment clients over a period of 30 years. They found that the Silent Generation value prestige (status) and intrinsic (autonomy) values more than younger workers (Baby Boomers, Gen Xers). Younger workers, in contrast, placed more importance on extrinsic (work conditions, security, compensation) and social (coworkers) values than older workers. The data was cross-sectional in nature, and it is unclear if the differences reflected aging or generational effects. The authors cautioned that different generations may be interpreting work values differently from each other, based on the respective generations' points of view and perceptions. There appears to be some support for this assertion. For example, Lester et al. (2012) reported that when different generations were asked to perceive how much the other generations value a particular work value, the results indicated that those perceptions are often inaccurate. The discrepancy between perceived and espoused (actual) values may thus be attributed to perceptual differences in what the values may represent to each generation.

Twenge et al. (2010) examined the work values among high school seniors from 1976, 1991, and 2006 respectively, and reported a rise in extrinsic values over time, peaking with the youngest cohort (i.e., Millennial generation). In a Canadian study comparing students aged 25 in 1985 and in 1996 (i.e., Gen Xers and Millennials), Krahn and Galambos (2014) reported that Millennials similarly valued extrinsic rewards more, and they also had stronger job entitlements (i.e., an expectation of a well-paying job, especially with rising levels of education). Collectively, these studies suggest that younger generations (with Millennials more than Gen Xers) exhibited stronger attraction to extrinsic work values, while older generations appeared to emphasize intrinsic and prestige work values.

Furthermore, although Millennials have been purported to "want to save the world" (Johnson & Ng, 2015) and are said to espouse stronger altruistic values than previous generations, empirical studies do not appear to support this view. Twenge et al. (2010) reported that Millennials, in fact, expressed lower altruistic values (i.e., helping other behavior) than Baby Boomers. Leveson and Joiner (2014), in a study of business students, reported that Millennials were willing to trade off social responsibility in exchange for greater extrinsic rewards at work. Twenge (2010) concluded that there was no generational difference in altruistic values in her review of past research.

Twenge et al. (2010) also documented that preference for leisure time increased over time, while work centrality decreased with more recent generations. Consistent with this trend, Becton et al. (2014) reported that Millennials and Gen Xers were less willing to undertake overtime work than Baby Boomers, when asked. In another study using high-school students between 1976 and 2007, Twenge and Kasser (2013) found attraction to materialism to be on the rise, peaking with Gen Xers and Millennials, and an emphasis on material rewards was associated with declining work centrality.

Taken together, the studies demonstrate differences in work values espoused by different generations. The general pattern that is evident in these studies indicates that, in general, younger generations of workers — particularly for Millennials — tend to exhibit a strong preference for extrinsic aspects of work (e.g., material rewards) and leisure time, and have low work centrality; while older generations tend to emphasize intrinsic aspects of work, prestige, and also report higher work centrality.

Psychological Contracts

A recent body of research has focused on generational differences in psychological contracts, defined as an employee's beliefs about the reciprocal obligations between that employee and his or her organization, where these obligations are based on perceived promises and not necessarily recognized by agents of the organization (Morrison & Robinson, 1997, p. 229). Researchers such as Lub, Bijvank, Bal, Blomme, and Schalk (2012) have argued that different generations perceive their psychological contracts differently, due to the different expectations and values that they hold in relation to work. Indeed, psychological contract theory has suggested that psychological contracts are affected by pre-employment experiences such as societal events (Rousseau, 2001), and thus might be age (and therefore, generation) related (Bal, De Lange, Jansen, & van der Velde, 2008; Lub et al., 2012). Researchers have suggested therefore that different generations will differ in their perceptions of both employer and employee obligations because of their different formative experiences (Lub, Bal, Blomme, & Schalk, 2014). Support for this proposition has been found by Lub et al.'s (2012) survey research in that there were indeed generational differences in the nature of the psychological contract that respondents perceived was held with their organization.

Relatedly, researchers have also suggested that generations not only differ in the nature of their psychological contract but might also differ in both their perception of psychological contract fulfillment and their cognitive responses to psychological contract fulfillment or breach (Deepthi & Baral, 2013; Lub et al., 2014). Alternatively, Festing and Schafer (2014) suggested that the relationship between talent management practices and the psychological contract is moderated by generation. Specifically, they proposed that highly engaged talent management practices would have a greater affect on psychological contract fulfillment for Generation X and Y than for Baby Boomers. However these ideas have not been empirically examined.

HUMAN RESOURCE MANAGEMENT ISSUES ACROSS DIFFERENT GENERATIONS

In general, there are three major HRM challenges facing organizations that are related to generational differences, and Millennials — who are the largest workforce entrants — in particular. First, organizations are striving to attract and retain the Millennials while working to extend the careers of Baby Boomers. As the economy recovers, employers will be faced with a shortage of skilled workers and the competition for talent will intensify (Callanan & Greenhaus, 2008). This also raises a concern with knowledge transfer as the Baby Boomers exit the workforce in large numbers. Second, the changing nature of work and careers entail that the younger generation of workers may not follow the traditional career path, and will instead be embracing "protean" and boundaryless careers, which are notions of a modern career (McDonald & Hite, 2008). Person-organization fit may shift over time as a result of changing psychological contracts (Cennamo & Gardner, 2008), and career achievement is measured in terms of career satisfaction rather than the number of promotions and compensation (Mainiero & Sullivan, 2006). Consequently, Millennials may be switching jobs, careers, and organizations much more frequently than previous generations. Additionally, the younger generation of workers — notably, Gen Xers and Millennials — are much more likely to desire work/life balance as they experience different demands and have lower work centrality than the Baby Boomers (Ehrhart, Mayer, & Ziegert, 2012; McDonald & Hite, 2008). Third, the differences in work values that exist among the generations will inevitably result in generational conflict in the workplace. Glass (2007) noted that the differences in work values could result in intergenerational conflicts arising out of expectations, work ethics, attitudes, opposing perspectives, and motivations. In this regard, Millennials may find the leadership styles of Baby Boomers to be outmoded, while Baby Boomers may perceive Millennials to be impatient and lacking in respect for organizational structures and hierarchy. As Millennials begin to step into leadership roles, it would also be important to understand the leadership attributes they espouse (Murray, 2011). Consistent with this and an aging workforce, Millennials will soon be managing an increasingly older workforce, and the perceptions of each other may lead to further work-place conflicts (Arnold & Yue, 2012).

Attracting the Front End of a Multigenerational Workforce

What do younger workers want? Research on work values may provide an insight into what Millennials value in order to attract them to an organiza-tion. For example, Millennials' preference for extrinsic rewards suggests that good compensation and benefits are keys to enticing the younger gen-eration of workers to join an employer. In a Mercer survey of Gen Xers and Millennials, both generations rank compensation and benefits ahead of developmental opportunities and work environment (e.g., manager qual-ity), work/life balance (hours, location, travel), and company environment (senior management, diversity) (Corporate Leadership Council, 2004). Of note, "base pay" and "manager quality" ranked well ahead all other work attributes, while "project responsibility" and "risk-taking" ranked last for the Millennials. The emphases on base pay and low (work) responsibility are consistent with research findings that point to the Millennial generation as having low work centrality, but nonetheless feel entitled to guaranteed com-pensation and benefits. The link between the Millennials and job entitlement has been established in previous studies (Krahn & Galambos, 2014; Westerman et al., 2011). In another large-scale survey conducted in Canada, the Millennials also rank "opportunities for advancement" as the top work attribute Millennials consider to be important when accepting their first employment (Ng et al., 2010). According to Bottorff (2011), when indivi-duals are motivated by money and advancement, they are less likely to express loyalty to, and remain with, an employer. Thus, extrinsic rewards or work values − such as compensation and benefits, and advancement opportunities − can easily be duplicated and do not confer a long-term compe-titive advantage to employers when attracting Millennials. Consequently, the provision of high levels of compensation and promises of rapid advancement are not sustainable methods for attracting and retaining Millennial workers.

Additionally, although the literature frequently points to Millennials' enthusiasm for corporate social responsibility (Livingstone, 2014; Meistner, 2012; Murray & Ayoun, 2010) − such as the environment, poverty, ethics, and philanthropy – there is little evidence that such concerns translate into meaningful considerations when Millennials make job choice decisions. Indeed, Ng et al. (2010) reported that Canadian students ranked "personal impact" and "social responsibility" behind extrinsic rewards (e.g., advancement, salary, and benefits) and social values (good people to work with, good people to report to) when accepting their first employment. Rasch and Kowske (2012) examined the value placed on corporate social responsibility by Millennials, Gen Xers, and Baby Boomers, and found that the younger generation was no more committed than older generations, particularly in the United States. In Australia, Leveson and Joiner (2014) similarly reported that a large majority of Millennials were willing to trade off social responsibility for greater extrinsic benefits such as pay. Johnson and Ng (2015) studied sector-switching intentions among nonprofit workers – who are supposedly committed to an organization's mission and are intrinsically motivated – and reported that Millennial managers are willing to switch sectors on account of pay. While troubling, this is largely consistent with earlier findings that Millennials have low levels of altruism, and there was no evidence they were more altruistic than previous generations (Twenge, 2010; Twenge et al., 2010). Indeed, statements of corporate social responsibility, a commitment to diversity, and philanthropic records, while important, may have little effect in attracting Millennials to an organization (Kowske et al., 2010).

A key employer attribute that Millennials may find appealing is the provision of work/life balance. Indeed, Ehrhart et al. (2012) reported that Millennials' perception of work/life policies on organizational websites significantly predicted attraction to the organization as an employer. Although the study did not compare work/life balance with other organizational attributes, other studies which compare work value preferences among Millennials may provide an insight into the relative importance Millennials place on this organizational attribute. In a study of hospitality managers across three generations (Baby Boomers, Gen Xers, Millennials) in the United States, "way of life" was the most important work value among members of the Gen X and Millennial generations (Chen & Choi, 2008). Work/life balance also ranked highly (#5 among 16 work values and behind advancement, good people to work for/with, and training opportunities) among Millennials in a Canadian study by Ng et al. (2010). The relative high importance of work/life balance is consistent with Twenge et al.'s (2010) finding that Millennials have lower work centrality in favor of more leisure time, when compared to the Baby Boomers and Gen Xers. In general, Millennials appear to be most attracted to extrinsic rewards (e.g., pay and advancement), and to a lesser degree to the provision of work/life balance. Altruistic missions and corporate social responsibility appear to have the least effect when attracting Millennials to an organization.

In addition to offering what the younger generation of workers wants, it is also important for employers to utilize the appropriate channels to attract the Millennials. As the most recent workforce entrants, Millennials are often recruited directly from colleges and universities, particularly for knowledge work (Terjesen & Frey, 2008). In the past, employers participated in college career fairs and held information sessions to entice students on campus to apply for jobs, however, recent surveys suggest that only one-third of Millennials attend such fairs (Jowett, 2011). Students have found written materials (e.g., company brochures) to be less helpful, and employers often fail to convey the information students seek at career fairs. Millennials also have low expectations of their campus recruitment centers in assisting them to find jobs (Ng & Burke, 2006). As digital natives, Millennials infrequently read the print media, when compared to the Baby Boomers, and instead rely on the internet when looking for jobs. As a consequence, employers are already responding to Millennials' habits by adapting their recruiting methods and using the internet more frequently (e.g., social media recruiting) (Ehrhart et al., 2012; Sarringhaus, 2011). According to Wazed and Ng (2015), employers also benefit from having immediate and frequent access to a large talent pool, reducing their hiring costs and time, and enhancing their employment branding through social media recruiting.

Retaining the Back End of a Multigenerational Workforce

An emerging concern for organizations and employers is the rapidly aging workforce. Employers are concerned that when Baby Boomers exit the workforce, they also take away institutional knowledge and experience that are key to organizational success (Collins, 2003; Duxbury & Halinski, 2014). Although it is possible for Baby Boomers to mentor Millennials, the knowledge transfer from one generation to another may not occur in time before the Baby Boomers retire. Therefore, it is important for organizations to retain Baby Boomers in the workforce longer to facilitate knowledge transfer from one generation to the other. Retaining Baby Boomers in the workforce longer also assists with plugging the shortage of skilled workers, and reduces the strain on the retirement system (Walker, 2007).

However, older workers are also stigmatized on account of negative stereotypes such as poor health, an inflexible attitude, resistance to change, and low trainability (Maurer, Barbeite, Weiss, & Lippstreu, 2008). As a result, the work motivation, engagement, and job performance among older workers have been questioned (Kanfer & Ackerman, 2004; Stamov-Roβnagel & Hertel, 2010). Age discrimination and negative stereotypes against older workers may discourage Baby Boomers from staying in the workforce (Posthuma, Wagstaff, & Campion, 2012). Research has shown that older workers may be persuaded to stay in the workforce longer when they are treated fairly and when their contributions are valued because such attitudes foster a sense of belonging with the organization (Armstrong-Stassen & Schlosser, 2011; Cheung & Wu, 2013). Additionally, Brooke (2003), in a meta-analysis, found that investments in older workers (e.g., training) exceeded their costs (e.g., absenteeism, workplace injuries), and the return on investments in older workers exceeded those of younger workers. Ng and Law (2014) interviewed workers aged 55 and reported that older workers are quite resilient and resourceful in adapting to the work-place as they age. Specifically, they utilized a range of strategies from priori-tizing work to compensating for declining abilities through the use of technology. The authors also noted that older workers contribute in differ-ent ways and provide stocks of experience, perspectives, and "calmness" (p. 6) in the workplace. Despite the findings, employers often prioritize the potential in younger workers over the experience and institutional memory provided by older workers (Taylor, Brooke, McLoughlin, & Di Biase, 2010).

A number of approaches have been proposed to help retain Baby Boomers longer in the workforce, and to extend the back end of their careers. Many of the suggested approaches range from implementing flex-ible work arrangements, and retooling or retraining of older workers, to enhancing the benefits for older workers to entice them to continue working past their normal retirement age (Duxbury & Halinski, 2014; Hermansen, & Midtsundstad, 2015; Picchio & Van Ours, 2013; Stone & Tetrick, 2013). Kwok, Bates, and Ng (2016) explored existing collective agreements within union environments to identify areas that can encourage older workers to stay. The authors reviewed nursing collective agreements and suggested operational changes, process improvements, and new tech-nology to reduce the strain for older nurses, as well as empowering them by having older nurses select their own work schedules to be helpful. Murphy (2012) also proposed reverse mentoring, where younger and more junior employees are paired with older, and more senior workers in a mentoring relationship. Such arrangements have the benefit of knowledge transfer and the development of leadership skills among the Millennials, while older workers also benefit from learning about new technology and closing the intergenerational divide in terms of work values and attitudes. Another novel approach, based on life span research, helps individuals focus on the goals and opportunities based on their remaining time at work. Zacher and Frese (2009, 2011) referred to this as *future time perspective* (FTP), where older workers develop future plans and possibilities. This provides older workers a sense of purpose, direction, and meaning, even at a later stage of one's life cycle. Furthermore, mentoring of younger workers (Murphy, 2012) also provides older workers with a sense of purpose and functional exchange. This perspective is particularly helpful to Baby Boomers, who derive their satisfaction from work centrality, staying connected, receiving recognition, and contributing to society (Twenge et al., 2010). This, in turn, improves older workers' subjective wellbeing and motivation to remain in the workforce. To that end, Zacher (2015) has called for more research using life span theory and FTP for studying generational differences.

Changing Nature of Work and Careers

Over the past two decades, globalization, technological advancement, and increasing worker mobility have resulted in changes to how work is performed (Burke & Ng, 2006). Historically, individuals would graduate from college and pursue a traditional career path, one that is characterized by climbing the corporate ladder with the occasional change in employers (Reitman & Schneer, 2003). However, economic, social, and technological changes have rendered traditional career paths to be obsolete. Long-term permanent employment is no longer the norm, technology has changed how work is performed, and successive generations have had to adapt to changing labor markets. Career researchers have pronounced traditional careers as dead, and reconceptualized the modern career as "protean" and "boundaryless" in nature (Briscoe & Finkelstein, 2009; Inkson, 2006). Protean career is used to describe how individuals begin to take charge of their own careers and retool or upgrade their skills to improve their employability (Hall, 1996, 2004). Likewise, boundaryless career refers to individuals who are increasingly mobile across organizations, geography, and mindsets (Arthur, 1994; Mirvis & Hall, 1996). Mainiero and Sullivan (2006) also proposed the "kaleidoscope" career concept, whereby individuals change their career patterns on the basis of authenticity, balance, and challenge to fit aspects of personal and work/life to form new work arrangements.

There is prima facie evidence to signify a shift in reconceptualizations of careers. Dries et al. (2008) surveyed students and workers across four generations in Belgium, and noted that people from different generations view careers differently. They used different prototypes of careers based on job security – bounded, staying, homeless, trapped, released, and boundaryless – and observed a decrease in the boundedness of careers with successive generations, where stability and job security were the norm. Interestingly, the respondents evaluated career success in terms of satisfaction, rather than salaries and promotions, suggesting new psychological contracts in employment relations. Sullivan, Forret, Carraher, and Mainiero (2009) compared career dimensions derived from the kaleidoscope model, between Baby Boomers and Gen Xers, and found that Gen Xers expressed a greater desire to achieve authenticity (alignment of personal values with organizational goals) and balance (work/life) than Baby Boomers. Both studies demonstrate the potential for how careers would unfold in different ways across different generations as a result of individual needs and environmental changes.

To capture changes in career patterns, Lyons, Schweitzer, Ng, and Kuron (2012) reviewed resumes and conducted interviews with 105 Canadians across four generations of workers. They found that younger generations (Gen Xers and Millennials) had significantly more job and organization changes than earlier generations. Most of these changes occur between 20–24 and 30–34 years of age, which Super (1957) referred to as career exploration and career establishment stages. Of note, the younger generation of workers was much more willing to accept non-upward career moves. The study provides early indications that career trajectories are no longer linear and upward, but that individuals are increasingly willing to make lateral and even downward career moves to enhance their career satisfaction (Dries et al., 2008), and to achieve a kaleidoscope career (Sullivan et al., 2009). In a follow-up study using professional workers, Lyons et al. (2015) confirmed their earlier findings. Millennials had twice as many job and organizational changes than Gen Xers, almost three times as many moves as Baby Boomers, and 4.5 times as many as the Silent Generation. The Silent Generation and Baby Boomers had significantly fewer involuntary moves than the younger generations, suggesting a more protean oriented approach to careers with successive generations.

The Quest for Work/Life Balance

Research on work/life balance suggests that Gen Xers and Millennials place higher importance on work/life balance than Baby Boomers (Broadbridge, 2003; Glass, 2007; Kerslake, 2005). And oft-cited rhetoric is that Baby Boomers are said to "live to work," whereas the Millennials "work to live" (Beutell & Wittig-Berman, 2008, p. 509). However, we know little about why Millennials value work/life balance, given that in most surveys (McDonald & Hite, 2008; Ng et al., 2010), they are of college age, are not yet married, and do not face the demands of raising a family.

Sok, Lub, and Blomme (2014) provided a detailed conceptual argument for generational differences in attitudes toward work/life balance. They suggested that Baby Boomers have high work centrality due to the economic circumstances during their formative years, and the traditional division of labor and relative stability within the homes that they grew up in. Gen Xers, on the other hand, grew up during increasing divorce rates, which led to them placing more value on their home life. Millennials grew up in dual income households and a gender-egalitarian environment, as well as increasing technological advancement, and therefore experienced more blurred work-family boundaries than previous generations and value family life. Notably, men and women's priorities have become more similar, suggesting that work-family balance has become more problematic for younger generations (Sok et al., 2014).

In a Canadian study, Lyons, Ng, and Schweitzer (2011) surveyed Baby Boomers, Gen Xers, and Millennials, and found that Baby Boomers and Gen Xers experienced greater career interference with home responsibilities than the Millennials. Gen Xers reported that families kept them from devoting more time to their careers. In addition, Gen Xers faced demands of eldercare as well as raising a family, which led them to report the lowest satisfaction with balancing their career and personal lives. In fact, Gen Xers reported that their career expectations on pay, advancement, and developmental opportunities are not being met. Indeed, in two separate studies, Leiter, Jackson, and Shaughnessy (2009), as well as Leiter, Price, and Spence Laschinger (2010) compared stress levels between Baby Boomers and Gen Xers, and found that Gen Xers reported more stress and negative experiences (e.g., exhaustion) than Baby Boomers because of competing work/life demands.

Millennials, on the other hand, reported that personal interests and activities (e.g., hobbies) interfered with their careers more frequently than

Baby Boomers. Indeed, past research suggests that Millennials have a desire for more leisure time (and twitter breaks) rather than work/life balance, which may see them following a more cyclical career, i.e., interrupting careers with travel than past generations (Corporate Leadership Council, 2004; Twenge et al., 2010). As the Baby Boomers — who are the parents of Millennials — age, the Millennials can also expect to face the same work/life demands as Gen Xers in balancing their careers with raising their own families (in place of leisure), as well as caring for their aging parents (Duxbury & Dole, 2015). Given that Baby Boomers did not face the same degree of work/life conflict during their career span, employers will need to integrate work/life balance into individual careers and work arrangements for Gen Xers and Millennial workers (Sullivan & Mainiero, 2007).

Leadership Preferences across Generations

The literature on generational differences in leadership preferences has been surprisingly sparse and mixed (Murray, 2011). According to Jackson (2012), the Silent Generation has a strong preference for traditional command and control leadership in the workplace. They respect rules and authority, and follow a hierarchical organizational structure. Like the Silent Generation, Baby Boomers also respect power and accomplishments. In contrast, Gen Xers question authority and prefer collaboration and a more horizontal organizational structure. Similarly, Millennials value autonomy and independent decision-making, and like the Gen Xers, they would prefer a decentralized organizational structure. While Jackson's characterization of the generational differences in attitudes toward authority and organizational structure is helpful, it would also be important to understand specific leadership attributes that different generations value and respect (Balda & Mora, 2011).

In this regard, Sessa, Kabacoff, Deal, and Brown (2007), using 40 leadership attributes, found significant differences in six of the top 12 rankings — credible, listens well, farsighted, focused, dedicated, and optimistic — between generations. Some of the findings corroborate with past literature. In particular, the Silent generation value "delegation" more than the other groups, likely because they follow the command and control mode of leadership. Gen Xers and Millennials value "focus" and "dedication" as key leadership attributes, and thus have little respect for authority if respect is not earned. Baby Boomers value "feedback" more than Millennials (which contradicts the notion that Millennials want frequent feedback; Ng et al., 2010), although it is unclear if this is providing feedback or receiving feedback.

In another study, Arsenault (2004) asked 790 people across the Silent Generation, Baby Boomers, Gen Xers, and Millennials to rank 10 admired characteristics of leaders. This research also found differences across the generations. Gen Xers and Millennials valued "determination" and "ambition" in leaders more than the Silent Generation and Baby Boomers. Baby Boomers and Gen Xers ranked "competence" as an important leadership characteristic, more than Millennials. All four generations also rated "honesty" as the most admired leadership characteristic, although the Silent Generation and Baby Boomers had higher honesty scores than Gen Xers and Millennials. In general, older generations (i.e., the Silent Generation and Baby Boomers) preferred "honesty" and "loyalty" in their leaders, while the younger generations valued "determination" and "ambition."

However, other research suggests that the different generations hold relatively similar views on the characteristics of successful leaders. Ahn and Ettner (2014) compared the responses on key leadership attributes – integrity, good judgment, leadership by example, decision-making, trust, justice/fairness, humility, and sense of urgency – between executives (with 20 or more years of experience) and MBA students (i.e., Millennials). The study found few differences, other than integrity (executives scored higher) and trust (students scored higher). The authors suggested that certain leadership values were foundational and had become institutionalized across generations. The pattern across these studies suggests that older generations (Silent Generation and Baby Boomers) tend to emphasize honesty and integrity more than the younger generation. Deal et al. (2012) studied leadership preferences among different generations in India, South Africa, the United Kingdom, and the United States and reported few significant differences in terms of how leadership is perceived across generations and countries. Given the limited number of studies that has been conducted on generational differences and leadership, these findings should best be treated as tentative and exploratory.

FUTURE DIRECTIONS OF GENERATIONAL RESEARCH

At the moment, we do know enough about the different generations on various attitudinal and behavioral outcomes as they relate to careers and the workplace. Although critics argue that the effect sizes in the differences are small (Becton et al., 2014; Benson & Brown, 2011; Costanza & Finkelstein, 2015), there are sufficient research studies that point to meaningful and material differences across the four generations with respect to their work values, attitudes, and career expectations (Cogin, 2012; Ng, Lyons, & Schweitzer, 2012; Twenge, 2010; Twenge & Campbell, 2012). Furthermore, we also have early predictions on how careers are unfolding for successive generations with the changing nature of work and careers (Lyons et al., 2012, 2015). At the moment, the most pressing challenge facing organizations and employers is managing an intergenerational workforce within the context of a shortage of skilled workers. This involves attracting and retaining Millennial workers, extending the careers for Baby Boomers, successfully managing knowledge transfer, and navigating the intergenerational dynamics in the workplace. We reviewed key literature on these issues in this chapter and offer suggestions for future research.

The next logical stage in understanding generational differences in the workplace would be to focus on how to tackle these issues within the context of methodological and practical challenges faced by researchers and practitioners. Based on our review of the current state of the literature on generations, we raise four important concerns to guide future work on generational research: (1) identifying and modernizing workplace policies and practice, (2) ensuring sustainability of current employment models while maintaining equity and fairness across generations, (3) facilitating future research with empirical work, and (4) integrating the effects of globalization in generational research.

First, many of the existing organizational policies and HRM practices have been crafted by Baby Boomers to organize the workplace during their tenure. In this regard, the younger generation of workers may view these policies and practices as outmoded given greater work/family demands, shifting nature of careers, and technological advances. The younger generation of workers are already (or will be) facing work/family demands, thus, existing work/life balance policies which penalize individual careers will need to be reconsidered. As society becomes increasingly more egalitarian, gender roles may be weakened, and men may take on more family care responsibilities than previous generations (Holland, 2015; Singleton & Maher, 2004), resulting in a greater demand for family-friendly policies. Men are equally as likely to sacrifice their careers for family (Holland, 2015). Furthermore, existing compensation and benefit policies which reward long-term employment (e.g., through vesting periods) may act as a deterrent when attracting younger workers who are expecting to have cyclical careers. Project-based work and short-term assignments may be the norm (Cross, Borgatti, & Parker, 2002; Davidson, 2015), and employers should consider more strategic compensation policies to attract the best talent, rather than attempting to retain workers over long periods of employment. In the past, working 9–5 has been the norm, but increasingly, younger workers have been reported to start work late in the day, but they also remain at work later (Marikar, 2013). Through the use of technology, many are plugged into work outside of traditional hours, and blurring the lines between work and leisure, but also making it difficult for organizations to set work rules and time off. Based on these examples, organizations and employers will need to overhaul existing workplace practices to adapt to a new generation of workers and the changing nature of work and organizations.

Second, many of the employment arrangements such as compensation and pension plans are deemed to be unsustainable as a result of shifting demographics. As the economy recovers, many employers have sought to reduce costs by hiring younger workers (i.e., Millennials) at lower wages (OECD, 2015; Thompson, 2015). Employers adopt a two-tier system in part because of an increasing number of more expensive older workers. Baby Boomers continue to enjoy higher levels of compensation on account of seniority, while new workforce entrants such as Millennials find themselves being paid less for doing the same amount and type of work (CBC News, 2013; Henderson, 2013). Many unions have also resorted to two-tiered collective agreements in order to save jobs and ensure sufficient membership among younger workers. When Baby Boomers retire, they also live longer and consequently place a heavier burden on pension plans than past generations. As a result, pension plans have moved from defined benefit (i.e., guaranteed to the pensioner) to defined contributions (based on what the pensioner contributes) (Ovsey, 2012). The changing nature of work and careers (e.g., project-based, short-term employment) will see the younger generation of workers face a wage penalty (Maume & Wilson, 2015), and forgoing the quality of life enjoyed by their Baby Boomer parents. The two-tiered system has led to concerns of equity and fairness across different generations, as the new and younger generation of workers is left behind. Unions continue to struggle in their efforts to organize Millennials (Stanberry, 2011), and this may lead to deteriorating quantity and quality of future work (Loughlin & Barling, 2001).

Relatedly, by the time the last of the Baby Boomers have exited the workforce, Gen Z (which we have introduced earlier) will be the next generation that will take the place of the Millennials in influencing and affecting the workplace. At the moment, we know little about their work values, attitudes, and career expectations largely because they are still in school. However, popular media have begun speculating on their preferences and lifestyles ranging from their daily lives, use of technology, their ethical values, and what they will be like in the workplace (Benhamou, 2015; Boitnott, 2016; Williams, 2015). Of interest would be the types of careers they would be seeking, how they would define work, and the relative importance of work vis-à-vis the pursuit of a life. Furthermore, the question on whether traditional jobs as we know them will continue to exist, and what new jobs will be invented remains to be answered. It will be a challenge to forecast the types of skills sets that will be required, and what policies and practices organizations should have in place to prepare themselves for future workforce entrants.

Third, as indicated earlier in the chapter, researchers have faced challenges untangling the effects of age, period, and generational effects when identifying differences with successive generations. For example, Costanza and Finklestein (2015) recently raised concerns that there remains minimal empirical evidence supporting differences across successive generations, and why these differences exist, and yet there are lots of perceptions that these differences do exist. Indeed, our experience suggests that when we control for age in our research models, much of the "generational" effects were explained leaving us to wonder if there is a generational effect. Thus, we may be limited in our ability to detect true generational differences. In this regard, Lyons, Urick, Kuron, and Schweitzer (2015) suggested enlarging our research tool kit and using multiple methods to help us capture the generational phenomena. One such method is the retrospective account of careers undertaken by Lyons et al. (2012), although other methodologies, such as mixed-methods, may also be used. Another major shortcoming in generational research is the use of cross-sectional methods arising from limited data. Although Twenge and colleagues (Twenge & Campbell, 2001; Twenge et al., 2008; Twenge et al., 2010) have been successful at locating time series data and using CTMA, generational researchers should begin to collect longitudinal data to help address the limitations of cross-sectional research.

Finally, much of the literature on generations has been generated from studying demographic shifts following post-war boom in North America and Western Europe. The findings while important may have limited generalizability to other emerging populations such as China and India, which are contributing large numbers of workers to the new economy. Researchers have documented that the generational cohorts in Asian countries (e.g., Japan, China, India, South Korea) are different from those in popular literature, based on defining events that occur in the region (Srinivasan, 2012; Srinivasan, John, & Christine, 2014). For example, studies have also shown that national culture plays a significant role in shaping the work values and attitudes of the same generations between the east and west (see, e.g., Colakoglu & Caligiuri, 2012; Egri & Ralston, 2004; Yi, Ribbens, Fu, & Cheng, 2015). As a result, it would be erroneous to generalize much of what is reported in popular media in the west to understanding the generational differences elsewhere. This is particularly important for multinationals attempting to replicate home country human resource policies and practices when expanding their operations overseas.

Additionally, increasing cultural diversity arising from globalization and talent mobility will also require us to consider the heterogeneity within a generation when interpreting large-scale studies. Twenge and colleagues (Twenge & Foster, 2008; Twenge et al., 2008) detected that California has lower levels of (rising) self-esteem scores because of a large number of Asian-American students, due to Asian parenting styles (see Chua, 2011). Indeed, Lyons, Ng, and Schweitzer (2014) suggested that an examination of generational differences must take into account socio-demographic variables such as gender, immigration, socioeconomic status, and geography (urban/rural divide). For example, immigrant experiences or having been raised in a rural area would have some degree of influence over the development of one's values and attitudes, which in turn, may or may not conform with those of the same generational cohort. At the same time, an increasing number of international students from developing economies studying in the west and returning home (see Porschitz, Guo, & Alves, 2012) will also bring greater convergence of these values and attitudes between developing and developed countries. An understanding of socio-demographic variables can inform us of the direction and magnitude of how work values, attitudes, and careers expectations may shift with successive generations.

CONCLUSION

The purpose of this chapter is to review the current state of literature on generational research and to identify potential HRM issues that will impact workplace and organizational performance. Our aim is to document what we already know about the different generations, identify gaps in the current literature, and make suggestions for future work, as well as make projections on what else we should know, particularly on future generations. We also highlighted current challenges facing generational research particularly with respect to the conceptualization of the construct and methodological limitations. Although there has been a lot of attention on generational shifts, we caution that conclusions be drawn from well-designed and methodologically sound research studies in order to give the field greater legitimacy, rather relying on anecdotes and stereotypes from popular media. In closing, we encourage greater scholarship attention to understand the implications of generational shifts as they impact employers, organizations, management, and the world of work.

REFERENCES

Ahn, M. J., & Ettner, L. W. (2014). Are leadership values different across generations? *Journal of Management Development, 33*(10), 977–990.

Alsop, R. (2008). *The trophy kids grow up: How the millennial generation is shaking up the workplace*. San Francisco, CA: Jossey-Bass.

Armstrong-Stassen, M., & Schlosser, F. (2011). Perceived organizational membership and the retention of older workers. *Journal of Organizational Behavior, 32*(2), 319–344.

Arnold, S. L., & Yue, S. (2012). *Perception of age diversity in Singapore: Implications for managing a diverse workforce*. Cheltenham, UK: Edward Elgar.

Arsenault, P. M. (2004). Validating generational differences: A legitimate diversity and leadership issue. *Leadership and Organization Development Journal, 25*(1–2), 124–141.

Arthur, M. B. (1994). The boundaryless career: A new perspective for organizational inquiry. *Journal of Organizational Behavior, 15*(4), 295–306.

Ashforth, B. E., Harrison, S. H., & Corley, K. G. (2008). Identification in organizations: An examination of four fundamental questions. *Journal of Management, 34*(3), 325–374.

Bal, P. M., De Lange, A. H., Jansen, P. G. W., & van der Velde, M. E. G. (2008). Psychological contract breach and job attitudes: A meta-analysis of age as a moderator. *Journal of Vocational Behavior, 72*(1), 143–158.

Balda, J. B., & Mora, F. (2011). Adapting leadership theory and practice for the networked, millennial generation. *Journal of Leadership Studies, 5*(3), 13–24.

Becker, H. A. (1992). *Generations and their opportunities*. Amsterdam: Meulenhof.

Becton, J. B., Walker, H. J., & Jones-Farmer, A. (2014). Generational differences in workplace behavior. *Journal of Applied Social Psychology, 44*(3), 175–189.

Benhamou, L. (2015). Everything you need to know about Generation Z. *Business Insider*, February 12. Retrieved from http://www.businessinsider.com/afp-generation-z-born-in-the-digital-age-2015-2

Bennett, J., Pitt, M., & Price, S. (2012). Understanding the impact of generational issues in the workplace. *Facilities, 30*(7–8), 278–288.

Benson, J., & Brown, M. (2011). Generations at work: Are there differences and do they matter? *The International Journal of Human Resource Management, 22*(9), 1843–1865.

Beutell, N., & Wittig-Berman, U. (2008). Work family conflict and work-family synergy for Generation X, Baby Boomers and Matures: Generational differences, predictors and satisfaction outcomes. *Journal of Managerial Psychology, 23*(5), 507−523.

Boitnott, J. (2016). Generation Z and the workplace: What you need to know. *Inc.* January 27. Retrieved from http://www.inc.com/john-boitnott/generation-z-and-the-workplace-what-you-need-to-know-.html

Bottorff, L. M. (2011). *Work attribute importance and loyalty intention: Millennial generation psychological contract.* CMC Senior Theses. Paper 110.

Briscoe, J. P., & Finkelstein, L. M. (2009). The "new career" and organizational commitment: Do boundaryless and protean attitudes make a difference? *Career Development International, 14*(3), 242−260.

Broadbridge, A. (2003). The appeal of retail as a career 20 years on. *Journal of Retailing and Consumer Services, 10*(5), 287−296.

Brooke, L. (2003). Human resource costs and benefits of maintaining a mature-age workforce. *International Journal of Manpower, 24*(3), 260−283.

Brummelman, E., Thomaes, S., Nelemans, S. A., De Castro, B. O., Overbeek, G., & Bushman, B. J. (2015). Origins of narcissism in children. *Proceedings of the National Academy of Sciences, 112*(12), 3659−3662.

Bryant, L. O. (2005). Music, memory and nostalgia: Collective memories of cultural revolution songs in contemporary China. *The China Review, 5*(2), 151−175.

Burke, R. J., & Ng, E. (2006). The changing nature of work and organizations: Implications for human resource management. *Human Resource Management Review, 16*(2), 86−94.

Callanan, G. A., & Greenhaus, J. H. (2008). The baby boom generation and career management: A call to action. *Advances in Developing Human Resources, 10*(1), 70−85.

Campbell, W. K., Campbell, S. M., Siedor, L. E., & Twenge, J. M. (2015). Generational differences are real and useful. *Industrial and Organizational Psychology, 8*(3), 324−331.

CBC News. (2013). *Millennial generation earning less than their parents.* Retrieved from http://www.cbc.ca/news/business/millennial-generation-earning-less-than-their-parents-1.2444341

Cennamo, L., & Gardner, D. (2008). Generational differences in work values, outcomes and person-organisation values fit. *Journal of Managerial Psychology, 23*(8), 891−906.

Chen, P. J., & Choi, Y. (2008). Generational differences in work values: A study of hospitality management. *International Journal of Contemporary Hospitality Management, 20*(6), 595−615.

Cheung, F., & Wu, A. M. (2013). Older workers' successful aging and intention to stay. *Journal of Managerial Psychology, 28*(6), 645−660.

Chua, A. (2011). *Battle hymn of the tiger mother.* New York, NY: Bloomsbury Publishing.

Cogin, J. (2012). Are generational differences in work values fact or fiction? Multi-country evidence and implications. *The International Journal of Human Resource Management, 23*(11), 2268−2294.

Colakoglu, S., & Caligiuri, P. (2012). Cultural influences on Millennial MBA students' career goals: Evidence from 23 countries. In *Managing the new workforce: International perspectives on the millennial generation* (pp. 262−280). Cheltenham, UK: Edward Elgar Publishing.

Collins, G. A. (2003). Rethinking retirement in the context of an aging workforce. *Journal of Career Development, 30*(2), 145−157.

Corporate Leadership Council. (2004). *Generation X and Y employees.* Washington, DC: Corporate Executive Board.

Costanza, D. P., Badger, J. M., Fraser, R. L., Severt, J. B., & Gade, P. A. (2012). Generational differences in work-related attitudes: A meta-analysis. *Journal of Business and Psychology*, *27*(4), 375–394.

Costanza, D. P., & Finkelstein, L. M. (2015). Generationally based differences in the workplace: Is there a *there* there? *Industrial and Organizational Psychology*, *8*(3), 308–323.

Cross, R., Borgatti, S. P., & Parker, A. (2002). Making invisible work visible: Using social network analysis to support strategic collaboration. *California Management Review*, *44*(2), 25–46.

Crumpacker, M., & Crumpacker, J. M. (2007). Succession planning and generational stereotypes: Should HR consider age-based values and attitudes a relevant factor or a passing fad? *Public Personnel Management*, *36*(4), 349–369.

Culpin, V., Millar, C. C. J. M., & Peters, K. (2015). Multi-generational frames of reference: Managerial challenges of four social generations in the organisation. *Journal of managerial psychology*, *30*(1), 1–7.

Davidson, A. (2015). What Hollywood can teach us about the future of work. *New York Times*, May 5. Retrieved from http://www.nytimes.com/2015/05/10/magazine/what-hollywood-can-teach-us-about-the-future-of-work.html

Deal, J. J., Stawiski, S., Graves, L. M., Gentry, W. A., Ruderman, M., & Weber, T. J. (2012). Perceptions of authority and leadership: A cross-national, cross-generational investigation. In *Managing the new workforce: International perspectives on the millennial generation* (pp. 281–306). Cheltenham, UK: Edward Elgar Publishing.

Deepthi, U., & Baral, R. (2013). Understanding the role of generational differences in psychological contract fulfillment and its impact on employees cognitive responses. *Review of HRM*, *2*(April), 74–84.

Dencker, J. C., Joshi, A., & Martocchio, J. J. (2007). Employee benefits as context for intergenerational conflict. *Human Resource Management Review*, *17*(2), 208–220.

Dries, N., Pepermans, R., & De Kerpel, E. (2008). Exploring four generations' beliefs about career: Is "satisfied" the new "successful"? *Journal of Managerial Psychology*, *23*(8), 907–928.

Duggan, W. (2015). China's millennial monetization is coming. *Yahoo finance*. Retrieved from http://finance.yahoo.com/news/chinas-millennial-monetization-coming-180051639.html. Accessed on September 9.

Duxbury, L., & Dole, G. (2015). Squeezed in the middle: Balancing paid employment, childcare and eldercare. In *Flourishing in life, work and careers: Individual wellbeing and career experiences* (pp. 141–166). Cheltenham, UK: Edward Elgar Publishing.

Duxbury, L., & Halinski, M. (2014). Dealing with the "Grumpy Boomers": Re-engaging the disengaged and retaining talent. *Journal of Organizational Change Management*, *27*(4), 660–676.

Egri, C. P., & Ralston, D. A. (2004). Generation cohorts and personal values: A comparison of China and the United States. *Organization Science*, *15*(2), 210–220.

Ehrhart, K. H., Mayer, D. M., & Ziegert, J. C. (2012). Web-based recruitment in the Millennial generation: Work–life balance, website usability, and organizational attraction. *European Journal of Work and Organizational Psychology*, *21*(6), 850–874.

Eisner, S. P. (2005). Managing generation Y. *Advanced Management Journal*, *8*(2), 4–15.

Elizur, D. (1984). Facets of work values: A structural analysis of work outcomes. *Journal of Applied Psychology*, *69*(3), 379–389.

Eskilson, A., & Wiley, M. (1999). Solving for the X: Aspirations and expectations of college students. *Journal of Youth and Adolescence*, *28*(1), 51–70.

Eyerman, R., & Turner, B. (1998). Outline of a theory of generations. *European Journal of Social Theory, 1*(1), 91–106.

Festing, M., & Schafer, L. (2014). Generational challenges to talent management: A framework for talent retention based on the psychological contract perspective. *Journal of World Business, 49*(2), 262–271.

Foot, D. K., & Stoffman, D. (1998). *Boom, bust & echo 2000: Profiting from the demographic shift in the new millennium*. Toronto, ON: Macfarlane Walter & Ross.

Foster, J. D., Campbell, W. K., & Twenge, J. M. (2003). Individual differences in narcissism: Inflated self-views across the lifespan and around the world. *Journal of Research in Personality, 37*(6), 469–486.

Fry, R. (2015, May 11). *Millennials surpass Gen Xers as the largest generation in U.S. labor force*. Pew Research Centre. Retrieved from http://www.pewresearch.org/fact-tank/2015/05/11/millennials-surpass-gen-xers-as-the-largest-generation-in-u-s-labor-force/

Gentile, B., Twenge, J. M., & Campbell, W. K. (2010). Birth cohort differences in self-esteem, 1988–2008: A cross-temporal meta-analysis. *Review of General Psychology, 14*(3), 261–268.

Gentry, W. A., Griggs, T. L., Deal, J. J., Mondore, S. P., & Cox, B. D. (2011). A comparison of generational differences in endorsement of leadership practices with actual leadership skill level. *Consulting Psychology Journal: Practice and Research, 63*(1), 39–49.

Giancola, F. (2006). The generation gap: More myth than reality. *Human Resource Planning, 29*(4), 32–37.

Gibson, C. (2015). Gen Z, iGen, Founders: What should we call the post-millennials? *Washington Post*, December 3. Retrieved from https://www.washingtonpost.com/lifestyle/style/gen-z-igen-founders-what-should-we-call-the-post-millennials/2015/12/03/38a102b2-99d2-11e5-94f0-9eeaff906ef3_story.html?postshare=8391449617846120&tid=ss_tw

Gilleard, C. (2004). Cohorts and generations in the study of social change. *Social Theory and Health, 2*(1), 106–119.

Glass, A. (2007). Understanding generational differences for competitive success. *Journal of Industrial and Commercial Training, 39*(2), 98–103.

Halbwachs, M. (1980). *The collective memory*. New York, NY: Harper.

Half, R. (n.d.). *Get ready for Generation Z*. Springfield, MO: Enactus.

Hall, D. T. (1996). Protean careers of the 21st century. *The Academy of Management Executive, 10*(4), 8–16.

Hall, D. T. (2004). The protean career: A quarter-century journey. *Journal of vocational behavior, 65*(1), 1–13.

Hansen, J. I. C., & Leuty, M. E. (2012). Work values across generations. *Journal of Career Assessment, 20*(1), 34–52.

Henderson, J. M. (2013). *Millennials earn less than their parents and the recession isn't to blame*. Retrieved from http://www.forbes.com/sites/jmaureenhenderson/2013/11/30/millennials-earn-less-than-their-parents-and-the-recession-isnt-to-blame/#87ee64ef430b

Hermansen, Å., & Midtsundstad, T. (2015). Retaining older workers—analysis of company surveys from 2005 and 2010. *International Journal of Manpower, 36*(8), 1227–1247.

Hill, R. P. (2002). Managing across generations in the 21st century. *Journal of Management Inquiry, 11*(1), 60–66.

Holdbrook, M. B., & Schindler, R. M. (1989). Some exploratory findings on the development of musical tastes. *Journal of Consumer Research, 16*(1), 119–124.

Holdbrook, M. B., & Schindler, R. M. (1994). Age, sex and attitude toward the past as predictors of consumers' aesthetic tastes for cultural products. *Journal of Marketing Research, 31*(3), 412–422.

Holderman, J. F., & Walls, S. (2008). As Generations X, Y, and Z determine the Jury's Verdict, What is the Judge's role. *DePaul Law Review*, *58*(2), 343–356.

Holland, K. (2015). Millennial managers struggle for work-life balance, *CNBC*, May 5. Retrieved from http://www.cnbc.com/2015/05/05/millennial-managers-struggle-for-work-life-balance.html

Howe, N., & Strauss, W. (2009). *Millennials rising: The next great generation*. New York, NY: Vintage Books.

Hui-Chun, Y., & Miller, P. (2003). The generation gap and cultural influence: A Taiwan empirical investigation. *Cross-Cultural Management*, *10*(3), 23–41.

Hui-Chun, Y., & Miller, P. (2005). Leadership style: The X generation and Baby Boomers compared in different cultural contexts. *Leadership and Organisation Development*, *26*(1–2), 35–50.

Inkson, K. (2006). Protean and boundaryless careers as metaphors. *Journal of Vocational Behavior*, *69*(1), 48–63.

Jackson, S. L. (2012). Leveraging intergenerational diversity to meet business goals. In C. Scott & M. Byrd (Eds.), *Handbook of research on workforce diversity in a global society: Technologies and concepts: Technologies and concepts* (pp. 386–402). Hershey, PA: Business Science Reference.

Johnson, J. M., & Ng, E. S. (2015). Money talks or millennials walk the effect of compensation on nonprofit millennial workers sector-switching intentions. *Review of Public Personnel Administration*. doi:10.1177/0734371X15587980

Joshi, A., Dencker, J. C., Franz, G., & Martocchio, J. J. (2010). Unpacking generational identities in organizations. *Academy of Management Review*, *35*(3), 392–414.

Jowett, C. (2011). Special report – TalentEgg's 2011 gen Y recruitment insider. *Talent Egg*, August 16. Retrieved from http://talentegg.ca/blog/?p=1630

Kanfer, R., & Ackerman, P. L. (2004). Aging, adult development, and work motivation. *Academy of Management Review*, *29*(3), 440–458.

Kerslake, P. (2005). Words from the Ys. *Management*, *52*(4), 44–46.

Kligler-Vilenchik, N., Tsfati, Y., & Meyers, O. (2014). Setting the collective memory agenda: Examining mainstream media influence on individuals' perceptions of the past. *Memory Studies*, *7*(4), 484–499.

Kowske, B. J., Rasch, R., & Wiley, J. (2010). Millennials' (lack of) attitude problem: An empirical examination of generational effects on work attitudes. *Journal of Business and Psychology*, *25*(2), 265–279.

Krahn, H. J., & Galambos, N. L. (2014). Work values and beliefs of 'Generation X' and 'Generation Y'. *Journal of Youth Studies*, *17*(1), 92–112.

Kwok, C., Bates, K. A., & Ng, E. S. (2016). Managing and sustaining an ageing nursing workforce: Identifying opportunities and best practices within collective agreements in Canada. *Journal of Nursing Management*, *24*(4), 500–511.

Labi, S. (2008). Baby Bloomers: Our new age. *Sunday Telegraph*, December 14, p. 50.

Lancaster, L. C., & Stillman, D. (2009). *When generations collide*. New York, NY: Harper Collins.

Leiter, M. P., Jackson, N. J., & Shaughnessy, K. (2009). Contrasting burnout, turnover intention, control, value congruence and knowledge sharing between Baby Boomers and Generation X. *Journal of Nursing Management*, *17*(1), 100–109.

Leiter, M. P., Price, S. L., & Spence Laschinger, H. K. (2010). Generational differences in distress, attitudes and incivility among nurses. *Journal of Nursing Management*, *18*(8), 970–980.

Lester, S. W., Standifer, R. L., Schultz, N. J., & Windsor, J. M. (2012). Actual versus perceived generational differences at work an empirical examination. *Journal of Leadership & Organizational Studies, 19*(3), 341–354.

Leung, L. (2004). Net-generation attributes and seductive properties of the internet as predictors of online activities and internet addiction. *Cyber Psychology and Behavior, 7*(3), 333–348.

Leveson, L., & Joiner, T. A. (2014). Exploring corporate social responsibility values of millennial job-seeking students. *Education + Training, 56*(1), 21–34.

Lieber, L. D. (2010). How HR can assist in managing the four generations in today's workplace. *Employment Relations Today, 36*(4), 85–91.

Liebowitz, J., Ayyavoo, N., Nguyen, H., Carran, D., & Simien, J. (2007). Cross-generational knowledge flows in edge organizations. *Industrial Management & Data Systems, 107*(8), 1123–1153.

Livingstone, G. (2014). Want the best talent? Then be a good corporate citizen. *Globe and Mail,* November 4. Retrieved from http://www.theglobeandmail.com/report-on-business/careers/career-advice/life-at-work/doing-good-a-must-for-attracting-talent/article 21443330/

Loughlin, C., & Barling, J. (2001). Young workers' work values, attitudes, and behaviours. *Journal of Occupational and Organizational Psychology, 74*(4), 543–558.

Lub, X. D., Bal, M., Blomme, R. J., & Schalk, R. (2014). Why do generational differences in psychological contracts exist? In E. Parry (Ed.), *Generational diversity at work: New research perspectives* (pp. 37–51). Abingdon, UK: Routledge.

Lub, X. D., Bijvank, M. N., Bal, P. B., Blomme, R., & Schalk, R. (2012). Different or alike? Exploring the psychological contract and commitment of different generations of hospitality workers. *International Journal of Contemporary Hospitality Management, 24*(4), 553–573.

Lyons, S., Ng, E. S. W., Schweitzer, L., & Kuron, L. K. J. (2012). Intergenerational differences in work values, career anchors and organizational mobility. In *Proceedings of the International Society for the Study of Organizational and Work Values Conference,* June 24–27.

Lyons, S., Urick, M., Kuron, L., & Schweitzer, L. (2015). Generational differences in the workplace: There is complexity beyond the stereotypes. *Industrial and Organizational Psychology, 8*(3), 346–356.

Lyons, S. T., Duxbury, L. E., & Higgins, C. A. (2006). A comparison of the values and commitment of private sector, public sector, and parapublic sector employees. *Public Administration Review, 66*(4), 605–618.

Lyons, S. T., Higgins, C. A., & Duxbury, L. (2010). Work values: Development of a new three-dimensional structure based on confirmatory smallest space analysis. *Journal of Organizational Behavior, 31*(7), 969–1002.

Lyons, S. T., & Kuron, L. (2014). Generational differences in the workplace: A review of the evidence and directions for future research. *Journal of Organizational Behavior, 35*(S1), S139–S157.

Lyons, S. T., Ng, E. S., & Schweitzer, L. (2014). Changing demographics and the shifting nature of careers implications for research and human resource development. *Human Resource Development Review, 13*(2), 181–206.

Lyons, S. T., Ng, E. S. W., & Schweitzer, L. (2011). Summary report of key findings. *Generational Career Shift,* 1–53.

Lyons, S. T., Schweitzer, L., & Ng, E. S. (2015). How have careers changed? An investigation of changing career patterns across four generations. *Journal of Managerial Psychology*, *30*(1), 8–21.

Lyons, S. T., Schweitzer, L., Ng, E. S., & Kuron, L. K. (2012). Comparing apples to apples: A qualitative investigation of career mobility patterns across four generations. *Career Development International*, *17*(4), 333–357.

Mainiero, L., & Sullivan, S. (2006). *The kaleidoscope career*. Mountain view, CA: Davies-Black Publishing.

Mannheim, K. (1952). The problem of generations. In P. Kecskemeti (Ed.), *Essays on the sociology of knowledge* (pp. 378–404). London: Routledge.

Marikar, S. (2013). For Millennials, a generational divide. *New York Times*, December 20. Retrieved from http://www.nytimes.com/2013/12/22/fashion/Millenials-Millennials-Generation-Y.html?_r=0

Matthews, V. (2008). Generation Z. *Personnel Today*, *13*(4), 48–52.

Maume, D. J., & Wilson, G. (2015). Determinants of declining wage mobility in the new economy. *Work and Occupations*, *42*(1), 35–72.

Maurer, T. J., Barbeite, F. G., Weiss, E. M., & Lippstreu, M. (2008). New measures of stereotypical beliefs about older workers' ability and desire for development: Exploration among employees age 40 and over. *Journal of Managerial Psychology*, *23*(4), 395–418.

McCrae, R. R., Costa, P. T., Jr., Ostendorf, F., Angleitner, A., Hřebíčková, M., Avia, M. D., & Saunders, P. R. (2000). Nature over nurture: Temperament, personality, and life span development. *Journal of Personality and Social Psychology*, *78*(1), 173–186.

McCrae, R. R., Costa, P. T., Jr., Terracciano, A., Parker, W. D., Mills, C. J., De Fruyt, F., & Mervielde, I. (2002). Personality trait development from age 12 to age 18: Longitudinal, cross-sectional and cross-cultural analyses. *Journal of Personality and Social Psychology*, *83*(6), 1456–1468.

McDonald, K. S., & Hite, L. M. (2008). The next generation of career success: Implications for HRD. *Advances in Developing Human Resources*, *10*(1), 86–103.

McMullin, J., Comeau, T., & Jovic, E. (2007). Generational affinities and discourses of difference: A case study of highly skilled information technology workers. *British Journal of Sociology*, *58*(2), 297–316.

McNichols, D. (2010). Optimal knowledge transfer methods: A generation X perspective. *Journal of Knowledge Management*, *14*(1), 24–37.

Meistner, J. (2012). Corporate social responsibility: A lever for employee attraction and engagement. *Forbes*, June 7. Retrieved from http://www.forbes.com/sites/jeannemeister/2012/06/07/corporate-social-responsibility-a-lever-for-employee-attraction-engagement/#2715e4857a0b259219357511

Mencl, J., & Lester, S. W. (2014). More alike than different what generations value and how the values affect employee workplace perceptions. *Journal of Leadership & Organizational Studies*, *21*(3), 257–272.

Mirvis, P. H., & Hall, D. T. (1996). Psychological success and the boundaryless career. In M. B. Arthur & D. Rousseau (Eds.), *The boundaryless career: A new employment principle for a new organizational era* (pp. 237–255). New York, NY: Oxford University Press.

Morrison, E. W., & Robinson, S. L. (1997). When employees feel betrayed: A model of how psychological contract violation develops. *Academy of Management Review*, *22*(1), 226–256.

Murphy, W. M. (2012). Reverse mentoring at work: Fostering cross-generational learning and developing millennial leaders. *Human Resource Management*, *51*(4), 549–573.

Murray, A. (2011). Mind the gap: Technology, millennial leadership and the cross-generational workforce. *The Australian Library Journal, 60*(1), 54–65.

Murray, D. W., & Ayoun, B. M. (2010). Hospitality student perceptions on the use of sustainable business practices as a means of signaling attractiveness and attracting future employees. *Journal of Human Resources in Hospitality & Tourism, 10*(1), 60–79.

Ng, E., Lyons, S. T., & Schweitzer, L. (Eds.). (2012). *Managing the new workforce: International perspectives on the millennial generation.* Cheltenham, UK: Edward Elgar Publishing.

Ng, E. S., & Burke, R. J. (2006). The next generation at work-business students' views, values and job search strategy: Implications for universities and employers. *Education + Training, 48*(7), 478–492.

Ng, E. S., & Law, A. (2014). Keeping up! Older workers' adaptation in the workplace after age 55. *La Revue canadienne du vieillissement* [Canadian Journal on Aging], *33*(1), 1–14.

Ng, E. S., & McGinnis Johnson, J. (2015). Millennials: Who are they, how are they different, and why should we care. In *The multigenerational workforce: Challenges and opportunities for organisations* (pp. 121–137). Cheltenham, UK: Edward Elgar Publishing.

Ng, E. S., Schweitzer, L., & Lyons, S. T. (2010). New generation, great expectations: A field study of the millennial generation. *Journal of Business and Psychology, 25*(2), 281–292.

Ng, E. S., & Sears, G. J. (2010). What women and ethnic minorities want. Work values and labor market confidence: A self-determination perspective. *The International Journal of Human Resource Management, 21*(5), 676–698.

Nielsen. (2014). *Money matters: Upscale Millennials are saving for tomorrow.* Retrieved from http://www.nielsen.com/us/en/insights/news/2014/money-matters-upscale-millennials-are-saving-for-tomorrow.html. Accessed on April 15.

OECD. (2015). *In it together. Why less inequality benefits all.* Retrieved from http://www.keepeek.com/Digital-Asset-Management/oecd/employment/in-it-together-why-less-inequality-benefits-all_9789264235120-en#page4

Ovsey, D. (2012). Will two-tiered pensions lead to two-tiered productivity? *National Post,* October 18. Retrieved from http://business.financialpost.com/executive/will-two-tiered-pensions-lead-to-two-tiered-productivity

Parker, B., & Chusmir, L. (1990). A generational and sex-based view of managerial work values. *Psychological Reports, 66,* 947–950.

Parker-Pope, T. (2010). An ugly toll of technology: Impatience and forgetfulness. *New York Times,* June 6.

Parry, E. (2014). *Generational diversity at work: New research perspectives.* Abingdon, UK: Routledge.

Parry, E., Unite, J., Chudzikowski, K., Briscoe, J. P., & Shen, Y. (2014). Generational differences in the factors influencing career success across countries. In E. Parry (Ed.), *Generational diversity at work: New research perspectives* (pp. 204–231). Abingdon, UK: Routledge.

Parry, E., & Urwin, P. (2011). Generational differences in work values: A review of theory and evidence. *International Journal of Management Reviews, 13*(1), 79–96.

Picchio, M., & Van Ours, J. C. (2013). Retaining through training even for older workers. *Economics of Education Review, 32*(1), 29–48.

Piktialis, D. S., & Greenes, K. A. (2008). *Bridging the gaps: How to transfer knowledge in today's multigenerational workplace.* Retrieved from http://tech.tac-atc.ca/private/education/pdfs/Multigenerational.pdf

Porschitz, E. T., Guo, C., & Alves, J. (2012). 'Going through the Mist': Early career transitions of Chinese millennial returnees. In *Managing the new workforce: International perspectives on the millennial generation* (pp. 86–106). Cheltenham, UK: Edward Elgar Publishing Limited.

Posthuma, R. A., Wagstaff, M. F., & Campion, M. A. (2012). Age stereotypes and workplace age discrimination. In *The Oxford handbook of work and aging* (pp. 298–312). New York, NY: Oxford University Press.

Pritchard, K., & Whiting, R. (2014). Baby Boomers and the lost generation: On the discursive construction of generations at work. *Organization Studies, 35*(11), 1605–1626.

Rasch, R., & Kowske, B. (2012). Will millennials save the world through work? International generational differences in the relative importance of corporate social responsibility and business ethics to turnover intentions. In *Managing the new workforce: International perspectives in the millennial generation* (pp. 222–241). Cheltenham, UK: Edward Elgar Publishing.

Reeves, T. C., & Oh, E. (2008). Generational differences. In J. M. Spector, M. D. Merrill, J. van Merrienboer, & M. P. Driscoll (Eds.), *Handbook of research on educational communications and technology* (3rd ed., pp. 295–303). Mahwah, NJ: Lawrence Erlbaum.

Reitman, F., & Schneer, J. A. (2003). The promised path: A longitudinal study of managerial careers. *Journal of Managerial Psychology, 18*(1), 60–75.

Rhodes, S. (1983). Age-related differences in work-attitudes and behaviour: A review and conceptual analysis. *Psychological Bulletin, 93*(2), 328–367.

Roberto, K. J., & Biggan, J. R. (2014). Keen, groovy, wicked or phat: Generational stereotyping and social identity. In E. Parry (Ed.), *Generational diversity at work: New research perspectives*. Abingdon, UK: Routledge.

Robertson, M. (2009). Young "netizens" creating public citizenship in cyberspace. *International Research in Geographical and Environmental Education, 18*(4), 287–293.

Ros, M., Schwartz, S. H., & Surkiss, S. (1999). Basic individual values, work values, and the meaning of work. *Applied Psychology, 48*(1), 49–71.

Rousseau, D. M. (2001). Schema, promises and mutuality: The building blocks of the psychological contact. *Journal of Occupational and Organizational Psychology, 74*(4), 511–542.

Rudolph, C. W. (2015). A note on the folly of cross-sectional operationalizations of generations. *Industrial and Organizational Psychology, 8*(3), 362–366.

Rudolph, C. W., & Zacher, H. (2015). Intergenerational perceptions and conflicts in multi-age and multigenerational work environments. In L. M. Finkelstein, D. M. Truxillo, F. Fraccaroli, & R. Kanfer (Eds.), *Facing the challenges of a multi-age workforce: A use-inspired approach* (pp. 253–282). Mahwah, NJ: Lawrence Erlbaum Associates.

Sarringhaus, M. M. (2011). The great divide: Social media's role in bridging healthcare's generational shift. *Journal of Healthcare Management, 56*(4), 235–244.

Schuman, H., & Corning, A. (2012). Generational memory and the critical period: Evidence for national and world events. *Public Opinion Quarterly, 76*(1), 1–31.

Schuman, H., & Scott, J. (1989). Generations and collective memories. *American Sociological Review, 54*(3), 359–381.

Sessa, V., Kabacoff, R., Deal, J., & Brown, H. (2007). Research tools for the psychologist manager: Generational differences in leader values and leadership behaviours. *Psychologist Manager Journal, 10*(1), 47–74.

Singleton, A., & Maher, J. (2004). The "new man" is in the house: Young men, social change, and housework. *The Journal of Men's Studies, 12*(3), 227–240.

Smola, K. W., & Sutton, C. D. (2002). Generational differences: Revisiting generational work values for the new millennium. *Journal of Organizational Behavior, 23*(4), 363–382.

Sok, J. M. H., Lub, X. D., & Blomme, R. J. (2014). Work-home values: The interplay between historical trends and generational work-home values. In E. Parry (Ed.), *Generational diversity at work: New research perspectives* (pp. 52–66). Abingdon, UK: Routledge.

Srinivasan, V. (2012). Multi generations in the workforce: Building collaboration. *IIMB Management Review, 24*(1), 48–66.

Srinivasan, V., John, D. A., & Christine, M. N. (2014). Generational cohorts and personal values. In E. Parry (Ed.), *Generational diversity at work: New research perspectives*. Abingdon, UK: Routledge.

Stamov-Roβnagel, C., & Hertel, G. (2010). Older workers' motivation: Against the myth of general decline. *Management Decision, 48*(6), 894–906.

Stanberry, D. M. (2011). Youth and organizing: Why unions will struggle to organize the millennials. *Case Western Reserve Journal of Law, Technology & Internet, 2*, 103–115.

Statistics Canada. (2011). *Generations in Canada*. Ottawa: Statistics Canada. Retrieved from http://www12.statcan.gc.ca/census-recensement/2011/as-sa/98-311-x/98-311-x2011003_2-eng.cfm

Stein, J. (2013). *Millennials: The me me me generation*. New York, NY: Time Warner.

Stokes, B. (2015). *Who are Europe's millennials?* PEW Research Center. Retrieved from http://www.pewresearch.org/fact-tank/2015/02/09/who-are-europes-millennials/. Accessed on February 9.

Stone, D., & Tetrick, L. (2013). Understanding and facilitating age diversity in organizations. *Journal of Managerial Psychology, 28*(7/8), 725–728.

Sullivan, S. E., Forret, M. L., Carraher, S. M., & Mainiero, L. A. (2009). Using the kaleidoscope career model to examine generational differences in work attitudes. *Career Development International, 14*(3), 284–302.

Sullivan, S. E., & Mainiero, L. A. (2007). Kaleidoscope careers: Benchmarking ideas for fostering family-friendly workplaces. *Organizational Dynamics, 36*(1), 45–62.

Super, D. E. (1957). *The psychology of careers* (Vol. 195). New York, NY: Harper & Row.

Tajfel, H. (Ed.). (1978). *Differentiation between social groups: Studies in the social psychology of intergroup relations* (Vol. xv, 474 pp.). Oxford, England: Academic Press.

Taylor, P., Brooke, L., McLoughlin, C., & Di Biase, T. (2010). Older workers and organizational change: Corporate memory versus potentiality. *International Journal of Manpower, 31*(3), 374–386.

Terjesen, S., & Frey, R. V. (2008). Attracting and retaining Generation Y knowledge worker talent. In V. Vaiman & C. Vance (Eds.), *Smart talent management: Building knowledge assets for competitive advantage* (pp. 66–90). Cheltenham, UK: Edward Elgar Publishing.

Thompson, C., & Gregory, J. B. (2012). Managing millennials: A framework for improving attraction, motivation, and retention. *The Psychologist-Manager Journal, 15*(4), 237–246.

Thompson, D. (2015). The economy is still terrible for young people. *The Atlantic*, May 19. Retrieved from http://www.theatlantic.com/business/archive/2015/05/the-new-normal-for-young-workers/393560/

Turner, B. (1998). Ageing and generational conflicts: A reply to Sarah Irwin. *British Journal of Sociology, 49*(2), 299–304.

Twenge, J. M. (2000). The age of anxiety? The birth cohort change in anxiety and neuroticism, 1952–1993. *Journal of Personality and Social Psychology, 79*(6), 1007.

Twenge, J. M. (2010). A review of the empirical evidence on generational differences in work attitudes. *Journal of Business and Psychology, 25*(2), 201–210.

Twenge, J. M. (2013). The evidence for generation me and against generation we. *Emerging Adulthood, 1*(1), 11–16.

Twenge, J. M., & Campbell, S. M. (2008). Generational differences in psychological traits and their impact on the workplace. *Journal of Managerial Psychology, 23*(8), 862–877.

Twenge, J. M., & Campbell, S. M. (2012). Who are the millennials? Empirical evidence for generational differences in work values, attitudes and personality. In *Managing the new workforce: International perspectives on the millennial generation* (pp. 152–180). Cheltenham, UK: Edward Elgar Publishing.

Twenge, J. M., Campbell, S. M., Hoffman, B. J., & Lance, C. E. (2010). Generational differences in work values: Leisure and extrinsic values increasing, social and intrinsic values decreasing. *Journal of Management, 36*(5), 1117–1142.

Twenge, J. M., & Campbell, W. K. (2001). Age and birth cohort differences in self-esteem: A cross-temporal meta-analysis. *Personality and Social Psychology Review, 5*(4), 321–344.

Twenge, J. M., & Campbell, W. K. (2008). Increases in positive self-views among high school students birth-cohort changes in anticipated performance, self-satisfaction, self-liking, and self-competence. *Psychological Science, 19*(11), 1082–1086.

Twenge, J. M., & Campbell, W. K. (2009). *The narcissism epidemic: Living in the age of entitlement.* New York, NY: Simon and Schuster.

Twenge, J. M., Campbell, W. K., & Freeman, E. C. (2012). Generational differences in young adults' life goals, concern for others, and civic orientation, 1966–2009. *Journal of Personality and Social Psychology, 102*(5), 1045.

Twenge, J. M., Campbell, W. K., & Gentile, B. (2012). Generational increases in agentic self-evaluations among American college students, 1966–2009. *Self and Identity, 11*(4), 409–427.

Twenge, J. M., & Foster, J. D. (2008). Mapping the scale of the narcissism epidemic: Increases in narcissism 2002–2007 within ethnic groups. *Journal of Research in Personality, 42*(6), 1619–1622.

Twenge, J. M., Gentile, B., DeWall, C. N., Ma, D., Lacefield, K., & Schurtz, D. R. (2010). Birth cohort increases in psychopathology among young Americans, 1938–2007: A cross-temporal meta-analysis of the MMPI. *Clinical Psychology Review, 30*(2), 145–154.

Twenge, J. M., & Kasser, T. (2013). Generational changes in materialism and work centrality, 1976–2007 associations with temporal changes in societal insecurity and materialistic role modeling. *Personality and Social Psychology Bulletin, 39*(7), 883–897.

Twenge, J. M., Konrath, S., Foster, J. D., Campbell, K. W., & Bushman, B. J. (2008). Egos inflating over time: A cross-temporal meta-analysis of the Narcissistic personality inventory. *Journal of Personality, 76*(4), 875–902.

Urick, M. J., & Hollensbe, E. C. (2014). Toward and identity-based perspective of generations. In E. Parry (Ed.), *Generational diversity at work: New research perspectives.* Abingdon, UK: Routledge.

Urwin, P., Buscha, F., & Parry, E. (2014). Back to basics: Is there a significant generational dimension and where does it 'cut'? In E. Parry (Ed.), *Generational diversity at work: New research perspectives* (pp. 81–94). Abingdon, UK: Routledge.

Walker, D. M. (2007). Older workers: Some best practices and strategies for engaging and retaining older workers. GAO-07-433T. GAO Reports, February 28, 1, 17.

Wazed, S., & Ng, E. S. (2015). College recruiting using social media: How to increase applicant reach and reduce recruiting costs. *Strategic HR Review, 14*(4), 135–141.

Westerman, J. W., Bergman, J. Z., Bergman, S. M., & Daly, J. P. (2011). Are universities creating millennial narcissistic employees? An empirical examination of narcissism in business students and its implications. *Journal of Management Education, 36*(1), 5–32.

Whiteoak, J. W., Crawford, N. G., & Mapstone, R. H. (2006). Impact of gender and generational differences in work values and attitudes in an Arab culture. *Thunderbird International Business Review, 48*(1), 77–91.

Williams, A. (2015). Move over, millennials, here comes Generation Z. *New York Times,* September 18. Retrieved from http://www.nytimes.com/2015/09/20/fashion/move-over-millennials-here-comes-generation-z.html

Williams, K. C., & Page, R. A. (2011). Marketing to generations. *Journal of Behavioural Studies in Business, 3*, 1–17.

Wong, M., Gardiner, E., Lang, W., & Coulon, L. (2008). Generational differences in personality and motivation: Do they exist and what are the implications for the workplace? *Journal of Managerial Psychology, 23*(8), 878–890.

Yi, X., Ribbens, B., Fu, L., & Cheng, W. (2015). Variation in career and workplace attitudes by generation, gender, and culture differences in career perceptions in the United States and China. *Employee Relations, 37*(1), 66–82.

Zacher, H. (2015). Using lifespan developmental theory and methods as a viable alternative to the study of generational differences at work. *Industrial and Organizational Psychology, 8*(3), 342–346.

Zacher, H., & Frese, M. (2009). Remaining time and opportunities at work: Relationships between age, work characteristics, and occupational future time perspective. *Psychology and Aging, 24*(2), 487.

Zacher, H., & Frese, M. (2011). Maintaining a focus on opportunities at work: The interplay between age, job complexity, and the use of selection, optimization, and compensation strategies. *Journal of Organizational Behavior, 32*(2), 291–318.

Zytowski, D. G. (1970). The concept of work values. *Vocational Guidance Quarterly, 18*(3), 176–186.

WORKPLACE FLEXIBILITY ACROSS THE LIFESPAN

P. Matthijs Bal and Paul G. W. Jansen

ABSTRACT

As demographic changes impact the workplace, governments, organizations, and workers are looking for ways to sustain optimal working lives at higher ages. Workplace flexibility has been introduced as a potential way workers can have more satisfying working lives until their retirement ages. This chapter presents a critical review of the literature on workplace flexibility across the lifespan. It discusses how flexibility has been conceptualized across different disciplines, and postulates a definition that captures the joint roles of employer and employee in negotiating workplace flexibility that contributes to both employee and organization benefits. Moreover, it reviews how flexibility has been theorized and investigated in relation to older workers. The chapter ends with a future research agenda for advancing understanding of how workplace flexibility may enhance working experiences of older workers, and in particular focuses on the critical investigation of uses of flexibility in relation to older workers.

Keywords: Workplace flexibility; older workers; aging; lifespan; flexible work arrangements

Research in Personnel and Human Resources Management, Volume 34, 43–99
ISSN: 0742-7301/doi:10.1108/S0742-730120160000034009

Flexibility can be regarded as one of the key concepts of the contemporary workplace (Bird, 2015). Organizations try to become more flexible and adaptable to ever-changing economic circumstances (Volberda, 1996; Way et al., 2015), while employees are expected to be more flexible in how they approach their jobs and careers (Hill, Grzywacz, et al., 2008). Moreover, employees are increasingly looking for more flexibility in how they balance their work with their personal lives (Allen, Johnson, Kiburz, & Shockley, 2013; Ferguson, Carlson, & Kacmar, 2015), and in how they develop their careers (Moen & Sweet, 2004). Finally, governments across the world have increasingly responded to these trends by declaring flexibility the keyword for the future workforce and workplace (Johnson, 2011). In all these instances the denotation "flexibility" refers to a different object and consequently has a different meaning.

It is not surprising that the increasing popularity of the allegedly multi-interpretational term flexibility has coincided with rapid demographic changes in the workforce, including the aging of populations across the world (Kooij, 2015; Zacher, 2015). These demographic changes have caused governments, organizations, and employees to take a different position in how work and careers are both conceived and realized when life expectancy will rise to 100 years and above. However, current retirement systems are largely based on people retiring at 65 years (Wang & Shultz, 2010). One of the more immediate consequences of the aging population is that the ratio of working versus nonworking people is declining rapidly, causing more nonworking people to be dependent upon a smaller number of people in jobs (Johnson, 2011). As these changes have put greater pressure on the affordability of pensions in many countries worldwide, governments have been engaging in the process of stimulating longer careers and ceasing with financially supporting early retirement. However, whereas the need for people to work beyond retirement has increased, it has yet been proven difficult to effectively address the issue of continuing working and extending retirement (Wang & Shi, 2014). Many older workers still have (private) early retirement plans, low willingness and intentions to continue working, and many older workers who lose their jobs at higher ages experience many difficulties in finding new jobs, and hence have a high probability of remaining unemployed (Johnson, 2011; Klehe, Koen, & De Pater, 2012; Wang & Shi, 2014).

One of the potential avenues for governments, organizations, and employees to address these issues is through the concept of flexibility (Putnam, Myers, & Gailliard, 2014; Siegenthaler & Brenner, 2001). It has been argued that flexibility could provide a useful tool for both

organizations and employees to enhance motivation, fulfilment, and productivity in later life, and to ensure older workers to be able and willing to
continue working (Bal, De Jong, Jansen, & Bakker, 2012). Hence, when
organizations want to retain and motivate their older workers, HR-systems
have to be adapted to allow more flexibility in how employees develop
their careers and how they balance work obligations with personal lives.
Governments have already taken steps to adapt laws and regulations in
order to enable organizations and workers to more flexibly arrange
employment relationships (Platman, 2004a).

Notwithstanding the potential relevance of flexibility for older workers
and late-career decisions (Wang & Shultz, 2010), there are a number of
issues regarding how flexibility can be used for older workers, and the role
it plays across the lifespan. First, as alluded to above, the definition of flexibility is rather vague, which limits its potential use for understanding how
it operates with regards to the motivation, well-being, and productivity of
workers across the lifespan. The term flexibility has been used in many
different fields, including organizational psychology (Allen et al., 2013;
Ferguson et al., 2015), sociology (Hyman, Scholarios, & Baldry, 2005;
Kalleberg, 2003; Vallas, 1999), strategic HRM (Way et al., 2015; Wright &
Snell, 1998), strategy (Sanchez, 1995; Volberda, 1996), and the careers
literature (Moen & Sweet, 2004). Flexibility has been used differently across
these fields, and thus carries different meanings which potentially contra-
dict each other (Putnam et al., 2014). Thus, understanding how flexibility
operates across the lifespan requires an understanding of how flexibility is
used in these different fields. The aim of this chapter, therefore, is to review
and advance understanding of workplace flexibility across the lifespan,
and in particular how workplace flexibility operates in the motivation,
well-being, and productivity of older workers. To do so, we will discuss the
various meanings and uses of the term flexibility in different literatures,
and incorporate these different conceptualizations and perspectives in relation to how workplace flexibility across the lifespan has been investigated.
We will first discuss the conceptualizations of workplace flexibility, and
discuss both employer and employee perspectives on flexibility. We will
postulate a working definition of workplace flexibility that includes both
employer and employee perspectives. Moreover, we review theories and
models used to explain how flexibility operates in the workplace, and relate
prominent lifespan theories of aging to the role of flexibility at work.
Subsequently, we review empirical studies on the role of workplace flexibility for older workers to ascertain the current empirical knowledge pertaining to the role of workplace flexibility for older workers. Finally, we

propose a future research agenda based on the review of the studies, and postulate specific recommendations for further investigation and use of workplace flexibility.

CONCEPTUALIZATIONS OF WORKPLACE FLEXIBILITY

Before we explore the conceptualization of workplace flexibility across different literatures, it is needed to understand the meaning of flexibility in its broader sense. A dictionary definition of the term "flexibility" concerns "the ability and/or willingness to easily modify, change or compromise" (Oxford Dictionary, 2015). These attributes refer to the psychological characteristics of what flexibility entails, while another, more physical, definition of flexibility concerns "the quality of bending easily without breaking" (Oxford Dictionary, 2015). In this chapter, and in line with most prominent definitions of workplace flexibility in the literature (De Menezes & Kelliher, 2011; Hill, Grzywacz, et al., 2008), we will primarily focus on the former aspect of flexibility, and ignore the changes in physical and muscular flexibility that comes with age (see, e.g., Seco et al., 2013). However, the latter definition includes an important aspect of flexibility that may be inherent to assumptions organizations may have regarding workplace flexibility (Kelliher & Anderson, 2010; Putnam et al., 2014), which is about the ability and willingness to bend without breaking. This may implicitly refer to employees' abilities and motivation to work more hours, conduct more tasks, and adapt easily when performing multiple roles in the organization (Way et al., 2015).

Translating flexibility to the workplace, and in particular the meaning of flexibility for workers, results in two perspectives on flexibility. On the one hand, flexibility may enable workers to reduce or rebalance workload, whereby actively external control is exercised over one's work. Workers are active shapers of their jobs and use flexibility to align jobs with their personalities (Kooij, 2015). On the other hand, flexibility may entail the ability of workers to conduct more work, and see their job descriptions expanded, involving more working hours and more effort. Hence, workers have to employ internal control mechanisms, and according to this perspective, workers are passive recipients of work. This distinction aligns with that of Heckhausen, Wrosch, and Schulz (2010), who in their theory of lifespan development described how people may use either primary control mechanisms (i.e., actively changing their environment) or secondary control mechanisms (i.e., reactively changing oneself) to achieve goal attainment across the lifespan. Flexibility may enable these mechanisms, through either allowing employees to adapt their jobs toward individual preferences (and thus exerting active, primary, externally-oriented control) or via demanding them to be more able to change to circumstances and conduct more work (and thus exerting passive, secondary, internally oriented control). Here, employees are expected to bend, stretch, and accept changes and increasing work pressure as part of contemporary working lives (Putnam et al., 2014). While until the 1980s flexibility was understood as being able to bend and return to a stable state, it has been more and more conceptualized as a state of continuous bending and adaptation to changing circumstances, without a stable point to return to (Kociatkiewicz & Kostera, 2014). Hence, flexibility is currently regarded as a permanent state attributed to organization and employee.

The key differentiation of the concept of flexibility in an HRM perspective in relation to other concepts, such as proactivity, job crafting, and readiness to change, is that flexibility is not only an attribute of people, but can be a characteristic of the job, the workplace, or the organization as well. This has led to a wide range of uses of the term, including organizational flexibility (Sanchez, 1995), flexible work arrangements (Allen et al., 2013), and flexibility HRM (Bal & De Lange, 2015; Chang, Gong, Way, & Jia, 2013). As the term flexibility has been used among different disciplines, the chances increase that the term is stretched toward a meaning that captures many variations, which is a typical case of concept stretching, which impedes construct clarity (Suddaby, 2010). The result is that the denotation flexibility is used loosely across and within fields, such that it may be unclear what flexibility specifically entails. What does it mean to be flexible, and how does one achieve flexibility as a person, or as an organization? Who or what should be flexible? These questions pertain to the idea of flexibility as something that, whether it is a characteristic of people or of systems, can be developed, maintained, or lost. However, there is still little understanding around how this functions in the workplace and in particular for older workers.

A more fundamental issue arises when we look at how primary control over workplace flexibility may lead to lower secondary control. Employees may enhance their working experiences using flexible work arrangements, but at the same time, this leads to a higher (self-inflicted) workload, and thus to lower internal regulation, as control over one's job and working hours decreases. This argument has been made earlier by Kelliher and

Anderson (2010), who showed that employees who were using flexible work practices were more likely to experience work intensification, while a review of Putnam et al. (2014) concluded that when employees had more autonomy resulting from flexible work arrangements, they were also likely to work harder and more hours, and experience less control over their work (see also Hill, Grzywacz, et al., 2008). We will discuss this apparent paradox in more detail later.

The origin of the concept of workplace flexibility stems from the idea of technological advancement leading to the need to more rapidly adapt to changing circumstances in the economic environment (Hinds, 2003; Tomaney, 1990). Given the increasingly rapid advancement of technology in society and the resulting hypercompetitiveness of markets across the world (Sanchez, 1995; Volberda, 1996), organizations are more under pressure to be adaptable and proactive toward these changes. As organizations are competing with each other, it becomes an essential organizational capability (Volberda, 1996) to be able to change organizational activities within short periods of time. Hence, a stream of research within the field of strategy has emerged since the 1990s on how organizations can become more flexible (Yu, Cadeaux, & Luo, 2015). One of the key features of organizational flexibility concerns the role of "*resource flexibility*," which should contribute to competitive advantage (Sanchez, 1995). This notion of flexibility in resources has been picked up by the strategic HRM literature, which introduced the concept of resource flexibility in (S-)HRM and flexibility HRM practices (Wright & Snell, 1998). Being closely tied to the strategy literature, flexibility HRM was originally conceptualized as the extent to which HRM practices can be different across units or locations within the same firm in order to allow the organization to become more responsive to changes in the environment (Wright & Snell, 1998). Flexibility in resources entails the idea that employees should be flexible toward how they can contribute to organizational goals, and that includes organizational use of flexible contracts, flexible job descriptions, and flexible organizational structures (Way et al., 2015). Two notions of organizational use of flexibility can be distinguished here; qualitative flexibility refers to having employees with broad behavioral repertoires, contributing to a broader quality of organizational skills, while quantitative flexibility refers to the organizational capability to hire and fire employees easily in order to adapt to the environment. While qualitative flexibility is associated with the skills of employees, quantitative flexibility is related to the amount of employees working for an organization at a particular moment.

Developing at the same time of the research on organizational flexibility, a stream of research appeared on flexible working schedules (Baltes, Briggs, Huff, Wright, & Neuman, 1999; De Menezes & Kelliher, 2011), which reflected the needs of many employees for nonstandard working times, and more flexibility in when and where they conducted their work in order to better balance work and life issues. This created a literature on *flexible work arrangements*, which primarily focuses on the role of flexibility for employees in choosing how they work and conduct their jobs. As this literature developed largely independent from the strategic (HRM) literature, different perspectives on the meaning of flexibility were consequently developed. A notable difference with the organizational flexibility literature is that this stream of research perceives the employee as actively constructing the job through choosing when and how to work. Therefore, as Hill, Grzywacz, et al. (2008) argued, workplace flexibility can be conceptualized from the organizational perspective as well as from the employees' perspective. Below, we will separately discuss in more detail how these perspectives overlap and differ from each other.

A final stream of research concerns *work boundary flexibility* (Ferguson et al., 2015). This research builds on boundary theory, which postulates that people maintain boundaries between work and private life, and work boundary flexibility refers to people's ability to change these boundaries at a particular moment (Ferguson et al., 2015; Glavin & Schieman, 2012). Hence, work boundary flexibility entails the idea that an employee can express agency over when work is conducted, and thus is able to change the boundaries between work and nonwork according to the demands of a given situation. This research aligns with the notion of psychological flexibility in the sense of a mental state of being able to change one's behavior in the pursuit of goals and values (Atkins & Parker, 2012; Bond, Flaxman, & Bunce, 2008). Thus while flexible work arrangements refer to organizational practices to allow the workers to flexibly arrange work, work boundary flexibility is a more psychological approach toward flexibility as a mental state. While this research has been silent on whether it is aimed at internal versus external control mechanisms, the notion that employees can maintain boundaries and be flexible in how they set their boundaries assumes an active approach toward work boundary flexibility. Yet, at the same time, the question is whether employees are in control over setting their boundaries or whether the organization may force employees in passively accepting boundary stretching.

In sum, there have been multiple conceptualizations of workplace flexibility, and these different conceptualizations may determine how workplace flexibility manifests for older workers. First, organizational perspectives focus on how organizations may become more flexible in a competitive market. Second, employee perspectives have focused on how flexibility may help workers to balance their work demands with private demands. A particular case of flexibility for workers is work boundary flexibility, which adds to understanding of workplace flexibility as a psychological mindset which can be perceived to be the opposite of cognitive rigidity (Atkins & Parker, 2012) The two main perspectives on flexibility (i.e., organizational and employee) will be included in the remainder of this chapter when we consider the role of flexibility HRM for older workers. We do not specifically discuss notions of work boundary flexibility, or psychological flexibility, as we were unable to locate studies investigating these concepts in relation to older workers.

Relevant to the context of the aging workforce is the notion of flexible retirement (Johnson, 2011). The literature has until recently taken a perspective on retirement as a decision-making process (Wang & Shi, 2014), which indicates that people make a motivated choice to retire at a specific moment in time, thereby gradually reducing their commitment to work and organization. However, increasingly retirement is being perceived as a process, which means that people gradually change their work roles and psychological perspectives on their work and careers (Dingemans & Henkens, 2014). Accordingly, the retirement process now involves many more flexible forms of employment relationships, often referred to as bridge employment (Dingemans, Henkens, & van Solinge, 2015). Bridge employment creates flexibility in how older workers transition from their work and career jobs toward full retirement, and may include a variety of work attachments, including part-time work, reduced working hours, and demotion (Wang, Zhan, Liu, & Shultz, 2008). This means that the question of flexibility across the lifespan, and in particular related to older workers, not solely pertains to aspects of the job which can be adjusted to older workers, but that complete jobs and HR-systems are adapted toward the employment of older workers. Before we will discuss the role of flexibility across the lifespan, we will first discuss in detail organizational and employee perspectives on workplace flexibility.

EMPLOYER PERSPECTIVES ON WORKPLACE FLEXIBILITY

The seminal work of Wright and Snell (1998) introduced the concept of flexibility in strategic HRM, and focused on two forms of organizational flexibility, based on the work of Sanchez (1995). Resource flexibility refers to the extent to which organizations can switch between resources or to which resources can be used alternatively. Coordination flexibility refers to the extent to which organizations can reconfigure the structure of the resources. Wright and Snell's (1998) translation of these types of organizational flexibility toward HRM practices includes the notion of HRM practices being different across units, locations, and teams, on the basis that HRM practices may have different utility depending on the context in which employees are conducting their work. Subsequent empirical research operationalized these types of flexibility in practices aimed at hiring and training employees such that they are able to conduct various roles in the organization (i.e., qualitative flexibility), and practices aimed at how quickly employees can be redeployed within an organization (i.e., quantitative flexibility; Chang et al., 2013). Other work took a person-based approach to flexibility by measuring employee skill and behavior flexibility, which focused on how broad the skills of the employees are, and how able employees are to adapt to changing work circumstances (Beltrán-Martín & Roca-Puig, 2013; Beltrán-Martín, Roca-Puig, Escrig-Tena, & Bou-Llusar, 2008; Bhattacharya, Gibson, & Doty, 2005). Dissatisfied with both of these approaches to flexibility HRM, Way and colleagues (2015), including the authors of the original SHRM piece on flexibility (Wright & Snell, 1998), developed a new measure of flexibility HRM, which included an aspect which was largely ignored in these earlier studies. In addition to items measuring the extent to which HR practices can be adapted to changing circumstances and to which extent employees are able to adapt accordingly, the measure included the use of contingent workers, and the organizational ability to quickly dismiss temporary workers who are no longer needed for achievement of organizational goals (Way et al., 2015, p. 1128–1129). Hence, this aspect heavily relies upon the extent to which organizations have quantitative flexibility, which is about how employment contracts are shaped, and whether workers are offered temporary or permanent contracts, the latter on the basis that they, when circumstances are changing, can be redeployed in other functions within the organization.

This addition has been important to understand the full scope of what is meant with organizational flexibility, and shows the inherent tensions which are present in the strategic HRM literature concerning flexibility in organizations. From an organizational perspective, it is important to be ready to change quickly and to adapt to changing circumstances if needed (Way et al., 2015). This is the ultimate meaning of organizational flexibility, and employee flexibility is supportive for the level of organizational flexibility (Wright & Snell, 1998). When organizations devote effort into training employees and to increase their behavioral flexibility by offering options for job sharing, job rotation and development, this may create a win-win situation, whereby organizations enhance their organizational capabilities (Volberda, 1996), and employees enhance their skills, motivation, and employability (Grant & Parker, 2009). However, this situation is only achieved when organizations offer permanent contracts to the employees, so that employees are motivated to invest in the organization and accept task enrichment. Yet, the use of contingent workers has been central to the conceptualization of the flexible organization (Wright & Snell, 1998), and the literature on organizational flexibility has emphasized the importance of having the opportunity to flexibly hire and dismiss employees in order to stay competitive.

This notion has among others been criticized in the sociology literature. The strategy and strategic HRM literatures too narrowly focus on the sur-vivors of the flexibilization of organizations, that is, the employees with permanent, fulltime contracts who receive training and opportunities to enrich their jobs (Legge, 1995; Vallas, 1999). Increasing organizational flex-ibility may lead to a distinction between core workers, who profit from qualitative flexibility (e.g., training that enables task enrichment), and per-ipheral workers, who face the consequences of quantitative flexibility (i.e., with increasing job insecurity). There is hardly any notion of these victims of the flexible organization, who are the people who are laid off and forced into temporary contracts. As many organizations are driven by the argu-ments of the business case (De Menezes & Kelliher, 2011), organizations and HR-managers will be inclined to perceive workplace flexibility primar-ily from the perspective of the organization, and the extent to which increased flexibility contributes to organizational performance (see, e.g., Martínez-Sánchez, Vela-Jiménez, Pérez-Pérez, & de-Luis-Carnicer, 2011). Hence, the question arises if organizations will still invest in arrangements for enhancement of employee flexibility when it does not (clearly) contri-bute to organizational goals. A study of Gardiner and Tomlinson (2009) indeed showed that organizations are more inclined to invest in flexibility for employees when it was aligned with strategic business rationales. In sum, the organizational perspective on flexibility relies heavily on the notion that flexibility of organizational structures, including HRM prac-tices, and employees can be enhanced in order to achieve higher perfor-mance and to survive in a competitive market. For employees, this includes a perspective on the possibility for enhancing skills and behavioral flexibil-ity, but also a perspective of being a resource, which can be used tempora-rily and dismissed when no longer needed.

EMPLOYEE PERSPECTIVES ON WORKPLACE FLEXIBILITY

Employee perspectives on flexibility have been developed largely independent from the literature on organizational flexibility and hence focus on a different aspect of flexibility. Hill, Grzywacz, et al. (2008, p. 151) define workplace flexibility from a worker perspective as the "degree to which workers are able to make choices to arrange core aspects of their professional lives." Flexibility in this meaning primarily refers to the free choice employees have to decide on how, when, and where they conduct their work. Hence, in contrast to employer perspective on flexibility which tends to perceive flexibility as being instrumental to organizational goals, here flexibility is primarily being instrumental to self-set employee goals. These goals have traditionally been related to work-life balance concerns (Allen et al., 2013), as the literature on flexible work arrangements until recently has been linked to the needs of women and young parents for work arrangements that would suit meeting the demands from work as well as from home (Ferguson et al., 2015). However, recent research has expanded the view of workplace flexibility being primarily useful for women and young parents, to a perspective of flexibility as being available to all employees within an organization, who may have different reasons for using flexibility (Bal, Van Kleef, & Jansen, 2015; Hyman et al., 2005). Thus, workplace flexibility from an employee perspective concerns the free choice of employees on deciding when, where, and how work will be conducted to meet work and personal needs. The "when" concerns the work schedules of an employee, which can be made more flexible by allowing employees to choose when they start and stop working, which days they work, and when they take breaks. Moreover, the "when" also refers to the opportunity for employees to work part-time or reduced hours during a particular period. The "where" concerns the location where an employee conduct (parts of) the work, which can be from the office, from home, or from any place relevant for the employee to conduct the job. Finally, the "how" concerns the distribution of tasks and responsibilities among employees, and may include the flexibility within teams to distribute tasks in line with workers' needs and preferences.

The concept of free choice is essential here, as a decision for a flexible employment relationship which is forced upon by the employer constitutes an arrangement in which the employee has no say. It is important to distinguish between flexibility *of* the employee (employer perspective), which is primarily the case in organizational perspectives, and flexibility *for* the employee (employee perspective), which is more aligned with employee perspectives. Workplace flexibility in relation to employees therefore can be understood from the perspective of the employer being able to change rapidly to meet the organizational goal of switching between resources or reconfiguring the structure of resources, up until the point where employees bend but not break (or do break when they are on temporary contracts with high job insecurity). But, workplace flexibility can also be understood as the organization, and with it its HRM-system and practices, to be flexible and guarantee flexibility of working conditions in favor of the employee (Hill, Grzywacz, et al., 2008). As long as free will is present in how flexibility is used in organizations, it can be regarded as contributing to the quality of work experiences. However, Putnam et al. (2014) argued that the execution of control is essential in this process. While flexibility may allow employees to have more autonomy over how they conduct their work, the control resides still outside the employee when targets are set within the hierarchy of the organization, and being imposed upon the employee. As we described in the introduction, there is a tension between the seemingly active, external regulation that flexibility may offer to employees, while they have to internally regulate themselves in order to meet performance goals set by the organization.

Therefore, enhanced autonomy as a result of increasing flexibility may even contribute to work intensification (Kelliher & Anderson, 2010), as flexible work schedules and flexible workspaces may imply that there are no boundaries anymore between work and private life, thereby decreasing external regulation options (cf. Ferguson et al., 2015). Thus the notion of increasing boundary flexibility may lead to a situation where the boundaries of work are stretched into the private spheres of people, who may struggle with maintaining a separation of the demands of their work with their private lives, a process exacerbated by the continuous availability of digital technologies. Hence, the control over work may seem to be increasing when employees have the availability of flexible work options also pertaining to external regulation, but control is still indirectly imposed on the worker through professional and cultural work norms (Putnam et al., 2014). Moreover, the more autonomy people have over key aspects of their work, the more energy has to be spent in maintenance of boundaries (Ferguson et al., 2015), and as energy is a limited resource, it can be depleted, and thus undermining self-regulation (Allen et al., 2013).

The employer's perspective may lead to a clash with the employee perspective, when organizational flexibility is narrowly translated toward the employee through an expansion of working times (Hyman et al., 2005;

Kelliher & Anderson, 2010). Another clash may arise when organizations train their employees to become flexible *within* the organization and to be able to conduct many different tasks, while employees may have specific needs toward development of their professional skills, aimed at increasing their employability *outside* the organization (Way et al., 2015). A final clash may arise when organizations strive for more flexibility through the use of contingent workers (i.e., using quantitative flexibility to shape employment relationships), who can be dismissed at any time, while employees have preferences for more stable employment relationships. Another issue arises when this is confronted with national regulations and law concerning the protection of labor contracts. This introduces a societal perspective on flexibility, in which not only regulation and law are designed given a particular perspective on workplace flexibility, but where the meaning of flexibility is defined given a particular ideological approach (Harvey, 2005). Hence, it is necessary to further explore the ideological underpinning of the concept flexibility, as it may inform our understanding of how flexibility is used at the workplace, and in particular in relation to older workers.

AN IDEOLOGICAL PERSPECTIVE ON FLEXIBILITY

The interest in workplace flexibility has not developed in a vacuum, but there are societal trends which have led to the increasing interest in organizations and employees for more flexibility. Therefore, to understand why organizations have become more interested in flexible employees, and why employees have become more interested in flexible work arrangements, an ideological perspective is needed to shape the wider context in which these developments have taken place. While Vallas (1999) points to the Fordist underpinnings of work until the 1960s and 1970s, a notable change has occurred since that era. From the 1980s onwards, rapid technological advances have demanded organizations to become more quickly adapting to changes in the environment. As product life cycles shortened, organizations could no longer rely upon stable environments, which among others has led to the rise of the "flexible specialization theory" (Vallas, 1999), which in essence means that organizations are driven primarily by the environment, and thus the environment is the driver of workplace change. It was Tomaney (1990), who already pointed toward the role of work intensification as an underlying rationale for the idea of flexibility as a management concept. This entails the rationale that employees should be flexible in skills so that they have the capacity to undertake a wide variety of tasks, while at the same time they should have unlimited flexibility as to how long they work (i.e., conducting unpaid overtime work), and thus mental capability to manage disappearing boundaries between work and nonwork. The essential question here is whether employees are in the position of refusing to be flexible, or whether they are actually forced by the organization to become completely flexible in their tasks and working times. An example is the mason on a permanent contract with a construction firm, who is fired and rehired on a contractor basis. This refers to enforced, quantitative flexibility by which market insecurity for the organization directly results in employment insecurity for the worker. Thus, workplace flexibility becomes an inherent part of the contemporary experience of work.

When flexibility is inherent to work and contemporary employment relationships, parallels can be drawn with wider societal trends, and in particular neoliberalism (Harvey, 2005), to the point where flexible work becomes a manifestation of dominant ideological paradigms in society. It is no coincidence that flexibility became more popular in the 1980s, a period of economic recession and high unemployment in many Western countries (Harvey, 2005). Organized labor movements, such as trade unions, were attacked and lost their power positions especially in the United States and the United Kingdom. This provided the opportunity for many organizations to engage in more flexible contracts with their employees, a trend that has progressed ever since, including the current rise of zero-hour contracts (Gov.uk, 2015; Karl, 2015; Pessoa & Van Reenen, 2014). However, neoliberal values, including unlimited entrepreneurial freedom and downscaling of government regulation of employee protection and security (Harvey, 2005; Seymour, 2014), could not be sold to the public without the rhetoric of flexible working arrangements for employees. Hence, greater freedom of labor was sold to the public as a virtue, with the option for individuals to more flexibly arrange their work with their personal lives, and thus to have control over their working lives. Hence, Harvey (2005) explicitly links employer perspectives on flexibility (i.e., to use employees as mere resources which can be dismissed when no longer necessary), with employee perspectives on flexibility (i.e., the chance to set one's own working conditions), with the latter being used to convince the public of the rhetoric of flexibility as constituting the future of work and employment relationships. However, long-term analyses have shown that this rhetoric of flexibility has primarily served organizations, rather than employees, as real wages have stagnated or decreased on average over the last 30 years (Harvey, 2005; Pessoa & Van Reenen, 2014), and income inequality has increased substantially

(Piketty, 2014). This economic-political analysis showed that flexibility is inherently related to neoliberal forces in society, which stress the freedom of organizations to operate, while deregulation limits the power and negotiation positions of (collective groups of) employees.

Subsequently, flexibility is not only debated at the organizational level but has been extended toward the societal level, where the flexible economy has been coined (i.e., low hiring and firing costs of workers, and few restrictions on changing work hours; Cuñat & Melitz, 2012). The opposite of economic flexibility has been coined rigidity (Cuñat & Melitz, 2012), and with it the negative connotation associated to the term *rigid*, as not being able to change. The question is where responsibility for employment security resides when workers in the flexible economy do not have job security anymore. Workers have to become "employable" (Van der Heijde & Van Der Heijden, 2006), but it is unclear whether employability is a right for employees (and thus a responsibility for organization or government to provide it), or a demand on employees, and thus the responsibility of workers themselves to become and remain employable. In the current economy, the latter seems to be the case (Bauman, 2013; Seymour, 2014).

Flexibility as inherently neoliberal value has even been extended to the level of the human being, and it is proposed that the norm of the flexible society and human being is now apparent (Bauman, 2013; Hinds, 2003). People, and certainly people at work, are expected in a neoliberal paradigm, to be ultimately flexible, to be able to adapt continuously to ever-changing circumstances, to be self-reliant, and to ensure one is not unemployed (Harvey, 2005; Morgan, 2015; Seymour, 2014). Flexibility becomes a characteristic of the new human being who is able to survive in a neoliberal society which is stripped of government protection, such as employment benefits and free education and health care (Morgan, 2015). This is mirrored in that flexibility takes no account of the losers, the have-nots, and the people with no chance of permanent and stable contracts (Bal & Lub, 2015; Bauman, 2013). It is not surprising how research within the domain of HRM has focused on such related constructs as proactivity (Grant & Parker, 2009), job crafting (Wrzesniewski & Dutton, 2001), employability (Van der Heijde & Van Der Heijden, 2006), active shaping (De Lange et al., 2010), boundaryless careers (Arthur, Khapova, & Wilderom, 2005), effectuation (Sarasvathy, 2001), life designing (Savickas et al., 2009), and idiosyncratic deals (Rousseau, 2005) in explaining how the contemporary worker has needed to become self-reliant in obtaining favorable working conditions. Flexibility fits within this picture, and to this extent has become a manifestation of neoliberalism at the workplace (Karl, 2015).

Flexibility, due to its conceptual ambiguity and vagueness, has been used rhetorically to sell increased organizational flexibility at the expense of the individual worker, but at the same time allow employees to more flexibly arrange their working conditions, as long as it contributes to or does not impede organizational performance (Gardiner & Tomlinson, 2009). According to Harvey (2005; Vallas, 1999), organizational flexibility is implicitly exchanged for opportunities for flexibility for employees. However, in this exchange, organizational flexibility entails greater job insecurity for noncore workers, and the risks of unemployment for the employee, and thus it comes at the expense of the employee (Harvey, 2005). This is important given the outlook of this chapter on flexibility across the lifespan, since, as we will see, this implicit exchange returns when we review the research on flexibility for older workers.

As this chapter's main focus is on the role of flexibility across the lifespan, we will now discuss theories and models explaining how flexibility is perceived by employees. As studies in the field of strategic HRM, which have focused on flexibility, primarily rely upon organizational representatives, such as directors or HR-managers (Way et al., 2015), they insufficiently describe how flexibility affects the work experiences of employees, and in particular older workers. We therefore review the literature on how employees experience workplace flexibility to understand how flexibility relates to the lifespan. To do so, we will be postulating a working definition of workplace flexibility that includes the explicit integration and negotiation of employer and worker interests.

WORKPLACE FLEXIBILITY FOR WORKERS

Workplace flexibility for workers entails the possibility to engage in decision-making concerning when, where, and how they work (Hill, Grzywacz, et al., 2008). These decisions are made striving for agreement between employee and organization (Bal et al., 2012). When employees engage in self-initiated shaping of their own working conditions, such as deciding when they start working and when they leave, it is denoted job crafting (Tims & Bakker, 2010). Workplace flexibility for workers occurs when organization and employee agree on whether employees have the space to arrange and decide on their working schedules, location, and tasks. Mutual agreement forms an essential part of how flexibility manifests in the workplace. Therefore, workplace flexibility is conceptually more closely related to idiosyncratic deals than job crafting as it aims to align employee perceptions of how they can apply flexibility in their work with organizational perceptions (Bal & Jansen, 2015).

A crucial distinction is between *availability* and *use* of workplace flexibility (Allen et al., 2013). While availability indicates whether the organization provides access to flexible work options to some or all of the employees in the firm, actual use refers to whether employees benefit from an arrangement. Availability is closely related to legal frameworks and regulation, as it determines whether workers have some entitlement toward the access of workplace flexibility, such as part-time working or flexible work schedules (Johnson, 2011). When flexibility is only available to some employees, such as women, and not others, this may be perceived to be discrimination, and therefore, may have detrimental effects for motivation and effectiveness of the program (Atkinson & Sandiford, 2016). Moreover, unequal access of flexibility to employees implies an establishment of a bureaucracy (Putnam et al., 2014), in which decisions have to be made as to who is entitled to a certain flexible work arrangement and who is not. Unequal access may have negative effects as people may feel unfairly treated when they do not have access (Greenberg, Roberge, Ho, & Rousseau, 2004). This is important for older workers, as traditionally, access to workplace flexibility for older workers has been regulated through certain ages (e.g., 50 or 55 years) at which a worker is entitled to flexibility, such as reduced working hours or exemption from working night shifts (Bal et al., 2012; Dingemans et al., 2015). Hence, a crucial aspect of availability concerns the extent to which options are available to all employees or to a limited group of workers.

Moreover, there may also be a gap between whether workplace flexibility arrangements are available to an employee, and whether the employees are actually using it. While some options may be available but not valued by the employee (such as teleworking; Bailey & Kurland, 2002), it may also be organizational cultures that hinder or facilitate use of flexibility (Bal et al., 2012). Yang and Zheng (2011) referred to decoupling, when organizations adopt flexibility programs as formal policies, but where, due to cultures that inhibit actual use of flexible work options, employees in reality do not use these flexibility arrangements. The study of Yang and Zheng (2011) showed that when organizations adopt flexibility, but when employees cannot really use it, employees felt to be performing worst in their jobs as compared to when employees could use them, or when the employees could not use them as the organization did not offer them. This shows that consistency between having flexibility available and actual implementation of flexibility is important for employees, as otherwise this may be perceived as a psychological contract breach (Morrison & Robinson, 1997).

Another dimension relevant for workplace flexibility is the type of flexibility. Allen et al. (2013), in their meta-analysis, distinguished between flex-time and flex-space. On the one hand, workplace flexibility offers employees to adapt their working times. Adaptations of working times may occur at daily level or may be arranged at an institutional level. Daily flexibility allows employees to choose when they start their working days and when they finish it (De Menezes & Kelliher, 2011), and more elaborate forms of workplace flexibility may allow employees to abolish working times, and be evaluated solely on output and performance targets (Ten Brummelhuis, Bakker, Hetland, & Keulemans, 2012). A more institutionalized approach to flexible working schedules is the opportunity to work part-time or reduced working hours. This allows a contractual agreement where the expectation of fulltime employment ceases to exist, and where part-time employment is regarded as a "normal" work arrangement. Part-time employment is increasing in popularity, and despite stereotypical perceptions of lower commitment, research has shown little evidence of systematic differences between part-time and fulltime workers (Thorsteinson, 2003). Furthermore, Bal and De Lange (2015) distinguished between regular and irregular flexibility, with the former referring to flexibility at a structural, daily level (such as changes in working times and reduced working hours), and the latter referring to irregular breaks from work, such as sabbaticals or working only part of the year (e.g., seasonal work). Hence, another important aspect of flex-time is whether it is related to employees' daily work schedules, or whether it concerns the more irregular breaks in which one can pursue alternative activities. While Bal and De Lange (2015) did not find many differences in the relationships of regular and irregular flexibility HRM in relation to employee engagement and job performance, future research might investigate the differential relationships of these aspects.

Another type of flexibility concerns flex-space (Allen et al., 2013). Flexibility in work locations allows employees to decide where they conduct their work. While there may be constraints within many jobs as to where tasks are completed (e.g., a border control employee has a very specific location for execution of the job), especially white-collar office workers may become more independent of the physical locations of offices to complete their work. Discretion over where to conduct work allows them to cope with work demands through completion of work at home, and thereby avoiding traffic jams, and possible interference with school times of children (Bailey & Kurland, 2002; De Menezes & Kelliher, 2011).

Finally, a type of workplace flexibility for older workers concerns early retirement and bridge employment options (Dingemans et al., 2015; Wang & Shi, 2014). Early retirement options offer employees the flexibility of ceasing working lives earlier than state pension age, while bridge employment options allow them to achieve a more flexible transition from fulltime work toward fulltime retirement through for instance reduced working hours, demotion, or the opportunity to work in another career until one's retirement (Armstrong-Stassen, 2008b). Recent research also investigated how older workers have more specific wishes as to how they arrange the transition from fulltime employment into full retirement, and found that in general four ways people may want to transition from work to employment: gradually reducing working hours, not changing anything until retirement, changing the content of one's job, and changing the context of one's job (such as working for another organization; Polat, Bal, & Jansen, 2012).

THEORIES AND MODELS OF WORKPLACE FLEXIBILITY

The primary theoretical underpinning of workplace flexibility for workers concerns the rebalancing of work with private life (Baltes et al., 1999). Baltes and colleagues (1999) explain this on the basis of the work adjustment model. Through more flexibility in how workers approach their working schedules and location, they may achieve greater correspondence between the requirements of a job on the one hand and their needs on the other hand. Hence, workplace flexibility is postulated to produce a greater fit between a person and the job (Bal et al., 2012; Moen, Kelly, & Huang, 2008). In addition, options for flexibility may be regarded as job characteristics, which in their own right may have a motivational effect as they provide employees with a sense of autonomy and control (Baltes et al., 1999; Moen et al., 2008). Flexibility, according to these models, is inherently positive for employees, as it contributes to a better work-life balance (Allen et al., 2013). However, flexibility may also be related to lower dedication to one's career, and attributions by others that one is not committed to the organization (Leslie, Manchester, Park, & Mehng, 2012; Rogier & Padgett, 2004). Hence, this shows the inherent contrast that may arise from flexibility arrangements between the employee, who is able to obtain more flexibility, and the employer, who questions the employees' commitment to the organization when flexibility is perceived to be negotiated to obtain a better work-life balance. Moreover, people with a low growth-need strength may have lower needs for autonomy (Baltes et al., 1999), and therefore flexibility may be less desirable for them. Especially older workers may have worked in fixed, regulated workplaces without flexibility, and therefore flexibility may have less initial attractiveness for older workers (Posthuma & Campion, 2009).

A theoretical perspective that explains the employer's perceptions on workplace flexibility for workers has been presented by institutional theory (Masuda et al., 2012), which postulates that organizations must adapt to pressures from the environment, such as cultural expectations. For instance, in cultures where gender equality is high, organizations will be more likely to offer flexible work arrangements (Lyness & Kropf, 2005). Hence, organizations do not solely use workplace flexibility in a self-enhancing way, that is, as the extent to which organizations can switch between resources or reconfigure the structure of resources. Instead, because organizations experience pressure from the environment, they also comply to the employee's perception of workplace flexibility as the degree to which the worker can decide when, where, and how work will be conducted to meet work and personal needs. In addition, neoinstitutional theory (McNamara, Pitt-Catsouphes, Brown, & Matz-Costa, 2012) explains that even though organizations may be pressured to incorporate workplace flexibility as perceived by workers, they may be more hesitant or resistant to fully implement these systems, which explains decoupling (Yang & Zheng, 2011), and the divergence between employers' and employees' perspectives on flexibility. As flexibility may be costly for organizations, they may refrain from implementing policies to enable employees to fully use flexibility at work.

As a result of this, McNamara et al. (2012) argued that many workers will obtain flexibility options through informal agreements rather than existing formal policies for workplace flexibility. Accordingly, research on informal agreements between employee and organization has increased substantially over the years (Liao, Wayne, & Rousseau, 2016; Rousseau, 2005). The central theoretical proposition of this research is that workers are not just passive recipients of working conditions, but active shapers of work and jobs (Bal et al., 2012; Kooij, 2015). Hence, employees proactively negotiate flexibility arrangements with their employer, outside and beyond existing regulations. Adding to the work adjustment model, this line of research shows that especially individualized agreements may create a stronger fit between a person and the job. A more institutionalized version of this notion has been offered in the work of Bal and colleagues, who showed that organizations that offer individualized career customization programs (Bal et al., 2015), or individualized HRM (Bal & Dorenbosch, 2015), may contribute to both employee outcomes (such as work engagement) and organizational outcomes (such as performance growth and reduction of sickness absence) by seeking a compromise between employees' and employers' perspectives of workplace flexibility. In sum, recent scientific approaches tend to stress the individualized nature of flexibility arrangements between employee and organization. This adds to the distinction between formal availability within an organization and employee use of workplace flexibility, such that the availability of flexibility is not a necessary requirement for employees to be able to use flexibility, as they might have individually negotiated it with the employer (Bal et al., 2012), or might have engaged in unauthorized crafting their job in a flexible way (Kooij, 2015).

Just as use does not imply prior availability, availability does not per se result in actual use. Research shows that the effects of the mere availability of HRM practices on outcomes to be psychologically-theoretically different from actual use. The impact of availability has traditionally been explained using signaling theory (Casper & Harris, 2008). This theory explains that in the absence of clear messages from the employer, employees use signals sent by the organization to interpret its benevolence toward the employees. When organizations have flexibility available, employees may interpret this favorably, and so perceive availability as a signal from the organization that it cares about the employees and wants to motivate and retain them. As employees feel more highly valued by their employer, they commit themselves and become more highly engaged in their work (Bal & De Lange, 2015). Moreover, social exchange theory (Blau, 1964) explains why actual use of flexibility relates to outcomes. When employees have the opportunity to actually use flexibility in their work, they perceive the relationships with their employer to be strengthened, as the employer in allowing more flexibility shows concern for the long-term well-being of the employee. The benevolent nature of the employer, shown in the willingness to grant flexibility to the employee, forms a stimulus for the social exchange relationship between them (Bal et al., 2015).

OUTCOMES OF WORKPLACE FLEXIBILITY FOR WORKERS

There have been multiple literature reviews on the outcomes of employee perspectives on flexible work arrangements over the last decades. The early meta-analysis of Baltes et al. (1999) showed that the relationships between flexible work schedules and productivity, job satisfaction and reduced absenteeism were positive, while flexibility in reduced work hours was positively related to employee performance, job satisfaction, and schedule satisfaction. Notwithstanding these initial positive results stemming from research in the 1980s and 1990s, the systematic review of De Menezes and Kelliher (2011) revealed a more nuanced picture and concluded that the "business case" for flexible working was lacking, as they found no systematic positive relationships between employee perspectives of workplace flexibility and organizational performance, albeit some indication for a reduction of sickness absenteeism following workplace flexibility. Moreover, they found that the link between flexible working and employee performance was unclear, and this relationship might be mediated as well as moderated by several factors, including job satisfaction as a mediator, and experiences with the use of flexibility as a potential moderator.

Allen and colleagues (2013) conducted a meta-analysis on the relationship between employee perceptions of workplace flexibility and work-family conflict, and concluded that while flexibility was related to lower work-to-home interference, it was unrelated to home-to-work interference. Hence, decreases of work-family conflict may be one of the primary aims of why employees use flexibility (Bailey & Kurland, 2002). Along similar lines, a study by Hornung, Rousseau, and Glaser (2008) showed that individualized flexibility deals for employees were related to lower work-family conflict. However, as the review of De Menezes and Kelliher (2011) showed, the relations of employee perceptions of workplace flexibility with outcomes tend to be inconsistent and mixed across studies. There are a range of factors that may explain this inconsistency, including work climate, the role of the supervisor, and attributions.

Factors Influencing the Impact of Flexibility

Putnam and colleagues (2014) explained that organizational climate may play an important role in relation to the effectiveness of workplace flexibility. Supportive work climates are crucially important in the extent to which employees are able to obtain flexibility, as well as to which they may successfully transfer negotiated arrangements to the workplace (Bal et al., 2012). As the research of Lai and colleagues (2009) has shown, the role of coworkers is important in the successful transfer of idiosyncratic deals to the workplace. When coworkers accept a negotiated flexibility deal, the deal will be more likely to be perceived as fair, such that the focal employee can manifest the deal in the workplace (Greenberg et al., 2004). Moreover, based on the same line of reasoning, Bal et al. (2012) argued and showed that i-deals will be more strongly related to motivation to continue working beyond retirement when there is a supportive climate for older workers, focusing on the continuous development and not on disengagement of workers when they become older. Hence, the literature on idiosyncratic deals informs the flexibility literature by showing the crucial role of organizational climate in influencing the degree to which employees perceive to be able to implement flexibility in their jobs.

Moreover, closely related to climate is the role of the supervisor. A study of Bal and colleagues (2015) showed that the effects of career customization, an institutionalized form of flexible career trajectories, on employees' work engagement and subsequent career success, was dependent upon whether the employees felt that their manager was supportive of the career customization program. This shows the role of managers in successfully translating flexibility programs toward employees (Leisink & Knies, 2011). When managers are unsupportive of flexibility use, workers will feel a threshold toward using it, as they might fear negative consequences for instance for performance appraisals. Accordingly, the meta-analysis of Kossek and colleagues (2011) showed that supervisory support was an important predictor of work-family support and subsequent reductions in work-family conflicts. Putnam et al. (2014), therefore, recommended flexibility to become part of the psychological contract between employees and their organizations, in which both parties look for agreements on how, when, and where work is conducted (Morrison & Robinson, 1997; Rousseau, 1995). This aligns with our earlier mentioned conceptualization of workplace flexibility as the negotiation between employee and organization. Establishing such a psychological contract requires the notion of flexibility as a right for employees, creating legitimacy for the existence of workplace flexibility for employees. This implies support in an institutional context, such as government regulation on workplace flexibility for employees, and added by collective labor agreements, and HR-policies.

However, including workplace flexibility for employees as part of the psychological contract does not have to imply that managers are supportive of flexibility use by employees. In fact, research has shown that the attributions supervisors make are predictive of how well use of flexibility arrangements contributes to employee commitment and career success (Leslie et al., 2012). In their study, Leslie and colleagues (2012) found that when managers attributed flexibility use of their subordinates to productivity motives (i.e., employees use flexibility to become more productive and efficient), rather than personal life motives (i.e., employees use flexibility to accommodate nonwork activities), employees were perceived to be more highly committed to the organization, and hence achieved more career success. Thus, and in line with the earlier described employer perspective on workplace flexibility, supervisors may have positive perceptions of flexibility primarily when it is established according to productivity motives, rather than family-oriented motives. These attributions made by supervisors as well as other stakeholders within and outside the organization are likely to determine the outcome of use of flexibility by workers. We expect this to be also important in relation to older workers' use of flexibility, which we now will discuss.

WORKPLACE FLEXIBILITY ACROSS THE LIFESPAN

Workplace flexibility has been linked to the aging workforce for some time as a way older workers can be motivated, retained, and made to maintain productivity at higher ages (Rau & Adams, 2005; Siegenthaler & Brenner, 2001). This represents a shift from the research on flexible work schedules which until then primarily focused on availability and use for women and young parents (Brewer, 2000). However, as life expectancy is increasing and retirement ages are slowly being increased across the world, organizations will consist of workers of a wide range of ages, and with them bringing their own more diverse needs and wishes as to how the employment relationship should be formed and developed (Kunze, Boehm, & Bruch, 2013). In response to these changes, there have been recent attempts to integrate gerontological theories with workplace theories to understand how the aging process affects people at work (Kooij, de Lange, Jansen, & Dikkers, 2008). There are two gerontological theories which are directly relevant to the flexibility across the lifespan topic, and beyond these theories, new theories have been developed to address directly the role of older workers in organizations. Specifically, SOC-theory (Baltes & Baltes, 1990) explains why older people have different needs compared to younger people, while the theory of aged heterogeneity (Nelson & Dannefer, 1992) explains why people become more different from their age-related peers when they become older. Moreover, the theory of work motivation across the lifespan explains how older workers are motivated differently in their work than younger workers (Kanfer & Ackerman, 2004; Kanfer, Beier, & Ackerman, 2013). Bridge employment theory (Wang & Shi, 2014) can be used to understand how older workers obtain flexible careers, and finally, we will also use the theory of successful aging to assess underlying notions of aging in relation to flexibility (Kooij, 2015; Zacher, 2015).

Selectivity, Optimization, and Compensation Theory

The SOC model of aging (Baltes & Baltes, 1990) postulates that with the aging process, people experience both losses and gains. For instance, as people become older, they generally decline in physical health and capabilities while they also perceive gains in experience and wisdom. To successfully cope with these losses and gains, people engage generally in three different strategies, *selection, optimization,* and *compensation* (Baltes, 1997). People select fewer goals in life, by prioritizing what they deem as important. They will also abandon goals which are no longer attainable when they become older. Moreover, they optimize efforts and achievements within those fewer, selected goals. For instance, people try to accumulate and gain resources in order to achieve successfully the remaining goals they have set (Zacher & Frese, 2011). Finally, people compensate for losses by employing alternative means to achieve goals. For instance, people may take more breaks from work. Hence, the SOC model argues that people use different strategies to cope with the changes they experience as a result of the aging process. The SOC model has been used as well to explain changes in people's motivation and goal attainment (Ebner, Freund, & Baltes, 2006; Freund, 2006), as well as how these strategies link to work attitudes and behaviors (Bal, Kooij, & De Jong, 2013; Yeung & Fung, 2009; Zacher & Frese, 2011). Translated to the notion of workplace flexibility, the SOC model may provide a first indication of why people, as they become older, value more flexibility at work. As people experience work-related losses, such as the physical capabilities to conduct work, or the perseverance of working long hours, workplace flexibility may provide older workers the tools to employ SOC strategies to cope with these losses. Accordingly, a study by Bal et al. (2013) indeed found that HRM practices aimed at workplace flexibility, such as reduced working, contributed to higher employee engagement, and commitment among workers who were focused on selection and compensation strategies at work. Thus, the SOC model presents a first indication of how workplace flexibility may contribute to older workers' motivation at work, as the latter facilitates them in adjusting SOC strategies with how they fulfill their work roles. However, the literature on SOC strategies remains rather silent on the specific ages at which specific strategies become important to people. An explanation of why this is theoretically irrelevant is presented by the theory of aged heterogeneity (Bal & Jansen, 2015; Nelson & Dannefer, 1992).

The Theory of Aged Heterogeneity

Nelson and Dannefer (1992) reviewed empirical gerontological studies and concluded that in 65% of the studies a pattern of increasing variability with age was observed. These observations were found across physical, cognitive, and personality domains, and have led to the introduction of the notion of increasing heterogeneity with age in gerontological research as well as HRM research (Kooij et al., 2008). Subsequent work extended this perspective and concluded that with increasing age, people become more different from their age-related peers (Dannefer, 2003). This idea has also been integrated implicitly in theory on aging at work, which assumes that older workers may have large variations in their physical, psychological, and other capabilities (Kooij et al., 2008). While younger workers may be more alike in what they expect from their work, and what their work capabilities are, older workers tend to be more different from each other in those respects. This aligns with the popular idea that some people are able and willing to work into their 90s, while others are burnt out, and no longer motivated at 50 (Posthuma & Campion, 2009). Thus, as older workers are very different from each other, it is insufficient to take a one-size-fits-all approach toward the management of employment relationships with older workers. This idea was developed by Bal et al. (2012), who proposed that to enhance motivation to continue working, a flexible, individualized approach is needed toward workers. Bal and Jansen (2015) developed this idea further theoretically, and explained how idiosyncratic deals may be especially important for older workers in retaining them in the workforce and enabling them to continue working at higher ages. Thus, flexibility is postulated to benefit in particular older workers theoretically, as increasing heterogeneity will be associated with increasing heterogeneous work-related needs as workers become older. Employee workplace flexibility in the sense of the choice to decide when, where, and how work is conducted may allow older workers to obtain a fit between their personal situation (i.e., the extent to which they still value work and are able to conduct work) and the demands that result from their jobs. In addition to these theories which may explain the utility of flexibility for older workers, there are also specific theories of aging at work which may inform how flexibility operates for older workers.

The Theory of Work Motivation across the Lifespan

One of the key issues regarding the retention of older people in the workforce pertains to their motivation to work and their motivation in their work (Kanfer & Ackerman, 2004; Kanfer et al., 2013). The theoretical work of Kanfer and colleagues (2013) was among the first in the field of organizational behavior and HRM to criticize the simplicity of the association between aging and decline, and introduced a theory based on four patterns related to the aging process: loss, growth, reorganization, and exchange. While people generally experience a loss in fluid intellectual abilities, they also experience growth in crystallized intellectual abilities (i.e., experiential knowledge). In addition to these (classic) changes associated with age, they also pointed toward the role of reorganization of goals, including a shift from knowledge-related goals toward emotional goals when people become older and experience time as running out (Kanfer & Ackerman, 2004; Kooij, Bal, & Kanfer, 2014). Moreover, people also may perceive an exchange of primacy of motives during the aging process, that is, some motives (such as achievement striving) are exchanged for other motives during late adulthood (such as generativity). Despite the broadness of the framework (Kanfer et al., 2013), the general lesson is that workplace flexibility as a concept has much potential to be integrated with theoretical frameworks on aging at work. The changes that people experience, such as losses and reorganization of goals, fit within the idea that increasing flexibility may contribute to the motivation of workers at higher ages. Flexibility, therefore, may contribute to both motivation to work (i.e., motivation to remain employed at higher ages) and motivation at work (i.e., motivation within a specific job), as long as flexibility aligns with the changes that people experience over time. In particular during the later stages of one's career and approaching retirement age, flexibility may be influential in how people experience their work. Accordingly, bridge employment theory (Dingemans et al., 2015) offers a framework of understanding choices and needs at these later stages during one's career.

Bridge Employment Theory

While not a specific theory as to how and why people engage in bridge employment, bridge employment can be regarded as a specific form of workplace flexibility for older workers. Bridge employment departs from the view that retirement is not so much a decision about at what moment a person desires to cease working, but a *process* which leads to a final situation where someone fully withdraws from work (Feldman & Beehr, 2011). During this process, people may decide not to transition from full-time employment into fulltime retirement instantly, but to gradually shift and to engage in some type of alternative employment (Shultz, 2003). Notwithstanding that some workers are forced into bridge employment as they lack the financial means to retire early and may be laid off from their career jobs (Shultz, 2003), bridge employment may offer a flexible way how people transition from full employment into retirement. Bridge employment may include working beyond state pension age, and is traditionally differentiated in career and noncareer bridge employment (Gobeski & Beehr, 2009; Wang et al., 2008). Research shows that the likelihood that people will be working in career bridge jobs versus non-career bridge jobs is predicted by different variables, such as job satisfaction, availability of job characteristics, and having skills in a certain domain that are specifically career-related (Gobeski & Beehr, 2009; Wang et al., 2008). Beyond these studies on predictors of bridge employment, it can be argued that retirement is now increasingly perceived not as a single point in time related to state pension age, but as a process in which people gradually withdraw from work. During this process, people may be focused on flexibility in their work as well on more flexible careers (Moen & Sweet, 2004; Platman, 2004a); both allow people to create a more flexible relationship between themselves and their work and jobs. While there is hardly any explicit mentioning in the bridge employment literature regarding the role of flexibility, it can be considered a specific form of workplace flexibility for older workers in that they can decide when, where, and how work will be conducted to meet work and personal needs during late-career stages. Such needs refer to the extent to which they are willing and able to engage in working within their career jobs, or whether they have needs and wishes to pursue alternatives, such as an accountant who starts working in childcare (Gobeski & Beehr, 2009). In sum, the previously mentioned theories all point toward the essential role that workplace flexibility (for employees) plays for the motivation and retention of older workers. A final perspective which will be discussed is that of successful aging, and in particular critical notions toward concepts of successful and productive aging.

A Critical Perspective on Successful Aging

One of the areas within the research on aging at work which has integrated some flexibility notion has been the work on "successful aging" (Kooij,

2015; Zacher, 2015). This concept has been developed in the 1980s, and recent attempts have been made to conceptualize the notion of successful aging at work, which is broadly defined as relative positive deviations in employees' age-related trajectories of work outcomes, such as well-being or performance, as compared to other employees of the same age (Zacher, 2015, p. 6). The work of Kooij (2015; Kooij, Tims & Kanfer, 2015) focuses in particular on the role of job crafting in how older workers may shape their jobs more in line with their needs and abilities. Older workers may engage in a wide range of proactive behaviors, through which they may achieve higher fit with their jobs and careers, and thereby age successfully. In line with their work, it could be postulated that proactive behaviors among older workers could be aligned with the opportunity to obtain workplace flexibility, such that older workers may age successfully, and thereby are motivated to continue working and maintain their well-being at higher ages. The successful aging theory thus proposes that it is not only through workplace flexibility that people may achieve fit with their work as it allows them to age successfully but also that older people may be more inclined to engage in proactive behaviors that lead them to have more flexibility in their work (for instance through job crafting), and as a result achieve successful aging (e.g., maintaining performance and engagement). Hence, the theory of successful aging presupposes active regulation by older workers of their work and proactive behavior to create more flexible jobs.

There are two problems with the conceptualization of successful aging with respect to the role of flexibility. Following Zacher's (2015) definition, someone's successful aging is defined not just as maintaining health and quality of life at higher age, but successful aging is particularly defined in comparison to others (i.e., other older workers). As aging is associated with declines and losses, it is the positive deviations in these losses as compared to other aging people at work that constitutes successful aging (Zacher, 2015). Successful aging is not alone in this conceptualization, as similar streams of research have been developed on healthy aging (Beckingham & Watt, 1995), sustainable aging (De Lange, Kooij, & Van der Heijden, 2015), and productive aging (Morrow-Howell, Hinterlong, & Sherraden, 2001). Notable in these conceptualizations is that the terminology around success and productivity impose a normative view on the aging process. Successful and productive aging impose the norm that workers have to be engaged in work at higher ages, no matter one's personal circumstances. Accordingly, there is an increasing tendency to focus on the proactive roles that older workers play or should play when negotiating and creating favorable work conditions for successful ageing (Kooij, 2015; Kooij et al., 2015). Older workers *need* to become proactive in order to be able to competitively retain their jobs, engage in work, and perform well, and thus to age successfully. Since the number of jobs remains limited, and despite obvious individual differences in abilities and aging patterns (Nelson & Dannefer, 1992), older workers are essentially competing with one another. When an older worker is unable to engage in work, for instance because of physical declines, this is consequently perceived to be failure as the norm of successful aging is to remain active and engaged in work. Hence, while active aging may constitute a healthy way of approaching the aging process, it is extrapolated to become the societal norm for every older worker (Dillaway & Byrnes, 2009).

Beyond this normative view, the responsibility for successful aging is increasingly individualized. Research on coverage of the aging process in popular media (Rozanova, 2010) has revealed how successful aging is perceived to be a personal choice, carrying individual responsibility, and the continued engagement in work as a manifestation of one's successes in life and work. There is little acknowledgment of the role of different circumstances, luck, and genetic predispositions in maintaining health and productivity at higher ages, thereby individualizing and drawing individual responsibility toward the aging process. The next step is to personally blame individuals who do not age successfully, and therefore could be stripped away from benefits, such as unemployment, pension, and health care benefits (Dillaway & Byrnes, 2009). Extending this logic, the increase of the state retirement age across many countries (Johnson, 2011) is translated into a personal responsibility of older people to ensure that they remain employed, as pension benefits will only be rewarded at higher ages. A problem arises with this individualization of responsibility for successful aging, as it undermines the organizational responsibility, or duty of care, to ensure the employability and workability of older workers (Schumann, 2001). It is not surprising that an image has been established of the greedy older worker who is no longer willing to work (Dillaway & Byrnes, 2009), as it shifts away the focus on the role of governments and organizations in providing societal and organizational preconditions for the employability of older workers (and thus the responsibility to ensure workplace flexibility). Ultimately, it is the joint responsibility of government, organization, and worker to ensure employability and workability through for instance lifelong learning, sustainable employment, and possibly the use of workplace flexibility across the lifespan.

Yet, it has been proven difficult to extend working lives of older workers in a way that sustains well-being of workers (Dingemans & Henkens, 2014; Johnson, 2011). Older workers may use suboptimal strategies to stay employed and search jobs at higher ages and may lack up-to-date skills and knowledge to remain employed (Klehe et al., 2012). Moreover, the critical literature on aging also points toward the underlying power relations that establish societal and organizational norms about aging and the role of individual responsibility and proactivity. These norms shift a focus of aging of the workforce as one of the "normal" processes within organizations toward perceiving older workers as a problem, who have to be incentivized to work and continue working, while at the same time shifting the responsibility for this to each older worker individually (Katz & Calasanti, 2015). These societal and organizational norms regarding successful aging align with employer perspectives on workplace flexibility, as it primarily focuses on how organizations may become more adaptable to changes in the environment by having the opportunity to hire and dismiss workers freely along with the needs of the company (Way et al., 2015; Wright & Snell, 1998). Hence, there is a need to formulate a perspective on "successful" aging without its emphasis of a solely individual responsibility for workplace flexibility, and in which workplace flexibility therefore is conceptualized aligning with a less one-sided, employer-oriented perspective on aging at work. To do so, we will first review the available empirical work on workplace flexibility for older workers, and evaluate the outcomes of existing studies in light of the previous discussions.

A REVIEW OF EMPIRICAL STUDIES ON WORKPLACE FLEXIBILITY FOR OLDER WORKERS

To obtain an overview of the current state of knowledge and understanding of how workplace flexibility specifically unfolds for older workers, we reviewed all published empirical work that examined the relationships between the two constructs. We performed a systematic review, in which we searched for any study looking at workplace flexibility and older workers. We entered key words into search engines, such as Ebscohost and Google Scholar, and looked for any study that investigated flexibility or flexible working or flexible arrangements. We also went through the reference lists of earlier review papers (Allen et al., 2013; Baltes et al., 1999;

De Menezes & Kelliher, 2011; Putnam et al., 2014). We omitted any study that did not investigate workplace flexibility but rather work-family conflict (Shacklock, Brunetto, & Nelson, 2009). We also excluded papers which did not focus on flexibility options, but we did include studies on individualized flexibility options (Bal et al., 2012, 2015). After searching the papers, we distinguished them into studies that investigated employee perceptions of flexibility and employer perception of flexibility. All of these studies were aimed at investigation of how workplace flexibility for employees was predicted by a range of factors (such as employee age), or how it affects work outcomes (such as work engagement). One study included both perceptions (Atkinson & Sandiford, 2016), but after reading the chapter, we deemed it more appropriate to categorize this chapter as employer perception. Table 1 presents an overview of the studies on employee perceptions, while Table 2 presents an overview of the studies from the employer perceptions on workplace flexibility for older workers. We found eleven studies from the employee perspective and six from the employer perspective. The tables show the study designs, the context of the sample, the measure of workplace flexibility, the findings of the studies, and the implications for understanding of workplace flexibility for older workers.

Employee Perceptions on Workplace Flexibility for Older Workers

Of the 11 studies we traced on employees' perspectives on workplace flexibility for older workers, 10 were based on cross-sectional or longitudinal survey studies of employees, and one was based on a vignette study among older workers (Rau & Adams, 2005). Most studies measured employee perceptions of availability of flexibility options, while some others measured actual use of flexibility at work, including flexibility i-deals (Bal et al., 2012), and use of flexible careers (Bal et al., 2015). Two studies measured importance or value of flexibility for older workers (Armstrong-Stassen, 2008b; Hill, Jacob, et al., 2008), and the vignette study measured availability of flexible work schedules in a job ad. Finally, Pitt-Catsouphes and Matz-Costa (2008) measured flexibility fit, which indicated the extent to which workers felt they had the level of flexibility in their work that they needed. Table 1 shows the findings and implications of each single study.

Summarizing the results from these 11 studies, there are four general implications for understanding of workplace flexibility for older workers. Generally, studies show that workplace flexibility is less available to older workers. The panel study of Golden (2008) among a large sample of US

Table 1. Overview of Studies on Employee Perspectives on Flexibility HRM.

Authors	Study Design	Study Context	Flexibility HRM Measure	Findings	Implications
Armstrong-Stassen (2008b)	Study 1: Cross-sectional survey	284 Canadian employees over 50 (171 in career jobs, 113 in bridge jobs)	Availability of flexible work options (FWOs)	Employees in bridge jobs perceived higher availability of FWOs than employees in career jobs, except for unpaid leave, which was rated higher by employees in career jobs	Generally FWOs are more likely to be available to employees in bridge jobs than in career jobs
Armstrong-Stassen (2008b)	Cross-sectional survey	609 Canadians over 50 (198 in career jobs, 90 in post-retirement jobs, and 321 retirees)	Importance and availability of flexible work options	People in post-retirement jobs rated flexible work options as more important to stay in the workforce compared to people in career jobs. People in post-retirement jobs reported higher availability of flexible work options compared to people in career jobs	FWOs are more important for people in post-retirement jobs to remain in the workforce, and perceive FWOs to be more available than people in career jobs
Bal et al. (2012)	Cross-sectional survey	1083 employees in Dutch health care organizations	Flexibility i-deals	Age is negatively related to flexibility i-deals. Flexibility i-deals are positively related to motivation to continue working beyond retirement	Older workers negotiate fewer flexibility i-deals, while these flexibility i-deals are important in relation to the motivation to continue working

Table 1. (Continued)

Authors	Study Design	Study Context	Flexibility HRM Measure	Findings	Implications
Bal and De Lange (2015)	Study 1: longitudinal survey	Study 1: 695 US employees	Study 1: Irregular and regular flexibility HRM availability and use	Study 1: Employee engagement mediates the relationships between availability of flexibility and job performance. Flexibility is more strongly related to engagement among younger workers, while availability of irregular flexibility and use of regular flexibility are more strongly related to job performance among older workers	Availability of flexibility is directly related to employee engagement and job performance. While use of flexibility is more important to enhance younger workers' engagement, it is more important for older workers to retain their job performance
	Study 2: cross-national survey	Study 2: 2,158 employees in 11 countries across the world	Study 2: Flexibility HRM availability and use	Study 2: Employee engagement mediates the relationships between availability of flexibility and job performance. Use of flexibility was more strongly related to engagement among younger workers	

	Method	Sample	Focus	Findings	Conclusion
Bal et al. (2015)	Longitudinal survey	496 Dutch employees (403 in common career trajectory, 93 in customized careers)	Mass career customization use	MCC use is more strongly related to work engagement and subsequently salary and bonuses for older workers, but only when the manager supports MCC use	Career customization is beneficial for older workers' work engagement and remuneration, but only when they feel supported by the manager to use career customization
Cebulla et al. (2007)	Cross-sectional survey	5,512 UK employees (pre-state pension age and post-state pension age workers)	Availability and use of flexible work options	Both pre- and post-state pension age workers have limited up-take of FWOs. Older workers were more likely to work in organizations that offer FWOs	There is a limited use of flexible work options, and older workers are more inclined to work in organizations where they are available
Golden (2008)	Panel survey	51,358 US employees	Availability of flexible work schedule	Age is negatively related to availability of flexible work schedules	Older workers tend to perceive lower availability of flexible work schedules
Hill, Jacob, et al. (2008)	Cross-sectional survey	41,118 US employees	Use and value of flexibility options	Gender differences in the use of flexibility are highest with young children, where women are more likely to use flexibility. These differences disappear in later life stages (with older children) Women tend to value flexibility higher than men, across the lifespan	Gender differences exist across the lifespan in how much employees use and value flexibility options, with women generally using more flexibility and valuing flexibility higher

Table 1. (*Continued*)

Authors	Study Design	Study Context	Flexibility HRM Measure	Findings	Implications
Pitt-Catsouphes and Matz-Costa (2008)	Cross-sectional survey	49,209 US employees	Flexibility fit	Flexibility fit is more strongly related to employee engagement among older workers	Older workers become more highly engaged when they have flexibility fit than younger workers
Rau and Adams (2005)	Vignette study	120 US university retirees with a desire to work	Flexible work schedule availability in a job ad	Organizational attractiveness was higher for retirees when job ads included the possibility for flexible work schedules, especially when there are opportunities for mentoring and when there are equal employment opportunities	Flexibility is an important requirement for retirees to consider applying for a job
Van Solinge and Henkens (2014)	Cross-sectional survey	1,450 workers above 50 in four large Dutch organizations	Availability of workplace flexibility (schedule and working from home)	Availability of workplace flexibility does not relate significantly to retirement intention or actual retirement	Compared to other predictors, flexibility did not predict retirement intentions or actual retirement

Note: When no sector is mentioned, respondents work in several different sectors.

Table 2. Overview of Studies on Employer Perspectives on Flexibility HRM.

Authors	Study Design	Study Context	Flexibility HRM Measure	Findings	Implications
Atkinson and Sandiford (2016)	Owner and employee interviews	46 UK owner-manager and workers in small firms	Existence and availability of flexible work arrangements	Flexibility is opportunistically used by organizations in recruitment. Older workers need and value flexibility, and obtain these in small firms primarily via i-deals	While flexibility is important for older workers, employers are hesitant to formally introduce it, and prefer i-deals
Bal and Dorenbosch (2015)	Employer survey	4,591 Dutch organization representatives	Individualized HRM availability and use (work schedules)	Sickness absence and employee turnover were lower among organizations with a high percentage of older workers who used individualized work schedules	In organizations with many older workers, individualized work schedules may decrease sickness absence and employee turnover
Beck (2013)	Employer interviews	32 UK interviews, of which 19 employers	Flexibility	Flexibility may be important to retain older workers, to cut costs, and to avoid costly redundancy payouts. Flexibility is also important to balance content of a job with abilities	Employers support flexibility when they perceive to benefit from having a flexible workforce.
Earl and Taylor (2015)	Employer interviews	97 Australian HR directors and managers	Availability and use of flexible working policies for older women workers	Workplace flexibility may enhance work-life balance and engagement of older workers. Flexibility, however, is also related to lower income and loss of status for older workers	The benefits of flexibility outweigh the costs for older workers

Table 2. (*Continued*)

Authors	Study Design	Study Context	Flexibility HRM Measure	Findings	Implications
Matz-Costa and Pitt-Catsouphes (2010)	Employer survey	578 US organizational representatives	Availability of flexible work options	Percentage of workforce older than 55 was unrelated to availability of flexible work options	Organizations with many older workers are not offering more flexible work options
Sweet, Pitt-Catsouphes, et al. (2014)	Employer survey	545 US HR-representatives	Availability of flexible move work arrangements, reduced work arrangements, and pause work arrangements	Proportion of older workers is not related to availability of flexibility to most or all employees	Organizations do not respond with higher availability of flexibility when the proportion of older workers is higher

employees revealed a negative relationship between age and having access to flexible work schedules. Moreover, the study of Bal et al. (2012) shows a negative correlation between age and flexibility i-deals, indicating that older workers are less likely to negotiate i-deals concerning flexibility at work. However, research also shows that older workers in bridge jobs have higher access to flexible work options than older workers in career jobs (Armstrong-Stassen, 2008a, 2008b). This is striking given that the attractiveness of jobs increases when flexibility is part of the job, as the vignette study among retirees showed (Rau & Adams, 2005). Moreover, Armstrong-Stassen (2008b) showed that flexibility is important for people in bridge jobs to remain employed and not to retire. The study of Hill, Jacob et al. (2008) contributed to these findings by showing that in particular older women value flexibility more than older men at work.

Furthermore, the studies generally showed positive relationships between flexibility and a range of employee outcomes. The study of Bal et al. (2012) showed that flexibility i-deals related to motivation to continue working beyond retirement, while the study of Bal and De Lange (2015) showed that flexibility was related to higher employee engagement and performance. Bal et al. (2015) found that use of flexible careers was related to higher employee engagement and subsequent career success, while Pitt-Catsouphes and Matz-Costa (2008) showed that flexibility fit was positively related to employee engagement. We found one exception, with the study of Van Solinge and Henkens (2014) not showing evidence that flexibility related to retirement intentions or actual retirement, while other job characteristics and personal circumstances (such as retirement income) were predictive of one's retirement intentions and actual retirement decision. Thus, this indicates that while workplace flexibility may contribute to older workers' positive work attitudes and behaviors, there is limited evidence that this leads to an actual postponing of retirement. The studies do, however, show that the relationships of flexibility with the outcomes (e.g., engagement, performance) are generally stronger for older workers. Bal and De Lange (2015) found stronger relationships for older workers between flexibility use and job performance, Bal et al. (2015) found that flexible careers were more strongly related to employee engagement among older workers (given that the manager supports flexible careers), and Pitt-Catsouphes and Matz-Costa (2008) found that flexibility fit was more strongly related to employee engagement among older workers. Hence, these studies tend to support that older workers may benefit more than younger workers from workplace flexibility in maintaining their engagement and performance in the job.

Finally, the studies show the potential relevance of the idea of fit in relation to flexibility. The study of Rau and Adams (2005) showed that organizational attractiveness was highest for older workers when there was flexibility available, but also options for mentoring and equal employment opportunities. Moreover, Pitt-Catsouphes and Matz-Costa (2008) showed that flexibility fit was predictive of employee engagement, indicating that it was not only having access to flexibility that is important, but the extent to which it fits with personal needs. Thus, when flexibility is aligned with other organizational practices and personal needs of employees, it is more strongly related to potentially relevant outcomes. In sum, the employee studies on workplace flexibility for older workers show that flexibility is generally less available to older workers, while it may predict important outcomes, and may even be more strongly predictive of outcomes for older workers, especially when there is fit with other characteristics in the organization.

Employer Perceptions on Workplace Flexibility for Older Workers

Six studies were found that focused on employers' views on how workplace flexibility could be implemented for older workers. These studies aimed at investigating the organizational need for implementation of workplace flexibility for workers. Three were survey studies and the other three were interview studies. The survey studies measured availability and use of flexibility practices, while in the interview studies, flexibility was included in a broader way, encompassing an HR practice available in the organization. There are a number of general implications resulting from these studies. First, the studies by Matz-Costa and Pitt-Catsouphes (2010) and Sweet, Pitt-Catsouphes, Besen, and Golden (2014) show that organizations with higher proportions of older workers are not more likely to offer flexibility options to workers. This is consistent with the findings from the employee perspective studies, which reported lower perceived availability of flexibility with age. Second, and also confirming the findings from the employees' studies, Bal and Dorenbosch (2015) found that especially organizations with many older workers had lower sickness absence and employee turnover when they used individualized flexible work schedules. This shows that flexibility may especially be beneficial in organizations with many older workers.

The studies also showed a picture of organizations using flexible work options in recruitment practices to attract a wider range of applicants

(Atkinson & Sandiford, 2016). Hence, workplace flexibility for older workers was used to achieve organizational goals (i.e., improving performance through better applicants). While in the interview studies, there was general agreement of the value of flexibility for older workers (Atkinson & Sandiford, 2016; Beck, 2013; Earl & Taylor, 2015), it was also recognized that formal practices were difficult to implement, and therefore organizations primarily used informal flexibility i-deals rather than implementing formal practices. The disadvantage of informal practices is the risk of arbitrariness in making decisions and the potential lack of understanding or willingness among less proactive older workers to negotiate informal agreements. Moreover, the use of flexibility by older workers was often related to *reductions* in income and retirement benefits as well as loss of status within the organization, which contributes to the idea of the use of flexibility to maintain organizational performance (Earl & Taylor, 2015). Finally, flexibility was also used by organization to cut costs, especially during the economic crisis (Beck, 2013), and therefore may also be used to force older workers into workload reductions, such that they would not have to be dismissed, but they would be affected through the loss of income and other benefits.

In sum, the limited amount of employer studies show that on the one hand, employers recognize the benefits of flexibility for older workers and workplace flexibility may have positive consequences for organizational outcomes, such as sickness absence and turnover (Bal & Dorenbosch, 2015). Yet, on the other hand, organizations have not responded with increasing the availability of flexibility for older workers (Matz-Costa & Pitt-Catsouphes, 2010; Sweet, Pitt-Catsouphes, et al., 2014), and there even is a tendency to use flexibility as rhetoric to be more attractive to applicants and to be more responsive to environmental changes by forcing people into flexible work schedules. This is largely in line with the earlier described theoretical perspectives on workplace flexibility from an employer's perspective (Way et al., 2015).

Comparison between Employee and Employer Perspectives

Notwithstanding the differences in study designs that have been used to study employee and employer perspectives and the higher number of studies focusing on employee perceptions, there are a number of notable similarities and differences between the two sets of studies. First, the studies on employee perceptions are aligned with the described theories on work-related aging processes, which postulate that with the aging process, people become increasingly different and hence place higher value in individualizing working conditions and obtaining more flexibility at work. The results of these studies show that older workers value flexibility, and when they have access or use it, become more highly engaged and productive. These studies tend to stress the positive aspects of flexibility for older workers. The employer studies are more nuanced and show the difficulties that arise in the different interests of employers and employees concerning the role of flexibility at work, and the reality where employers are only offering flexibility when it aligns with business interests. This underlines the employer view based on the strategic HRM perspective which postulates that flexibility offers a useful way for organizations to stay competitive in an ever-changing market (Volberda, 1996; Wright & Snell, 1998). When flexible work arrangements contribute to employees' engagement and performance (Bal & De Lange, 2015), they may contribute to organizational performance as well (Bal & Dorenbosch, 2015), thereby providing a "business case" for flexibility (De Menezes & Kelliher, 2011). Thus, even though flexibility may be beneficial for older workers in terms of maintaining their health and engagement, it is largely used across these studies to ascertain how older workers may contribute to organizational goals. Hence, flexibility is an instrument for organizations to find a way toward viability, competitiveness, and performance, while flexibility is being described for workers as a way to retain engagement, particularly at higher age (Cebulla, Butt, & Lyon, 2007).

While older workers value flexibility as it increases their external regulation (or primary control mechanisms; Heckhausen et al., 2010), employers tend to emphasize the importance of flexibility of older workers to be able to contribute to organizational goals. Notable is that across the reviewed studies, there is little acknowledgment of the interests of the *other* party; neither do older workers generally acknowledge the organizational or societal need to continue working, while organizations generally do not take into account the importance of employment for older workers, or the need to adapt jobs toward the abilities and needs of older workers. This aligns with the earlier mentioned difference between organizational qualitative and quantitative flexibility (Wright & Snell, 1998). While there may be a societal need for workers to extend their working lives as life expectancy continues to increase (Johnson, 2011), organizational responses have largely focused on increasing quantitative flexibility (i.e., through easily hiring and firing employees). With the societal need for extending working lives, and the potential role of workplace flexibility, currently the focus on qualitative flexibility (i.e., internal training and development, task enrichment) remains underemphasized, and is undermined by the dominance of quantitative flexibility. The consequence is that ageing workers increasingly become less engaged in lifelong learning, which ultimately results in lower levels of human resources development across society, as workers are primarily engaged in retaining jobs rather than developing themselves in/across organizations (Brewer, 2000).

CONCLUSIONS AND FUTURE RESEARCH

In this chapter, we have critically reviewed conceptualizations of and research on workplace flexibility for older workers. Our review points toward a number of crucial issues pertaining to the conceptualization, measurement, and use of the term workplace flexibility across and within different disciplines. Moreover, as our review shows, the majority of studies are similar in that they focus on the positive aspects of flexibility in its relationships with outcomes such as employee engagement and performance. Many studies neglect the more critical aspects of workplace flexibility and aging, such as the tensions that arise between the interests of older workers and those of organizations. Moreover, studies also ignore the potential ideological connotations which have been associated with these concepts. The disadvantage of this is that research on flexibility can be used to legitimize a certain perspective on the responsibility of ensuring flexibility of workers (Bauman, 2013). To advance theory and understanding of these issues, we discuss a number of areas for future research.

Conceptualizations of Workplace Flexibility

First, we have observed a use and conceptualization of the term flexibility which is fundamentally different across disciplines. Generally, two conceptualizations can be distinguished, with a focus on either organizational (employer) flexibility as in adaptive to changes in the environment (Way et al., 2015) or flexibility for employees as in having leeway to change one's schedules, work locations, and ways one conduct the job (Hill, Grzywacz, et al., 2008). While there is no fundamental problem with having different perspectives on a particular phenomenon (Suddaby, 2010), a tension arises when these views conflict and lead to contradictory findings. This is notable in research on flexibility for older workers, with a body of research pointing toward the potential positive roles (employee) flexibility for older workers may have (Siegenthaler & Brenner, 2001), while another body of literature shows the instrumental role of (employer) flexibility for organizational goals (Atkinson & Sandiford, 2016; Beck, 2013). The important notion here is that these conflicting conceptualizations should be taken into account when studying the role of workplace flexibility for older workers.

The point to be made here is that employer and employee perspectives on flexibility cannot be seen as separate dimensions which are unrelated to each other. They have been developed and are influencing the employment relationship in a joint process, where the rise of employer flexibility, and in particular the opportunity to put employees in uncertain, insecure contracts, was legitimized with the promise of more flexibility for workers (Harvey, 2005; Seymour, 2014). Therefore, their rise has occurred simultaneously, and research on workplace flexibility should take this into account as well. Research on how flexible work arrangements may contribute to working lives of older workers should not neglect that this flexibility co-occurs with a rise in employment insecurity for older workers, and increasing difficulties with finding new jobs when unemployed (Klehe et al., 2012). Consequently, researchers should not one-sidedly focus on the positive aspects of flexible work options for older workers, but instead realize that flexibility should not only be studied as an isolated phenomenon of within-individual psychological processes. Instead, we plea for a broad employer-employee exchange perspective with investigation of different types of institutional (governmental, organizational, labor unions) pressures toward the establishment of the employment relationship and the role of flexibility in it. Taking this one step further may inspire researchers not only to take into account the exchange of flexibility between parties but also to investigate alternatives, such as organizations where flexibility is positioned as a central principle, such as organizational democracies or volunteering organizations where employees are empowered to self-organize and have the flexibility needed to successfully conduct their work (Stohl & Cheney, 2001). This means that flexibility is not positioned as an outcome which is instrumental in organizational goals (and thus contributing to employee and organizational performance), but valued as an outcome as such since it is experienced as contributing to meaningful work.

Workplace Flexibility across the Lifespan

There is a need for more critical perspectives on both fields of workplace flexibility and aging at work (Putnam et al., 2014; Rozanova, 2010). As explained above, workplace flexibility may be a double-edged sword for older workers, as it may provide them with opportunities to regulate age-related changes in a flexible, adaptable way, but at the same time, it may be a manifestation of the individualized responsibility to take care of one's career, and a refusal of organizations to manage careers of older workers, or to create jobs which are suitable for older workers. At the same time, literatures on aging have relied intensely on notions of successful or productive aging (Kooij, 2015; Zacher, 2015), and the need for older people to remain active and employed during late adulthood. Again, these literatures have stressed the individual responsibility of people to remain employed, but also the "norm" that one should be active and proactive when one becomes older, and attributing blame to individuals who are unable to be productive at higher age, or to age successfully in line with the (Western) societal norms of self-directedness, independence, and activity (Katz & Calasanti, 2015). Future research therefore should take a critical approach, acknowledging the multi-faceted aspects of workplace flexibility and aging, and refrain from imposing normative views of successful aging on research (and research designs). Caution is therefore needed in researching flexibility for older workers, as different perspectives may offer different theoretical frameworks for understanding how workplace flexibility manifests for older workers. In particular, it is imperative that in future research the conditioning roles of government and organizations for an optimal tradeoff between employer/employee flexibility should be investigated.

More specifically, a more integrative model of workplace flexibility includes flexibility at three levels. At the societal level, governments have to ensure social security to enable a more flexible workforce (Johnson, 2011), which includes social benefits, and investments for people to return to work if unemployed due to flexibilization of contracts. At the organizational level, employers should ensure work security, which may replace job security, and include an exchange relationship consisting of guaranteed work for employee investment in development and learning. This indicates a willingness of organizations to engage in qualitative flexibility rather than quantitative flexibility, and thus aims at developing employees to be more flexible and employable. Finally, at the personal level, workers need to cooperate in building qualitative flexibility, through engaging in development activities, lifelong learning, which then may contribute to higher psychological flexibility (Atkins & Parker, 2012) and employability (Van der Heijde & Van Der Heijden, 2006).

Another issue at the organizational level pertains to whether organizations should implement age-specific practices (Kunze et al., 2013). Age-specific flexibility practices may include workload reductions from a certain age (such as above 50), which have been popular in many countries (Johnson, 2011). However, these possible flexibility practices are costly and may benefit older workers at the expense of younger workers. For instance, when older workers are exempt from night shifts (e.g., in health care), this may lead to younger workers having to conduct more night shifts, and thus potentially offloading the burden of less desirable working conditions to others. In addition, age-specific practices may lead to perceptions of entitlement, as regardless of individual needs, people may feel that they are entitled to a practice when they reach a specific age (Bal & Jansen, 2015). As research has shown, even though of similar ages, people may differ substantially in terms of how willing, able, and motivated they are at work (Kanfer et al., 2013; Kooij et al., 2008). Therefore, age-specific practices may be irrelevant when there is no perceived general age-related need for a practice. Hence, governments and organizations are increasingly reducing age-related practices, such as exempts, additional leave, and early retirement benefits, but these may not be replaced with other relevant, general, uniform, institutionalized practices. Instead, and as research has shown, organizations are increasingly refraining from implementing formal flexibility practices (Atkinson & Sandiford, 2016), and hence rely more on idiosyncratic deals (Bal & Jansen, 2015; Rousseau, 2005). This may be at odds with the findings from the review, which shows that older workers generally receive less flexibility, while it may contribute more strongly to their work attitudes and behaviors. A straightforward recommendation for employers is to increase availability of flexibility for older workers when there is a need or desire to retain older workers in the workforce and organizations. Employer perspectives, which not solely focus on organizational flexibility through contingent workers, may also contribute to this by offering skill-enhancing practices to older workers, which may contribute to both organizational adaptiveness and worker adaptiveness. Yet, our review shows that older workers are also less likely to negotiate individualized flexibility arrangements, which may be an avenue for organizations to focus on in the future, and provide more equal access among workers to individualized deals (Bal & Lub, 2015).

The switch from formal practices to idiosyncratic deals raises some important questions for future research. The interplay between formal flexibility practices and flexibility i-deals is in need of further investigation, as formal practices may generally be easier for employees to obtain than to negotiate idiosyncratic deals (Bal & Lub, 2015). Some older workers may have powerful positions in organizations, and therefore may easily obtain flexibility arrangements, while other older workers lack those powers, and thus will not be able to have flexibility in their work. However, workplace flexibility, as we defined it earlier in the chapter, results from the negotiation between employee and organization, and thus should be negotiated with mutual benefits in mind (Rousseau, 2005). Only through more explicit alignment of both employee and organizational interests, nepotism and cronyism can be avoided (Bal & Lub, 2015), and therefore may serve both employees, organizations, and other stakeholders (such as society and government).

Dynamics of Workplace Flexibility

Following the tendency to individualize workplace flexibility negotiations, another question should be raised, which concerns the stability and fluctuations of flexibility arrangements. Bal and De Lange (2015) introduced the idea of regular versus irregular flexibility, which referred to arrangements where people may have flexibility in their daily job activities, or whether they have the opportunity to have flexibility irregularly, such as sabbaticals or unpaid leave. Hence, flexibility may have different relevance as it is implemented in daily activities or whether it extends to larger conceptualizations of the employment relationship. In the latter case, there is a necessary involvement of institutions such as governments to ensure the structure of these practices. A related issue concerns whether arrangements are stable or fluctuating. For instance, when someone has negotiated a flexible work schedule, for how long is this agreement valid? Does workplace flexibility change when organizations are changing? This is especially in the context of workplace flexibility for older workers, as flexibility agreements made in the past may have limited relevance when workers become older. Moreover, there is now also evidence that employers are less likely to promote use of flexible work arrangements to workers in times of economic uncertainty (Sweet, Besen, Pitt-Catsouphes, & McNamara, 2014). However, research tends to assume workplace flexibility as being rather static, as an aspect of the job and organization that does not change. It is therefore important to investigate how employees' perceptions of their jobs change when they start using flexibility, and when flexibility is taken away from them. Hence, it is important to further study how people experience receiving, having, and losing flexibility at work to fully understand how it operates in the workplace. Taking a step further leads to the notion of flexible careers (Bal et al., 2015; Moen & Sweet, 2004), in which people move away from the traditional career trajectories within organizations (such as the up-or-out system in many consulting firms), toward a variety of forms (e.g., in and out, grow or go, or life-time employment) in which people make decisions about how they develop their careers within and across organizations (see also the notion of boundaryless careers; Arthur et al., 2005). Bridge employment in this expanded view on the flexible career is integrated toward a hyper-flexible career form in which people over their careers make decisions on how they fit work with the other aspects in their lives, such as eldercare and volunteer work (Bal & Jansen, 2015; Polat et al., 2012). However, flexible careers should also be investigated critically, as flexible careers may be associated with greater freedom from organizational constraints, but at the same time they also come with greater responsibility for workers to take care of their own knowledge-building, experience obsolescence, income, and well-being (Platman, 2004b). In sum, the flexibility literature is in need of a more dynamic perspective on how workplace flexibility operates over longer time for both workers and employers. As flexibility is potentially increasingly negotiated in idiosyncratic ways, this may offer organizations and employees the opportunity to better align mutual needs and benefits, such that traditional practices which may have had limited relevance as aging entails so many interindividual differences. At the same time, older workers may become pressured to individually obtain flexibility, which may be easier for the more proactive and employable employees, potentially creating another inequality between the "haves" and the "have-nots." Future research may shed more light on these issues.

Methodological Challenges

The flexibility literature across the lifespan also needs to address some methodological issues pertaining to how flexibility is measured and operationalized. A traditional way of measuring flexibility for workers is by asking whether practices are available and whether workers take advantage of these practices (Allen et al., 2013). In line with our definition, measurement should try to integrate both employee and employer perspectives on flexibility, and include the negotiation of flexibility in its conceptualization and measurement. However, an important issue for measurement of workplace flexibility also pertains to what it means for workers to use a practice. To what extent do people decide on a daily level where and when they conduct their work, and how they conduct it, or is flexibility more about the perception of workers that they are in control, and that they have the ability to do so? Moreover, to which extent do people then fluctuate their daily rhythms, or are they more likely to stick to certain routines? In other words, is workplace flexibility about the daily decisions concerning how work is conducted, or is it about the employees' perceptions that they in control over their work schedules? Likewise, research may inform whether there is alignment or contradiction in the views from the employer or manager versus the views from the employee. Research of Yang and Zheng (2011) already showed that decoupling, where organizations claim they implement flexibility but in reality refrain from it, was associated with lower perceptions of performance. Future research may also show whether and how managers agree with their employees in the flexibility arrangements, and ascertain whether employee perceptions of flexibility actually concern idiosyncratic deals (with mutual agreement) or job crafting (i.e., unauthorized shaping of one's job).

Furthermore, flexibility in its own right may be valued by employees, as it signals the employers' willingness to create a basis around which work and life are organized. Therefore, workplace flexibility may be investigated as an outcome of a process where organizations and workers negotiate and find agreement in the ways work is distributed, conducted, and managed, through which conceptualizations of the flexible organization (Sanchez, 1995) may be aligned with worker needs and preferences (Putnam et al., 2014). In this case, employee workplace flexibility would be a constitutive element of the total rewards bundle. It is important that in future research both conceptualizations are taken into account, especially when researching the relevance and fluctuations of workplace flexibility for workers given the current uncertain economic circumstances (Sweet, Besen, et al., 2014).

REFERENCES

Allen, T. D., Johnson, R. C., Kiburz, K. M., & Shockley, K. M. (2013). Work–family conflict and flexible work arrangements: Deconstructing flexibility. *Personnel Psychology*, *66*, 345–376.

Armstrong-Stassen, M. (2008a). Human resource practices for mature workers—and why aren't employers using them? *Asia Pacific Journal of Human Resources, 46*, 334–352.

Armstrong-Stassen, M. (2008b). Organisational practices and the post-retirement employment experience of older workers. *Human Resource Management Journal, 18*, 36–53.

Arthur, M. B., Khapova, S., & Wilderom, C. (2005). Career success in a boundaryless career world. *Journal of Organizational Behavior, 26*, 177–202.

Atkins, P., & Parker, S. (2012). Understanding individual compassion in organizations: The role of appraisals and psychological flexibility. *Academy of Management Review, 37*, 524–546.

Atkinson, C., & Sandiford, P. (2016). An exploration of older worker flexible working arrangements in smaller firms. *Human Resource Management Journal, 26*, 12–28.

Bailey, D. E., & Kurland, N. B. (2002). A review of telework research: Findings, new directions, and lessons for the study of modern work. *Journal of Organizational Behavior, 23*, 383–400.

Bal, P. M., De Jong, S. B., Jansen, P. G., & Bakker, A. B. (2012). Motivating employees to work beyond retirement: A multi-level study of the role of i-deals and unit climate. *Journal of Management Studies, 49*, 306–331.

Bal, P. M., & De Lange, A. H. (2015). From flexibility human resource management to employee engagement and perceived job performance across the lifespan: A multisample study. *Journal of Occupational and Organizational Psychology, 88*, 126–154.

Bal, P. M., & Dorenbosch, L. (2015). Age-related differences in the relations between individualised HRM and organisational performance: A large-scale employer survey. *Human Resource Management Journal, 25*, 41–61.

Bal, P. M., & Jansen, P. G. W. (2015). Idiosyncratic deals for older workers: Increased heterogeneity among older workers enhance the need for i-deals. In P. M. Bal, D. T. A. M. Kooij, & D. M. Rousseau (Eds.), *Aging workers and the employee-employer relationship* (pp. 129–144). Amsterdam: Springer International Publishing.

Bal, P. M., Kooij, D. T., & De Jong, S. B. (2013). How do developmental and accommodative HRM enhance employee engagement and commitment? The role of psychological contract and SOC strategies. *Journal of Management Studies, 50*, 545–572.

Bal, P. M., & Lub, X. D. (2015). Individualization of work arrangements: A contextualized perspective on the rise and use of i-deals. In P. M. Bal & D. M. Rousseau (Eds.), *Idiosyncratic deals between employees and organizations: Conceptual issues, applications, and the role of coworkers* (pp. 9–23). London: Psychology Press.

Bal, P. M., Van Kleef, M., & Jansen, P. G. (2015). The impact of career customization on work outcomes: Boundary conditions of manager support and employee age. *Journal of Organizational Behavior, 36*, 421–440.

Baltes, B. B., Briggs, T. E., Huff, J. W., Wright, J. A., & Neuman, G. A. (1999). Flexible and compressed workweek schedules: A meta-analysis of their effects on work-related criteria. *Journal of Applied Psychology, 84*, 496–513.

Baltes, P. B. (1997). On the incomplete architecture of human ontogeny: Selection, optimization, and compensation as foundation of developmental theory. *American Psychologist, 52*, 366–380.

Baltes, P. B., & Baltes, M. M. (1990). Psychological perspectives on successful aging: The model of selective optimization with compensation. In P. B. Baltes & M. M. Baltes (Eds.), *Successful aging: Perspectives from the behavioral sciences* (pp. 1–34). New York, NY: Cambridge University Press.

Bauman, Z. (2013). *Liquid modernity*. New York, NY: Wiley.

Beck, V. (2013). Employers' use of older workers in the recession. *Employee Relations, 35,* 257–271.

Beckingham, A. C., & Watt, S. (1995). Daring to grow old: Lessons in healthy aging and empowerment. *Educational Gerontology: An International Quarterly, 21,* 479–495.

Beltrán-Martín, I., & Roca-Puig, V. (2013). Promoting employee flexibility through HR practices. *Human Resource Management, 52,* 645–674.

Beltrán-Martín, I., Roca-Puig, V., Escrig-Tena, A., & Bou-Llusar, J. C. (2008). Human resource flexibility as a mediating variable between high performance work systems and performance. *Journal of Management, 34,* 1009–1044.

Bhattacharya, M., Gibson, D. E., & Doty, D. H. (2005). The effects of flexibility in employee skills, employee behaviors, and human resource practices on firm performance. *Journal of Management, 31,* 622–640.

Bird, J. (2015). Flexibility crucial in attracting millennials. *Financial Times.* Retrieved from http://www.ft.com/cms/s/2/9672854a-5545-11e5-b029-b9d50a74fd14.html#axzz3nmYuo Dk0. Accessed on October 6, 2015.

Blau, P. M. (1964). *Exchange and power in social life.* New York, NY: Wiley.

Bond, F. W., Flaxman, P. E., & Bunce, D. (2008). The influence of psychological flexibility on work redesign: Mediated moderation of a work reorganization intervention. *Journal of Applied Psychology, 93,* 645–654.

Brewer, A. M. (2000). Work design for flexible work scheduling: Barriers and gender implications. *Gender, Work & Organization, 7,* 33–44.

Casper, W. J., & Harris, C. M. (2008). Work-life benefits and organizational attachment: Self-interest utility and signaling theory models. *Journal of Vocational Behavior, 72,* 95–109.

Cebulla, A., Butt, S., & Lyon, N. (2007). Working beyond the state pension age in the United Kingdom: The role of working time flexibility and the effects on the home. *Ageing and Society, 27,* 849–867.

Chang, S., Gong, Y., Way, S. A., & Jia, L. (2013). Flexibility-oriented HRM systems, absorptive capacity, and market responsiveness and firm innovativeness. *Journal of Management, 39,* 1924–1951.

Cuñat, A., & Melitz, M. J. (2012). Volatility, labor market flexibility, and the pattern of comparative advantage. *Journal of the European Economic Association, 10,* 225–254.

Dannefer, D. (2003). Cumulative advantage/disadvantage and the life course: Cross-fertilizing age and social science theory. *The Journals of Gerontology Series B: Psychological Sciences and Social Sciences, 58,* S327–S337.

De Lange, A. H., Kooij, D. T. A. M., & Van der Heijden, B. I. J. M. (2015). Human resource management and sustainability at work across the lifespan: An integrative perspective. In L. Finkelstein, D. Truxillo, F. Fraccaroli, & R. Kanfer (Eds.), *Facing the challenges of a multi-age workforce. A use-inspired approach.* SIOP Organizational Frontiers Series. London: Psychology Press.

De Lange, A. H., Taris, T., Jansen, P. G. W., Kompier, M., Houtman, I., & Bongers, P. (2010). On the relationships among work characteristics and learning-related behavior: Does age matter? *Journal of Organizational Behavior, 31,* 925–950.

De Menezes, L. M., & Kelliher, C. (2011). Flexible working and performance: A systematic review of the evidence for a business case. *International Journal of Management Reviews, 13,* 452–474.

Dillaway, H. E., & Byrnes, M. (2009). Reconsidering successful aging: A call for renewed and expanded academic critiques and conceptualizations. *Journal of Applied Gerontology*, *28*, 702–722.

Dingemans, E., & Henkens, K. (2014). Involuntary retirement, bridge employment, and satisfaction with life: A longitudinal investigation. *Journal of Organizational Behavior*, *35*, 575–591.

Dingemans, E., Henkens, K., & van Solinge, H. (2015). Access to bridge employment: Who finds and who does not find work after retirement? *The Gerontologist*, in press.

Earl, C., & Taylor, P. (2015). Is workplace flexibility good policy? Evaluating the efficacy of age management strategies for older women workers. *Work, Aging and Retirement*, *1*, 214–226.

Ebner, N. C., Freund, A. M., & Baltes, P. B. (2006). Developmental changes in personal goal orientation from young to late adulthood: From striving for gains to maintenance and prevention of losses. *Psychology and Aging*, *21*, 664–678.

Feldman, D. C., & Beehr, T. A. (2011). A three-phase model of retirement decision making. *American Psychologist*, *66*, 193–203.

Ferguson, M., Carlson, D., & Kacmar, K. M. (2015). Flexing work boundaries: The spillover and crossover of workplace support. *Personnel Psychology*, *68*, 581–614.

Freund, A. M. (2006). Age-differential motivational consequences of optimization versus compensation focus in younger and older adults. *Psychology and Aging*, *21*, 240–252.

Gardiner, J., & Tomlinson, J. (2009). Organisational approaches to flexible working: Perspectives of equality and diversity managers in the UK. *Equal Opportunities International*, *28*, 671–686.

Glavin, P., & Schieman, S. (2012). Work–family role blurring and work–family conflict: The moderating influence of job resources and job demands. *Work and Occupations*, *39*, 71–98.

Gobeski, K. T., & Beehr, T. A. (2009). How retirees work: Predictors of different types of bridge employment. *Journal of Organizational Behavior*, *30*, 401–425.

Golden, L. (2008). Limited access: Disparities in flexible work schedules and work-at-home. *Journal of Family and Economic Issues*, *29*, 86–109.

Gov.uk. (2015). Retrieved from https://www.gov.uk/contract-types-and-employer-responsibilities/zero-hour-contracts. Accessed on October 23, 2015.

Grant, A. M., & Parker, S. K. (2009). Redesigning work design theories: The rise of relational and proactive perspectives. *The Academy of Management Annals*, *3*, 317–375.

Greenberg, J., Roberge, M. E., Ho, V. T., & Rousseau, D. M. (2004). Fairness as an "i-deal": Justice in under-the-table employment arrangements. *Research in Personnel and Human Resources Management*, *22*, 1–34.

Harvey, D. (2005). *A brief history of neoliberalism*. Oxford, UK: Oxford University Press.

Heckhausen, J., Wrosch, C., & Schulz, R. (2010). A motivational theory of life-span development. *Psychological Review*, *117*, 32–60.

Hill, E. J., Grzywacz, J. G., Allen, S., Blanchard, V. L., Matz-Costa, C., Shulkin, S., & Pitt-Catsouphes, M. (2008). Defining and conceptualizing workplace flexibility. *Community, Work and Family*, *11*, 149–163.

Hill, E. J., Jacob, J. I., Shannon, L. L., Brennan, R. T., Blanchard, V. L., & Martinengo, G. (2008). Exploring the relationship of workplace flexibility, gender, and life stage to family-to-work conflict, and stress and burnout. *Community, Work and Family*, *11*, 165–181.

Hinds, M. (2003). *The triumph of the flexible society: The connectivity revolution and resistance to change.* Westport, CT: Greenwood Publishing Group.

Hornung, S., Rousseau, D. M., & Glaser, J. (2008). Creating flexible work arrangements through idiosyncratic deals. *Journal of Applied Psychology, 93,* 655–664.

Hyman, J., Scholarios, D., & Baldry, C. (2005). Getting on or getting by? Employee flexibility and coping strategies for home and work. *Work, Employment & Society, 19,* 705–725.

Johnson, R. W. (2011). Phased retirement and workplace flexibility for older adults: Opportunities and challenges. *The ANNALS of the American Academy of Political and Social Science, 638,* 68–85.

Kalleberg, A. L. (2003). Flexible firms and labor market segmentation. Effects of workplace restructuring on jobs and workers. *Work and Occupations, 30,* 154–175.

Kanfer, R., & Ackerman, P. L. (2004). Aging, adult development, and work motivation. *Academy of Management Review, 29,* 440–458.

Kanfer, R., Beier, M. E., & Ackerman, P. L. (2013). Goals and motivation related to work in later adulthood: An organizing framework. *European Journal of Work and Organizational Psychology, 22,* 253–264.

Karl, A. G. (2015). The zero hour of the neoliberal novel. *Textual Practice, 29,* 335–355.

Katz, S., & Calasanti, T. (2015). Critical perspectives on successful aging: Does it "appeal more than it illuminates"? *The Gerontologist, 55,* 26–33.

Kelliher, C., & Anderson, D. (2010). Doing more with less? Flexible working practices and the intensification of work. *Human Relations, 63,* 83–106.

Klehe, U. C., Koen, J., & De Pater, I. E. (2012). Ending on the scrap heap? In J. W. Hedge & W. C. Borman (Eds.), *The Oxford handbook of work and aging* (pp. 313–340). Oxford, UK: Oxford University Press.

Kociatkiewicz, J., & Kostera, M. (2014). *Liquid organization: Zygmunt Bauman and organization theory.* London: Routledge.

Kooij, D., de Lange, A., Jansen, P., & Dikkers, J. (2008). Older workers' motivation to continue to work: Five meanings of age: A conceptual review. *Journal of Managerial Psychology, 23,* 364–394.

Kooij, D. T. (2015). Successful aging at work: The active role of employees. *Work, Aging and Retirement, 1,* 309–319.

Kooij, D. T., Bal, P. M., & Kanfer, R. (2014). Future time perspective and promotion focus as determinants of intraindividual change in work motivation. *Psychology and Aging, 29,* 319–328.

Kooij, D. T., Tims, M., & Kanfer, R. (2015). Successful aging at work: The role of job crafting. In P. M. Bal, D. T. A. M. Kooij, & D. M. Rousseau (Eds.), *Aging workers and the employee-employer relationship* (pp. 145–161). London: Springer International Publishing.

Kossek, E. E., Pichler, S., Bodner, T., & Hammer, L. B. (2011). Workplace social support and work–family conflict: A meta-analysis clarifying the influence of general and work–family-specific supervisor and organizational support. *Personnel Psychology, 64,* 289–313.

Kunze, F., Boehm, S., & Bruch, H. (2013). Organizational performance consequences of age diversity: Inspecting the role of diversity-friendly HR policies and top managers' negative age stereotypes. *Journal of Management Studies, 50,* 413–442.

Lai, L., Rousseau, D. M., & Chang, K. T. T. (2009). Idiosyncratic deals: Coworkers as interested third parties. *Journal of Applied Psychology, 94,* 547–556.

Legge, K. (1995). *Human resource management: Rhetorics and realities: Anniversary edition.* London: Palgrave Macmillan.

Leisink, P. L., & Knies, E. (2011). Line managers' support for older workers. *The International Journal of Human Resource Management, 22,* 1902–1917.

Leslie, L. M., Manchester, C. F., Park, T. Y., & Mehng, S. A. (2012). Flexible work practices: A source of career premiums or penalties? *Academy of Management Journal, 55,* 1407–1428.

Liao, C., Wayne, S. J., & Rousseau, D. M. (2016). Idiosyncratic deals in contemporary organizations: A qualitative and meta-analytical review. *Journal of Organizational Behavior, 37*(S1), S9–S29.

Lyness, K. S., & Kropf, M. B. (2005). The relationships of national gender equality and organizational support with work-family balance: A study of European managers. *Human Relations, 58,* 33–60.

Martínez-Sánchez, A., Vela-Jiménez, M. J., Pérez-Pérez, M., & de-Luis-Carnicer, P. (2011). The dynamics of labour flexibility: Relationships between employment type and innovativeness. *Journal of Management Studies, 48,* 715–736.

Masuda, A. D., Poelmans, S. A., Allen, T. D., Spector, P. E., Lapierre, L. M., Cooper, C. L., & Moreno-Velazquez, I. (2012). Flexible work arrangements availability and their relationship with work-to-family conflict, job satisfaction, and turnover intentions: A comparison of three country clusters. *Applied Psychology, 61,* 1–29.

Matz-Costa, C., & Pitt-Catsouphes, M. (2010). Workplace flexibility as an organizational response to the aging of the workforce: A comparison of nonprofit and for-profit organizations. *Journal of Social Service Research, 36,* 68–80.

McNamara, T. K., Pitt-Catsouphes, M., Brown, M., & Matz-Costa, C. (2012). Access to and utilization of flexible work options. *Industrial Relations, 51,* 936–965.

Moen, P., Kelly, E., & Huang, Q. (2008). Work, family and life-course fit: Does control over work time matter? *Journal of Vocational Behavior, 73,* 414–425.

Moen, P., & Sweet, S. (2004). From 'work–family' to 'flexible careers': A life course reframing. *Community, Work & Family, 7,* 209–226.

Morgan, G. (2015). Elites, varieties of capitalism and the crisis of neo-liberalism. In G. Morgan, P. Hirsch, & S. Quack (Eds.), *Elites on trial* (Vol. 43, pp. 55–80). Research in the Sociology of Organizations. Bingley, UK: Emerald Group Publishing Limited.

Morrison, E. W., & Robinson, S. L. (1997). When employees feel betrayed: A model of how psychological contract violation develops. *Academy of Management Review, 22,* 226–256.

Morrow-Howell, N., Hinterlong, J., & Sherraden, M. (2001). *Productive aging: Concepts and challenges.* Baltimore, MD: JHU Press.

Nelson, E. A., & Dannefer, D. (1992). Aged heterogeneity: Fact or fiction? The fate of diversity in gerontological research. *The Gerontologist, 32,* 17–23.

Oxford Dictionary. (2015). *Oxford English dictionary.* Oxford, UK: Oxford University Press.

Pessoa, J. P., & Van Reenen, J. (2014). The UK productivity and jobs puzzle: Does the answer lie in wage flexibility? *The Economic Journal, 124,* 433–452.

Piketty, T. (2014). *Capital in the twenty-first century.* Cambridge, MA: Harvard University Press.

Pitt-Catsouphes, M., & Matz-Costa, C. (2008). The multi-generational workforce: Workplace flexibility and engagement. *Community, Work and Family, 11,* 215–229.

Platman, K. (2004a). Flexible employment in later life: Public policy panaceas in the search for mechanisms to extend working lives. *Social Policy and Society, 3*, 181–188.

Platman, K. (2004b). 'Portfolio careers' and the search for flexibility in later life. *Work, Employment & Society, 18*, 573–599.

Polat, T., Bal, P. M., & Jansen, P. G. (2012). After-retirement work profiles: How do employees want to continue working after retirement? *Gedrag & Organisatie, 25*, 66–86.

Posthuma, R. A., & Campion, M. A. (2009). Age stereotypes in the workplace: Common stereotypes, moderators, and future research directions. *Journal of Management, 35*, 158–188.

Putnam, L. L., Myers, K. K., & Gailliard, B. M. (2014). Examining the tensions in workplace flexibility and exploring options for new directions. *Human Relations, 67*, 413–440.

Rau, B. L., & Adams, G. A. (2005). Attracting retirees to apply: Desired organizational characteristics of bridge employment. *Journal of Organizational Behavior, 26*, 649–660.

Rogier, S. A., & Padgett, M. Y. (2004). The impact of utilizing a flexible work schedule on the perceived career advancement potential of women. *Human Resource Development Quarterly, 15*, 89–106.

Rousseau, D. M. (1995). *Psychological contracts in organizations: Understanding written and unwritten agreements.* Thousand Oaks, CA: Sage.

Rousseau, D. M. (2005). *I-deals, idiosyncratic deals employees bargain for themselves.* Armonk, NY: ME Sharpe.

Rozanova, J. (2010). Discourse of successful aging in The Globe & Mail: Insights from critical gerontology. *Journal of Aging Studies, 24*, 213–222.

Sanchez, R. (1995). Strategic flexibility in product competition. *Strategic Management Journal, 16*, 135–159.

Sarasvathy, S. D. (2001). Causation and effectuation: Toward a theoretical shift from economic inevitability to entrepreneurial contingency. *Academy of Management Review, 26*, 243–263.

Savickas, M. L., Nota, L., Rossier, J., Dauwalder, J.-P., Duarte, M. E., Guichard, J., ... & Van Vianen, A. E. (2009). Life designing: A paradigm for career construction in the 21st century. *Journal of Vocational Behavior, 75*, 239–250.

Schumann, P. L. (2001). A moral principles framework for human resource management ethics. *Human Resource Management Review, 11*, 93–111.

Seco, J., Abecia, L. C., Echevarría, E., Barbero, I., Torres-Unda, J., Rodriguez, V., & Calvo, J. I. (2013). A long-term physical activity training program increases strength and flexibility, and improves balance in older adults. *Rehabilitation Nursing, 38*, 37–47.

Seymour, R. (2014). *Against austerity.* London: Pluto Press.

Shacklock, K., Brunetto, Y., & Nelson, S. (2009). The different variables that affect older males' and females' intentions to continue working. *Asia Pacific Journal of Human Resources, 47*, 79–101.

Shultz, K. S. (2003). Bridge employment: Work after retirement. In G. A. Adams & T. A. Beehr (Eds.), *Retirement: Reasons, processes, and results* (pp. 214–241). New York, NY: Springer.

Siegenthaler, J. K., & Brenner, A. M. (2001). Flexible work schedules, older workers, and retirement. *Journal of Aging & Social Policy, 12*, 19–34.

Stohl, C., & Cheney, G. (2001). Participatory processes/paradoxical practices communication and the dilemmas of organizational democracy. *Management Communication Quarterly*, *14*, 349–407.

Suddaby, R. (2010). Editor's comments: Construct clarity in theories of management and organization. *Academy of Management Review*, *35*, 346–357.

Sweet, S., Besen, E., Pitt-Catsouphes, M., & McNamara, T. K. (2014). Do options for job flexibility diminish in times of economic uncertainty? *Work, Employment, and Society*, *28*, 882–903.

Sweet, S., Pitt-Catsouphes, M., Besen, E., & Golden, L. (2014). Explaining organizational variation in flexible work arrangements: Why the pattern and scale of availability matter. *Community, Work & Family*, *17*, 115–141.

Ten Brummelhuis, L. L., Bakker, A. B., Hetland, J., & Keulemans, L. (2012). Do new ways of working foster work engagement? *Psicothema*, *24*, 113–120.

Thorsteinson, T. J. (2003). Job attitudes of part-time vs. full-time workers: A meta-analytic review. *Journal of Occupational and Organizational Psychology*, *76*, 151–177.

Tims, M., & Bakker, A. B. (2010). Job crafting: Towards a new model of individual job redesign. *SA Journal of Industrial Psychology*, *36*, 1–9.

Tomaney, J. (1990). The reality of workplace flexibility. *Capital & Class*, *14*, 29–60.

Vallas, S. P. (1999). Rethinking post-Fordism: The meaning of workplace flexibility. *Sociological Theory*, *17*, 68–101.

Van der Heijde, C. M., & Van Der Heijden, B. I. (2006). A competence-based and multidimensional operationalization and measurement of employability. *Human Resource Management*, *45*, 449–476.

Van Solinge, H., & Henkens, K. (2014). Work-related factors as predictors in the retirement decision-making process of older workers in the Netherlands. *Ageing and Society*, *34*, 1551–1574.

Volberda, H. W. (1996). Toward the flexible form: How to remain vital in hypercompetitive environments. *Organization Science*, *7*, 359–374.

Wang, M., & Shi, J. (2014). Psychological research on retirement. *Annual Review of Psychology*, *65*, 209–233.

Wang, M., & Shultz, K. S. (2010). Employee retirement: A review and recommendations for future investigation. *Journal of Management*, *36*, 172–206.

Wang, M., Zhan, Y., Liu, S., & Shultz, K. S. (2008). Antecedents of bridge employment: A longitudinal investigation. *Journal of Applied Psychology*, *93*, 818–830.

Way, S. A., Tracey, J. B., Fay, C. H., Wright, P. M., Snell, S. A., Chang, S., & Gong, Y. (2015). Validation of a multidimensional HR flexibility measure. *Journal of Management*, *41*, 1098–1131.

Wright, P. M., & Snell, S. A. (1998). Toward a unifying framework for exploring fit and flexibility in strategic human resource management. *Academy of Management Review*, *23*, 756–772.

Wrzesniewski, A., & Dutton, J. E. (2001). Crafting a job: Revisioning employees as active crafters of their work. *Academy of Management Review*, *26*, 179–201.

Yang, S., & Zheng, L. (2011). The paradox of de-coupling: A study of flexible work program and workers' productivity. *Social Science Research*, *40*, 299–311.

Yeung, D. Y., & Fung, H. H. (2009). Aging and work: How do SOC strategies contribute to job performance across adulthood? *Psychology and Aging*, *24*, 927–940.

Yu, K., Cadeaux, J., & Luo, B. N. (2015). Operational flexibility: Review and meta-analysis. *International Journal of Production Economics, 169*, 190–202.

Zacher, H. (2015). Successful aging at work. *Work, Aging and Retirement, 1*, 4–25.

Zacher, H., & Frese, M. (2011). Maintaining a focus on opportunities at work: The interplay between age, job complexity, and the use of selection, optimization, and compensation strategies. *Journal of Organizational Behavior, 32*, 291–318.

UNDERSTANDING AND REDUCING WORKPLACE DISCRIMINATION

Ho Kwan Cheung, ☆ Eden King, Alex Lindsey, Ashley Membere, Hannah M. Markell and Molly Kilcullen

ABSTRACT

Even more than 50 years after the Civil Rights Act of 1964 prohibited discrimination toward a number of groups in employment settings in the United States, workplace discrimination remains a persistent problem in organizations. This chapter provides a comprehensive review and analysis of contemporary theory and evidence on the nature, causes, and consequences of discrimination before synthesizing potential methods for its reduction. We note the strengths and weaknesses of this scholarship and highlight meaningful future directions. In so doing, we hope to both inform and inspire organizational and scholarly efforts to understand and eliminate workplace discrimination.

Keywords: Discrimination; diversity; equal employment; diversity management

☆ Authors contributed equally and authorship was determined alphabetically

Research in Personnel and Human Resources Management, Volume 34, 101–152
Copyright © 2016 by Emerald Group Publishing Limited
All rights of reproduction in any form reserved
ISSN: 0742-7301/doi:10.1108/S0742-730120160000034010

Any worker can encounter insults, demotions, docked payrolls and blocked opportunities. When these kinds of actions are directed toward members of particular social groups because of their identities, however, a larger social problem – that of workplace discrimination – is revealed. Unfortunately, despite the prohibition of employment discrimination on the basis of race, color, religion, sex, or national origin by the Civil Rights Act of 1964, people from disadvantaged social groups continue to report unfair treatment at work. Indeed, a total of 88,778 charges of discrimination were received by the Equal Employment Opportunity Commission in 2014, yielding $22.5 million in monetary relief for litigated cases (Equal Employment Opportunity Commission [EEOC], 2015). These concerns are magnified in the increasingly diverse workplace; the Bureau of Labor Statistics reports that the composition of the U.S. workforce is approximately 47% women, 21% ethnic minority, and 10% people with disabilities (U.S. Bureau of Labor Statistics, 2015).

Human resource scholars and practitioners are attuned to these statistics and have built a large body of relevant knowledge. For example, the Society for Human Resource Management identified demographic changes and cultural integration as critical themes in its strategic initiative to shape the future of work (Society for Human Resource Management [SHRM], 2013). As another example, a review of articles published in the *Journal Applied Psychology* since its 1917 inception discovered over 500 papers on employment discrimination (Colella & King, 2015). The overarching goal of this chapter is to reflect on the major conclusions and questions that have emerged from this body of work. To do so, we define discrimination and specify its potential targets before considering its proximal and distal causes and consequences. We further synthesize theory and evidence that guide efforts to reduce discrimination and avoid its consequences. Overall, this review fulfills dual purposes to inform and inspire practical and scholarly efforts to understand and eliminate discrimination in the workplace.

DEFINING WORKPLACE DISCRIMINATION

The United Nations' International Labor Organization (2015) defined employment discrimination as "any distinction, exclusion or preference made on the basis of race, colour, sex, religion, political opinion, national extraction or social origin, which has the effect of nullifying or impairing equality of opportunity or treatment in employment or occupation." This conceptualization reflects global recognition of the persistence of unfair employment experiences of people from a variety of social groups. It is also consistent with the social psychological distinctions between discrimination, prejudice, and stereotypes that place discrimination as the behavioral manifestation of biased cognitions (stereotypes) and attitudes (prejudice) toward individuals as a function of their social group membership.

Yet, this definition is also limited in two important ways. Indeed, Shen and Dhanani (2015) clarified that, "the research literature has generally adopted a broader conceptualization of workplace discrimination, including behaviors outside of organizational practices (e.g., interpersonal treatment by coworkers and customers) as well as encompassing discrimination based on social characteristics that are not always legally protected (e.g., weight, sexual orientation, physical attractiveness)." Thus, the U.N. definition is first limited by its omission of other likely targets of discrimination such as gay and lesbian people, people with disabilities, and ex-convicts (see Ruggs et al., 2013). Second, this definition is also limited by its emphasis on equal opportunity more so than interpersonal experiences that vary with social identity characteristics. In this chapter, we consider a broad range of social groups whose members are unfairly targeted by discrimination and a variety of behavioral indicators of discrimination. This broader view of discrimination can be understood through common typologies applied to its operationalization and through its placement in a larger nomological network.

Dominant Typologies of Discrimination

These broad definitions have informed typologies of discrimination which tend to cluster discriminatory actions according to their conspicuousness. Here we discuss three separate approaches to understanding types of discrimination: *subtle versus overt, interpersonal versus formal, and microaggressions.* These perspectives represent shared scholarly understanding that the manifestation of contemporary discrimination is much less conspicuous than that of the past, but also indicate some disagreement in which behavioral distinctions are most important to emphasize.

The first, most inclusive classification scheme designates some discriminatory actions as *overt* and others as *subtle* in nature. Overt discrimination involves blatant, unambiguous actions that directly convey denigration of a person as a function of their social group membership. This can be contrasted with subtle discrimination, which includes "actions that are ambiguous in intent to harm, difficult to detect, low in intensity, and often unintentional" (Jones, Peddie, Gilrane, King, & Gray, in press). It is further important to note that these actions are, "entrenched in common, everyday interactions, taking the shape of harassment, jokes, incivility, avoidance, and other types of disrespectful treatment" (Van Laer & Janssens, 2011, p. 1205). The subtle-overt distinction can be aligned with research in social cognition that articulates the ways that implicit (unconscious) and explicit (conscious) biases operate (Dovidio, Gaertner, Kawakami, & Hodson, 2002); much like cognitions operate in unconscious and conscious forms, so too do discriminatory behaviors. This may explain why a large body of research has accumulated from this perspective, including studies examining different patterns in perceiving (Operario & Fiske, 2001) and responding to subtle and overt discrimination (Deitch, Barsky, Butz, Chan, Brief, & Bradley, 2003).

The second typology that has received substantial scholarly attention is one that distinguishes between formal and interpersonal manifestations of discrimination (Hebl, Foster, Mannix, & Dovidio, 2002). Whereas formal discrimination can be understood as behavior that is generally illegal and structurally oriented (such as a decision not to hire or promote someone on the basis of their social identity), interpersonal discrimination involves unhelpful, disrespectful, or hostile behaviors in everyday interactions. Research using this typology has demonstrated, for example, that gay and lesbian job applicants (Hebl et al., 2002) and obese shoppers (King, Shapiro, Hebl, Singletary, & Turner, 2006) encounter interpersonal, but not formal, forms of discrimination. Although formal and interpersonal discrimination are often described using terms that overlap with overtness and subtlety, they are not entirely aligned; discrimination can be formal and subtle or interpersonal and overt (Lindsey et al., 2015).

A third, emerging typology focuses on these everyday interactions and behaviors from the perspective of microaggressions, "brief and common-place daily verbal, behavioral, or environmental indignities, whether intentional or unintentional, that communicate hostile, derogatory, or negative racial slights and insults toward the target person or group" (Sue et al., 2007, p. 273). These behaviors can be classified as microassaults (i.e., attacks intended to harm the target), microinsults (i.e., rude or insensitive comments about a person's identity), and microinvalidations (i.e., actions that minimize others' feelings or experiences). Less empirical work has been conducted to support this theoretical framework compared to the other typologies, but Constantine (2007) showed that clients' perceptions of therapists' microaggressions were correlated with poorer quality therapeutic relationships.

It is noteworthy that aspects of these distinctions may be captured by the overarching concept of *modern discrimination*. Indeed, Marchiondo, Ran, and Cortina (2015) describe modern discrimination as being potentially unconscious and, "characterized by subtle, low-intensity behaviors that isolate or handicap others" and "often nonverbal in nature but can manifest through verbal and paraverbal (e.g., intonation, volume) behavior." This conceptualization encompasses the subtle and interpersonal forms of discrimination and both microinvalidations and microinsults, and thus can be distinguished from traditional forms of discrimination that were more overt, formal, and severe in nature.

Nomological Network

These types of discrimination can also be understood in relation to other highly related and commonly studied constructs in personnel psychology. In particular, we identify conceptual overlap and distinctiveness between discrimination and the concepts of *adverse impact, harassment,* and *incivility*.

Adverse impact is a particular type of formal discrimination that may or may not be subtle in nature. Adverse impact emerges when members of particular social identity groups receive fewer opportunities or valued outcomes as the result of an employment device or procedure (such as a cognitive ability test or interview). Substantial attention in personnel psychology has been paid to the factors that give rise to adverse impact (Colella & King, 2015), due in large part to evolving civil rights statutes and legal precedents that specify the conditions and outcomes that are prohibited. The disparities of focus in adverse impact analyses are undoubtedly indicators of discrimination; that is, adverse impact is one way that discrimination manifests. It is not, however, the only way that discrimination is expressed.

Indeed, harassment on the basis of gender or sex, racio-ethnicity, and sexual orientation are very different manifestations of discrimination. The EEOC (2015) specifies that "Harassment can include 'sexual harassment' or unwelcome sexual advances, requests for sexual favors, and other verbal or physical harassment of a sexual nature," and further clarifies that, "Harassment does not have to be of a sexual nature, however, and can include offensive remarks about a person's sex." Sexual harassment, which has received a great deal of scholarly and public scrutiny, is thus a specific form of discrimination that is sexual in nature. This may take the form of overt and formal discrimination when sexual favors are expected or requested in exchange for employment outcomes in the case of quid pro quo harassment. Sexual harassment may also be more subtle and interpersonal in nature when it emerges as behaviors that create a hostile work environment. Indeed, hostile work environment claims are characterized by some of the same kinds of rude, disrespectful, and insensitive behaviors that characterize modern discrimination more generally (King et al., 2011).

The interpersonal aspects of modern discrimination itself can be equated in many ways to a targeted form of incivility (Cortina, 2008). Although incivility is generally understood as low-intensity behaviors that violate social norms and injure targets without clear intent to harm, incivility that is *selective* is directed toward particular others because of their social group memberships; Cortina (2008) argued that selective incivility represents subtle manifestations of gender and racial discrimination. Moreover, like selective incivility, behaviors that are considered to be representative of social undermining (e.g., "behavior intended to hinder, over time, the ability to establish and maintain positive interpersonal relationships, work-related success, and favorable reputation" (Duffy, Ganster, & Pagon, 2002, p. 332)) and abusive supervision (e.g., the "sustained display of hostile verbal and nonverbal behaviors, excluding physical contact" (Tepper, 2000, p. 178)) can also be considered to be markers of discrimination if they are disproportionately or intentionally targeted at people as a function of their social group membership (see Hershcovis, 2011). Drawing from these closely related, but not entirely overlapping, areas of scholarship builds a broader understanding of factors that give rise to discrimination toward a variety of targets, its outcomes, and strategies for its reduction.

WHO IS TARGETED?

Before reviewing research regarding the specific targets of discrimination, we must make a distinction between groups that fall under the protection of U.S. federal antidiscrimination laws and those who do not. Whether or not a group has legal protection may shape differences in the antecedents, incidences, consequences and remediation strategies regarding workplace discrimination. Under Title VII of the Civil Rights Act of 1964, employers are prohibited from discriminating against individuals based on their race, color, sex, religion, or national origin. As of 1967, the Age Discrimination in Employment Act forbids employers from discriminating against individuals who are 40 years or older. The Pregnancy Discrimination Act of 1978 protects against sex discrimination based on pregnancy. In 1990, the Americans with Disabilities Act (ADA) extended further protections to workers with disabilities. However, even with these laws and regulations in place, individuals from these groups still experience discrimination in the workplace as shown by sheer number of cases overseen by the EEOC (EEOC, 2015). Additionally, lesbian, gay, bisexual, and transgender (LGBT) individuals, working parents, and ex-convicts also have their own unique experiences with workplace discrimination that may be impacted by their lack of explicit federal legal protection. We choose to focus on these groups in particular as the EEOC states that these groups should be protected based on Title VII (EEOC, 2007, 2012, 2015).

Protected Classes

Racial Minorities

Racial discrimination charges made up approximately 35% of the charges overseen by the EEOC in the last 18 years (EEOC, 2015). Most of the research concerning racial discrimination focuses on the experiences of racial minorities such Black Americans, Latinos, and Asian Americans. In terms of formal discrimination, studies have found that racial minorities are less likely to receive job and interview offers than Whites despite equal qualifications (Bertrand, Mullainathan, & Shafir, 2004; Derous, Nguyen, & Ryan, 2009; Derous, Ryan, & Serlie, 2015; King, Mendoza, Madera, Hebl, & Knight, 2006). Biases against racial minorities have also been found for perceptions of job fit (Steward & Cunningham, 2015), performance evaluations (McKay, Avery, & Morris, 2008; McKay & McDaniel, 2006), promotion opportunities (Elvira & Zatzick, 2002; McBrier, & Wilson, 2004; Wilson & Maume, 2013), and leadership evaluations (Chung-Herrera & Lankau, 2005; Rosette, Leonardelli, & Phillips, 2008; Sy et al., 2010).

Racial minorities can also suffer from interpersonal discrimination in organizations (De Castro, Gee, & Takeuchi, 2008; Deitch et al., 2003; Lewis & Gunn, 2007; Raver & Nishii, 2010). Studies have found that racial minorities can be the targets of racial microaggressions (Kern & Grandey, 2009; King et al., 2011; Sue, Lin, Torino, Capodilupo, & Rivera, 2009; Wang, Leu, & Shoda, 2011), subtler forms of incivility from coworkers and supervisors (Cortina, Kabat-Farr, Leskinen, Huerta, & Magley, 2013; Cunningham, Miner, & McDonald, 2013), and exclusion from social and informal networks (Gray, Kurihara, Hommen, & Feldman, 2007; Hodson, Roscigno, & Lopez, 2006).

Sex

Similar to race, sex discrimination charges made up about 30% of EEOC charges from 1997 to 2014 (EEOC, 2015). Studies have found that women face formal discrimination in the selection process, particularly in prototypically masculine jobs and industries: women are less likely to be recommended for hire for masculine-typed occupations (Davison & Burke, 2000; Moss-Racusin, Dovidio, Brescoll, Graham, & Handelsman, 2012). Women also encounter formal discrimination beyond the selection process as they receive lower performance evaluations compared to men (Foschi, Lai, & Sigerson, 1994; Swim, Borgida, Maruyama, & Myers, 1989; Thomas-Hunt & Phillips, 2004). This can be exacerbated by the sex-type of the occupation as women in more masculine jobs are evaluated more harshly compared to their male counterparts (Boldry, Wood, & Kashy, 2001; Eagly, Karau, & Makhijani, 1995; Eagly, Makhijani & Klonsky, 1992; Heilman, Wallen, Fuchs, & Tamkins, 2004). Managers also give female workers fewer promotion opportunities (Blau & DeVaro, 2007; Lyness & Heilman, 2006; Roth, Purvis, & Bobko, 2012), which can block them from obtaining leadership positions (De Pater, Van Vianen, & Bechtoldt, 2010; Eagly & Carli, 2007). Additionally, women are targets of wage discrimination. Although the Equal Pay Act of 1963 protects against wage discrimination based on sex, women still earn around 20% less than men and this wage gap holds across race, organization level, and age (Catalyst, 2015).

Women can also be targets of interpersonal discrimination within the workplace. Women are more likely to report being targets of sexual harassment compared to men (Lewis & Gunn, 2007; Salin, 2003; Yamada, Cappadocia, & Pepler, 2014). Women are also more likely to report being targets of incivility compared to men (Cortina et al., 2002, 2013; Cortina, Magley, Williams, & Langhout, 2001; Richman et al., 1999) and certain women may be more susceptible to incivility compared to others (Cortina et al., 2013).

Religion

EEOC charges involving religious discrimination have been steadily increasing throughout the years from less than 2.5% in the 1990s to 4% post-2001 (EEOC, 2015). Most of the research on religious discrimination has focused on the interpersonal realm (Ghumman, Ryan, Barclay, & Markel, 2013). For example, Muslim and Jewish workers were more likely to report that they were the target of jokes about their religion on the job (Taylor, 2002). A field study found that Muslim female applicants wearing traditional attire had more negative and shorter interactions with hiring managers compared to women who were not wearing such attire (King & Ahmad, 2010). Muslim women wearing the hijab also report lower expectations of callbacks when applying for jobs compared to women not wearing the hijab (Ghumman & Jackson, 2010). Moreover, religious minorities may face backlash in the form of discrimination when asking for accommodations that do not align with the typical workweek set up by their employers. For example, Muslim workers may need to ask for specific days off during the month of Ramadan or Jewish workers who are Orthodox may request time off on the Jewish Shabbat as opposed to a Sunday (Ghumman et al., 2013).

Age
Charges of age discrimination have also increased steadily from 18% in 1999 to 23% in 2014 (EEOC, 2015). Experimental studies have found that older workers were more likely to face biases in the hiring process compared to their younger counterparts (Bendick, Brown, & Wall, 1999). Additionally, older workers were also more likely than younger workers to receive harsher performance evaluations when their performance was low (Rupp, Vodanovich, & Crede, 2006). A recent meta-analysis echoes these findings, as results showed that older workers were less likely to be hired for jobs, received lower performance evaluations, and had fewer opportunities for promotion when compared to younger workers (Bal, Reiss, Rudolph, & Baltes, 2011).

Mixed results have been found regarding experiences of interpersonal discrimination for older workers, however. Competing studies have found that both older and younger workers face harassment in the workplace (Cortina et al., 2001; Einarsen & Skogstad, 1996). Furthermore, although some studies have found older workers are perceived as more aloof and lacking in interpersonal skills (Bal et al., 2011), others have contradicted these findings (Ng & Feldman, 2012).

Disability
EEOC charges regarding disability discrimination have fluctuated over the years with a low of 20% of total cases in the early 2000s to a dramatic increase to 29% in 2014 (EEOC, 2015). There are a large number of disabilities that can evoke discrimination that range from completely visible to completely invisible in nature. Visible disabilities are readily signaled to others by some type of visual cue such as a wheelchair or hearing aids

(Saal, Martinez, & Smith, 2014). Invisible disabilities include a wide range of both physical or psychological conditions that have no visual cues or features that be readily attributed to an obvious disability; examples include chronic pain and psychological disorders (Santuzzi, Waltz, Finkelstein, & Rupp, 2014). Reviews of discrimination allegations against individuals with disabilities have noted that most allegations have been related to formal discrimination matters such as hiring, terms of employment, and accommodations (Chan, McMahon, Cheing, Rosenthal, & Bezyak, 2005; McMahon & Shaw, 2005). Yet, individuals with invisible disabilities may face greater amounts of formal discrimination. For example, a study found that job applicants with physical disabilities were evaluated more positively than those with invisible mental disabilities (Premeaux, 2001). Coworkers may engage in interpersonal discrimination as individuals with disabilities may be victims of backlash when they ask their employers for special accommodations (Colella, 2001).

National Origin
EEOC charges regarding national origin made up around 10%−11% of charges in recent years (EEOC, 2015). Although they are provided federal protections under Title VII, relatively sparse research has been conducted regarding workplace discrimination against immigrants. Immigration status can be divided into many distinct categories that can affect the type and severity of discrimination someone faces. In their review of research about discrimination aimed against immigrants, Binggeli, Dietz, and Krings (2013) noted that undocumented immigrants and asylum seekers deal with more formal discrimination regarding wages and compensation (Marfleet & Blustein, 2011; Schultheiss, Watts, Sterland, & O'Neill, 2011), while highly qualified immigrants are more likely to face issues of subtle discrimination (Baltes & Rudolph, 2010; Hakak, Holzinger, & Zikic, 2010; Petersen & Dietz, 2005). Additionally, instances of discrimination may change depending on what country the immigrant worker is from and their accent (Hosoda, Nguyen, & Stone-Romero, 2012; Hosoda & Stone-Romero, 2010; Purkiss, Perrewé, Gillespie, Mayes, & Ferris, 2006).

Unprotected Classes

LGBT Workers
Although the United States has made numerous strides in civil rights for LGBT individuals in recent years such as establishing marriage equality,

LGBT individuals still face discrimination in the workplace. As of 2015, only 18 states and the District of Columbia have employment laws that protect against workplace discrimination for both gender identity and sexual orientation (Human Rights Campaign Foundation, 2015). Even though the Employment Non-Discrimination Act, which seeks to protect individuals from discrimination based on their sexual orientation and gender identity, has been proposed to Congress on numerous occasions, there is currently no federal law in place protecting LGBT workers.

In terms of formal discrimination, gay workers reported earning lower wages than did heterosexual men (Badgett, 1995; Baumle & Poston, 2011). LGBT individuals also tend to receive fewer callbacks from prospective employers (Weichselbaumer, 2003), lower performance evaluations, and can be seen as less competent compared to heterosexual workers (Horvath & Ryan, 2003). As for interpersonal discrimination, a field study conducted by Hebl et al. (2002) found that gay applicants were treated with more hostility compared to other applicants. Additionally, a number of LGBT workers report facing interpersonal discrimination in the forms of harassment and exclusion (Colvin, 2004, 2009).

Although gay, lesbian, and bisexual individuals are targets of discrimination based on their sexual orientation, transgender individuals face discrimination due to their gender identity diverging from their assigned birth sex (Collins, McFadden, Rocco, & Mathis, 2015). Transgender workers have vastly different workplace experiences compared to gay, lesbian, and bisexual employees and have reported facing workplace discrimination (Levitt & Ippolito, 2014; Lombardi, Wilchins, Priesing, & Malouf, 2002). Transgender workers can face many instances of formal workplace discrimination such as lower rates of hiring (Grant et al., 2011), lower wages (Badgett, Lau, Sears, & Ho, 2007), being demoted post-transition (Sangganjanavanich, 2009), and facing termination due to their gender identity (Budge, Tebbe, & Howard, 2010; Hartzell, Frazer, Wertz, & Davis, 2009). Transgender workers can also face interpersonal discrimination in overt forms such as microaggressions (e.g., use of the wrong pronouns) and threats (Budge et al., 2010) or in subtler forms such as being isolated and disrespected by coworkers and the subject of gossip (Brewster, Velez, Mennicke, & Tebbe, 2014; Dietert & Dentice, 2009; Sangganjanavanich, 2009). Additionally, discrimination experiences can differ between trans men and trans women. For example, trans men report higher salaries post-transition, while trans women report a decrease in salary (Schilt & Wiswall, 2008) and lower perceived competence (Schilt & Connell, 2007).

Parental Status

Parents are an additional group that can face workplace discrimination with no explicit protection through federal regulations. Mothers are more likely to face instances of incivility compared to fathers and men and women without children (Miner, Pesonen, Smittick, Seigel, & Clark, 2014). Field studies have found that pregnant female job applicants encountered more interpersonal discrimination compared to their nonpregnant counterparts (Hebl, King, Glick, Singletary, & Kazama, 2007; Morgan, Walker, Hebl, & King, 2013). Mothers are also more susceptible to some aspects of formal discrimination compared to others. Indeed, studies have found that mothers are less likely to receive hiring recommendations and callbacks compared to women without children (Correll, Benard, & Paik, 2007; Cuddy, Fiske, & Glick, 2004; Heilman & Okimoto, 2008) and fathers (Fuegen, Biernat, Haines, & Deaux, 2004). Similar results have been found for pregnant women (Bragger, Kutcher, Morgan, & Firth, 2002; Halpert, Wilson, & Hickman, 1993; Masser, Grass, & Nesic, 2007). Although research has found that fathers receive lower evaluations in some interpersonal dimensions, such as perceived commitment, compared to men without children (Fuegen et al., 2004), the effects seem to be exacerbated for mothers overall.

Ex-Convicts

One population of emerging interest in the employment realm is ex-convicts. A large number of ex-convicts have been seeking employment in recent years (National Reentry Resource Center, 2014). However, since there is no federal legislation protecting their rights, ex-convicts attempting to re-enter the workforce may face formal discrimination from employers. In their theoretical paper, Young and Powell (2015) proposed a variety of factors that could affect the selection process for ex-convicts. For example, biases could differ depending on the time of crime that was committed. White-collar offenders are perceived as more competent in news reports (Riley, Elgin, Lawrence, & Matlack, 2014) and have been sought out by companies and government agencies that deal with sensitive information (Bort, 2012; Zakaria, 2011). Other possible factors that could affect hiring biases against ex-convicts include the seriousness of the crime, how recently it was committed, and demographic characteristics of the perpetrator (Young & Powell, 2015).

Global Perspective

Our review of the targets of discrimination has intentionally focused on experiences within the United States. However, instances of workplace discrimination may vary depending on the country of focus. For example, the United Kingdom has federal regulations in place that protect individuals from discrimination based on their sexual orientation (Badgett & Frank, 2007), so instances of formal discrimination against LGBT workers may be fewer than in the United States. However, there are many countries where non-heterosexual orientations are illegal and this may have profound effects on instances of workplace discrimination (Rupar, 2014). Differences in gender egalitarianism and parental leave policies may engender reductions in workplace sex and parental status discrimination in non-U.S. countries (Ray, Gornick, & Schmitt, 2008; Schwab et al., 2015). Additionally, certain countries are more racially homogenous compared to the United States, so the type of racial discrimination workers face may change due to differences in racial identity (Dikötter, 1994). Future research should examine the roles that country and culture play in manifestations of certain types of discrimination in a broad range of countries outside of the United States. This research path may be of increased interest due to the increased amount of globalization within the workforce and amount of intercultural communication between workers.

Future Directions

Although we have illustrated the major research findings regarding workplace discrimination, further work needs to be done. For example, although immigrants may face discrimination for not being native citizens, the manifestation of said discrimination may change depending on where they are originally from. Future research should examine how experiences of discrimination differ depending on reason for immigration and country of origin. The changes in demographics of the workforce may also present an opportunity for further research. Scholars should take note of the aging workforce in the United States in order to come to more consistent findings regarding formal and interpersonal forms of age discrimination (Finkelstein & Truxillo, 2013). Additionally, employees can be members of multiple protected or unprotected classes at once. Studies have found that racial minority women are more likely to be targets of incivility than White women or racial minority men (Cortina et al., 2013). Future studies should examine the differences between women with multiple stigmatized identities and how it impacts their experiences with discrimination in the workplace. By examining the differences in discrimination aimed at these groups, we may find out more about the antecedents, consequences, and remediation strategies that are unique to them.

ANTECEDENTS OF DISCRIMINATION

Our understanding of employment discrimination hinges on a thorough comprehension of the range of factors that lead to it. These factors include individual, organizational, and societal features that differentially influence conscious (explicit) and unconscious (implicit) forms of discrimination. In this summary we outline the factors lead people to consciously or unconsciously discriminate at each of these three levels (see Table 1).

Antecedents of Conscious Discrimination

Individual Level

When one thinks of discrimination, frequently one thinks of the classic case in which an individual intentionally denies another person goods, services, or opportunities based upon demographic characteristics (Deitch et al., 2003). This conscious discrimination is not usually thought of in terms of individual level traits, but rather "good vs. bad" behavior. However, there are certain personality traits that can predict this type of discrimination across individuals, such as Social Dominance Orientation (SDO; Sidanius & Pratto, 1999), and Right Wing Authoritarianism (RWA; Altemeyer, 1981, 1988; Petersen & Dietz, 2000), which operate through two distinct mechanisms (Crawford, Jussim, Cain, & Cohen, 2013). RWA comes from viewing the world as dangerous and threatening place, whereas SDO derives from viewing the world as a competitive place (Duckitt, 2006).

Table 1. Categories of Antecedents of Discrimination.

Level	Unconscious	Sources	Conscious	Sources
Individual	Social categorization stereotypes	Fiske (2000)	Right wing Authoritarianism	Petersen and Dietz, (2000); Crawford et al. (2013)
	Modern/aversive racist views	Deitch (2003); Dovidio and Gaertner (2004)	Social dominance orientation	Umphress et al. (2008); Crawford et al. (2013)
Organizational	Homosocial reproduction	Kanter (1977a, 1977b); Reskin (2000)	Organizational climate	Gelfand et al. (2007)
	Token dynamic	Kanter (1977a); King et al. (2010)		
Societal	Collectivistic vs. individualistic	Chatman and Spataro (2005)	Business justification	Brief et al. (2000)

SDO is defined as an individual's desire to adhere to the traditional societal hierarchy by supporting the dominance of "superior" groups and the subjugation of "inferior" groups (Sidanius & Pratto, 1999). Individuals higher in SDO view the world as a "competitive jungle" (Crawford et al., 2013, p. 164) and are as such motivated to maintain the current societal status hierarchies (Duckitt, 2006). Interestingly, this applies not only to members of the high-status group (e.g., Whites, men, heterosexuals), but SDO can also be present in members of the lower-status groups.

Unsurprisingly, SDO is associated with prejudice and negative responses toward lower-status groups; including members of ethnic/racial minorities, women, and individuals with disabilities (Duckitt, 2006). Given their competitive view of the world, this is particularly true when those groups are viewed as a threat to the current social order (Crawford et al., 2013). Thus, being higher in SDO is predictive of consciously discriminating against members of low-status groups in order to maintain the status quo (Crawford et al., 2013; Umphress, Simmons, Boswell, & del Triana, 2008). An example of this would be not choosing the most qualified candidate because of his or her low-status (Umphress et al., 2008), or endorsing discrimination against low-status groups and unequal distribution of resources in a hypothetical setting (Kteily, Ho, & Sidanius, 2012).

Importantly, even individuals belonging to low-status groups can be high in SDO (Umphress et al., 2008). This phenomenon operates via several socio-psychological mechanisms, including outgroup favoritism and group debilitating behavior (Umphress et al., 2008). Outgroup favoritism occurs when the low-status group internalizes the denigration of their own group, and chooses to identify with the high-status outgroup (Tafjel & Turner, 1986). Another explanation of this phenomenon can be found in system justification theory (Jost, 2001), which suggests that outgroup favoritism is the result of rationalizing the status quo, as humans are predisposed to want to justify the social system in which they exist. A related theory, the "belief in a just world" theory, states that as humans we want to believe that our world is fair and that people are deserving of what they receive in life. For example, some individuals believe that the poor are poor because they do not work hard enough (Jost & Hunyady, 2003), neglecting to acknowledge the societal structures that impose poverty on certain groups of people. This belief can be espoused by successful individuals but also by the impoverished themselves. SDO plays a role in each of these explanatory mechanisms, as it is the desire to maintain societal systems of marginalization that drives the need to rationalize them.

A related trait, RWA leads to conscious discrimination via a different mechanism than SDO. Rather than viewing the world as competitive and hoping to increase status by subjugating "lesser groups," those high in RWA see the world as an overall threatening place and seek comfort in conforming to traditional standards (Duckitt, 2006). Thus, it is not necessarily the desire to promote oneself, but rather the hope to maintain stability in a confusing world, that motivates the discriminatory behaviors of those high in RWA. RWA has been shown to predict racial, gender, and weight, discrimination (Crawford et al., 2013; O'Brien, Latner, Ebneter, & Hunter, 2013; Petersen & Dietz, 2008; Umphress et al., 2008). Importantly, RWA has also been shown to predict discrimination in personnel selection (O'Brien et al., 2013; Petersen & Dietz, 2000). The literature suggests that those high in RWA are especially likely to discriminate when an authority figure instructs them to do so (Petersen & Dietz, 2000, 2008). This leads us to a discussion of the next level of employment discrimination antecedents: the organizational level.

Organizational Level
The level of structure within a human resources system can impact the extent of conscious discrimination observed in the organization. When formal antidiscrimination policies are in place, employees are less likely to go against these policies and commit conscious acts of discrimination (Delaney & Lundy, 1996). For example, organizations with Equal Employment Opportunity (EEO) diversity officers and those that have adopted the formal policy of specifically targeting minorities for recruitment exhibit less discrimination. Conversely, organizations without these structures allow for loopholes through which prejudiced individuals can justify discriminatory decisions and policies (Gelfand, Nishii, Raver, & Schneider, 2007).

Societal Level
Societal attitudes refer to universal beliefs that are influenced by prevailing conditions such as governments, historical background, and cultural orientation. Societal prejudices can create and perpetuate what some organizations view as a business justification for discrimination (Brief, Dietz, Cohen, Pugh, & Vaslow, 2000). If it is perceived that society is unaccepting of a certain group, the business will adapt to that in order to serve its customers. This type of organizational pressure occurred with Blacks in the 1960s. Jobs involving sales, such as car dealerships and clothing stores, rationalized that they intentionally discriminated against colored people

because it "just would not work" from a customer's viewpoint. Organizations had to gear toward their customers to maximize profits, so they took into consideration their customer's potential prejudices and adjusted their employment accordingly.

This "matching assertion" functions on the premise that performance of staff is positively affected by the racial makeup of the personnel being similar to the customer population. In addition, sales performance significantly increases when there is racial diversity congruence, meaning that the diversity in the community is similar to the diversity in the organization (Richard, Stewart, Mckay, & Sackett, 2015). Justifications such as these may be seen as non-prejudiced and plausible by those who use them, even though they are explicitly racial in nature (Brief et al., 2000). This type of discrimination draws on the similarity-attraction paradigm (people are attracted to and seek membership in groups with members who are similar to them) and social identity theory (belonging to a group causes a person to identify with that group, conform to their norms, and discriminate against outgroups; Dwyer, Orlando, & Shepherd, 1998).

This type of discrimination is not limited to race; a recent example of how societal attitudes can influence discrimination involves the debate about LGBT marriage equality. In Indiana, the owners of a bakery refused to prepare a cake for the marriage of two men. They justified their decision by claiming to be doing right by their God and not wanting to be party to this different group's ceremony. The Colorado Court ultimately ruled against the baker, asserting that it is illegal to refuse service to a customer based on their sexual orientation (Larimer, 2015).

Antecedents of Unconscious Discrimination

The most pernicious forms of discrimination that occur in the contemporary workplace tend to be unconscious and committed unknowingly, as the perpetrators do not view themselves as prejudiced (McConahay, 1983). Understanding that the same factors that support unconscious discrimination can also exacerbate its conscious forms, we focus here on the individual, organizational, and societal factors that are most strongly associated with unconscious behaviors.

Individual Level
At the individual level, antecedents to this type of unconscious discrimination are related to strongly held attitudes (prejudices) and cognitive

processes. With respect to cognitive processes, social categorization theory and research has established that humans have a need to lessen processing demands by classifying others into groups (Tajfel, 1982). This is because we have evolved to be able to quickly categorize individuals in our surroundings as "safe" or "unsafe," "trustworthy" or "untrustworthy." Naturally, we are predisposed to favor our own ingroup. There are several possible explanations for this, most with roots in evolutionary psychology. Realistic conflict theory (Sherif, Harvey, White, Hood, & Sherif, 1988) describes this ingroup favoritism as the logical result of competition between groups, such that if groups are in competition for resources, you will favor members of your own group. Other theories posit that ingroup favoritism occurs because of a need for individuals to boost their own self-esteem, which is accomplished by building up reasons why your ingroup is better than the outgroup and making intergroup distinctions (Brown, 1999). This is true even when said group membership is determined arbitrarily (Tajfel, 1970). However, in reality, group membership is not determined based upon random assignment, but rather using physical or ideological qualities. Humans use this information to form cognitive schema and heuristics, thereby grouping people into categories.

In the context of personnel psychology, employers use stereotyping and categorization to make decisions about individuals, assuming a person's ambition and intelligence based on visible physical qualities such as race, weight, and gender (Agerström & Rooth, 2011; Browne & Kennelly, 1999). Humans are inherently prone to implicit stereotyping, which is defined as unconsciously attributing specific qualities to members of a particular group (Quillian, 2008). Even individuals that consciously deny prejudice can have automatic biases that conflict with their tolerant values (Devine, 2001).

In general, people tend to accentuate differences between categorized groups and minimize differences within. Two types of stereotyping, prescriptive and descriptive, can affect how a person categorizes groups. Individuals asserting how a certain group *should* behave are engaging in prescriptive stereotyping, while describing how a group *does* behave is descriptive stereotyping (Goldman, Gutek, Stein, & Lewis, 2006). Prescriptive racial stereotypes derive from historical social roles and inequalities. The content of these stereotypes varies with regard to two dimensions: the degree to which group members are perceived as warm (a person's intent) and the degree to which they are seen as competent (a person's capability; Fiske, Cuddy, Glick, Xu, & Devine, 2002). In part due to these cognitive processes, people have innate prejudices, which are unjustified or incorrect attitudes (usually negative) toward an individual based on their membership to a social group. Such stereotypes and prejudice can give rise to discrimination.

Typically, the expression of these prejudices is suppressed by anti-prejudiced norms; therefore, expressions of prejudices are typically accompanied with justifications to support the legitimacy of the claim. Justifications for the status quo (keeping the social order) and legitimizing myths can results in discrimination in organizations since typically these views favor dominant groups and suppress minorities. The justification-suppression model (JSM) suggests that "genuine" prejudices are not directly shown (restrained by values and norms), but are expressed when justifications release these suppressed prejudices (Crandall & Eshleman, 2003).

An increase in anti-discrimination laws, practices, and ideologies has led to a decrease in blatant and conscious prejudice expression (Cortina, 2008). Yet, unconscious biases perpetuate subtle discrimination. Aversive, "modern," prejudice is characterized by complex, ambivalent attitudes that result in avoidance of a certain group of people. This involves appealing to rules or stereotypes to rationalize or deny an aversion to a particular group. Aversive racists or sexists see their views as facts, rather than opinions. They claim to have egalitarian values, they outwardly condemn discrimination, and they deny being prejudiced (Cortina, 2008), yet experience negative emotions such as fear, uneasiness, disgust, or indifference when encountering people from other social groups. This causes them to unconsciously change their behavior when interacting with diverse groups. This behavior can be seen as degrading or offensive and can lead to racial discrimination, particularly in the workplace (Cortina, 2008).

Organizational Level

Many cognitive antecedents, such as social categorization, are influenced by factors outside of the individual, such as the environmental context and the social context of the organization (Gelfand et al., 2007; Reskin, 2000). The size of the organization, structure of the organization's Human Resources system, number of minorities in leadership positions, heterogeneity of teams, and the number of other minorities in a workplace can all influence the likelihood that unconscious discrimination will be expressed.

Indeed, the experiences of minorities within organizations are in part shaped by the racial and ethnic makeup of the organization itself (Avery, McKay, & Wilson, 2008). This can be explained via the framework of relational demography, which posits that greater demographic similarity to those in one's workplace leads to perceptions of the workplace as fair and supportive (Tsui, Egan, & Iii, 1992). Thus, underrepresented groups are more likely to experience the workplace as unfair and even discriminatory, particularly when these individuals belong to a low-status underrepresented group (Avery et al., 2008). This is especially true when individuals are one of very few members of their minority group.

When a minority group is severely underrepresented in the workplace the individuals belonging to that minority may experience tokenism. Tokenism is a special case of underrepresentation in the workplace (Goldman et al., 2006; Kanter, 1977a, 1977b). Importantly, as seen with underrepresentation more generally, the negative effects of tokenism are seen primarily when the tokens are from low-status group such as female police officers or construction workers (King, Hebl, George, & Matusik, 2010), and not a high-status group, such as male nurses (Budig, 2002).

Tokenism occurs when less than 15% of an organization or team's members belong to a given minority group (Kanter, 1977a). For example, take an engineering firm where five out of 50 employees are women. In this case, women are seen as tokens of their group within the organization, and they are scrutinized more closely as a result. As tokens, more attention is paid to their mistakes, whereas a dominant member can make a mistake without it reflecting on his group, a token's mistake is taken as evidence of her group's unsuitability (Kanter, 1977a). This is especially the case if there is already the stereotype that women are not as good at math or engineering-related tasks (which the male members may see as confirmed by the dearth of women working at the company), due to confirmation bias.

Furthermore, the majority members engage in a process of contrast, trying to distinguish themselves from the tokens. This is very isolating for the tokens as it can occur on both a social level (Goldman et al., 2006) and professional level. This process of negative contrast with the token group is very commonly a way in which organizational composition can perpetuate unconscious discrimination. When comparing the tokens to themselves, the majority members of the organization firm are inherently prone to seeing themselves as the more favorable group when comparing themselves to the tokens, thereby maintaining the belief that women are less capable than men. This may decrease the likelihood that women would be hired for these positions, thereby perpetuating the cycle of tokenism (Goldman et al., 2006; Kanter, 1977a).

Tokenism and the more general form of underrepresentation can be perpetuated through the Attraction-Selection-Attrition (ASA; Schneider, 1987) model. The ASA model predicts that all organizations are prone to move toward homogeneity, as individuals are likely to be attracted to organizations that they perceive consist of individuals like themselves. These individuals are then more likely to be selected, as the organization wants to hire employees who would "fit in" and then, the employees who leave are typically those who do not "fit in," often because they are dissimilar to the pervading culture and current employees (Jackson & Joshi, 2011). Thus, the current makeup of the organization with respect to various forms of diversity has serious consequences for who is attracted to joining the organization and who remains there for a substantial period of time. Though not consciously discriminatory, the ASA model combined with relational demography theory can explain how minority individuals may perceive discrimination in their workplaces and how those in positions of power can perpetuate underrepresentation.

Of particular interest in the scholarly literature is diversity climate — employees' perceptions of how valuable diversity is to an organization and the emphasis the organization places on promoting diversity and reducing discrimination (Pugh, Dietz, Brief, & Wiley, 2008). An organization with a positive diversity climate will typically have lower levels of discrimination because the organization is more attuned and committed to resolving the issues associated with the management of a diverse workforce (Cox, 1994; Gelfand et al., 2007). Diversity climate can be shaped in part by the gender, ethnic, and racial composition (McKay & Avery, 2006) of the organization and the region surrounding the organization (Pugh et al., 2008). The idea behind this is that in an organization with a negative diversity climate, prejudicial attitudes will discreetly dictate policy; HR principles will not be consistently applied and minorities may be isolated and consequently have difficulties finding mentors and climbing up the proverbial ladder (Gelfand et al., 2007). Consequently, organizational diversity climate can be seen as a key organizational level antecedent of discrimination.

Structural Factors
In addition to organizational cognitive processes, there are several organizational structural factors that often precede unconscious workplace discrimination. For example, organizational size can influence discrimination. Large companies are typically more inert than their smaller counterparts, and promote and select less often (Arvey, Azevedo, Ostgaard, & Raghuram, 1996). A smaller company is usually less structured in how it selects and promotes, and also does so more often — thereby providing more opportunities to reshape the demographics of the organization. An

informal system, however, can make it difficult for well-meaning individuals to overcome their unconsciously ingrained stereotypes when selecting, promoting, and conducting performance reviews.

Indeed, individuals in power typically promote and select candidates who resemble themselves (Fadil, 1995; Kanter, 1977a, 1977b). Again, through this process known as homosocial reproduction, or the "similar-to-me bias," the human desire to affiliate with similar individuals and view them more positively perpetuates the selection and promotion of those employees perceived as similar. To illustrate, if most managers are White, heterosexual, males, then they are likely to see other White, heterosexual, males as the most deserving of promotion (Gelfand et al., 2007). Through this process, they unconsciously deny other worthy employees of the promotion in unstructured human resource systems.

Societal Level

Certain societal factors also influence discriminatory employment practices, such as the national culture. Culture "shapes the cognitive schemas which ascribe meaning and values to motivational variables and guide our choices, commitments, and standards of behavior" (Erez, 1994, p. 582). These underlying societal features can lead to employers discriminating in the workplace as well as perceived discrimination by the employee (Chatman & Spataro, 2005). In particular, the degree to which organizations are embedded in societies that are characterized by high levels of power distance or low levels of gender egalitarianism are likely to perpetuate unconscious discrimination.

Power distance is "a value that differentiates individuals, groups, organizations, and nations based on the degree to which inequalities are accepted either as unavoidable or as functional" (Daniels & Greguras, 2014). Individuals low on power distance do not perceive distinctions based on power or social strata, whereas individuals higher on power distance believe that authority figures should be respected and revered. Specifically, in the workplace power distance is the perceived difference or inequality in the amount of power a supervisor has compared to their subordinate, and the magnitude of inequality that is accepted by both subordinate and supervisor is reinforced by culture (Bochner & Hesketh, 1994; Hofstede, 2001). The degree to which people within a culture endorse such ideologies likely corresponds with unconscious discrimination because abusive treatment from authorities is more common in high power distance cultures and this abusive treatment can manifest itself in the form of discrimination directed toward the subordinate (Hofstede, 1980; Tepper, 2007).

Similarly, cultural levels of gender egalitarianism, or the degree to which there is a minimizing of gender stereotyping and gender inequality in a culture, may also be associated with unconscious discrimination (Ott-Holland et al., 2013). Cultures that are low in egalitarianism likely are higher in discrimination. Egalitarians typically avoid discriminating behavior when they are dealing with members of a group that are perceived as being discriminated against (Dutton, 1976). In sum, there are a number of individual, organizational, and societal factors that give rise to conscious and unconscious discrimination. The consequences of these behaviors, in turn, involve both individuals and organizations.

CONSEQUENCES OF DISCRIMINATION

It is clear from our review that employment discrimination, driven by the human mind's natural tendency to socially categorize, is a pervasive issue that can affect a variety of targets. The official tally of 88,778 discrimination charges in a single year likely underrepresents the pervasiveness of workplace discrimination (EEOC, 2014). Moreover, the injustice of these experiences can have far-reaching consequences. In this section, we will review the major theories that explain key outcomes of discrimination and delve into its work- and health-related effects on individuals and organizations.

Theoretical Frameworks

Research on consequences of discrimination is grounded in a number of interrelated theories including (1) social exchange, (2) justice, (3) stress, and (4) attributional ambiguous. According to social exchange theory, the norm of reciprocity plays a major role in formation and maintenance of social relationships (Blau, 1964; Gouldner, 1960). People form relationships that are either economic or social in nature at work, the former being short-term, quid pro quo in nature while the latter involves long-term exchange of more intangible resources such as recognition and esteem (Podsakoff, MacKenzie, Paine, & Bachrach, 2000). Particularly in a social relationship, when individuals devote resources, they expect the other party to return that obligation in the future. This extends to justice theories such that individuals perceive justice when the norm of reciprocity is upheld and they experience equal social exchange (Masterson, Lewis, Goldman, & Taylor, 2000). When individuals are discriminated against on the basis of their social identity, the injustice is a violation of the norm of reciprocity, resulting in negative attitudes such as reduced satisfaction and commitment (Cohen-Charash & Spector, 2001).

Consequences of discrimination have also been examined in a stress framework, such as demand and resource models (Volpone & Avery, 2013) and the transactional stress model (Cassidy, O'Connor, Howe, & Warden, 2004). The link between stress and negative health outcomes was established long ago (Parasuraman & Alutto, 1984). The main argument for the application of stress models is that perception and experiences of discrimination can act as stressors to stigmatized individuals and negatively impact their health through stress activation and decrease of self-control resources that are otherwise used for engaging in healthy behaviors. Furthermore, according to minority stress theory, minority status itself can also act as a stressor to individuals as they are aware of the stigma and subsequent prejudice and discrimination against it (Meyer, 1995). Although initially developed to explain consequences of discrimination against LGBT people, the theory can be applied to other groups whose minority statuses are associated with negative social attitudes.

In addition, the ambiguous, subtle forms of modern discrimination are also linked theoretically to potential negative outcomes (Dipboye & Colella, 2005). Attributional ambiguity theory contends that individuals are uncertain whether discrimination has occurred when the act is subtle. Such ambiguity can lead to negative effect, lower self-esteem, and depression in members of stigmatized groups (Crocker, Cornwell, & Major, 1993; Major, Quinton, & Schmader, 2003) because individuals may blame themselves for the unfair treatment, which can impact their psychological well-being in the long run. While some have argued that these forms of discrimination are not as detrimental due to their seemingly trivial nature, research has shown that they are at least as damaging as traditionally overt forms of discrimination across a variety of outcomes, especially when accumulated over time (Jones et al., in press). This supports and extends attributional ambiguity theory by suggesting the extra cognitive load necessary to process and attribute subtle injustice can take an equal, if not greater, toll on targets' health and work outcomes.

Consistent with these major theories, research has shown that workplace discrimination is related to a series of negative consequences. Next, we will review these outcomes based on recent meta-analyses and empirical studies that describe these effects and their boundary conditions. While some of the studies reviewed pertain more to general discrimination instead of being workplace-specific, we contend that the conclusions are likely to translate into organizational contexts; research has shown that the relationships between perceived discrimination and major outcomes do not differ significantly across different settings (Jones et al., in press).

Individual Outcomes

Work Outcomes

Unsurprisingly, employment discrimination has a direct negative effect on key individual work outcomes. According to a recent meta-analysis based on 90 effect sizes, discrimination has several detrimental effects on important workplace variables such as performance, satisfaction, commitment, job stress, withdrawal, and career success (Jones et al., in press). Such effects are observed across a variety of target groups. For instance, studies on LGBT employees found that perceived discrimination is linked to lower job satisfaction, organizational commitment, organizational-based self-esteem, and increased turnover intentions (Ragins & Cornwell, 2001; Velez, Moradi, & Brewster, 2013). Bergman, Palmieri, Drasgow, and Ormerod (2012) also found that racial/ethnic harassment across five different racial/ethnic groups (White, Black, Hispanic, Asian, and Native American) was related to lower satisfaction toward work, supervisors, and opportunities, while King et al. (2010) found that gender discrimination is negatively related to helping behaviors. As a result of these negative work attitudes, individuals subsequently develop withdrawal behaviors including lateness, absenteeism, and eventually turnover intentions (Volpone & Avery, 2013).

Physical Health Outcomes

In addition to impacting important work outcomes, discrimination also has a detrimental impact upon individuals' physical health. Meta-analytic results on effects of both workplace and general perceived discrimination indicated that it can have a negative impact on physical health by heightening physiological stress response and increasing participation in unhealthy behaviors (Jones et al., in press; Pascoe & Richman, 2009). Specifically, individuals are more likely to experience cardiovascular reactivity, which leads to high blood pressure and other serious cardiovascular diseases (Smart Richman, Pek, Pascoe, & Bauer, 2010). In addition, individuals who regularly experience discrimination are also more likely to engage in risky health behaviors such as smoking, alcohol, and other substance use (Bennett, Wolin, Robinson, Fowler, & Edwards, 2005; Landrine & Klonoff, 1996).

Research has also suggested that the strength of the relationship between discrimination and outcomes does not vary across different types of discrimination. Specifically, effects on health outcomes do not seem to differ significantly between racial and gender discrimination or subtle and overt discrimination (Jones et al., in press). In addition, research was able to rule out the alternative explanation of health disparity due to demographic differences between subgroups. One study found that African Americans reported higher blood pressure when being discriminated against than when they were not (Krieger & Sidney, 1996), and another study found that perceived discrimination also predicted smoking behavior above and beyond other related demographic variables such as education, gender, income, and age (Landrine & Klonoff, 2000). A meta-analysis of 44 effect sizes between perceived racial discrimination and hypertension (Dolezsar, McGrath, Herzig, & Miller, 2014) showed that the effect was stronger for older, male, and less educated participants, suggesting individual demographic moderators may be important factors in the perceived discrimination-health relationship within each type of discrimination.

Psychological Health Outcomes
Compared to physical health, mental health has received more research attention across different target groups. Discrimination can severely impact individuals' psychological health through similar mechanisms as physical health by inducing stress that raises the level of cortisol in the body (Miller, Chen, & Zhou, 2007), which puts individuals at risk for mental conditions such as depression and schizophrenia (Bjorntorp & Rosmond, 1999; Nemeroff, 1996). Indeed, results from multiple meta-analyses indicate that there is a significant relationship between perceived discrimination and reduced mental health across a variety of target groups. For instance, Lee and Ahn (2011, 2012) found that across Asians and Hispanics, perceived discrimination has the strongest effect on anxiety, followed by depression and psychological distress. These findings are corroborated by Schmitt, Branscombe, Postmes, and Garcia (2014), who found the negative perceived discrimination-mental health relationship was stronger for different minority groups such as sexual minorities, people with mental and physical disabilities, and obese people. As individuals developmental conditions due to workplace discrimination, they may subsequently suffer further prejudice and discrimination due to the stigma associated with mental illnesses, which is associated with attributes such as incompetence,

dangerousness, and character weakness (Corrigan, Kerr, & Knudsen, 2005). This can instigate a vicious cycle of discrimination as individuals' perceived discrimination leads to the acquisition of additional stigmatized identities that perpetuates negative experiences and associated consequences.

Organizational Outcomes

Compared to individual outcomes, the impact of discrimination on organizational level is much less studied. When discrimination is widespread within an organization, aggregates of individual negative outcomes can translate into costly consequences at the organizational level from attraction phase to the retention phase of the employment cycle. The Civil Rights Act of 1964 and subsequent related laws and executive orders prohibit discrimination on the basis of sex, race, religion, national origin, and disability status. One of the most tangible consequences stemming from this legislation is employment discrimination lawsuits. According to EEOC statistics, total settlements for employment lawsuits cost $22.4 million in 2014, which does not include other exorbitant expenses such as investigation and litigation that can often go up to millions of dollars (EEOC, 2014).

In addition to the direct financial cost of litigation, employment discrimination also has a detrimental effect on organizational reputation, which can impact both the organization's performance and also their efforts to attract top talent in today's increasingly diverse culture. Specifically, employment discrimination lawsuits can signal that an organization does not value diversity (Smith, Morgan, King, Hebl, & Peddie, 2012; James & Wooten, 2006), which subsequently negatively influences potential applicants' perceptions of the organization and prevents them from being interested in being part of the organization (Robinson & Dechant, 1997). Furthermore, a negative public image associated with lawsuits can decrease public confidence and deter the public from consuming organization's products or services, which reduces revenue and stock prices (Goldman et al., 2006; Pruitt & Nethercutt, 2002).

Other sources of indirect financial costs associated with discrimination in the workplace include decreased productivity, increased turnover, and health insurance and disability compensation costs due to related negative health outcomes. When discrimination is commonplace, it can create a hostile work environment that is particularly conducive to highlighting faultlines, or dividers that create subgroups within teams and organizations, thereby creating conflict (Molleman, 2005). Given how costly the employment cycle can be from recruiting to training, high rates of employee turnover are particularly undesirable for organizations. As discussed earlier, individual consequences of discrimination such as reduced commitment and satisfaction (Mays & Cochran, 2001) and increased withdrawal behaviors (McKay & Avery, 2005) can impact organizational effectiveness when aggregated to higher level, affecting morale and diversity climate, ultimately leading to employee turnover. In addition, individual health outcomes associated with increased stress and strain may also increase costs of health insurance and disability compensation costs, furthering the financial loss associated with discrimination. Altogether, perceived discrimination, regardless of its subtlety and targets, is shown to have a far-reaching negative impact on both individual well-being and organizational performance, calling for the need for remediation strategies to mitigate these damaging effects.

STRATEGIES FOR DISCRIMINATION REDUCTION

Given the costly nature of discrimination and the factors that facilitate its persistence, it is critical to consider opportunities for reducing its emergence and associated consequences. In this section, we discuss strategies that individuals and organizations can use to aid in the goal of reducing discrimination against stigmatized populations in the workplace.

Individual Strategies

An emerging body of research is devoted to examining the boundary conditions that can attenuate the negative effects of discrimination. One key moderator that has received some attention is the role of support and coping strategies, both of which can be either adaptive or maladaptive. For instance, Pascoe and Richman (2009) found that having instrumental and emotional social support buffers the negative relationship between perceived discrimination and both physical and mental health outcomes. The same meta-analysis also found that active, approach coping strategies such as talking to friends can have a buffering effect while passive, avoidant coping strategies such as self-distraction can exacerbate the already-negative health outcomes resulting from discrimination. These similar results are observed in regards to work outcomes; those who actively reframe the situation were found to be absent less and have lower turnover intentions, while those who avoid the situation were found to experience lower engagement (Volpone & Avery, 2013). However, some studies do not find the moderating effect of social support on the relationship between perceived discrimination and work-life conflict (Minnotte, 2012). Similarly, coping did not attenuate the negative relationship between perceived weight discrimination and perceived career success (Randle, Mathis, & Cates, 2012). Altogether, although some research suggests that individuals should engage in active, approach coping in order to be less affected by perceived discrimination, the effects are not consistent and further investigation, perhaps in the form of meta-analysis, will be needed to conclude the moderating role of different types of coping and support on the relationship between discrimination and its consequences.

What is clear is that discrimination can be reduced by efforts on the part of targets of discrimination. While we do not wish to imply that the burden of prejudice reduction should fall on the shoulders of targets of discrimination, we as scientists have an opportunity to empower targets who would seek to make change. Accordingly, in the sections that follow we synthesize research on prejudice reduction strategies that can be used by both targets of prejudice and their allies.

Identity/Impression Management
Research has been inconsistent regarding the effects of identity management strategies. Importantly, we view identity management strategies as most appropriate for individuals managing stigmas that are relatively invisible in nature. While some studies have indicated that revealing one's stigmatized identity is related to positive outcomes such as higher well-being (Ilic et al., 2012) and concealing one's identity is related to decreased mental health (Gross & John, 2003; Pennebaker, Colder, & Sharp, 1990) and negative work outcomes (Ragins, Singh, & Cornwell, 2007), other studies suggested expressing one's identity is related to increase perceived prejudice and discrimination (Hebl et al., 2002), which can lead to the negative outcomes discussed above. On one hand, concealment and suppression may be especially detrimental to individuals' well-being due to the cognitive demand required to hide a part of themselves (Ragins, 2008), as well as the stress associated with being inauthentic (Clair, Beatty, & MacLean, 2005). However, expression of one's identity can also expose them to the danger of the negative outcomes of discrimination. Further research is needed to

examine possible moderators to explain these equivocal findings and to understand how individuals can best manage stigmatized identities at work. Future research should also examine what role allies might play in improving the workplace experiences of individuals with invisible stigmas (see Sabat et al., 2014).

Research on impression management provides us with several strategies that individuals possessing visible stigmas can utilize to create positive interpersonal experiences and potentially reduce discrimination against themselves in the workplace. One of these strategies is called acknowledgment, which is defined as recognizing and communicating a stigmatized identity when targets are interacting with others. An important nuance to these research findings is that the timing of acknowledgment seems to be important when predicting its prejudice reducing effect. Indeed, earlier acknowledgment has been shown to engender less prejudice when compared with acknowledgment later in time or not acknowledging at all (Hebl & Skorinko, 2005). Additionally, the effectiveness of acknowledgment may depend on the perceived controllability of the stigma in question (Hebl & Kleck, 2002). Specifically, this strategy may be more effective for those with stigmas that are perceived to be uncontrollable (e.g., genetic diseases) when compared to stigmas that are deemed to be more controllable. For example, to the extent that a perceiver believes obesity to be a controllable condition, acknowledgment may not be as helpful of a strategy for obese targets.

Another impression management strategy that has received some empirical support is called individuation (Fiske & Neuberg, 1990; Singletary & Hebl, 2009). The logic underlying this strategy is that (1) stereotypes are more likely to result in discrimination when information about a given target is lacking and (2) counterstereotypic information can distinguish a given individual from negative beliefs about people who possess their stigma. Research supports this underlying logic, suggesting that targets of discrimination can benefit from providing counterstereotypic information in social and workplace situations. For example, results of a field experiment in a selection context showed that ostensibly obese targets who refuted the stereotype that they are lazy received less discrimination compared to those that did not refute this stereotype (King et al., 2006). In another study, female leaders were evaluated more positively when described as both great leaders, conveying agency, and great mothers, refuting the stereotype of low communality (Heilman & Okimoto, 2007). Finally, when individuals in an FMRI scanner were told to look for unique information about a racial outgroup member, individuation promoted more thoughtful and less biased cognitive processing of target-related information (Wheeler & Fiske, 2005).

Prejudice Confrontation

Prejudice confrontation can be defined as "verbally or nonverbally expressing one's dissatisfaction with prejudicial and discriminatory treatment to the person who is responsible for the remark or behavior" (Shelton, Richeson, & Vorauer, 2006, p. 67). This strategy does not necessarily have to involved heated encounters as the name suggests, but rather can be enacted by asking a perpetrator to refrain from engaging in such discriminatory behavior in the future. Confrontation has been shown be effective in terms of reducing discriminatory responses when used by targets of discrimination and their allies (Czopp, Monteith, & Mark, 2006). Importantly, confrontation may be more effective when enacted by allies. For example, women who confront sexism may be dismissed and viewed as complainers, while male ally confronters may be seen as more objective (Kaiser & Miller, 2004; Rasinski & Czopp, 2010). Unfortunately, individuals report that they do not actually confront prejudice as often as they wish they would in a given situation. Research has shown that individuals may be particularly reticent to confront when they feel they cannot make a difference or when they perceive potential social costs for confronting (Good, Moss-Racusin, & Sanchez, 2012; Rattan & Dweck, 2010), which may be likely in workplace contexts. Given that discrimination has negative psychological consequences for both targets and bystanders (Schmader, Croft, Scarnier, Lickel, & Mendes, 2012), this lack of responding to discrimination is rather alarming. How can we encourage individuals to confront the discrimination they witness?

Seeking to answer this very question, the *confronting prejudiced responses* (CPR) model proposes several obstacles that might prevent individuals from confronting in various situations (Ashburn-Nardo, Morris, & Goodwin, 2008). In order to overcome these obstacles, the authors make several recommendations to promote confrontation in our workplaces. First, increase the detection of discrimination (especially more subtle manifestations of discrimination) through workplace diversity education. Second, help people understand that discrimination is an emergency that needs to be dealt with immediately, rather than waiting to deal with it later in time. Third, empower individuals to increase their perceptions of personal responsibility for handling instances of discrimination at work. Fourth and finally, teach people how to confront through behavioral monitoring training and practice (Ashburn-Nardo et al., 2008). If these barriers to confrontation can be overcome, it could create a self-regulating workplace over time where targets and allies readily communicate that discrimination is not to be tolerated, leading to a more inclusive climate overall. Confrontation behaviors are likely to reduce discrimination via social norm clarity, which means that individuals can serve as communicators of information regarding the social appropriateness of attitudes and behaviors, and that these social norms likely influence an individual's subsequent attitudes and behaviors (Martinez, 2012; Zitek & Hebl, 2007). Overall, we view prejudice confrontation as one of the most promising individual strategies for discrimination reduction given its documented success and the fact that it can be utilized by targets and allies alike.

Organizational Strategies

Organizations have the opportunity and responsibility to enact policies, procedures, and programs that reduce discrimination. In this section we describe the human resource systems that evidence suggests can be effective in reducing formal and interpersonal manifestations of discrimination in the workplace.

Reducing Formal Discrimination

A critical manifestation of formal employment discrimination takes the form of selection and promotion decisions that reflect adverse impact. One strategy for reducing adverse impact in selection is to use predictors that have smaller subgroup differences when compared to those created by cognitive ability tests. Although cognitive ability tests are among the best predictors of performance in the workplace, they also produce large subgroup differences that disadvantage racial and ethnic minorities (Hough, Oswald, & Ployhart, 2001). To the degree that other selection methods (e.g., interviews and personality measures) can be used with a degree of consistency, a reduction in subgroup differences, and thus a reduction in adverse impact overall, should be observed (Ployhart & Holtz, 2008; Schmitt & Quinn, 2009). A concern related to this strategy is that of a "validity tradeoff" wherein using alternative predictors reduces adverse impact but also weakens the potential of a selection battery to predict performance. A strategy that can partially alleviate this concern is to use multiple predictors in an effort to assess a full range of the knowledge, skills, and abilities needed to perform a job effectively. This strategy is particularly desirable in that it may reduce adverse impact while actually improving the validity of a selection system, but only to the extent that a wide variety of job-related, non-redundant predictors are selected (Ployhart & Holtz, 2008; Schmitt, Clause, & Pulakos, 1996).

Another discrimination reduction strategy is to modify tests through alternative items or modes of test stimuli (Schmitt & Quinn, 2009). As a starting point, it is important to identify and remove items that may be biased against a given marginalized group. This is a common-sense strategy that could accomplish multiple desirable goals, including increasing the face validity of selection tests for a variety of marginalized groups (Schmitt & Quinn, 2009). In addition, an organization might consider using video-based measures or computer simulations as opposed to traditional paper-and-pencil selection tests. Research has shown that this is an effective method for reducing adverse impact against racial and ethnic minorities, but more work needs to be done to examine the potential for this strategy to benefit other marginalized groups (Pulakos & Schmitt, 1996).

Other strategies for reducing adverse impact in selection focus on how employment decisions are made after data has already been collected. These strategies serve as alternatives to rank-order decision making, which typically used in organizations but could lead to more adverse impact. One such strategy involves banding or grouping selection test scores together into groups that are not meaningfully different from one another on a psychometric basis. Banding is a strategy that accounts for the unreliability of measures by creating ranges within which scores are not treated as significantly different from one another (Aguinis, 2004). Research has shown that banding can be an effective and efficient way of reducing subgroup differences in selection systems. However, it is important to note that the largest reductions in adverse impact are found when subgroup preferences are used within bands, which is often illegal (Ployhart & Holtz, 2008). Thus, there continues to be substantive controversy and debate surrounding the practice of banding (see Pyburn, Ployhart, & Kravitz, 2008). A similar strategy is to set cut scores for predictor measures in ways that reduce adverse impact without having much of an effect on predictive power. This strategy is similar to banding in that scores above a given cut score are not treated as significantly different from one another when making selection decisions. When utilizing this strategy, it is important that the cut score is decided upon based on the relationship between the criterion and the predictor in question as well as subject matter experts' judgments, as opposed to being set more arbitrarily (see Kehoe, 2009). Research has shown that adjusting cut scores in this manner can be an effective strategy for reducing adverse impact in selection decisions (Hoffman & Thornton, 1997).

Another tactic relates to how predictors and/or criterion measures are weighted in the selection process. The logic of this strategy is that by assigning more weight to predictor and/or criterion scales that demonstrate less adverse impact, we can improve the fairness of our selection systems. By utilizing this technique, organizations can enjoy the validity benefits of using a wide range of predictors while also avoiding adverse impact by weighting predictors and/or criterion measures that have the lowest subgroup differences. Research suggests this can be an effective strategy for reducing adverse impact in selection (DeCorte, 1999; Hattrup, Rock, & Scalia, 1997). Thus, this is certainly a strategy to consider for use in selection decisions. However, it is important to remember that this strategy will only be effective to the extent that there are already predictors that do not demonstrate considerable subgroup differences in the selection battery. Additionally, the validity of the selection system will only be improved to the extent that the predictors which are most job-related are given stronger weights. Finally, preliminary evidence suggests that rater trainings that reduce implicit bias may be an effective way to reduce formal discrimination in performance ratings (see Anderson et al., 2015).

Reducing Interpersonal Discrimination
The most common strategy through which organizations have worked to reduce interpersonal discrimination is the implementation of diversity training programs. Indeed, approximately two-thirds of human resource managers report using diversity training in their organizations (Esen, 2005). However, troubling reviews have revealed that (1) diversity training is not frequently assessed for effectiveness, (2) it has only small to moderate effects on trainees' immediate attitudes, (3) that other important outcomes – including discrimination – are often excluded, and (4) that the most common approaches to diversity training might not be effective in accomplishing their goals (Bezrukova, Jehn, & Spell, 2012; Kulik & Roberson, 2008). In this section, we first define diversity training before providing a nuanced analysis of what training strategies are most effective.

Diversity training can be defined as "a distinct set of programs aimed at facilitating positive intergroup interactions, reducing prejudice and discrimination, and enhancing the skills, knowledge, and motivation of people to interact with diverse others" (Bezrukova et al., 2012, p. 208). Importantly, diversity training differs from more traditional workplace training in that it deals with subjective and emotionally laden topics, such as one's presumably engrained attitudes about stigmatized groups (Hanover & Cellar, 1998). This is likely part of the reason that diversity training can sometimes result in backlash, where individuals react against the training, producing the opposite of desired training effects (see Legault, Gutsell, & Inzlicht, 2011). Diversity trainers hope to avoid such backlash, and instead pursue goals such as compliance, harmony, and (most desirably) inclusion (Rossett & Bickham, 1994). Findings have been mixed regarding the effectiveness of various diversity training initiatives. One factor that may be able to account for these inconsistencies is the type of outcome criterion chosen to indicate program success. Commonly measured outcomes include diversity knowledge, diversity attitudes, and diversity skills and behaviors. Given the focus of this chapter on workplace discrimination, we will focus our review of diversity training on its impact on behavioral outcomes and diversity skill.

Diversity skill is a critical diversity training outcome, which can be broadly defined as the behavior needed to effectively and ethically work with individuals who are not a member of one's ingroup (Avery & Thomas, 2004). This outcome is potentially the most important outcome to measure when assessing the effectiveness of any diversity training program; employees would need to possess these skills or gain them from training in order to effectively work with people from different backgrounds in the workplace. In other words, trainees need to gain these skills in order for researchers to see any sort of behavioral outcomes from diversity training. In spite of this, diversity skills and behavioral outcomes have received less attention in the evaluation of diversity training programs than both diversity attitudes and diversity knowledge outcomes (Kulik & Roberson, 2008).

One problem that has arisen in studies that use this outcome to assess the effectiveness of diversity training programs is that few studies use objective behavioral outcomes (e.g., actually displaying a learned skill in the work setting). Rather, many studies have settled for using a self-report measure that asks participants to assess what skills they learned from the training (DeMeuse, Hostager, & O'Neill, 2006). This method could be viewed as biased in that the goals of diversity training programs tend to be transparent to participants, which could lead them to respond in a socially desirable way to the self-assessing outcome measures. Indeed, studies using the skills subscale of the Multicultural Awareness-Knowledge-Skills Survey (D'Andrea, Daniels, & Heck, 1991) as a self-assessing measure of diversity skill acquisition consistently show positive effects of diversity training of self-rated skill improvement, but the results are somewhat mixed in the few cases that objective behavioral criteria are used (Kulik & Roberson, 2008). Supportive behaviors for a variety of minority groups can also be measured directly. For instance, Madera, King, and Hebl (2013) developed a scale of self-reported supportive behaviors toward LGBT individuals (e.g., "Been to a social or community event supporting gay and lesbian individuals") that could easily be adapted for a wide range of stigmatized populations. While such scales are relatively new to the literature, we would argue that these objective indicators of supportive behaviors should be focused on more explicitly in future diversity training work.

One reassuring piece of evidence for diversity training promoting diversity skills and behaviors in the workplace is some work done by Roberson, Kulik, and Pepper (2003), which revealed that the focus of the diversity training program can have an effect on objective behavioral outcomes. In this study the researchers were able to show that when the focus of diversity training was to learn diversity skills (instead of just to gain diversity awareness), the training was much more effective in producing objective diversity skills behaviors (measured by responses to critical incidents that could very well occur in the workplace). Additionally, some recent work has shown that perspective taking (i.e., actively considering the experiences of others) may be an effective training method for improving prosocial behaviors toward African Americans and sexual orientation minorities (Lindsey, King, Hebl, & Levine, 2015). While these studies provide support for the idea that diversity training can have a positive effect on diversity behaviors and discrimination outcomes, much more work needs to be done to replicate these results and show that diversity training truly does teach people the skills they need to work with others from different backgrounds.

Future Research Directions

Importantly, we have focused this section on the discrimination reduction strategies that have received the most empirical investigation, but the list of tactics covered here is by no means exhaustive (see Lindsey, King, McCausland, Jones, & Dunleavy, 2013 for a more complete list of discrimination reduction strategies across the employment cycle). One area that appears ripe for future research is the investigation of which strategies can reduce formal discrimination toward specific marginalized groups in the workplace. Most work to this point has focused on race and gender differences. We would recommend expanding this narrow view of diversity to include religious minorities, LGBT individuals, individuals with disabilities, and protected veterans, which are all stigmatized groups that have received substantially less attention in the literature (Ruggs et al., 2013). Similarly, future research should explore the generalizability of findings regarding identity management, impression management, and prejudice confrontation strategies. Indeed, more work must be conducted to determine (1) whether these are viable strategies to teach targets in the workplace by incorporating them into diversity training programs, (2) if there are other behaviors allies can engage in to assist, and (3) if the effectiveness of these strategies can generalize across various stigmas. Finally, the diversity training literature desperately needs a unifying theoretical framework to explain what activities are likely to be beneficial, what the processes that give rise to prosocial change are, and what the boundary conditions of these effects may be.

CONCLUSION

The body of work summarized here confirms the persistent challenges of workplace discrimination in terms of its complex forms, numerous targets, pernicious antecedents, and far-reaching consequences. Yet, our review also identifies emerging evidence that can be leveraged toward overcoming these challenges. It is critical that scholars and practitioners continue to build knowledge regarding the manifestations, antecedents and outcomes of discrimination, particularly as it pertains to understudied targets and higher levels of analysis such as ecological environments and regional cultures. Perhaps even more crucial, however, is the question of how to intervene in these processes. Robust and compelling answers to this question are necessary for genuine progress toward equality.

REFERENCES

Agerström, J., & Rooth, D. O. (2011). The role of automatic obesity stereotypes in real hiring discrimination. *Journal of Applied Psychology, 96*(4), 790.

Aguinis, H. (2004). *Test score banding in human resource selection: Legal, technical, and societal issues.* Westport, CT: Quorum.

Altemeyer, B. (1981). *Right-wing authoritarianism.* Winnipeg: University of Manitoba Press.

Altemeyer, B. (1988). *Enemies of freedom: Understanding right-wing authoritarianism.* The Jossey-Bass social and behavioral science series and The Jossey-Bass public administration series. San Francisco, CA: Jossey-Bass.

Anderson, A. J., Ahmad, A. S., King, E. B., Lindsey, A. P., Feyre, R., Ragone, S., & Kim, S. (2015). The effectiveness of three training strategies to reduce the influence of bias in evaluations of female leaders. *Journal of Applied Social Psychology, 45,* 522–529.

Arvey, R. D., Azevedo, R. E., Ostgaard, D. J., & Raghuram, S. (1996). The implications of a diverse labor market on human resource planning. In E. E. Kossek & S. A. Lobel

(Eds.), *Managing diversity: Human resource strategies for transforming the workplace* (pp. 51–73). Cambridge, MA: Blackwell.

Ashburn-Nardo, L., Morris, K. A., & Goodwin, S. A. (2008). The confronting prejudiced responses (CPR) model: Applying CPR in organizations. *Academy of Management: Learning and Education, 7*, 332–342.

Avery, D. R., McKay, P. F., & Wilson, D. C. (2008). What are the odds? How demographic similarity affects the prevalence of perceived employment discrimination. *Journal of Applied Psychology, 93*, 235–249.

Avery, D. R., & Thomas, K. M. (2004). Blending content and contact: The roles of diversity curriculum and campus heterogeneity in fostering diversity management competency. *Academy of Management Learning & Education, 3*, 380–396.

Badgett, M. L. (1995). The wage effects of sexual orientation discrimination. Industrial & *Labor Relations Review, 48*, 726–739.

Badgett, M. L., & Frank, J. (2007). *Sexual orientation discrimination: An international* perspective. New York, NY: Routledge.

Badgett, M. V. L., Lau, H., Sears, B., & Ho, D. (2007). *Bias in the workplace: Consistent evidence of sexual orientation and gender identity discrimination.* The Williams Institute. Retrieved from http://escholarship.ucop.edu/uc/item/5h3731xr

Bal, A. C., Reiss, A. E., Rudolph, C. W., & Baltes, B. B. (2011). Examining positive and negative perceptions of older workers: A meta-analysis. *The Journals of Gerontology Series B: Psychological Sciences and Social Sciences, 66*, 687–698.

Baltes, B. B., & Rudolph, C. W. (2010). Examining the effect of negative Turkish stereotypes on evaluative workplace outcomes in Germany. *Journal of Managerial Psychology, 25*, 148–158.

Baumle, A. K., & Poston, D. L. (2011). The economic cost of homosexuality: Multilevel analyses. *Social Forces, 89*, 1005–1031.

Bendick, M., Jr., Brown, L. E., & Wall, K. (1999). No foot in the door: An experimental study of employment discrimination against older workers. *Journal of Aging & Social Policy, 10*, 5–23.

Bennett, G. G., Wolin, K. Y., Robinson, E. L., Fowler, S., & Edwards, C. L. (2005). Perceived racial/ethnic harassment and tobacco use among African American young adults. *American Journal of Public Health, 95*, 238–240.

Bergman, M. E., Palmieri, P. A., Drasgow, F., & Ormerod, A. J. (2012). Racial/ethnic harassment and discrimination, its antecedents, and its effect on job-related outcomes. *Journal of Occupational Health Psychology, 17*, 65–78.

Bertrand, M., Mullainathan, S., & Shafir, E. (2004). A behavioral-economics view of poverty. *American Economic Review, 94*, 419–423.

Bezrukova, K., Jehn, K. A., & Spell, C. S. (2012). Reviewing diversity training: Where we have been and where we should go. *Academy of Management Learning & Education, 11*, 207–227.

Binggeli, S., Dietz, J., & Krings, F. (2013). Immigrants: A forgotten minority. Industrial *and Organizational Psychology, 6*, 107–113.

Bjorntorp, P., & Rosmond, R. (1999). Hypothalamic origin of the metabolic syndrome X. *Annals of the New York Academy of Sciences, 892*, 297–307.

Blau, F. D., & DeVaro, J. (2007). New evidence on gender differences in promotion rates: An empirical analysis of a sample of new hires. *Industrial Relations: A Journal of Economy and Society, 46*, 511–550.

Blau, P. M. (1964). Social exchange. In *Exchange and power in social life* (pp. 88–114). Sydney: Wiley.

Bochner, S., & Hesketh, B. (1994). Power distance, individualism/collectivism, and job-related attitudes in a culturally diverse work group. *Journal of Cross-Cultural Psychology*, *25*(2), 233–257.

Boldry, J., Wood, W., & Kashy, D. A. (2001). Gender stereotypes and the evaluation of men and women in military training. *Journal of Social Issues*, *57*, 689–705.

Bort, J. (2012). McAfee hires famous computer hacker to break into cars. *Business Insider*, August 20. Retrieved from http://www.businessinsider.com/mcafee-hires-famous-computer-hacker-to-break-into-cars-2012-8

Bragger, J. D., Kutcher, E., Morgan, J., & Firth, P. (2002). The effects of the structured interview on reducing biases against pregnant job applicants. *Sex Roles*, *46*, 215–226.

Brewster, M. E., Velez, B. L., Mennicke, A., & Tebbe, E. (2014). Voices from beyond: A thematic content analysis of transgender employees' workplace experiences. *Psychology of Sexual Orientation and Gender Diversity*, *1*, 159.

Brief, A. P., Dietz, J., Cohen, R. R., Pugh, S. D., & Vaslow, J. B. (2000). Just doing business: Modern racism and obedience to authority as explanations for employment discrimination. *Organizational Behavior and Human Decision Processes*, *81*, 72–97.

Brown, R. (1999). Social identity theory: Past achievements, current problems and future challenges. *European Journal of Social Psychology*, *29*, 634–667.

Browne, I., & Kennelly, I. (1999). Stereotypes and realities: Images of Black women in the labor market. In I. Brown (Ed.), *Latinas and African American women at work* (pp. 302–326). New York, NY: Russell Sage Foundation.

Budge, S. L., Tebbe, E. N., & Howard, K. A. (2010). The work experiences of transgender individuals: Negotiating the transition and career decision-making processes. *Journal of Counseling Psychology*, *57*, 377–393.

Budig, M. J. (2002). Male advantage and the gender composition of jobs: Who rides the glass escalator. *Social Problems*, *49*, 258.

Cassidy, C., O'Connor, R. C., Howe, C., & Warden, D. (2004). Perceived discrimination and psychological distress: the role of personal and ethnic self-esteem. *Journal of Counseling Psychology*, *51*, 329–339.

Catalyst. (2015). Catalyst quick take: Women's earnings and income. *Catalyst*. Retrieved from http://www.catalyst.org/knowledge/womens-earnings-and-income

Chan, F., McMahon, B. T., Cheing, G., Rosenthal, D. A., & Bezyak, J. (2005). Drivers of workplace discrimination against people with disabilities: The utility of attribution theory. *Work*, *25*, 77–88.

Chatman, J. A., & Spataro, S. E. (2005). Using self-categorization theory to understand relational demography-based variations in people's responsiveness to organizational culture. *Academy of Management Journal*, *48*, 321–331.

Chung-Herrera, B. G., & Lankau, M. J. (2005). Are we there yet? An assessment of fit between stereotypes of minority managers and the successful-manager prototype. *Journal of Applied Social Psychology*, *35*, 2029–2056.

Clair, J. A., Beatty, J. E., & MacLean, T. L. (2005). Out of sight but not out of mind: Managing invisible social identities in the workplace. *Academy of Management Review*, *30*, 78–95.

Cohen-Charash, Y., & Spector, P. E. (2001). The role of justice in organizations: A meta-analysis. *Organizational behavior and human decision processes*, *86*, 278–321.

Colella, A. (2001). Coworker distributive fairness judgments of the workplace accommodation of employees with disabilities. *Academy of Management Review, 26*, 100–116.

Colella, A. J., & King, E. B. (2015). *Handbook of workplace discrimination.* Oxford: Oxford University Press.

Collins, J. C., McFadden, C., Rocco, T. S., & Mathis, M. K. (2015). The problem of transgender marginalization and exclusion critical actions for human resource development. *Human Resource Development Review, 14*, 205–226.

Colvin, R. (2004). *The extent of sexual orientation discrimination in Topeka, KS.* New York, NY: National Gay and Lesbian Task Force Policy Institute. Retrieved from http://www.thetaskforce.org/static_html/downloads/reports/reports/TopekaDiscrimination.pdf

Colvin, R. (2009). Adding sexual orientation to New York state's human rights law: Initial information about implementation and effectiveness. *Journal of Homosexuality, 56*, 485–498.

Constantine, M. G. (2007). Racial microaggressions against African American clients in cross-racial counseling relationships. *Journal of Counseling Psychology, 54*, 1–16.

Correll, S. J., Benard, S., & Paik, I. (2007). Getting a job: Is there a motherhood penalty? *American Journal of Sociology, 112*, 1297–1339.

Corrigan, P. W., Kerr, A., & Knudsen, L. (2005). The stigma of mental illness: explanatory models and methods for change. *Applied and Preventive Psychology, 11*, 179–190.

Cortina, L. M. (2008). Unseen injustice: Incivility as modern discrimination in organizations. *Academy of Management Review, 33*, 55–75.

Cortina, L. M., Kabat-Farr, D., Leskinen, E. A., Huerta, M., & Magley, V. J. (2013). Selective incivility as modern discrimination in organizations evidence and impact. *Journal of Management, 39*, 1579–1605.

Cortina, L. M., Lonsway, K. A., Magley, V. J., Freeman, L. V., Collinsworth, L. L., Hunter, M., & Fitzgerald, L. F. (2002). What's gender got to do with it? Incivility in the federal courts. *Law & Social Inquiry, 27*, 235–270.

Cortina, L. M., Magley, V. J., Williams, J. H., & Langhout, R. D. (2001). Incivility in the workplace: Incidence and impact. *Journal of Occupational Health Psychology, 6*, 64–80.

Cox, T. (1994). *Cultural diversity in organizations: Theory, research and practice.* San Francisco, CA: Berrett-Koehler Publishers.

Crandall, C., & Eshleman, A. (2003). A justification-suppression model of the expression and experience of prejudice. *Psychological Bulletin, 129*, 414–446.

Crawford, J. T., Jussim, L., Cain, T. R., & Cohen, F. (2013). Right-wing authoritarianism and social dominance orientation differentially predict biased evaluations of media reports: Dual-process model and media reports. *Journal of Applied Social Psychology, 43*, 163–174.

Crocker, J., Cornwell, B., & Major, B. (1993). The stigma of overweight: Affective consequences of attributional ambiguity. *Journal of Personality and Social Psychology, 64*, 60–70.

Cuddy, A. J., Fiske, S. T., & Glick, P. (2004). When professionals become mothers, warmth doesn't cut the ice. *Journal of Social Issues, 60*, 701–718.

Cunningham, G. B., Miner, K., & McDonald, J. (2013). Being different and suffering the consequences: The influence of head coach–player racial dissimilarity on experienced incivility. *International Review for the Sociology of Sport, 48*, 689–705.

Czopp, A. M., Monteith, M., & Mark, A. Y. (2006). Standing up for a change: Reducing bias through interpersonal confrontation. *Journal of Personality and Social Psychology, 90*, 784–803.

D'Andrea, M., Daniels, J., & Heck, R. (1991). Evaluating the impact of multicultural counseling training. *Journal of Counseling and Development, 70*, 143–150.

Daniels, M. A., & Greguras, G. J. (2014). Exploring the nature of power distance implications for micro-and macro-level theories, processes, and outcomes. *Journal of Management, 40*, 1202–1229.

Davison, H. K., & Burke, M. J. (2000). Sex discrimination in simulated employment contexts: A meta-analytic investigation. *Journal of Vocational Behavior, 56*, 225–248.

De Castro, A. B., Gee, G. C., & Takeuchi, D. T. (2008). Workplace discrimination and health among Filipinos in the United States. *American Journal of Public Health, 98*, 520–526.

De Pater, I. E., Van Vianen, A. E., & Bechtoldt, M. N. (2010). Gender differences in job challenge: A matter of task allocation. *Gender, Work & Organization, 17*, 433–453.

DeCorte, W. (1999). Weighting job performance predictors to both maximize the quality of the selected workforce and control the level of adverse impact. *Journal of Applied Psychology, 84*, 695–702.

Deitch, E. A., Barsky, A., Butz, R. M., Chan, S., Brief, A. P., & Bradley, J. C. (2003). Subtle yet significant: The existence and impact of everyday racial discrimination in the workplace. *Human Relations, 56*(11), 1299–1324.

Delaney, J. T., & Lundy, M. C. (1996). Unions, collective bargaining, and the diversity paradox. *Managing Diversity: Human Resource Strategies for Transforming the Workplace* (pp. 245–272). Cambridge, MA: Blackwell Publishers.

DeMeuse, K. P., Hostager, T. J., & O'Neill, K. S. (2006). A longitudinal evaluation of senior managers' perceptions and attitudes of a workplace diversity training program. *Human Resource Planning, 30*, 38–46.

Derous, E., Nguyen, H. H., & Ryan, A. M. (2009). Hiring discrimination against Arab minorities: Interactions between prejudice and job characteristics. *Human Performance, 22*, 297–320.

Derous, E., Ryan, A. M., & Serlie, A. W. (2015). Double jeopardy upon resume screening: When Achmed is less employable than Aisha. *Personnel Psychology, 68*, 659–696.

Devine, P. G. (2001). Implicit prejudice and stereotyping: How automatic are they? Introduction to the special section. *Journal of Personality and Social Psychology, 81*(5), 757.

Dietert, M., & Dentice, D. (2009). Gender identity issues and workplace discrimination: The transgender experience. *Journal of Workplace Rights, 14*, 121–140.

Dikötter, F. (1994). Racial identities in China: Context and meaning. *The China Quarterly, 138*, 404–412.

Dipboye, R. L., & Colella, A. (2005). *Discrimination at work: The psychological and organizational bases.* Mahwah, NJ: Lawrence Erlbaum Associates.

Dolezsar, C. M., McGrath, J. J., Herzig, A. J., & Miller, S. B. (2014). Perceived racial discrimination and hypertension: A comprehensive systematic review. *Health Psychology, 33*, 20–34.

Dovidio, J. F., Gaertner, S. E., Kawakami, K., & Hodson, G. (2002). Why can't we just get along? Interpersonal biases and interracial distrust. *Cultural Diversity and Ethnic Minority Psychology, 8*, 88.

Dovidio, J. F., & Gaertner, S. L. (2004). Aversive racism. *Advances in Experimental Social Psychology, 36*, 1–52.

Duckitt, J. (2006). Differential effects of right wing authoritarianism and social dominance orientation on outgroup attitudes and their mediation by threat from and competitiveness to outgroups. *Personality and Social Psychology Bulletin, 32*, 684–696.

Duffy, M. K., Ganster, D. C., & Pagon, M. (2002). Social undermining in the workplace. *Academy of Management Journal, 45*, 331–351.

Dutton, D. (1976). Tokenism, reverse discrimination, and egalitarianism in interracial behavior. *Journal of Social Issues, 32*, 93–107.

Dwyer, S., Orlando, R., & Shepherd, C. D. (1998). An exploratory study of gender and age matching in the salesperson-prospective customer dyad: Testing similarity-performance predictions. *Journal of Personal Selling & Sales Management, 18*(4), 55–69.

Eagly, A. H., & Carli, L. L. (2007). *Through the labyrinth: The truth about how women* become leaders. Cambridge, MA: Harvard Business Press.

Eagly, A. H., Karau, S. J., & Makhijani, M. G. (1995). Gender and the effectiveness of leaders: A meta-analysis. *Psychological Bulletin, 117*, 125–145.

Eagly, A. H., Makhijani, M. G., & Klonsky, B. G. (1992). Gender and the evaluation of leaders: A meta-analysis. *Psychological Bulletin, 111*, 3–22.

Einarsen, S., & Skogstad, A. (1996). Bullying at work: Epidemiological findings in public and private organizations. *European Journal of Work and Organizational Psychology, 5*, 185–201.

Elvira, M. M., & Zatzick, C. D. (2002). Who's displaced first? The role of race in layoff decisions. *Industrial Relations, 41*, 329–361.

Equal Employment Opportunity Commission. (2007, May 23). *Employment guidance: Unlawful disparate treatment of workers with caregiving responsibilities*, No. 915.002. Retrieved from http://www.eeoc.gov/policy/docs/caregiving.html

Equal Employment Opportunity Commission. (2012, April 25). *Consideration of arrest and conviction records in employment decisions under Title VII of the Civil Rights Act of 1964*, No. 915.002. Retrieved from http://www.eeoc.gov/laws/guidance/arrest_conviction.cfm

Equal Employment Opportunity Commission. (2015, August 27). *Fact sheet: Recent EEOC litigation regarding Title VII & LGBT-related discrimination*, No. 915.002. Retrieved from http://www.eeoc.gov/eeoc/litigation/selected/lgbt_facts.cfm

Equal Employment Opportunity Commission (EEOC). (2014). *Charge statistics FY 1997 through FY 2014*. Retrieved from http://eeoc.gov/eeoc/statistics/enforcement/charges.cfm

Erez, M. (1994). Towards a model of cross-cultural I/O psychology. *Handbook of Industrial and Organizational Psychology, 4*, 569–607.

Esen, E. (2005). 2005 workplace diversity practices. Survey report. Society for Human Resource Management.

Fadil, P. A. (1995). The effect of cultural stereotypes on leader attributions of minority subordinates. *Journal of Managerial Issues*, 193–208.

Finkelstein, L., & Truxillo, D. (2013). Age discrimination research is alive and well, even if it doesn't live where you'd expect. *Industrial and Organizational Psychology, 6*, 100–102.

Fiske, S. T. (2000). Stereotyping, prejudice, and discrimination at the seam between the centuries: Evolution, culture, mind, and brain. *European Journal of Social Psychology, 30*(3), 299–322.

Fiske, S., Cuddy, A., Glick, P., Xu, J., & Devine, P. (2002). A model of (often mixed) stereotype content: Competence and warmth respectively follow from perceived status and competition. *Journal of Personality and Social Psychology, 82*, 878–902.

Fiske, S. T., & Neuberg, S. L. (1990). A continuum of impression formation, from category-based to individuating processes: Influences of information and motivation on attention and interpretation. *Advances in Experimental Social Psychology, 23*, 1–74.

Foschi, M., Lai, L., & Sigerson, K. (1994). Gender and double standards in the assessment of job applicants. *Social Psychology Quarterly, 57*, 326–339.

Fuegen, K., Biernat, M., Haines, E., & Deaux, K. (2004). Mothers and fathers in the workplace: How gender and parental status influence judgments of job-related competence. *Journal of Social Issues, 60*, 737–754.

Gelfand, M. J., Nishii, L. H., Raver, J. L., & Schneider, B. (2007). Discrimination in organizations: An organizational-level systems perspective. In R. L. Dipboye & A. Colella (Eds.), *Discrimination at Work: The psychological and organizational bases*. New York, NY: Taylor & Francis Group.

Ghumman, S., & Jackson, L. (2010). The downside of religious attire: The Muslim headscarf and expectations of obtaining employment. *Journal of Organizational Behavior, 31*, 4–23.

Ghumman, S., Ryan, A. M., Barclay, L. A., & Markel, K. S. (2013). Religious discrimination in the workplace: A review and examination of current and future trends. *Journal of Business and Psychology, 28*, 439–454.

Goldman, B. M., Gutek, B. A., Stein, J. H., & Lewis, K. (2006). Employment discrimination in organizations: Antecedents and consequences. *Journal of Management, 32*, 786–830.

Good, J. J., Moss-Racusin, C. A., & Sanchez, D. T. (2012). When do we confront? Perceptions of costs and benefits predict confronting discrimination on behalf of the self and others. *Psychology of Women Quarterly, 36*, 210–226.

Gouldner, A. W. (1960). The norm of reciprocity: A preliminary statement. *American Sociological Review*, 161–178.

Grant, J. M., Mottet, L. A., Tanis, J., Harrison, J., Herman, J. L., & Keisling, M. (2011). *Injustice at every turn: A report of the national transgender discrimination survey*. Washington, DC: National Center for Transgender Equality and National Gay and Lesbian Task Force.

Gray, M., Kurihara, T., Hommen, L., & Feldman, J. (2007). Networks of exclusion: Job segmentation and social networks in the knowledge economy. *Equal Opportunities International, 26*, 144–161.

Gross, J. J., & John, O. P. (2003). Individual differences in two emotion regulation processes: Implications for affect, relationships, and well-being. *Journal of Personality and Social Psychology, 85*, 348–362.

Hakak, L. T., Holzinger, I., & Zikic, J. (2010). Barriers and paths to success: Latin American MBAs' views of employment in Canada. *Journal of Managerial Psychology, 25*, 159–176.

Halpert, J. A., Wilson, M. L., & Hickman, J. L. (1993). Pregnancy as a source of bias in performance appraisals. *Journal of Organizational Behavior, 14*, 649–663.

Hanover, J., & Cellar, D. F. (1998). Environmental factors and the effectiveness of workforce diversity training. *Human Resource Development Quarterly, 9*(2), 105–124.

Hartzell, E., Frazer, M. S., Wertz, K., & Davis, M. (2009). The state of transgender California. Results from the 2008 California transgender economic health survey. Transgender Law Center, San Francisco, CA.

Hattrup, K., Rock, J., & Scalia, C. (1997). The effects of varying conceptualizations of job performance on adverse impact, minority hiring, and predicted performance. *Journal of Applied Psychology, 82*, 656–664.

Hebl, M., & Kleck, R. E. (2002). Acknowledging one's stigma in the interview setting: Effective strategy or liability? *Journal of Applied Social Psychology, 32*, 223–249.

Hebl, M. R., Foster, J. B., Mannix, L. M., & Dovidio, J. F. (2002). Formal and interpersonal discrimination: A field study of bias toward homosexual applicants. *Personality and Social Psychology Bulletin, 28*, 815–825.

Hebl, M. R., King, E. B., Glick, P., Singletary, S. L., & Kazama, S. (2007). Hostile and benevolent reactions toward pregnant women: Complementary interpersonal punishments and
rewards that maintain traditional roles. *Journal of Applied Psychology*, *92*, 1499−1511.

Hebl, M. R., & Skorinko, J. (2005). Acknowledging one's physical disability in the interview:
Does "when" make a difference? *Journal of Applied Social Psychology*, *35*, 2477−2492.

Heilman, M. E., & Okimoto, T. G. (2007). Why are women penalized for success at male
tasks? The implied communality deficit. *Journal of Applied Psychology*, *92*, 81−92.

Heilman, M. E., & Okimoto, T. G. (2008). Motherhood: A potential source of bias in employment decisions. *Journal of Applied Psychology*, *93*, 189−198.

Heilman, M. E., Wallen, A. S., Fuchs, D., & Tamkins, M. M. (2004). Penalties for success:
Reactions to women who succeed at male gender-typed tasks. *Journal of Applied
Psychology*, *89*, 416−427.

Hershcovis, M. S. (2011). "Incivility, social undermining, bullying … oh my!": A call to
reconcile constructs within workplace aggression research. *Journal of Organizational
Behavior*, *32*, 499−519.

Hodson, R., Roscigno, V. J., & Lopez, S. H. (2006). Chaos and the abuse of power workplace
bullying in organizational and interactional context. *Work and Occupations*, *33*,
382−416.

Hoffman, C. C., & Thornton, C. G. (1997). Examining selection utility where competing predictors differ in adverse impact. *Personnel Psychology*, *50*, 455−470.

Hofstede, G. (2001). *Culture's consequences: Comparing values, behaviors, institutions, and
organizations across nations.* Thousand Oaks, CA: Sage.

Hofstede, G. H. (1980). *Culture's consequences: International differences in work-related values.*
Beverly Hills, CA: Sage.

Horvath, M., & Ryan, A. M. (2003). Antecedents and potential moderators of the relationship
between attitudes and hiring discrimination on the basis of sexual orientation. *Sex
Roles*, *48*, 115−130.

Hosoda, M., Nguyen, L. T., & Stone-Romero, E. F. (2012). The effect of Hispanic accents on
employment decisions. *Journal of Managerial Psychology*, *27*, 347−364.

Hosoda, M., & Stone-Romero, E. (2010). The effects of foreign accents on employment-related
decisions. *Journal of Managerial Psychology*, *25*, 113−132.

Hough, L. M., Oswald, F. L., & Ployhart, R. E. (2001). Determinants, detection, and ameli-
oration of adverse impact in personnel selection procedures: Issues, evidence, and lessons learned. *International Journal of Selection and Assessment*, *9*, 152−194.

Human Rights Campaign Foundation. (2015). *Corporate equality index 2016: Rating American
workplaces on lesbian, gay, bisexual and transgender equality.* Retrieved from
http://hrc-assets.s3-website-us-east-1.amazonaws.com//files/assets/resources/CEI-2016-
FullReport.pdf

Ilic, M., Reinecke, J., Bohner, G., Hans-Onno, R., Beblo, T., Driessen, M., … Corrigan, P. W.
(2012). Protecting self-esteem from stigma: A test of different strategies for coping with
the stigma of mental illness. *International Journal of Social Psychiatry*, *58*, 246−257.

Jackson, S., & Joshi, A. (2011). Work team diversity. In S. Zedeck (Ed.), *APA handbook of
industrial and organizational psychology, Vol. 1: Building and developing the organization. APA handbooks in psychology* (pp. 651–686). Washington, DC: American
Psychological Association.

James, E. H., & Wooten, L. P. (2006). Diversity crises: How firms manage discrimination lawsuits. *Academy of Management Journal*, *49*, 1103−1118.

Jones, K. P., Peddie, C. I., Gilrane, V. L., King, E. B., & Gray, A. (in press). Not so subtle: A meta-analysis of the correlates of subtle and overt discrimination. *Journal of Management.*

Jost, J., & Hunyady, O. (2003). The psychology of system justification and the palliative function of ideology. *European Review of Social Psychology, 13,* 111–153.

Jost, J. T. (2001). *Outgroup favoritism and the theory of system justification: A paradigm for investigating the effects of socioeconomic success on stereotype content.* In cognitive social psychology: The Princeton symposium on the legacy and future of social cognition (pp. 89–102).

Kaiser, C. R., & Miller, C. T. (2004). A stress and coping perspective on confronting sexism. *Psychology of Women Quarterly, 28,* 168–178.

Kanter, R. M. (1977a). *Men and women of the corporation.* New York, NY: Basic Books.

Kanter, R. M. (1977b). Some effects of proportions on group life. *American Journal of Sociology, 82,* 965–990.

Kehoe, J. F. (2009). Cut scores and adverse impact. In J. L. Outtz (Ed.), *Adverse impact: Implications for organizational staffing and high stakes selection* (pp. 289–322). New York, NY: Taylor & Francis Group.

Kern, J. H., & Grandey, A. A. (2009). Customer incivility as a social stressor: The role of race and racial identity for service employees. *Journal of Occupational Health Psychology, 14,* 46–57.

King, E. B., & Ahmad, A. S. (2010). An experimental field study of interpersonal discrimination toward Muslim job applicants. *Personnel Psychology, 63,* 881–906.

King, E. B., Dunleavy, D. G., Dunleavy, E. M., Jaffer, S., Morgan, W. B., Elder, K., & Graebner, R. (2011). Discrimination in the 21st century: Are science and the law aligned? *Psychology, Public Policy, and Law, 17,* 54–75.

King, E. B., Hebl, M. R., George, J. M., & Matusik, S. F. (2010). Understanding tokenism: Negative consequences of perceived gender discrimination in male-dominated organizations. *Journal of Management, 36,* 482–510.

King, E. B., Mendoza, S. A., Madera, J. M., Hebl, M. R., & Knight, J. L. (2006). What's in a name? A multiracial investigation of the role of occupational stereotypes in selection decisions. *Journal of Applied Social Psychology, 36,* 1145–1159.

King, E. B., Shapiro, J., Hebl, M. R., Singletary, S. L., & Turner, S. L. (2006). The stigma of obesity in customer service: A mechanism for remediation and bottom-line consequences of interpersonal discrimination. *Journal of Applied Psychology, 91,* 579–593.

Krieger, N., & Sidney, S. (1996). Racial discrimination and blood pressure: The CARDIA Study of young black and white adults. *American Journal of Public Health, 86,* 1370–1378.

Kteily, N., Ho, A. K., & Sidanius, J. (2012). Hierarchy in the mind: The predictive power of social dominance orientation across social contexts and domains. *Journal of Experimental Social Psychology, 48,* 543–549.

Kulik, C. T., & Roberson, L. (2008). Common goals and golden opportunities: Evaluation of diversity education in academic and organizational settings. *Academy of Management Learning & Education, 7,* 309–331.

Landrine, H., & Klonoff, E. A. (1996). The schedule of racist events: A measure of racial discrimination and a study of its negative physical and mental health consequences. *Journal of Black Psychology, 22,* 144–168.

Landrine, H., & Klonoff, E. A. (2000). Racial segregation and cigarette smoking among Blacks: findings at the individual level. *Journal of Health Psychology, 5,* 211–219.

Larimer, S. (2015). *Colorado court rules against baker who refused same-sex marriage cake order*. Retrieved from http://www.chicagotribune.com/news/nationworld/ct-colorado-baker-same-sex-marriage-cake-20150815-story.html. Accessed on December 13, 2015.

Lee, D. L., & Ahn, S. (2011). Racial discrimination and Asian mental health: A meta-analysis. *The Counseling Psychologist, 39*, 463−489.

Lee, D. L., & Ahn, S. (2012). Discrimination against Latina/os: A meta-analysis of individual-level resources and outcomes. *The Counseling Psychologist, 40*, 28−65.

Legault, L., Gutsell, J. N., & Inzlicht, M. (2011). Ironic effects of antiprejudice messages: How motivational interventions can reduce (but also increase) prejudice. *Psychological Science, 22*, 1472−1477.

Levitt, H. M., & Ippolito, M. R. (2014). Being transgender: Navigating minority stressors and developing authentic self-presentation. *Psychology of Women Quarterly, 38*, 46−64.

Lewis, D., & Gunn, R. (2007). Workplace bullying in the public sector: Understanding the racial dimension. *Public Administration, 85*, 641−665.

Lindsey, A., King, E., Cheung, H., Hebl, M., Lynch, S., & Mancini, V. (2015). When do women respond against discrimination? Exploring factors of subtlety, form, and focus. *Journal of Applied Social Psychology, 45*, 649−661.

Lindsey, A., King, E., Hebl, M., & Levine, N. (2015). The impact of method, motivation, and empathy on diversity training effectiveness. *Journal of Business and Psychology, 30*, 605−617.

Lindsey, A., King, E., McCausland, T., Jones, K., & Dunleavy, E. (2013). What we know and don't: Eradicating employment discrimination 50 years after the Civil Rights Act. *Industrial and Organizational Psychology: Perspectives of Science and Practice, 6*, 391−413.

Lombardi, E. L., Wilchins, R. A., Priesing, D., & Malouf, D. (2002). Gender violence: Transgender experiences with violence and discrimination. *Journal of Homosexuality, 42*, 89−101.

Lyness, K. S., & Heilman, M. E. (2006). When fit is fundamental: Performance evaluations and promotions of upper-level female and male managers. *Journal of Applied Psychology, 91*, 777−785.

Madera, J. M., King, E. B., & Hebl, M. R. (2013). Enhancing the effects of sexual orientation diversity training: The effects of setting goals and training mentors on attitudes and behaviors. *Journal of Business and Psychology, 28*, 79−91.

Major, B., Quinton, W. J., & Schmader, T. (2003). Attributions to discrimination and self-esteem: Impact of group identification and situational ambiguity. *Journal of Experimental Social Psychology, 39*, 220−231.

Marchiondo, L. A., Ran, S., & Cortina, L. (2015). Modern discrimination. In A. Colella & E. King (Eds.), *Oxford handbook of workplace discrimination*. Oxford: Oxford University Press.

Marfleet, P., & Blustein, D. L. (2011). 'Needed not wanted': An interdisciplinary examination of the work-related challenges faced by irregular migrants. *Journal of Vocational Behavior, 78*, 381−389.

Martinez, L. (2012). *Confronting bias: How targets and allies can address prejudice against gay men in the workplace*. Doctoral dissertation. Retrieved from ProQuest Dissertations & Theses Global (3534266).

Masser, B., Grass, K., & Nesic, M. (2007). 'We like you, but we don't want you'—The impact of pregnancy in the workplace. *Sex Roles, 57*, 703−712.

Masterson, S. S., Lewis, K., Goldman, B. M., & Taylor, M. S. (2000). Integrating justice and social exchange: The differing effects of fair procedures and treatment on work relationships. *Academy of Management Journal, 43*, 738–748.

Mays, V. M., & Cochran, S. D. (2001). Mental health correlates of perceived discrimination among lesbian, gay, and bisexual adults in the United States. *American Journal of Public Health, 91*, 1869–1876.

McBrier, D. B., & Wilson, G. (2004). Going down? Race and downward occupational mobility for white-collar workers in the 1990s. *Work and Occupations, 31*, 283–322.

McConahay, J. B. (1983). Modern racism and modern discrimination: The effects of race, racial attitudes, and context on simulated hiring decisions. *Personality and Social Psychology Bulletin, 9*, 551–558.

McKay, P. F., & Avery, D. R. (2005). Warning! Diversity recruitment could backfire. *Journal of Management Inquiry, 14*, 330–336.

McKay, P. F., & Avery, D. R. (2006). What has race got to do with it? Unraveling the role of racioethnicity in job seekers'reactions to site visits. *Personnel Psychology, 59*(2), 395–429.

McKay, P. F., Avery, D. R., & Morris, M. A. (2008). Mean racial-ethnic differences in employee sales performance: The moderating role of diversity climate. *Personnel Psychology, 61*, 349–374.

McKay, P. F., & McDaniel, M. A. (2006). A reexamination of black-white mean differences in work performance: More data, more moderators. *Journal of Applied Psychology, 91*, 538.

McMahon, B. T., & Shaw, L. (2005). Workplace discrimination and disability. *Journal of Vocational Rehabilitation, 23*, 137–143.

Meyer, I. H. (1995). Minority stress and mental health in gay men. *Journal of Health, 36*, 38–56.

Miller, G. E., Chen, E., & Zhou, E. S. (2007). If it goes up, must it come down? Chronic stress and the hypothalamic-pituitary-adrenocortical axis in humans. *Psychological Bulletin, 133*, 25–45.

Miner, K. N., Pesonen, A. D., Smittick, A. L., Seigel, M. L., & Clark, E. K. (2014). Does being a mom help or hurt? Workplace incivility as a function of motherhood status. *Journal of Occupational Health Psychology, 19*, 60–73.

Minnotte, K. L. (2012). Perceived discrimination and work-to-life conflict among workers in the United States. *The Sociological Quarterly, 53*, 188–210.

Molleman, E. (2005). Diversity in demographic characteristics, abilities and personality traits: Do faultlines affect team functioning? *Group Decision and Negotiation, 14*, 173–193.

Morgan, W. B., Walker, S. S., Hebl, M. M. R., & King, E. B. (2013). A field experiment: Reducing interpersonal discrimination toward pregnant job applicants. *Journal of Applied Psychology, 98*, 799–809.

Moss-Racusin, C. A., Dovidio, J. F., Brescoll, V. L., Graham, M. J., & Handelsman, J. (2012). Science faculty's subtle gender biases favor male students. *Proceedings of the National Academy of Sciences, 109*, 16474–16479.

National Reentry Resource Center. (2014). *Reentry facts.* Lexington, KY: The Council of State Governments. Retrieved from http://csgjusticecenter.org/nrrc/facts-and-trends/

Nemeroff, C. B. (1996). The Corticotropin-Releasing Factor (CRF) hypothesis of depression: New findings and new directions. *Molecular Psychiatry, 1*, 336–342.

Ng, T. W., & Feldman, D. C. (2012). Evaluating six common stereotypes about older workers with meta-analytical data. *Personnel Psychology, 65*, 821–858.

O'Brien, K. S., Latner, J. D., Ebneter, D., & Hunter, J. A. (2013). Obesity discrimination: The role of physical appearance, personal ideology, and anti-fat prejudice. *International Journal of Obesity, 37,* 455–460.

Operario, D., & Fiske, S. T. (2001). Ethnic identity moderates perceptions of prejudice: Judgments of personal versus group discrimination and subtle versus blatant bias. *Personality and Social Psychology Bulletin, 27,* 550–561.

Ott-Holland, C., Huang, J., Ryan, A., Elizondo, F., Wadlington, P., & Tracey, T. J. G. (2013). Culture and vocational interests: The moderating role of collectivism and gender egalitarianism. *Journal of Counseling Psychology, 60,* 569–581.

Parasuraman, S., & Alutto, J. A. (1984). Sources and outcomes of stress in organizational settings: Toward the development of a structural model. *Academy of Management Journal, 27,* 330–350.

Pascoe, E. A., & Richman, L. S. (2009). Perceived discrimination and health: A meta-analytic review. *Psychological Bulletin, 135,* 531–554.

Pennebaker, J. W., Colder, M., & Sharp, L. K. (1990). Accelerating the coping process. *Journal of Personality and Social Psychology, 58,* 528–537.

Petersen, L.-E., & Dietz, J. (2000). Social discrimination in a personnel selection context: The effects of an authority's instruction to discriminate and followers' authoritarianism. *Journal of Applied Social Psychology, 30,* 206–220.

Petersen, L.-E., & Dietz, J. (2005). Prejudice and enforcement of workforce homogeneity as explanations for employment discrimination. *Journal of Applied Social Psychology, 35,* 144–159.

Petersen, L.-E., & Dietz, J. (2008). Employment discrimination: Authority figures' demographic preferences and followers' affective organizational commitment. *Journal of Applied Psychology, 93,* 1287–1300.

Ployhart, R. E., & Holtz, B. C. (2008). The diversity-validity dilemma: Strategies for reducing racioethnic and sex subgroup differences and adverse impact in selection. *Personnel Psychology, 61,* 153–172.

Podsakoff, P. M., MacKenzie, S B., Paine, J. B., & Bachrach, D. G. (2000). Organizational citizenship behaviors: A critical review of the theoretical and empirical literature and suggestions for future research. *Journal of Management, 26*(3), 513–563.

Premeaux, S. F. (2001). Impact of applicant disability on selection: The role of disability type, physical attractiveness, and proximity. *Journal of Business and Psychology, 16,* 291–298.

Pruitt, S. W., & Nethercutt, L. L. (2002). The Texaco racial discrimination case and shareholder wealth. *Journal of Labor Research, 23,* 685–693.

Pugh, S. D., Dietz, J., Brief, A. P., & Wiley, J. W. (2008). Looking inside and out: The impact of employee and community demographic composition on organizational diversity climate. *Journal of Applied Psychology, 93*(6), 1422.

Pulakos, E. D., & Schmitt, N. (1996). An evaluation of two strategies for reducing adverse impact and their effects on criterion-related validity. *Human Performance, 9,* 241–258.

Purkiss, S. L. S., Perrewé, P. L., Gillespie, T. L., Mayes, B. T., & Ferris, G. R. (2006). Implicit sources of bias in employment interview judgments and decisions. *Organizational Behavior and Human Decision Processes, 101,* 152–167.

Pyburn, K. M., Jr., Ployhart, R. E., & Kravitz, D. A. (2008). The diversity–validity dilemma: Overview and legal context. *Personnel Psychology, 61,* 143–151.

Quillian, L. (2008). Does unconscious racism exist? *Social Psychology Quarterly, 71*(1), 6–11.

Ragins, B. R. (2008). Disclosure disconnects: Antecedents and consequences of disclosing invisible stigmas across life domains. *Academy of Management Review, 33,* 194–215.

Ragins, B. R., & Cornwell, J. M. (2001). Pink triangles: Antecedents and consequences of perceived workplace discrimination against gay and lesbian employees. *Journal of Applied Psychology, 86,* 1244.

Ragins, B. R., Singh, R., & Cornwell, J. M. (2007). Making the invisible visible: Fear and disclosure of sexual orientation at work. *Journal of Applied Psychology, 92,* 1103.

Randle, N., Mathis, C., & Cates, D. (2012). Cooping to repair the career damage of workplace weight discrimination. *Journal of Organizational Culture, Communications & Conflict, 16,* 89–106.

Rasinski, H. M., & Czopp, A. M. (2010). The effect of target status on witnesses' reactions to confrontations of bias. *Basic and Applied Social Psychology, 32,* 8–16.

Rattan, A., & Dweck, C. S. (2010). Who confronts prejudice? The role of implicit theories in the motivation to confront prejudice. *Psychological Science, 21,* 952–959.

Raver, J. L., & Nishii, L. H. (2010). Once, twice, or three times as harmful? Ethnic harassment, gender harassment, and generalized workplace harassment. *Journal of Applied Psychology, 95,* 236–254.

Ray, R., Gornick, J. C., & Schmitt, J. (2008). *Parental leave policies in 21 countries: Assessing generosity and gender equality.* Washington, DC: Center for Economic and Policy Research. Retrieved from http://www.lisdatacenter.org/wp-content/uploads/parent-leave-report1.pdf

Reskin, B. F. (2000). The proximate causes of employment discrimination. *Contemporary Sociology, 29,* 319.

Richard, O., Stewart, M., Mckay, P., & Sackett, T. (2015). The impact of store-unit-community racial diversity congruence on store-unit sales performance. *Journal of Management.*

Richman, J. A., Rospenda, K. M., Nawyn, S. J., Flaherty, J. A., Fendrich, M., Drum, M. L., & Johnson, T. P. (1999). Sexual harassment and generalized workplace abuse among university employees: Prevalence and mental health correlates. *American Journal of Public Health, 89,* 358–363.

Riley, M., Elgin, B., Lawrence, D., & Matlack, C. (2014). Missed alarms and 40 million stolen credit card numbers: How Target blew it. *Bloomberg Businessweek,* p. 13.

Roberson, L., Kulik, C. T., & Pepper, M. B. (2003). Using needs assessment to resolve controversies in diversity training design. *Group and Organization Management, 28,* 148–174.

Robinson, G., & Dechant, K. (1997). Building a business case for diversity. *The Academy of Management Executive, 11,* 21–31.

Rosette, A. S., Leonardelli, G. J., & Phillips, K. W. (2008). The White standard: Racial bias in leader categorization. *Journal of Applied Psychology, 93,* 758.

Rossett, A., & Bickham, T. (1994). Diversity training: Hope, faith and cynicism. *Training, 31,* 40–46.

Roth, P. L., Purvis, K. L., & Bobko, P. (2012). A meta-analysis of gender group differences for measures of job performance in field studies. *Journal of Management, 38,* 719–739.

Ruggs, E. N., Law, C., Cox, C. B., Roehling, M. V., Wiener, R. L., Hebl, M. R., & Barron, L. (2013). Gone fishing: I–O psychologists' missed opportunities to understand marginalized employees' experiences with discrimination. *Industrial and Organizational Psychology, 6,* 39–60.

Rupar, T. (2014). Here are the 10 countries where homosexuality may be punished by death. *The Washington Post,* February 24. Retrieved from https://www.washingtonpost.com/

news/worldviews/wp/2014/02/24/here-are-the-10-countries-where-homosexuality-may-be-punished-by-death/

Rupp, D. E., Vodanovich, S. J., & Crede, M. (2006). Age bias in the workplace: The impact of ageism and causal attributions. *Journal of Applied Social Psychology, 36*, 1337–1364.

Saal, K., Martinez, L. R., & Smith, N. A. (2014). Visible disabilities: Acknowledging the utility of acknowledgment. *Industrial and Organizational Psychology, 7*, 242–248.

Sabat, I. E., Lindsey, A., Membere, A., Anderson, A., Ahmad, A., King, E., & Bolunmez, B. (2014). Invisible disabilities: Unique strategies for workplace allies. *Industrial and Organizational Psychology: Perspectives of Science and Practice, 7*, 259–265.

Salin, D. (2003). Ways of explaining workplace bullying: A review of enabling, motivation and precipitating structures and processes in the work environment. *Human Relations, 56*, 1213–1232.

Sangganjanavanich, V. F. (2009). Career development practitioners as advocates for transgender individuals: Understanding gender transition. *Journal of Employment Counseling, 46*, 128–135.

Santuzzi, A. M., Waltz, P. R., Finkelstein, L. M., & Rupp, D. E. (2014). Invisible disabilities: Unique challenges for employees and organizations. *Industrial and Organizational Psychology, 7*, 204–219.

Schilt, K., & Connell, C. (2007). Do workplace gender transitions make gender trouble? *Gender, Work & Organization, 14*, 596–618.

Schilt, K., & Wiswall, M. (2008). Before and after: Gender transitions, human capital, and workplace experiences. *The B.E. Journal of Economic Analysis & Policy, 8*, 1–28.

Schmader, T., Croft, A., Scarnier, M., Lickel, B., & Mendes, W. B. (2012). Implicit and explicit emotional reactions to witnessing prejudice. *Group Processes & Intergroup Relations, 15*, 379–392.

Schmitt, M. T., Branscombe, N. R., Postmes, T., & Garcia, A. (2014). The consequences of perceived discrimination for psychological well-being: A meta-analytic review. *Psychological Bulletin, 140*, 921–948.

Schmitt, N., Clause, C. S., & Pulakos, E. D. (1996). Subgroup differences associated with different measures of some common job-relevant constructs. *International review of industrial and organizational psychology* (Vol. 11, pp. 115–139). New York, NY: Wiley.

Schmitt, N., & Quinn, A. (2009). Reductions in measured subgroup mean differences: What is possible? *Implications of Organizational Staffing and High Stakes, 31*, 425–451.

Schneider, B. (1987). The people make the place. *Personnel Psychology, 40*(3), 437–453.

Schultheiss, D. E., Watts, J., Sterland, L., & O'Neill, M. (2011). Career, migration and the life CV: A relational cultural analysis. *Journal of Vocational Behavior, 78*, 334–341.

Schwab, K., Samans, R., Zahidi, S., Bekhouche, Y., Ugarte, P. P., Ratcheva, V., ... Tyson, L. D. (2015). *The global gender gap report 2015.* Geneva: World Economic Forum. Retrieved from http://www3.weforum.org/docs/GGGR2015/cover.pdf

Shelton, J. N., Richeson, J. A., & Vorauer, J. D. (2006). Threatened identities and interethnic interactions. In W. Stroebe & M. Hewstone (Eds.), *European review of social psychology* (Vol. 17, pp. 312–358). New York, NY: Psychology Press.

Shen, W., & Dhanani, L. (2015). Measuring and defining discrimination. In A. J. Colella & E. B. King (Eds.), *The Oxford handbook of workplace discrimination.* Oxford, UK: Oxford University Press.

Sherif, M., Harvey, O. J., White, B. J., Hood, W. R., & Sherif, C. W. (1988). *The robbers cave experiment: Intergroup conflict and cooperation.* Middletown, CT: Wesleyan University Press.

Sidanius, J., & Pratto (1999). *Social dominance: An intergroup theory of social hierarchy and oppression.* New York, NY: Cambridge University Press.

Singletary, S. L., & Hebl, M. R. (2009). Compensatory strategies for reducing interpersonal discrimination: The effectiveness of acknowledgments, increased positivity, and individuating information. *Journal of Applied Psychology, 94,* 797–805.

Smart Richman, L., Pek, J., Pascoe, E., & Bauer, D. J. (2010). The effects of perceived discrimination on ambulatory blood pressure and affective responses to interpersonal stress modeled over 24 hours. *Health Psychology, 29,* 403–411.

Smith, A. N., Morgan, W. B., King, E. B., Hebl, M. R., & Peddie, C. I. (2012). The ins and outs of diversity management: The effect of authenticity on outsider perceptions and insider behaviors. *Journal of Applied Social Psychology, 42,* E21–E55.

Society for Human Resource Management. (2013). *Shaping the future.* Retrieved from http://www.shrm.org/about/foundation/shapingthefuture/pages/futoreofhr.aspx

Steward, A. D., & Cunningham, G. B. (2015). Racial identity and its impact on job applicants. *Journal of Sport Management, 29,* 245–256.

Sue, D. W., Capodilupo, C. M., Torino, G. C., Bucceri, J. M., Holder, A. M. B., Nadal, K. L., & Esquilin, M. (2007). Racial microaggression in everyday life: Implications for clinical practice. *American Psychologist, 62,* 271–286.

Sue, D. W., Lin, A. I., Torino, G. C., Capodilupo, C. M., & Rivera, D. P. (2009). Racial microaggressions and difficult dialogues on race in the classroom. *Cultural Diversity and Ethnic Minority Psychology, 15,* 183–190.

Swim, J., Borgida, E., Maruyama, G., & Myers, D. G. (1989). Joan McKay versus John McKay: Do gender stereotypes bias evaluations? *Psychological Bulletin, 105,* 409–429.

Sy, T., Shore, L. M., Strauss, J., Shore, T. H., Tram, S., Whiteley, P., & Ikeda-Muromachi, K. (2010). Leadership perceptions as a function of race–occupation fit: The case of Asian Americans. *Journal of Applied Psychology, 95,* 902–919.

Tajfel, H. (1970). Experiments in intergroup discrimination. *Scientific American, 223,* 96–102.

Tajfel, H. (1982). Social psychology of intergroup relations. *Annual Review of Psychology, 33*(1), 1–39.

Tajfel, H., & Turner, J. C. (1986). The social identity theory of intergroup behavior. In S. Worshel & W. Austin (Eds.), *The psychology of intergroup relations.* Chicago, IL: Nelson-Hall.

Taylor, H. (2002). *Workplace discrimination against, and jokes about, African Americans, gays, Jews, Muslims, and others.* New York, NY: Harris Interactive. Retrieved from http://media.theharrispoll.com/documents/Harris-Interactive-Poll-Research-Workplace-Discrimination-Against-and-Jokes-About-A-2002-11.pdf

Tepper, B. J. (2000). Consequences of abusive supervision. *Academy of Management Journal, 43,* 178–190.

Tepper, B. J. (2007). Abusive supervision in work organizations: Review, synthesis, and research agenda. *Journal of Management, 33*(3), 261–289.

Thomas-Hunt, M. C., & Phillips, K. W. (2004). When what you know is not enough: Expertise and gender dynamics in task groups. *Personality and Social Psychology Bulletin, 30,* 1585–1598.

Tsui, A. S., Egan, T. D., & Iii, C. A. O. (1992). Being different: Relational demography and organizational attachment. *Administrative Science Quarterly, 37,* 549. Retrieved from http://doi.org/10.2307/2393472

U.S. Bureau of Labor Statistics. (2015). *Labor force statistics from current population survey.* Retrieved from http://www.bls.gov/cps/demographics.htm

Umphress, E. E., Simmons, A. L., Boswell, W. R., & del Triana, M. C. (2008). Managing discrimination in selection: The influence of directives from an authority and social dominance orientation. *Journal of Applied Psychology, 93*, 982–993.

United Nations' International Labor Organization. (2015). Retrieved from http://www.ilo.org/global/about-the-ilo/lang–en/index.htm

Van Laer, K., & Janssens, M. (2011). Ethnic minority professionals' experiences with subtle discrimination in the workplace. *Human Relations, 64*, 1203–1227.

Velez, B. L., Moradi, B., & Brewster, M. E. (2013). Testing the tenets of minority stress theory in workplace contexts. *Journal of Counseling Psychology, 60*, 532–542.

Volpone, S. D., & Avery, D. R. (2013). It's self defense: How perceived discrimination promotes employee withdrawal. *Journal of Occupational Health Psychology, 18*, 430–448.

Wang, J., Leu, J., & Shoda, Y. (2011). When the seemingly innocuous "stings": Racial microaggressions and their emotional consequences. *Personality and Social Psychology Bulletin, 37*, 1666–1678.

Weichselbaumer, D. (2003). Sexual orientation discrimination in hiring. *Labour* Economics, *10*, 629–642.

Wheeler, M. E., & Fiske, S. T. (2005). Controlling racial prejudice: Social-cognitive goals affect amygdala and stereotype activation. *Psychological Science, 16*, 56–83.

Wilson, G., & Maume, D. (2013). Men's race-based mobility into management: Analyses at the blue collar and white collar job levels. *Research in Social Stratification and Mobility, 33*, 1–12.

Yamada, S., Cappadocia, M. C., & Pepler, D. (2014). Workplace bullying in Canadian graduate psychology programs: Student perspectives of student–supervisor relationships. *Training and Education in Professional Psychology, 8*, 58.

Young, N. C., & Powell, G. N. (2015). Hiring ex-offenders: A theoretical model. Human *Resource Management Review, 25*, 298–312.

Zakaria, T. (2011). U.S. Government hankers for hackers. *Reuters*, August 2. Retrieved from http://www.reuters.com/article/2011/08/02/idUSN1E7701KK20110802#TF289XiiGom mqrgs.97

Zitek, E. M., & Hebl, M. R. (2007). The role of social norm clarity in the influenced expression of prejudice over time. *Journal of Experimental Social Psychology, 43*, 867–876.

SOCIAL MEDIA USE IN HRM

Donald H. Kluemper, Arjun Mitra and
Siting Wang ☆

ABSTRACT

Over the past decade, the rapid evolution of social media has impacted the field of human resource management in numerous ways. In response, scholars and practitioners have sought to begin an investigation of the myriad of ways that social media impacts organizations. To date, research evidence on a range of HR-related topics are just beginning to emerge, but are scattered across a range of diverse literatures. The principal aim of this chapter is to review the current literature on the study of social media in HRM and to integrate these disparate emerging literatures. During our review, we discuss the existent research, describe the theoretical foundations of such work, and summarize key research findings and themes into a coherent social media framework relevant to HRM. Finally, we offer recommendations for future work that can enhance knowledge of social media's impact in organizations.

Keywords: Social media; social networking web sites; human resource management

---

☆ The second and third authors contributed equally.

Research in Personnel and Human Resources Management, Volume 34, 153–207
Copyright © 2016 by Emerald Group Publishing Limited
All rights of reproduction in any form reserved
ISSN: 0742-7301/doi:10.1108/S0742-730120160000034011

Due to the recent and rapid evolution of social media, scientific study has been substantially outpaced by organizational practice, creating a situation in which relevant organizational phenomena are understudied. As such, numerous opportunities exist to engage in academic research within a broad range of areas in which social media and human resource management intersect. Recent interest in the topic has emerged across a wide range of research disciplines, such as industrial/organizational psychology and management (McFarland & Ployhart, 2015), law (Brandenburg, 2008), information technology (Willey, White, Domagalski, & Ford, 2012), marketing (Lebrecque, Markos, & Milne, 2011), and psychology (Back et al., 2010). Although much of the existing research relates specifically to social networking web sites (SNWs) and employment selection (Kluemper, 2013), this chapter will focus on a full range of social media topics that relate to human resource management. This chapter will attempt to describe a wide range of ways in which social media impacts human resource management, review and integrate the literature in these diverse areas, summarize key research findings, and offer recommendations for future research in the field of human resource management.

Social media are digital Web 2.0 applications that facilitate interactive information, user-created content, and collaboration (see Elefant, 2011). Social media exists entirely on the Internet or portals that can access the Internet (e.g., computers, tablets, and cell phones). Applications are different technological mechanisms to connect people and information. The most popular and well-known social media applications are SNWs. SNWs are a subset of social media and meet the following three broad criteria: (1) they are an online service that allows users to build a profile within the network, (2) they allow users to build a list of other users that they share a connection with, and (3) they allow users to view and to navigate the information created by other users on the social network (Boyd & Ellison, 2007). Because of these unique features, SNWs have been the focus of academic research in the area of employment selection (Van Iddekinge, Lanivich, Roth, & Junco, in press). However, SNWs are only a subset of the broader domain of social media that will be explored in this chapter.

We chose to organize HRM-related social media concepts into four categories. The first includes external organizational stakeholders, such as branding, organizational image, and attraction of job applicants. The second includes employment selection using SNWs, which includes a range of topics such as privacy, discrimination, negligent hiring, validity, reliability, generalizability, impression management, applicant reactions, and possible screening approaches. The third category consists of social media use to improve organizational functioning and includes the topics of productivity, engagement and teamwork, training, knowledge management, social capital, organizational culture, and leadership. The final category introduces how social media may lead to counterproductive work behaviors such as cyberloafing and the potential for employee disciplinary action.

To better explain the types of social media relevant to each of the HRM topics, we drew from Kaplan and Haenlein's (2010) classification scheme for social media based on a set of theories in the field of media research: "social presence/media richness" and "self-presentation/self-disclosure." Social presence theory relates to the acoustic, visual, and physical contact that can be achieved (Short, Williams, & Christie, 1976), while media richness theory (Daft & Lengel, 1986) states that (social) media differ in the degree of richness they possess, such as the amount of information transmitted in a given time interval. For the social dimension, self-presentation represents the desire to control the impressions others form (Goffman, 1959), while self-disclosure represents the revelation of personal information (e.g., thoughts, feelings, likes, dislikes). Kaplan and Haenlein (2010) create a classification scheme by creating three categories for "social presence/media richness" (low, medium, high) and two categories for "self-presentation/self-disclosure" (low, high). This creates six categories of social media: (1) blogs (low/high), (2) SNWs (medium/high), (3) virtual social worlds (high/high), (4) collaborative projects (low/low), (5) content communities (medium/low), and (6) virtual game worlds (high/low). We expand on this classification scheme, including aspects of social media that are related to human resource management, such as project management systems, information sharing systems, virtual learning environments, and engagement development platforms (see Table 1).

Using this expanded classification scheme of different types of social media, we identify the categories of social media that are pertinent to each of the HRM-related concepts (see Table 2). More specifically, we identify the types of social media relevant to each of 13 different HRM-related concepts. For example, only SNWs (medium "social presence/media richness" and high "self-presentation/self-disclosure") are relevant for employment selection, while all six categories of social media are relevant for cyberloafing. As such, a central aim of this chapter is to clarify the types of social media relevant to a broad range of HRM-related literatures.

Table 1.   Forms of Social Media.

| | | Social Presence/Media Richness | | |
		Low	Medium	High
Self-presentation/ Self-disclosure	High	Blogs, mobile applications (e.g., Foursquare, Pinterest), project management systems, collaborative software	Social networking web sites (e.g., Facebook, LinkedIn, Twitter, Tumblr, MySpace)	Virtual learning environment (Moodle, OLAT), virtual social worlds (e.g., Second Life)
	Low	Collaborative projects (e.g., Wikipedia), information sharing systems (e.g., BookCrossing)	Content communities (e.g., YouTube, Glassdoor, Reddit, Flickr, Slideshare)	Engagement development platforms (e.g., AvayaLive Engage, IntoSite), Virtual game worlds (e.g., World of Warcraft)

Source: Adapted from Kaplan and Haenlein (2010).

Table 2.   Applications of Social Media in HRM.

| Social Presence/Media Richness | Low | Medium | High | Low | Medium | High |
Self-Presentation/Self-Disclosure	Low	Low	Low	High	High	High
Branding		✓		✓	✓	
Organizational image		✓		✓	✓	
Applicant attraction		✓		✓	✓	
Employment selection					✓	
Employee productivity	✓	✓	✓	✓	✓	✓
Employee engagement and teamwork			✓	✓	✓	
Employee training	✓	✓	✓	✓	✓	✓
Knowledge management	✓	✓		✓	✓	✓
Social capital				✓	✓	✓
Organizational culture	✓	✓	✓	✓	✓	✓
Leadership	✓	✓	✓	✓	✓	✓
Cyberloafing	✓	✓	✓	✓	✓	✓
Disciplinary action					✓	

Note: The six categories correspond to the six categories in Table 1.

SOCIAL MEDIA AND EXTERNAL ORGANIZATIONAL STAKEHOLDERS

Branding

Social media use is prevalent in the field of marketing. The goal of branding in any social media strategy serves the organization both internally and externally. The social media branding strategy (a) builds a sense of membership or citizenship with the organization, (b) encourages the acceptance and communication of brand values, and (c) encourages the audience to engage in dialogue and promote the brand (Yan, 2011). Through branding efforts, social media provides new opportunities for organizational stakeholders to be informed, identify common interests, coordinate interventions, share information, organize interest groups more effectively, express and share opinions and demands, and monitor company behavior while shortening the response time available for corporations to respond to inquiries (Kane, Fichman, Gallaugher, & Glaser, 2009). As such, social media can increase stakeholder engagement in organizational issues and company responses to these relevant online communities (Hoffmann & Lutz, 2015). Of the six social media categories, blogs, mobile applications, content communities, and SNWs has relevant to branding like Facebook, Twitter, LinkedIn, Yelp, and Glassdoor (see Table 2). Though generally beyond the scope of human resource management, one important organizational stakeholder is the perspective job applicant. As such, organizational image is an important factor related to social media.

Organizational Image Impacting Job Applicants

Rynes and Cable (2003) suggest that a viable strategy to improve organizational image is to provide more information about the organization on an organization's web site. Cober, Brown, Blumental, Doverspike, and Levy (2000) conducted an examination of organizational web sites and found that compensation, culture, and developmental information are commonly communicated through organizational web sites. Over 90% of large U.S. companies report using their company web site to communicate job and organization information to potential job applicants (Capelli, 2001). Beyond web sites, various sources of social media (e.g., LinkedIn) may also be used to convey such organizational information. Based on Kaplan and

Haenlein's (2010) categories, blogs, mobile applications, content communities, and SNWs are also relevant to conveying organizational image to
job applicants (see Table 2).

From an employee recruitment perspective, organizations using employee
testimonials via social media combine the benefits of controlling the information presented to job seekers with interpersonal sources of information
afforded by social media (Van Hoye & Lievens, 2007). Moreover, information on various social media generally is not an organization's self-
presentation created to attract job seekers (Lievens & Harris, 2003). Like
many rating applications and online forums, such as Yelp and Glassdoor,
people can easily find information as well as provide opinions about an
organization. Because this media is published by a third party, the information is not sanitized or sanctioned by the organization (Cable & Yu,
2006). Negative information can spread quickly and on a massive scale,
thereby impacting an organization's reputation (McFarland & Ployhart,
2015). This may harm new employees' attraction to and assimilation into
an organization, perhaps contributing to recruitment problems, turnover,
and poor job attitudes.

Conversely, social media can reduce recruitment costs by up to 95%
over traditional recruitment sources and reduces hiring cycle time by
roughly 25% (Cober et al., 2000). As recruitment via social media dramatically increases the size of the applicant pool, attracting qualified candidates
becomes more complicated (Boehle, 2000). Leaders should embrace the
trend that employee social media activities increasingly shape organizational reputation. Reputation will no longer be dominantly influenced and
managed by communications departments, but by an organization's entire
workforce (Dreher, 2014). With each employee having the opportunity to
participate in online conversations, all organizational stakeholders become
more equal contributors to the reputation of the firm. Social media in company branding efforts can be helpful in building a good reputation. This is
important due to the established link between a positive corporate reputation and applicant intentions to apply for a job (Sivertzen, Nilsen, &
Olafsen, 2013). Allan, Mahto, and Otondo (2007) find that organization
image is important for shaping applicant evaluations of an organization
and its employment opportunities, in that image was positively related to
attitudes toward the organization and indirectly related to intentions to
pursue employment through attitudes. This is particularly striking in a
social media context, where job seekers access different types of information in the order the information is interesting to them. Social media allows

organizations to weave complex visual, auditory, and cognitive recruitment messages that are broadly distributed.

As such, from the organization's perspective, along with potential downside risks, social media provides the opportunity to communicate practically unlimited information about the organization, to communicate this information via multiple channels, and to communicate this information to a vast number of geographically dispersed job seekers at a relatively low cost (Cober, Brown, Keeping, & Levy, 2004; Cober et al., 2000). This capability highlights the importance of variables stemming from social media that have not been previously examined in the recruitment literature.

Organizational Attraction of Job Applicants

Switching now from the organizational to the recruiter/applicant perspective, recruiter blogs have long lauded the benefits of social media for recruitment purposes (McFarland & Ployhart, 2015). Social media affords the opportunity for employers to advertise job postings through employee networks, enabling employees to spread the word about job openings. This is a digital version of word-of-mouth but faster, larger in scale, and is more geographically distributed (McFarland & Ployhart, 2015). Based on Kaplan and Haenlein's (2010) categories, these digital versions of word-of-mouth include blogs, mobile applications, content communities, and SNWs (see Table 2). For job seekers in the early information-gathering stage, recruitment-targeted social media may be particularly relevant as job seekers attempt to narrow down a manageable set of organizations to pursue employment. Social media provides these seekers the ability to engage in extremely cost-effective searches to garner extensive information about organizations of interest (Allan et al., 2007). Professional, well-designed social media may help prospective applicants find information of interest and provide positive signals about the organization and its potential as an employer (Allan et al., 2007). Beyond active job seekers, leveraging social media may be a critical source for the recruitment of passive job candidates (McFarland & Ployhart, 2015).

It is important to note that perceptions of media richness, rather than objective characteristics, relate to changes in people's beliefs. This evidence suggests that richer media leads to more effective communication not just because a greater amount of information is transmitted but also because people are more likely to accept and internalize information from sources they perceive as rich (Cable & Yu, 2006). In general, face-to-face interactions and telephone calls are believed to be richer than webpages (Markus, 1994). In a recruitment context, these criteria suggest that face-to-face interactions with company representatives should be seen by applicants as more rich than the viewing of a company's web site or browsing an electronic bulletin board (Cable & Yu, 2006). Career fairs allow instant feedback in the form of questions and answers, permit multiple cues including verbal messages and body gestures, and can be tailored to each job seeker's interests and questions. Conversely, company web sites and electronic bulletin boards have less media richness because they generally are not customized to individual job seekers, do not allow for timely feedback, and are often text-based with no opportunity for verbal inflection or nonverbal cues (Cable & Yu, 2006).

As such, paying attention to social media use for recruitment purposes may be akin to training interviewers. Contact with online recruitment sources may also be as relevant as contact with organizational agents, such as interviewers, thereby influencing early attraction to the organization (Allan et al., 2007). Barber (1998) described early job pursuit decisions such that individuals are exposed to recruitment efforts from organizations that they may or may not have some existing mental image about. These individuals then use the information conveyed to make the first critical job search decision – whether to pursue employment with a particular organization.

In the context of social media recruiting, signaling theory suggests that without other information about an organization, applicants draw inferences about the organization based on cues gained from social media (Braddy, Meade, & Kroustalis, 2008). This generally occurs because applicants assume that social media characteristics are representative of the entire organization (Rynes, Bretz, & Gerhart, 1991). For example, if an organization maintains a social media presence that is not user friendly, job seekers may use this information to form a general negative impression of the organization because they assume it is indicative of how other practices and policies at the organization are implemented.

Issues related to person-organization fit are impacted by social media-based recruitment. This is particularly salient because it is now possible for potential applicants to provide information regarding their value preferences via the Web and to receive tailored feedback regarding their potential fit with the organization (Dineen, Ash, & Noe, 2002), thereby extending P-O fit research because this research has primarily considered P-O fit that is inferred by individuals rather than explicitly provided in the form of tailored feedback from the organization. Recruitment web sites provide real-time feedback about the job seeker's fit with an organization, which influences applicant attraction to the organization (Hu, Su, & Chen, 2007).

Job applicants and employers alike have historically had a great deal of control over the information and image presented to each other, resulting in information asymmetries (Bangerter, Roulin, & König, 2012; Sivertzen et al., 2013). In contrast, social media breaks down information barriers (McFarland & Ployhart, 2015). Web sites such as Glassdoor consist of employees rating the quality of their employing organization, allowing candidates to search postings and learn about the company culture (McFarland & Ployhart, 2015). Thus, future research that focuses on social media recruitment design features and content beyond the control of the organization would be very valuable.

SOCIAL NETWORKING WEB SITES AND EMPLOYMENT SELECTION

Mangla (2009) recounts an encounter of a 22-year-old master's degree student from California. The student allegedly posted on her Twitter feed, "Cisco just offered me a job! Now I have to weigh the utility of a fatty paycheck against the daily commute to San Jose and hating the work." A Cisco employee responded to the tweet. The applicant then turned down the job, likely because she believed that Cisco would withdraw the offer. One of the largest areas of research at the nexus of social media and HRM is that of employment selection. This area is said to be the "Wild West" world of personnel selection (Davison, Bing, Kluemper, & Roth, in press). Social media in selection occurs when organizational representatives view SNWs such as LinkedIn and/or Facebook (see Table 2) in the employment selection process, leading to the acceptance or rejection of job applicants (Kluemper, in press). As with any selection approach that has been developed within the past century, there are a wide range of issues that collectively provide information about the value and risk of such an approach. These issues generally relate to the extent that the approach will benefit the workplace (improved company performance and/or improved worker well-being) while taking into account associated risks and liabilities (e.g., privacy and discrimination) (Kluemper, Davison, Cao, & Wu, 2015). This section addresses a large number of these interrelated issues.

Career Builder, Reppler, Microsoft, and the Society for Human Resource Management conducted practitioner surveys to provide valuable information from which conclusions and trends may be drawn about SNW screening practices. CareerBuilder.com conducted a study of 2,667 U.S. hiring managers. Results showed that 45% of employers use SNWs to research job candidates, a jump of 22% from just a year earlier (Forty-five Percent of Employers, 2009). The industries with the highest use of SNWs are information technology (63%) and professional and business services (53%). Some SNWs were evaluated more frequently than others, with 29% using Facebook, 26% using LinkedIn, 21% using MySpace, and 7% using Twitter. After screening job applicants, 35% of employers reported rejecting candidates based on information uncovered from the search. Top reasons given for rejecting applicants include the applicant having provocative or inappropriate photos or information, content about drinking or drug use, bad-mouthing a previous employer, poor communication skills, discriminatory comments, lying about qualifications, and sharing confidential information from a previous employer. Conversely, 18% of employers reported hiring a candidate because of favorable information found. Top reasons given include a positive personality, good organizational fit, the profile supported the applicants' job qualifications, strong applicant creativity, good apparent communication skills, a well-rounded applicant, other SNW users posted positive information about the applicant, and that SNW information revealed applicant awards and accolades.

A survey of 300 hiring managers conducted by Reppler.com found that 91% of hiring managers use SNWs to screen applicants. The most common SNWs were Facebook (76%), Twitter (53%), and LinkedIn (48%). In this survey, 69% of respondents indicated eliminating candidates due to negative SNW information, while 68% reported hiring a candidate due to observing positive information. Reasons given for eliminating and accepting applicants were similar to those found in the Career Builder survey earlier.

Microsoft sanctioned a multinational survey to examine the role of online information in the hiring process (Cross-tab Marketing Services, 2010), though screening any online information is somewhat broader than screening SNWs. The survey included 1,345 consumers and 1,106 HR professionals, hiring managers, or recruiters. These respondents were equally drawn from the United States, the United Kingdom, Germany, and France. Results reveal that the percentage of hiring managers who use online information and the percentage of companies with policies requiring such screening is highest in the United States (79% and 75%, respectively) followed by the United Kingdom (47% and 48%, respectively), Germany (59% and 21%, respectively), and France (23% and 21%, respectively). Further, 70% of U.S. hiring managers report having rejected job applicants based on online information, 41% for the United Kingdom, 16% for

Germany, and 14% for France. Also, roughly a third of consumers took no steps to manage their online reputation, but consumers who did take steps to manage their digital reputation were much less concerned about online searches.

Finally, the Society for Human Resource Management (SHRM, 2011) surveyed 541 HR professionals responsible for staffing. Results indicate that 67% have never used SNWs to screen applicants and do not plan to do so, 4% used them previously but will not in the future, 11% never have but plan to, and 18% reported using SNWs to screen applicants currently. Notably, for-profit organizations are more likely to utilize SNW screening than their nonprofit and governmental counterparts. For example, 44% of privately owned for-profit organizations reported using SNWs to screen applicants. The top reason provided as to why these organizations conduct screen SNWs is the perception that hiring managers can obtain more information about an applicant than can be gained with a resume and cover letter. Further, the most frequently used SNWs were LinkedIn (85%), Facebook (78%), far more than MySpace (13%), Twitter (11%), and other SNWs.

Based on these surveys, common themes, trends, and some inconsistencies emerge. A common theme is that SNW screening is prevalent (though more-so in the United States than in other countries). Further, the prevalence of SNW screening may depend on the type of job and/or industry of the applicant being evaluated (e.g., for-profits and the technology and business sectors). Trends seem to include a shift from viewing SNWs such as Facebook to more professional web sites such as LinkedIn (Kluemper, McLarty, & Rosen, 2013; McLarty, Kluemper, & Rosen, 2013). Also, HR driven SNW screening policies appear to be on the rise. As far as inconsistencies, it is difficult to determine whether SNW screening is increasing or decreasing. One possibility is that both are true (Kluemper, 2013). It seems plausible that HR representatives may be less likely to use SNWs for screening purposes (likely due to the legal and other risks associated with such use), while non-HR hiring managers may be more likely to screen using SNWs (perhaps due to the ease of accessing what they perceive as a potential treasure trove of information about the job applicant). These themes, trends, and inconsistencies underscore the need for extensive academic study and debate regarding each of the issues.

Privacy

The issue of SNW privacy is particularly controversial, as the rapid evolution of technology has presented unique legal and ethical challenges

(Kluemper, 2013). The fourth Amendment to the U.S. Constitution implies an expectation of privacy. However, it is a current debate whether SNW users have a reasonable expectation of privacy protected by law (Brandenburg, 2008). There is widespread disagreement as to what is private and public with SNWs. Applicants may view obtaining SNW information as an invasion of privacy, while organizations may view SNWs as legitimate public information (Gustafson, 2012). In this vein, just 33% of HR managers are concerned about invading the privacy of applicants via SNWs (SHRM, 2011). Case law has established that web sites viewable to the public do not have a reasonable expectation of privacy (*J. S., v. Bethlehem Area Sch. Dist.*, 2000) though monitoring private Internet chat rooms is illegal (*Pietrylo v. Hillstone Restaurant Group*, 2008). To add further confusion, an expectation of privacy may depend in part on the nature of the job, while job applicants have less of an expectation of privacy from that of employees (Woska, 2007).

On the one hand, organizations have a duty to protect stakeholders from injury initiated by employees that the employer knows or "should have known" to pose a risk to others. Thus, organizations that fail to conduct thorough background investigations may be liable for damages under the tort of negligent hiring (Woska, 2007), particularly for high-profile positions and those that have the potential to adversely impact others (e.g., law enforcement). On the other hand, several existing statutes may be relevant to SNW screening. The U.S. Fair Credit Reporting Act may apply to companies that search SNWs like Facebook, particularly for information that is intended to be private (Juffras, 2010). The Stored Communications Act may be relevant, as it makes the intentional access of online databases illegal (Brandenburg, 2008), which may include SNWs. The European Union's Data Privacy Directive of 1995 extends to SNWs and requires consent by EU applicants (Massey, 2009). Further, SNW screening for employment purposes could violate the particular web site's terms of use (Willey et al., 2012).

Smith and Kidder (2010) identify several ways that hiring managers can gain access to SNWs such as Facebook even when pages are set as private, such as "friending" applicants, asking existing employees to report on friends, or by employing students from the same university as a way of gaining access to applicant profiles. Recent media reports of companies asking applicants for SNW login information and a tactic termed "over the shoulder" screening (in which applicants are required to log on during the application process so that hiring managers can review private online information) has led to applicant anger and frustration, resulting in a wide range of recent legislation and guidance on the issue.

Several states have now passed legislation which, in general, makes it illegal for an employer to request an applicant to provide a password (or other related account information) or to demand access to an applicant's profile on a social networking web site. To respect applicant privacy, organizations should consider notifying prospective applicants that social media searches may be conducted so that the applicant is aware that there is no expectation of privacy, or even go one step further by obtaining written informed consent (Kaslow, Patterson, & Gottlieb, 2011).

Discrimination

The SHRM survey (2011) indicates that 66% of HR managers are concerned about legal risks associated with SNW screening. These include issues about protected characteristics such as age, race, gender, and religious affiliation. Further, many recent academic publications identify issues of discrimination pertaining to SNW screening (Brown & Vaughn, 2011; Davison, Maraist, Hamilton, & Bing, 2012; Gustafson, 2012; Kluemper & Rosen, 2009; Kluemper, Rosen, & Mossholder, 2012; Roth, Bobko, Van Iddekinge, & Thatcher, 2016; Slovensky & Ross, 2012; Smith & Kidder, 2010; Willey et al., 2012). There are two basic forms in which discrimination can occur during the selection process: disparate treatment, when an applicant is treated differently based on a protected class status, and adverse impact, a facially neutral employment practice that has the result of disproportionately affecting an underrepresented group. SNW screening creates a more substantial risk of disparate treatment than many other selection methods. This is due to the prevalence protected class status information on SNWs, such as religion or certain disabilities not found in a resume or in-person interview (Davison et al., 2012). Disparate impact may occur, for example, with older and socioeconomically disadvantaged groups (e.g., Spanish-dominant Hispanics) who have less access to SNWs (Davison et al., 2012).

Facebook users themselves report that the following information is available on their SNW profiles: sexual orientation, relationship status, birth date, religious beliefs, and political affiliation (Karl, Peluchette, & Schlaegel, 2010). Further, gender and race are associated with the types of SNWs a user is likely to adopt (Pike, 2011) while older individuals are less likely to adopt SNWs altogether (Smith & Kidder, 2010). Those older SNW users are likely to post information in different ways and may not be as comfortable when posting personal information (Epstein, 2008). This may be a particularly relevant issue, given that the job applicant and hiring manager are often from different generations (Smith & Kidder, 2010). Also, the information available on SNWs may lead to similarity bias by the individual doing the hiring (Smith & Kidder, 2010), which represents an additional factor that may lead to discriminatory hiring.

The primary U.S. Federal laws relating to SNW discrimination on the basis race, color, religion, sex, gender, nation of origin, disability, and age are Title VII of the Civil Right Act, the Americans with Disabilities Act, and the Age Discrimination in Employment Act. For example, Title VII dictates that preemployment inquiries are not lawful if they disproportionately eliminate from consideration applicants based on protected class status not justified through business necessity/job relatedness (Woska, 2007). Beyond U.S. Federal law, most states have established legal protection for sexual orientation as well as other characteristics. Finally, though the types of groups who enjoy legal protection differs by country, many countries provide similar or expanded legal protection from employment discrimination for various groups (Myors et al., 2008).

Thus, due to the prevalence of SNW screening and the likelihood that discrimination occurs in SNW screening context, it is likely that SNW-related discrimination cases will arise (Gustafson, 2012). Roth and colleagues (2016) found no articles that reported empirical data on adverse impact when screening SNWs. The chapter provides convincing evidence that a lower representation of underrepresented groups as it relates to Internet access may bias the rater, potentially leading to adverse impact. Increasingly, organizations recognize the value of keeping records of social media use to defend against potential legal claims for defamation, discrimination, or to comply with government regulations (Vega, 2010). Future research into the issue of discrimination via SNW screening is needed, particularly given the likely dynamic rate of change in both social media technologies and related regulation.

Negligent Hiring

Organizations should conduct reasonable background checks when screening applicants because failure to do so incurs legal liability for employers (Kluemper, 2013). In particular, organizations involved in public safety may find themselves defending a lawsuit when employees engage in illegal behavior and it is discovered that information about prior illegal behavior was available at the time of hire (Levashina & Campion, 2009). As such, failing to screen SNWs may itself incur legal liability, particularly for companies in particular industries (Slovensky & Ross, 2012). Thus, if an employer identifies (or should have identified) potential disqualifying SNW information about a job applicant but still hires the individual, the employer could be sued for negligent hiring if the employee later harms a coworker, customer, client, or other stakeholder (Davison et al., 2012).

Validity

There are several forms of validity, each relevant to SNW screening (Kluemper, 2013), such as construct validity, content validity, convergent validity, concurrent validity, face validity, criterion-related validity, and incremental validity. First, in the context of SNWs, screeners may be casually scanning profiles, thus not attempting to measure anything in particular. If they are attempting to measure a particular set of constructs, the question becomes whether this operationalization actually measures what it claims to. Construct validity consists of whether the operationalization of a construct actually measures what it purports to measure. Content validity assesses whether the measure comprehensively covers all aspects of this construct. Convergent validity evaluates whether the measure correlates with other measures that it is theoretically predicted to correlate with, while concurrent validity assesses whether a construct correlates with other measures of the same construct. Face validity measures whether a measure appears to measure what it claims to be measuring. Though each of these forms of validity are important, in the context of SNW screening, a critical form of validity is criterion-related or predictive validity, such that there is a correlation between what is assessed via SNWs and relevant outcomes. Job relatedness has been identified as an important aspect of SNW screening (Smith & Kidder, 2010). Criterion-related validity establishes that a selection test is job-related (i.e., the construct being measured related to a core function of the job in question). In the context of employment selection, the most relevant outcome is task performance, such that the SNW evaluation is able to identify and weed out individuals that would otherwise yield lower levels of performance on the job. Finally, incremental validity, whether a new test adds predictive value beyond existing methods, needs to be evaluated in relation to application blanks, biodata, self-report personality tests, etc. (Roth et al., 2016).

To further stress the importance of criterion-related validity, any selection test that fails to provide criterion-related validity serves little purpose in an employment selection system. This should be the first and most important hurdle for SNW screening (Kluemper, 2013). If SNWs cannot be shown to establish criterion-related validity, particularly given the legal issues, these assessments serve little purpose. With that said, several established selection methods (e.g., interviews, cognitive ability tests, personality tests) have been studied across hundreds if not thousands of academic studies attempting to demonstrate and improve criterion-related validity. SNW screening is in its infancy and practice has outstripped research in this area. There are two implications of this. First, academics need to study this phenomenon to learn whether SNW screening has criterion-related validity and/or design ways to improve criterion-related validity. Second, practitioners should be aware that little evidence exists regarding this important issue. This should serve as a warning that current SNW screening approaches may not yield valid and legally defensible results, despite being intuitively appealing to those currently engaging in SNW screening.

This is not to say that the potential for criterion-related validity does not exist. Although 45% of HR managers believe that information about job candidates taken from SNWs may not be relevant to job performance (SHRM, 2011), SNWs may reveal unique job-relevant applicant information, such as education, work history, and professional membership (Davison et al., 2012). Though little evidence yet exists, it stands to reason that the presence of information about, for example,, drug use, discriminatory comments, or misrepresentations of qualifications (Forty-five Percent of Employers, 2009) might identify individuals with low levels of future job performance or other negative organizational outcomes. In this vein, the criterion-related validity of SNWs should also be assessed in relation to other variables beyond task performance, such as organizational citizenship behavior, workplace deviance, lateness, absenteeism, turnover (Roth et al., 2016). Further, there are various issues which may harm the validity of a selection method, such as a lack of reliability, low generalizability, and applicant impression management. These potential threats to validity are particularly relevant to SNW screening.

Reliability

Reliability represents various ways to demonstrate that a measure is consistent and is a necessary, but not sufficient, condition for validity. In other words, reliably assessing a construct does not mean the approach is valid, but failing to establish consistency of measurement, by definition, indicates that the selection method lacks validity. Three types of reliability are germane to SNW screening (Kluemper, 2013): test-retest reliability (consistent from one test administration to the next), inter-rater reliability (the degree to which test scores are consistent when measurements are taken by different evaluators), and internal consistency reliability (the consistency of results across independent pieces of information within an assessment).

SNW information can be inaccurate (Smith & Kidder, 2010), such as information that is false (Davison et al., 2012) or widely exaggerated, perhaps even inaccurately posted by others without the users' knowledge or consent. In addition, there is the potential to mistake another user's identity with that of the applicant's, differences in information across multiple user accounts, and the creation of imitation accounts (Slovensky & Ross, 2012), thereby creating further inconsistencies. The variability in the type and amount of information available via SNWs prevents a completely standardized approach to collecting profile information (Brown & Vaughn, 2011) and requires evaluators to deal with incomplete information (Roth et al., 2016). In support of this notion, 48% of HR managers are concerned about the inability to verify information from an applicant's SNW, while 34% are concerned that not all job candidates have information available on SNWs (SHRM, 2011).

In addition, changes in one's behaviors across the phases of one's life (Slovensky & Ross, 2012) potentially lead to inconsistent SNW screening results over time, potentially harming test-retest reliability. This incomplete information and inconsistencies across SNW profiles likely leads to differences in evaluative judgments from independent raters, a potential problem for inter-rater reliability. Finally, information (or entire SNW profiles) that may be present for one job applicant may not be present for all applicants, thereby creating a challenge to the generation of internal consistency reliability. Thus, problems associated with reliability when screening SNWs must be taken into consideration and create a series of problems for potential viability of SNW screening.

Generalizability

The concept of generalizability implies that what may be valid or reliable in one context may not be in a different context. One aspect of SNW screening that relates to generalizability is that there are numerous SNWs with divergent purposes, user demographics, ability to restrict access, and volume and type of information provided (Kluemper, 2013). For example, there are numerous differences between Facebook and LinkedIn regarding a wide range of issues. Facebook (when compared to LinkedIn) has more users, generally has more information, is typically geared toward "friends" (rather than professional "connections"), is more likely to have restricted access, and is the focus of much of the legislation described earlier. LinkedIn, on the other hand, is more like an expanded resume and is used for the explicit purpose of connecting professionally, including that of recruitment and selection. Therefore, on just about any aspect of SNW screening, issues regarding Facebook or MySpace may not be germane to LinkedIn or Twitter, and vice versa.

Another aspect of generalizability relates to the potentially divergent relevance of SNW screening for various occupations. For example, SNW screening may be more prevalent with IT, professional, and business service positions (Forty-five Percent of Employers, 2009). As such, SNW screening may be more widespread, and/or more widely accepted by applicants in certain industries such as military suppliers, banking, child care, and private security firms (Slovensky & Ross, 2012). Further, it stands to reason that certain aspects of SNW information may be more relevant to some jobs than others. For instance, it may be more job-relevant to screen out gang members as prison guards, discriminatory police officers, drug users in industrial manufacturing, and those who share confidential information about employers in high security jobs (Kluemper, 2013). Thus, the extensiveness of related approaches such as background checks should reflect the severity of the risk posed to organizational stakeholders if the applicant is hired (Woska, 2007). In addition, all professions are not equivalent with regard to privacy rights. For example, according to the Department of Labor, the Employee Polygraph Protection Act of 1988 applies to most private employers, but does not cover federal, state, local government agencies, and private employers related to national security. It stands to reason that selected occupations (e.g., national security) may be more likely (perhaps even legally compelled) to conduct more invasive SNW screening, such as "friending" and "over the shoulder" screening (Kluemper, 2013). It should also be noted that these practices will likely evoke lawsuits due to privacy concerns. Legislation and case law will continue to emerge on this issue. For these reasons, organizations lacking a strong justification to engage in invasive SNW screening practices should avoid them.

Finally, the little we now know about SNW screening is largely based on findings from young college students in the United States (Kluemper,

2013). Although this may be the most relevant context in which to begin study (e.g., Facebook began primarily with U.S. college students), a more generalizable range of age groups, national cultures, occupations, and industries need to be considered in future research.

Impression Management

As noted by the Vice President of HR at CareerBuilder.com Rosemary Haefner, "Social networking is a great way to make connections with potential job opportunities and promote your personal brand across the Internet" "Make sure you are using this resource to your advantage by conveying a professional image and underscoring your qualifications" (Forty-five Percent of Employers, 2009). However, little is known about the prevalence of impression management (personal branding) via SNWs such as Facebook and LinkedIn, particularly for employment purposes. It has been suggested that SNW users engage in self-presentation to influence the impressions of others (Karl et al., 2010) and some content can be manipulated by users to present themselves in a more favorable manner (Kluemper et al., 2012). Users can clean up SNWs to remove embarrassing or offensive content (Davison et al., 2012), even utilizing "SNW scrubbing" firms to help manage their SNW information (Shiller, 2010). Pike (2011) found that the more value a user places on self-presentation via SNWs, the more suitable the candidate will be perceived by a hiring manager. Further, Bohnert and Ross (2010) conducted a laboratory study using evaluations of hypothetical job candidates and concluded that individuals with positive SNW profiles that were more family oriented or professional were seen as more suitable for employment than those with party oriented SNW pro-files. Thus, developing a favorable online presence seems to have a positive impact on hiring decisions.

Although SNW users may attempt to impress others, these distortions may depend on the intended viewer (Davison, Maraist, & Bing, 2011) such that users may be creating them for specific audiences or blurring personal, family, and professional identities (Pike, 2011). SNW users engage in impression management, but are often misdirected or insufficient in their efforts. In particular, SNW users find impression management difficult, particularly during life changes or when attempting to manage multiple audiences (Lebrecque et al., 2011). Further, it has been suggested that information might be more accurate on certain SNWs (e.g., Facebook) because one's connections can directly comment on inaccurate information

(Davison et al., 2011). This context has the potential to yield less censored SNW information (Davison et al., 2012). Kluemper and Rosen (2009) argue that SNWs may be less susceptible to socially desirable responding than other selection methods such as personality tests. Kluemper et al. (2012) argue that faking SNW information runs counter to the fundamental purpose of certain SNWs (i.e., Facebook) and that some information may be difficult to fake via social media, such as information posted to a user's web site by others, number of friends, and the content of photos. Thus, some hiring managers may focus on SNW information written by "friends" of the applicant, as such information may be seen as less subject to impression management attempts (Slovensky & Ross, 2012). In support of this perspective, Back and colleagues (2010) found that ratings of Big Five personality via SNWs is far more closely aligned with actual personality rather than ideal-self ratings of personality, indicating that SNWs accurately represent user personality traits. Further, there is a strong correlation between a SNW users' online and offline identity, but a weak relationship between an applicants' SNW identity and self-presentation on a resume (Pike, 2011).

Thus, it appears that at least some form of impression management via SNWs is possible and may have a favorable impact on hiring decisions. However, manipulating other aspects of a profile may be difficult or even impossible and, further, that SNW users may choose not to alter their profiles for the reasons described earlier. Because impression management may harm validity, it is important that future research seek to better understand the characteristics of those who choose to engage in SNW impression management, the extent that it is done, and in what contexts.

Some users may use SNWS for the purpose of personal branding, such that personal profiles may be designed with the intention of networking for job opportunities. This is likely the case for SNWs such as LinkedIn and may be increasingly true for SNWs such as Facebook (Kluemper, 2013). In this vein, applicants with positive profiles may wish that their SNW profile is evaluated, believing that this may provide some advantage in the job search process. It is clear that the nature of the content of SNWs such as Facebook has changed dramatically in recent years. For example, the nature of the information posted in the first few years of Facebook was generally geared toward college peers. However, that online behavior changed when the nature of college student network connections changed to include parents and coworkers (Kluemper, 2013). It is difficult to predict how these divergent SNW platforms (e.g., Facebook and LinkedIn) and intended audiences (e.g., employers) will change over time. However, it is clear that the use of different social media platforms associated with different parts of our lives creates a tension related to balancing multiple online identities.

In addition, social media are increasingly becoming a more salient part of our personal and professional identities. For example, Schwartz and Halegoua (2015) note that Foursquare users understand their check-ins are part of their presentation of their online persona. Using multiple social media platforms including sub-groups of acquaintances associated with different platforms are strategies noted by Frampton and Child (2013) as allowing individuals to manage their privacy. Knight and Weedon (2014) support this notion by arguing that social media allows individuals to perform various roles on our multimodal lives, as a professional, a parent, an acquaintance, and a colleague. Conversely, Qualman (2012) expresses concern about how social media is breaking down what he terms a "social schizophrenia" in an individual's identity. According to Qualman, it is problematic for an employee to express different identities within the virtual world offered by social media – what he terms as "party and work personalities." In the SNW screening context, this relates to the issue of applicant reactions when potential employers access such information. As such, future research is needed to investigate the impact of these multiple online identities.

Applicant Reactions

Applicants who become aware that their social media information has been evaluated by an employer may view the organization's selection procedure as unfair. This position is supported by the Manpower survey that reports 56% of job applicants would view an organization as unethical for considering their social media profiles when hiring and 43% reported they would "feel outraged" if a firm used their social media information to screen them prior to making a hiring decision (Slovensky & Ross, 2012). As such, applicants, if they become aware that SNW information has been used by a hiring manager, may develop perceptions of informational, distributive, and procedural injustice possibly resulting in a reduction of applicant attraction to the organization (Slovensky & Ross, 2012). Applicants have been shown to have more favorable views of certain selection approaches (e.g., job interviews, job knowledge tests, and work sample tests) than others (e.g., cognitive ability tests, personality tests, and college transcripts) (Reeve & Schultz, 2004), such that applicants who view the hiring process as intrusive or lacking validity may be more likely to perceive the process as unfair and potentially file a lawsuit (Wallace, Page, & Lippstreu, 2006).

Applicants might perceive that they have more of a right to SNW privacy than the law provides, leading qualified applicants to remove themselves from consideration from a job. Further, these negative applicant reactions may be contagious, affecting firm reputation via others in the users' social network (Davison et al., 2012). Black, Johnson, Takach, and Stone (2012) have developed a theoretical model regarding applicant reactions to SNW screening. The authors provide theoretical rational and hypotheses regarding potential negative applicant reactions to social network screening due to informational, procedural, socio-cultural, and individual factors. These factors are posited to result in negative organizational consequences such as fewer job acceptances, applicants' propensity to sue, and damage to company reputation.

Empirical research regarding applicant reactions to SNW screening has begun to emerge. Gustafson (2012) found that undergraduate students view Facebook screening as unfair, but that these negative perceptions were reduced when applicants were asked permission to access the SNW. Siebert, Downes, and Chrostopher (2012) found that the use of social network screening did not impact organizational attractiveness or intentions to pursue employment, even though social network screening did negatively impact applicant attitudes toward the selection procedure. However, more invasive social network screening procedures (i.e., requiring the acceptance of a friend request from the hiring manager) had negative effects on applicant reactions. Sanchez, Roberts, Freeman, and Clayton (2012) found no negative effects of SNW screening on five applicant reaction variables: perceptions of SNW checks, organizational attractiveness, job pursuit intentions, procedural justice, and informational justice. Further, participants' perceptions to SNW checks were, counter to the hypotheses, positively related to the applicant reaction constructs. The authors explain these findings by arguing that college-age applicants generally expect employers to screen SNW profiles. Thus, little is known about applicant reactions to SNW screening. A wider range of academic study is needed to better understand these issues.

Approaches to SNW Screening

Assessing personality via SNWs is one of the primary approaches used by hiring managers (Davison et al., 2012; Pike, 2011). This is not surprising, as undergraduate students higher in conscientiousness, agreeableness, and emotional stability are shown to be less likely to report posting problematic content on SNW profiles (Karl et al., 2010). Kluemper and Rosen (2009) conducted a study of the Big Five personality traits, intelligence, and grade point average, based on Facebook profiles. Results indicate that each of these characteristics can be reliably assessed via SNW profiles. Further, more intelligent and emotionally stable raters were shown to be more accurate in the evaluation of SNW profiles than their less intelligent and neurotic counterparts.

Kluemper et al. (2012) provide evidence from two studies that Facebook can be used by trained evaluators to reliably assess various personality traits, traits shown in existing literature to predict academic and job success and to be legally defensible for selection purposes. Study 1 results conclude that Facebook-rated personality (1) correlates with traditional self-reported personality, (2) demonstrates internal consistency and inter-rater reliability for personality and hireability, (3) correlates with evaluator preferences to hire the Facebook user, and (4) correlates with supervisor ratings of job performance for a sub-sample of Facebook users who were employed six months later. Study 2 results conclude that Facebook-rated personality (1) correlates with traditional self-reported personality tests, (2) demonstrates internal consistency and inter-rater reliability, (3) is stronger than self-reported personality and IQ in predicting academic success, and (4) provides incremental prediction of academic performance beyond what was obtained from self-rated personality and intelligence tests combined. Taken together, these studies provide initial evidence that information available on Facebook can be used to identify individuals who are more successful in college and on the job.

It has also been suggested that SNWs might be able to assess particular aspects of knowledge, skills, abilities, and other characteristics (KSAOs) beyond personality traits. Possible KSAOs that might be assessed via SNWs include fluency in a particular language, technical proficiencies, creative outlets, teamwork skills (Smith & Kidder, 2010), network ability, creativity (Davison et al., 2012), communication, interpersonal, leadership, persuasion, and negotiation skills (Roth et al., 2016). Written communication, including grammar, spelling, and composition may be assessed, though informal writing may not represent the applicant's workplace communication style (Davison et al., 2012). However, some KSAO information obtained via SNWs is likely to be largely redundant with information obtained via established screening techniques (Davison et al., 2012). For example, typical poor grammar and misspellings may not provide value beyond other selection methods, such as writing samples (Davison et al., 2012). More work is needed in this area to identify whether these KSAOs can be accurately assessed via SNW screening and whether criterion-related validity can be established.

A recent study by Van Iddekinge and colleagues (2013) found that Facebook ratings of KSAOs did not predict job performance. That is, the validity of actual recruiters looking at job applicant Facebook pages was empirically unrelated to job performance. Although this study used college recruiters to rate student Facebook profiles and obtained supervisor ratings of job performance one year later, this study utilized only one untrained evaluator per profile, with different evaluators across profiles, which likely results in subsequent unreliability of assessment (Davison, Bing, Kluemper, & Roth, in press). Further, the KSAOs measured were not necessarily relevant to each of the wide range of students' subsequent occupations.

Given the divergent results from Kluemper and colleagues and Van Iddekinge and colleagues, minimal and conflicting evidence exists with regard to the validity of using Facebook profiles for selection purposes. Based on these preliminary results, it seems that personality testing may be superior to assessing KSAOs, at least when using Facebook. Further, it may be that Facebook is superior as a means to predict academic performance rather than job performance, yielding potential implications for academic selection versus employment selection. Future research needs to shed light on these open questions.

Another approach is that of biographical data. Biodata identifies questions about life and work experiences and is based on the premise that past behaviors, opinions, values, beliefs, and attitudes will predict future behavior. Biodata has been shown to have moderate criterion-related validity and is generally legally defensible (Mumford, Costanza, Connelly, & Johnson, 1996). As such, it has been suggested that SNW screening has strong similarities to Davison et al. (2012) and would benefit from an approach based on the biodata literature (Slovensky & Ross, 2012).

Another potential approach is person-organizational fit. It is widely acknowledged that hiring managers may try to measure person-organization fit via SNW screening (Davison et al., 2012; Roth et al., 2016; Slovensky & Ross, 2012). However, this approach likely tends to be more subjective than other approaches discussed here, so demonstrating criterion-related validity in the SNW context presents a challenge for a P/O fit approach. An approach to P/O fit would need to be highly structured, such as formally assessing fit characteristics like innovation, team orientation, and achievement orientation at the organizational level, then assessing them via SNW profiles (Kluemper, 2013).

Probably the most common current approach to SNW screening is to view profiles for potential disqualifying information. This approach resembles a type of background check. While it seems feasible that applicants with SNW information pertaining to drug use, discriminatory comments, misrepresented qualifications, or shared confidential information about a current employer (Forty-five Percent of Employers, 2009) might provide a strong basis to reject an applicant. Relatedly, a primary concern of some organizations may be related to public relations, such that potential employees have a "clean" online presence not likely to harm the organization if public access information is viewed by company stakeholders. However, other information used to disqualify candidates might be more idiosyncratic and subjective. For example, drinking is legal in the United States for individuals at least 21 years of age. Drinking socially does not necessarily equate to drinking on the job (which is likely against company policy). Some SNW screeners, particularly when there are no specific established criteria with which to assess, may use this information to eliminate a candidate from contention. Other screeners may consider the photo appropriate in a social context or even view the applicant more favorably due to an impression that the applicant gets along well with others or has a wider range of network connections (Kluemper, 2013). Eliminating candidates based on "gut feel" is less likely to be valid and more likely to involve disparate treatment or adverse impact. With any of these potential SNW screening approaches, there are several best practices that should improve validity and/or decrease legal risks.

This section endeavored to elucidate the current state of research and practice regarding SNW screening. In doing so, a large number of issues were outlined regarding this practice, such as privacy, discrimination, negligent hiring, validity, reliability, generalizability, impression management, and applicant reactions. Various established selection methods have addressed similar issues in past research, and thus SNW screening may be further informed through a more detailed investigation of personality testing, structured interviews, cognitive ability tests, and various approaches dealing with personal information. These approaches yield a range of best practices that should be incorporated into organizational social screening policies. In general, the absence of such accumulation of knowledge in the area of SNW screening should result in caution on the part of practitioners attempting screen SNWs for hiring purposes. At the same time, several avenues for academic research are highlighted and sorely needed this nascent area.

Social Media Policies

Another take-away from the review of SNW screening is the need for social media and SNW screening policies. The purpose of social media policies is to communicate organizational, legal, and regulatory rules to employees and leaders at all organizational levels, to convey a clear understanding of appropriate and lawful social media use at work, and to aid companies in demonstrating compliance to courts, regulators, and other stakeholders (Altimeter, 2011; Flynn, 2012). Social media policies are increasingly salient as part of organizational governance. To minimize potential resistance to such policies, Johnston (2015) suggests engaging employees as part of the development process and the format should focus on clarity, simplicity, and tone.

Organizations should carefully consider their social media policies as the short-term lack of productivity may be used by employees to restore and maintain work-life balance, which fosters positive employee attitudes organization and long-term productivity gains (Moqbel, Nevo, & Kock, 2013). Social media screening policies must be written broadly enough to adapt to changing technologies, yet specific enough to deal with a myriad of situations that may result from applicants and employees (Slovensky & Ross, 2012). Obtained information should be securely stored and should conform to the various laws within country and jurisdiction. Further, the value of the information should be balanced against ethical standards and considerations of company reputation (Slovensky & Ross, 2012).

SOCIAL MEDIA TO ENHANCE ORGANIZATIONAL PERFORMANCE

Employee Productivity

Brodkin (2008) found that about a quarter of businesses block employee access to SNWs due to concerns about wasting time, leaking confidential information, and becoming more vulnerable to computer viruses. Job incumbents face the challenge of remaining productive at work while simultaneously being distracted by social media (Akinbode, Opayemi, & Sokefun, 2013). Information overload, which may result from social media, might also impact employee productivity (Al-Busaidi, 2014). One outcome of our high-tech society is that multitasking is becoming normal in all parts of life, with societal pressures to continue working professionally in what would have previously been personal time and to stay connected socially while at work (Turkle, 2011).

Social media use may be seen by employers as a risk of reduced productivity (D'Abate & Eddy, 2007). However, the use of social networking sites by employees can help enhance job satisfaction directly and organizational commitment indirectly, leading to improved job performance (Moqbel et al., 2013). Vuori and Okkonen (2012) provide empirical support for the importance of employee perceptions of task overload and ease of use, such that the best way to motivate employees to use a social media platform for knowledge sharing is to assure them that by using the platform eases their workload, rather than increasing it. Leidner, Koch, and Gonzalez (2010) found that the ability of employees to access Facebook at work increases retention and organizational commitment − particularly for new hires, as this allows for a social connection with family, friends, and other coworkers while in the workplace, leading to a better work-life balance (Leidner et al., 2010). For example, Ellison, Steinfield, and Lampe (2007) found a strong association between the prevalence of Facebook use and social capital and that using social media can help certain users to improve self-esteem and life satisfaction.

As such, social media can impact employee performance either positively or negatively, as a time waster or a way to improve job-related attitudes, as a stressor or as stress relief. Of the six social media categories, all have the potential to impact job performance (see Table 2), though the different types of social media (e.g., Facebook vs. Wikipedia) will have differential impacts on performance depending on how each are used. The remaining HRM-related concepts all have performance implications and each will focus on different ways that social media will have an impact.

Employee Engagement and Teamwork

Perhaps the greatest risk of social media may be choosing not to utilize this emerging technology (Timimi, 2013). Social media provides organizations with an outlet that fosters engagement and dialogue in ways that company web sites fail to achieve (Walters, Burnett, Lamm, & Lucas, 2009). Social media helps employees to connect, inform, inspire, and track other employees to collaboratively create, find, share, and evaluate the available information (Nov, Naaman, & Ye, 2010). Murphy (2010) note that the characteristics of social media facilitates organizations to foster employee engagement, promote information sharing for problem solving, improve and enhance business agility, minimize task duplication, promote stronger engagement initiatives with senior employees, gain sustainable competitive advantage in numerous human resource management functions ranging from talent acquisition and talent deployment to leadership development and succession planning. In these ways, social media helps to improve employee engagement.

Social media facilitates organizations to successfully engage its employees through a platform of dialogue exchange integrating employees into the internal culture of the organization through a sense of community building and a vision sharing process (Parry & Solidoro, 2013). For example, internal online social groups monitored by organizations can enable employees to share grievances and also post innovative ideas for change management thus replacing the traditional use of suggestion boxes (Parry & Solidoro, 2013). Similarly, online help forms within the organizations, such as company blogs, can help bring employees from different business units together via a common platform where they can post their work-related problems or issues to receive a range of creative approaches to solve these issues. Such forums will not only help achieve diverse viewpoints on issues from employees operating in different functional areas or business units but also enable organizations to strengthen their internal climate and build a sense of belongingness and connectedness among employees.

McFarland and Ployhart (2015) identify teamwork as relevant to social media, though team dynamics may be quite different in social media contexts (Bell & Kozlowski, 2002; Hoch & Kozlowski, 2014). Social networking is not simply one tool or approach; rather, it is comprised of a wide array of tools that facilitate "social constructivism," that is, the potential for individuals who are separated by time and/or location to collaborate on a common project. In this vein, the virtual team literature can be used to help inform research on social media (Bell & Kozlowski, 2002; Hoch & Kozlowski, 2014; Maznevski & Chudoba, 2000). As such, social media allows users to develop and maintain relationships with coworkers with similar needs, interests, or problems (Cho, Chen, & Chung, 2010; Lee & Ma, 2011). In short, social media can serve as a medium through which to help foster employee engagement through more effective teamwork.

A 2008 study by the Aberdeen group notes that companies which make use of different social networking tools like wikis, blogs, organizational web sites, online forums, etc. achieved an annual increment of 18% in engagement levels of their employees compared to only 1% rise in employees of those organizations which did not use any form of social media (Aberdeen Group, 2008). Similarly, another study conducted in 2012 by APCI and Gagen McDonald revealed that 58% of the employees that responded with a desire to work for an organization that uses social media, 86% of them would refer or recommend their friends and acquaintances to work for these companies, 61% reported that working in organizations which use social media would increase collaboration levels, and 60% reported that they find such organizations to be driven by innovation. The study also reported that employees working in organizations which use social media technology are more likely to support their company in a time of crisis (APCI & McDonald, 2012).

In sum, enhanced employee engagement using social media technologies should enhance individual performance. Different types of social media may be relevant to engagement and teamwork, such as blogs, project management systems, collaborative software, SNWs, and engagement development platforms (see Table 2). In addition, the utilization of these technologies in the workplace should foster relationships among coworkers, thereby enhancing team performance as well. Timimi (2013) provide three criteria to foster employee engagement via social media: (1) clear social media guidelines, (2) meaningful new hire social media orientation, and (3) effective employee social media training. Hence, the use of social media to improve employee engagement and teamwork has multiple benefits and we call for more scientific research on how organizations can leverage the unexploited potential of social media to increase engagement and teamwork.

Training

Minocha (2009) argues that social media assists employees in gaining transferable skills that are useful for current and future work contexts, such as team-working skills and online collaboration and communication skills. While some works show no difference in learning achievement between employees who receive online versus face-to-face training (Clark, 1983; Locyker, Patterson, & Harper, 2001; Yang & Lin, 2011), other work shows that social media may be beneficial for learning (Weber, 2015). A benefit that distinguishes online from instructor-led training is the possibility for trainees to individualize learning experiences and have this training available when it is convenient (Filipczak, 1995). This individualization involves a shift in responsibility from trainers to learners because learners are empowered through control important features of the training (Brown, 2001).

Twitter, Facebook, YouTube, and other kinds of social media such as Webinars provide an online environment that allows leaners to share and seek information, discuss ideas, as well as transmit and innovate knowledge (Bingham & Conner, 2010; Puijenbroek, Poell, Kroon, & Timmerman, 2014). Meanwhile, trainers can offer updates, follow-up tips, and various training-related activities through social media, such as blogs and wikis (Bozarth, 2010). As an example, the social media platforms "Second Life" and "Lotus Workplace" give companies the option to create virtual training workplaces to allow employees to virtually meet, hold events, practice corporate communications, conduct training sessions, all in an immersive virtual learning environment. As such, a wide range of social media may be used for training purposes, including collaborative software, wikis, SNWs, content communities, virtual learning environments including virtual social worlds, and engagement development platforms, thus encompassing all six of the social media categories in Table 2. Intertwined with the concept of using social media for organizational training purposes is the more well-studied topic of knowledge management.

Knowledge Management

Knowledge sharing is defined as "the act of making knowledge available to others within the organization" (Ipe, 2003, p. 341). Fostering knowledge sharing among employees is a three-folded challenge (Hannon, 1997): Employees may not know that the knowledge they possess might be of value to the company, they may not be motivated to share it, and there may be no mechanism to share knowledge to others in the company. Social media offers a promising set of tools for group collaboration, providing integrated platforms for communication, collaboration, and knowledge exchange (Al-Busaidi, 2014) and therefore provides a useful mechanism for knowledge generation and dissemination (von Krogh, 2012), and sharing (Vuori & Okkonen, 2012).

Social media facilitates knowledge sharing by increasing knowledge reuse by employees and by eliminating the reliance on rigid organizational structures. Whereas, before social media, the majority of knowledge was shared during formal briefings, now each employee has complete visibility into how colleagues manage knowledge. This includes access to sources, identifying when different functional areas are working on the same problem from different perspectives, and accessing materials that can be easily be repurposed for other objectives (Yates & Paquette, 2011). As such, social media can create a network capable of supporting workers in knowledge sharing, potentially filling gaps in skills, competencies and knowledge within the organization (Alberghini, Cricelli, & Grimaldi, 2014). Wikis, online community forums, and blogs create instant feedback loops as recipients of knowledge are able to share their reactions in real time with the author and other readers and in some cases, receiving clarification or new information to help them overcome knowledge boundaries (Yates & Paquette, 2011).

Hakami, Tam, Busalim, and Husin (2014) provide an excellent review of a broad range of factors that affect knowledge sharing through social media. Though a full review of these factors is beyond the scope of the chapter, these factors fall into three categories; technology, organizational/environmental, and individual/personal. Other research has focused on five leading social media characteristics that are related to knowledge sharing. These characteristics enable social media to foster knowledge sharing because they enhance visibility and promote knowledge creation and distribution by enabling participants to develop relationships and trust (Hakami et al., 2014).

1. User content generation: Allows users to create, edit, comment, annotate, evaluate, and distribute content.
2. Peer to peer communication: Globally interactive in real-time formats such as chatting, video/telephone conferencing.
3. Networking: Allows users to create virtual communities that enable individuals with similar interests to collectively interact online to share knowledge and experience, develop relationships, and freely discuss issues.
4. Multimedia orientation: Allows users to store and share content in various forms including text, image, audio, and video. Users easily share, tag, and comment on multimedia files.
5. User friendly: Designs that are simple, dynamic, attractive, and enjoyable, where users easily publish and customize multimedia.

Constantinides and Fountain (2008) classified the application of social media for knowledge management into five categories: web logs (e.g., online journals); SNWs; communities (web sites organizing and sharing specific contents); forums/bulletin boards (sites for exchanging ideas and information usually regarding particular interests); and content aggregators (applications allowing users to fully customize the web content they want to access). As such, social media enables employees to enrich knowledge management at various stages. Social media allows online knowledge sharing to shift from a centralized to a decentralized process, as individuals can post information any time in both informal and formal ways (Kane & Fichman, 2009). Social media also allows the knowledge sharing process to move from intermittent to continuous, as individuals can engage in ongoing online conversations (Ellison & Boyd, 2013).

Information may be created (e.g., on YouTube), debated and influenced (by blogs), disseminated and spread (by social networks), and stored for use as social capital (e.g., on wikis) (Sigala & Chalkiti, 2015). For example, Puijenbroek et al. (2014) report SNWs such as Twitter being used to show metrics like as healthcare conversions and Facebook being used to connect and share information and discuss ideas related to health and nursing. An example is the Learning Disability Nurse Facebook page which is a community of learning disability nurses who share work-related information. Another example of videos on social media used for learning are YouTube videos such as those shared via Tiered Electronic Distribution (TED), including TEDx and TED-ED and TedMed. Orzano, McInerney, Scharf, Tallia, and Crabtree (2008) suggest that tacit knowledge sharing is better facilitated by employing social tools that encourage interaction and socialization among individuals. Jarrahi and Sawyer (2013) showed that social media, such as Twitter, blogs, and LinkedIn, are effective platforms for sharing informal knowledge and innovative ideas within and across organizations through locating expertise, socializing, and networking.

Within a particular organization, incorporating social software onto current knowledge management platforms, organizations can create virtual communities of interests for employees to interact with each other to share the knowledge and information that improves productivity (Zhang, 2012). For instance, British Telecom, a proponent of enterprise social software, has adopted a series of social software applications, including a Wikipedia-style database named BTpedia, a central blogging tool, a podcasting tool, project management software, and an enterprise social networking platform (Hill, 2008). Similarly, Lockheed Martin developed a customized social media platform (UNITY). The motivation behind the introduction of UNITY was centered on knowledge management. Lockheed Martin was concerned about how to capture the knowledge of a retiring generation, with 50% of its workforce eligible to retire within 5–10 years (Lynch,

2008). This loss of talent raised key concerns about how to uncover the tacit knowledge of these employees (Murphy & Salomone, 2013). Additional drivers for Lockheed Martin to begin investing in social media include a concern about the slowdown of existing systems by e-mail, PowerPoint presentations and meetings, as well as the need to connect a large, geographically dispersed workforce (Rambling Tech, 2008).

Behringer and Sassenberg (2015) found that knowledge managers should consider individual differences in employees when assessing the importance of knowledge exchange via social media tools. These authors also draw on the importance of perceived usefulness of social media for improving knowledge exchange. Perceived usefulness can be facilitated by adapting the tool to the need of the user and by emphasizing the actual functionality of the tool. Employees will only consider using the tool if the benefits are apparent. Finally, these authors highlight the importance of self-efficacy as related to use. If employees do not feel confident in using the tool, they will not use them.

More creative people use social media for higher levels of knowledge management, because social networks empower people to acquire and debate knowledge with others, which they compare with existing personal knowledge for internalizing, adapting, accommodating, or assimilating new knowledge (Sigala & Chalkiti, 2015). In addition, social media enhances not only the functional but also the socio-affective aspects that support collaborative knowledge management processes, such as communication, peer pressure/recognition, trust building, and enrichment of bonds among members of social networks (Liu, Magjuka, Bonk, & Seung-Jee, 2007). For example, wikis and blogs allow collaboration and relationship building among individuals (Jonassen, 2000), while tagging enables the formation of social networks (Ullrich et al., 2008). Thus, a wide range of social media can be used for the purpose of knowledge management, such as blogs, collaborative software, information sharing systems, SNWs and content communities, and virtual learning environments (see Table 2).

Social Capital

Skeels and Grudin (2009) found that the primary reasons for using Facebook at work were to reconnect with past colleagues and friends, to build stronger working relationships, to maintain awareness and keep in touch, and to build social capital. People report joining Facebook and spending time on the site to keep in touch with old friends and to strengthen bonds with colleagues. Thus, individuals seek to maintain and increase their social capital via social media (Ellison et al., 2007). This social capital generated via social networks allows individuals to access information and opportunities (e.g., advice networks and job openings) that would otherwise be unavailable (Lin, 2001). Employees with a large and diverse social media network have more social capital than individuals with small, less diverse networks (Resnick, 2002). A survey conducted by McKinsey found that 75% of executives reported that their companies have invested in Web 2.0 tools which foster social networking behavior (Schneckenberg, 2009), thereby enhancing social capital.

Investing time and resources in social networks also helps employees to build norms of reciprocity and mutual trust among themselves which becomes crucial and helpful while engaging in collaborative activities (e.g., brainstorming or problem-solving in groups). This also improves task performance in cross-functional teams where members with different competencies pool resources to meet the common goal of the project. Scheufele and Shah (2000) classified social capital into three major domains: behavioral, intrapersonal, and interpersonal. While intrapersonal social capital focuses on individual employee's life satisfaction, interpersonal social capital measures the level of trust between employees (generalized trust) and behavioral social capital refers to the extent of individual employee's participation in civic and political activities (Scheufele & Shah, 2000). Past research has revealed that employees who use SNWs (like Facebook and Twitter) are more likely to feel an increased level of life satisfaction, happiness, and connectedness (Valkenburg, Peter, & Schouten, 2006). This indicates that employee participation in social networking activities has significant positive impact on the intrapersonal domain of social capital. This might be beneficial from the organization's point of view, as long-term enhancement of individual employee's happiness and life satisfaction will affect other work-related individual outcomes like increased work motivation and productivity levels, higher job satisfaction, and organizational commitment.

Williams (2006) found out that the nature of relationship within a social network can also be used to classify different types of social capital. Weak-tie social networks are used to connect employees from different spheres and work domains thus creating a platform of opportunities due to high amount of resource and information sharing. This is known as bridging social capital which although beneficial, lacks the emotional bonding that exists among employees in strong-tie social networks. Strong-tie social networks generate bonding social capital which involves creating a platform of similarities and interdependencies among employees thus leading to enhanced levels of emotional bonding and affect between them (Williams, 2006). Thus, future research should explore how organizations, through proper utilization of social media, can benefit in terms of building both bridging and bonding social capital among its employees.

For the development of social capital, self-disclosure is necessary to build interpersonal bonds. As such, the categories of social media that require high self-disclosure, such as collaborative software, SNWs, and virtual social worlds, are likely to foster social capital (see Table 2).

Organizational Culture

Social media shapes organizational culture such that formal organizational policies and practices that seek to create a particular culture may be distorted by informal interactions via social networks (McFarland & Ployhart, 2015). Beyond this potential to distort organizational efforts to foster a particular culture, numerous companies, including Best Buy and Dell, have successfully utilized social media to meet important organizational objectives, such as cost reduction, revenues generation, or stimulation of innovation (Huy & Shipilov, 2012). Therefore, whether haphazard and unintentional or when intentional and used holistically throughout the organization, social media becomes part of the organization's culture.

Social media can also be used by organizations to signal its internal workplace culture to external stakeholders (e.g., job applicants). When information asymmetry exists between organizations and stakeholders, companies can share information about its workplace culture like inclusive human resource policies or practices, social responsibility initiatives, or even mission and vision on company web sites in the form of employee testimonials, blogs, videos of top management teams sharing the ultimate goals and objectives of the organization. This helps create communication channels between the organization and stakeholders. These communication channels, in turn, inform stakeholders and make them more aware about the internal climate of the organization, getting information directly from the actual employees of the organization about the company.

Another way in which companies can leverage use of social media is to create an internal culture of high emotional capital. Huy and Shipilov (2012) noted that organizations in which the leadership team engages in developing emotional capital within the employee networks benefit in terms of better information flows, stronger collaboration, higher employee satisfaction and motivation levels, and reduced turnover intentions. Authentic leadership can be very helpful in building a strong culture of emotional capital where employees can identify with the leader and can engage in a one to one communication of ideas and information thus creating a stronger sense of belongingness (Huy & Shipilov, 2012). In this vein, organizational culture may be shaped via a wide range of social media platforms such as collaborative software, SNWs, virtual learning environments, information sharing systems, content communities, and engagement development platforms (see Table 2).

Leadership

Employees need a safe environment to share ideas, find solutions to problems, and have their opinions heard. When organizations fail to provide this environment in the workplace, employees may create their own (Gossett, 2006). Rather than attempting to silence the discussions taking place on counter institutional social media, leaders should consider these online forums to be a valuable and unique source of employee feedback. Other subtle acts of employee discontent and dissent generally occur in places that leaders cannot easily access. However, counter institutional social media make these discussions public and enable leaders to obtain this type of information they would normally not have access to. By monitoring and engaging in these forms of social media, leaders will be better able to understand and deal with employee concerns, potentially intervening before this catharsis culminates into organizational conflict (e.g., strikes, lawsuits). As such, it may be in a leaders' best interest to work within rather than in opposition to these forms of social media (Gossett, 2006).

With an effective use of social media, leaders help foster communication and connectivity among employees, increases transparency, and empowers employees by circumventing the organizational hierarchy (Paus, 2013). With ineffective uses of social media, such as when leaders use separate personal and private profiles, stakeholders develop doubts about the leaders' "true self," resulting in lower trust in the leader (Huy & Shipilov, 2012). As such, social media is particularly powerful for top-level leaders who do not interact with followers on a regular basis. Top-level leaders can project authenticity by displaying a single and consistent identity across personal and professional communications. CEO social media use describing the company's challenges and vision may engender support for the leader and organizational strategy (McFarland & Ployhart, 2015).

In support of this notion that effective social media use is important for leaders, Huy and Shipilov (2012) suggest that companies should utilize the following framework when deploying social media internally:

1. Identify leaders who are authentic and who employees trust.
2. Help these leaders to develop social media skills.
3. Ask these leaders to build social media communities that emphasize aspects of emotional capital such as authenticity, pride, attachment, and fun.
4. Deploy social media tools sequentially, starting with wikis and podcasts, and extend to more interactive social networking only after enough emotional capital has been built.
5. Expect instrumental benefits (such as improved information exchange, motivation, morale, reduced turnover) only after emotional capital has been developed with employees.

It can be concluded that leaders are critical for effective utilization of social media in organizations, providing useful tools to help recruit, select, and train employees, to create an organizational culture that minimizes cyberloafing, and to help foster employee engagement, teamwork, and social capital. Due to these wide ranging responsibilities, leaders need to understand and utilize any and all social media platforms (see Table 2).

SOCIAL MEDIA AND COUNTERPRODUCTIVE WORK BEHAVIORS

Cyberloafing

Cyberloafing is a set of behaviors at work in which an employee engages in electronically mediated activities, particularly through the use of the Internet, that his or her immediate supervisor would not consider job-related (Askew, Coovert, Vandello, Taing, & Bauer, 2011) and include online gambling, stock trading, online romance, chat, visiting pornographic web sites (Johnson & Indvik, 2004), watching YouTube and checking Facebook (Lim, 2002), online banking, using organizational technological resources for personal e-mail, gaming, or other purposes (Mastrangelo, Everton, & Jolton, 2006). Blau, Yang, and Ward-Cook (2006) found that cyberloafing is comprised of three factors: Internet surfing or browsing, nonwork-related use of e-mail, and behaviors requiring high degrees of interactivity (e.g., online gaming). As such, cyberloafing can involve any of the forms of social media (see Table 2). However, these forms of social media are nonwork-related in nature.

Blanchard and Henle (2008) define serious cyberloafing as a deviant behavior because it is likely to go against the norms of the organization. A high profile case of cyberloafing is the scandal at the Securities and Exchange Commission involving dozens of employees who spent sizable amounts of their workday viewing pornography (Simmons, 2010). Mastrangelo and colleagues (2006) separate cyberloafing behaviors as a function of their potential for harm, consisting of two concepts labeled as "counterproductive computer use" and "non-productive computer use." The former involves behaviors that may expose an organization to risk or liability (Mills, Hu, Beldona, & Clay, 2001) as a function of the misuse of a company's social media (e.g., illegal software downloading, distribution of pornography exposing the firm's systems to viruses, or "malware" through surfing). The latter consists of behaviors which are assessed as posing essentially little or no risk to a firm's systems (e.g., viewing SNWs). These behaviors represent a loss of productivity at work. Extending this model and paralleling the results of Robinson and Bennett's model of workplace deviance, social media-based cyberloafing equate to counterproductive behaviors which relate to each of the four quadrants (see Fig. 1 from Weatherbee & Kelloway, 2006). For example, nondestructive cyberloafing behaviors, such as idle web-surfing or when organizational members take e-breaks (Baker & Phillips, 2007), are situated in the production deviance quadrant. Cyberaggression is situated within the interpersonal aggression quadrant, hacking within the property deviance, and blame shifting or gossip in e-mail in the political deviance quadrant (Weatherbee, 2010). Supporting this link between cyberloafing and counterproductive work behaviors, Askew and colleagues (2014) found an empirical link between cyberloafing and withdrawal behaviors (absenteeism, lateness, extended breaks, leaving early, and a composite withdrawal variable) and conclude that cyberloafing appears to be a type of withdrawal behavior.

In addition, there is a new trend in the cyberloafing realm related to smart mobile phones – mobile cyberloafing as compared to classic forms of cyberloafing (via laptops and desktop computers). Many cyberloafing activities, today, are being redirected to mobile phones (Sheikh, Atashgah, & Adibzadegan, 2015). With "push notifications," "location-enabled apps," alerts, reminders, and connectivity options, mobile phones are becoming a dominant paradigm for cyberloafing as well as a significant source of distraction at work.

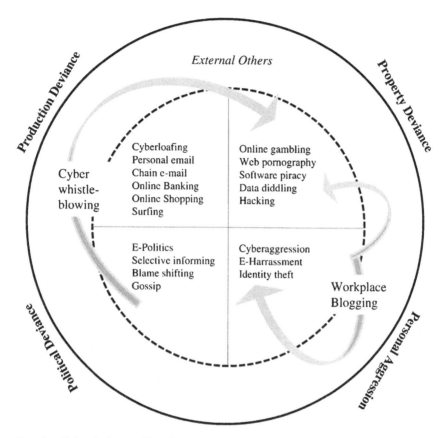

Fig. 1. Cyberdeviancy Typology and Effect-Shifts. *Source*: Weatherbee and Kelloway (2006); Adapted from Robinson and Bennett (1995).

Cyberloafing is a complex behavior which is likely to persist in organizations for the foreseeable future, particularly as additional social media applications are developed (Blanchard & Henle, 2008). It is likely that cyberloafing will become more prominent. As such, it is important to better understand the cyberloafing behaviors employees engage in and how we can minimize the negative effects of cyberloafing on worker productivity while still maintaining a positive culture in the workplace. In this vein, counterproductive use of social media by a particular employee may impact the culture of the organization, as the inter-connectedness of social media in the workplace serves to facilitate effects that generate reciprocal or escalatory patterns beyond the individual (Weatherbee, 2010).

Because cyberloafers may unwittingly visit sites which expose the organization to legal liabilities and to the dangers posed by computer viruses, cyberloafers may pose a greater "threat" to organizations relative to other types of loafers, in terms of productivity losses and costs incurred (Lim, 2002). Understanding the drivers of cyberloafing helps managers develop more effective Internet usage policies, enhance organizational culture, and increase employee autonomy and engagement to alleviate cyberloafing (Sheikh et al., 2015). Employees engage in cyberloafing behaviors because of personal attitudes about these practices, workplace norms, and the ability to hide cyberloafing. Blau et al. (2006) suggest social learning theory as an explanation for cyberloafing, noting that employees look to other coworkers as potential role models in the organization and that cyberloafing is learned through engaging in these behaviors that they see by others in the organizational environment. Liberman, Gwendolyn, McKenna, and Buffardi (2011) found that employee job attitudes, organizational characteristics (managerial support for social media usage and perceived cyberloafing of coworkers), participation in non-Internet loafing activities, and employee attitudes toward cyberloafing are related to employee tendency to cyberloaf. Also, Caplan (2007) found that more emotionally unstable individuals are more likely to spend time online to escape negative outcomes associated with face-to-face social interactions.

Cyberloafing by employees may affect organizations in several ways, such as companies having to increase IT expenditures, combating the exposure of their IT infrastructure to potential threats, and monitoring employee productivity more closely (Sharma & Gupta, 2003). Consequently, cyberloafers do not need to worry as much about the visibility of their loafing compared to the more traditional loafers (Lim, 2002). Organizational conditions conducive to cyberloafing include (a) their computer screens are not easily visible to coworkers or supervisors, (b) they can hear or see people approaching their work station, (c) they work in isolation, or (d) their computer activity is not monitored. In contrast to web site access self-efficacy, the ability to hide cyberloafing has been established as a predictor of cyberloafing (Askew, Coovert, Taing, Ilie, & Bauer, 2012).

Davis, Flett, and Besser (2002) suggest that a solution minimize cyberloafing is to be preventative rather than reactive. In organizations that offer employees open access to social media, carefully screen out job candidates likely to engage in such practices. Ugrin and Pearson (2013) concluded that organizational policies and Internet monitoring will be relatively ineffective at reducing cyberloafing unless employees know about others who have been caught and punished severely. More specifically, the authors found that personal e-mailing and viewing social media were deterred when the possibility of getting fired was coupled with a detection mechanism, knowledge of active enforcement in the past, and a perception that e-mailing is unacceptable. In this vein, organizations may adopt and implement various control mechanisms, such as social media policies and software systems designed to block access to certain web sites (Henle, Kohut, & Booth, 2009).

When organizations are distributively, procedurally, and interactionally unjust in how employees are treated, employees are more likely to legitimize their subsequent engagement in the act of cyberloafing. As this internal justification for behavior enables them to justify their otherwise deviant actions, employees are more likely to engage in cyberloafing (Lim, 2002). As such, an avenue to minimize employee cyberloafing is to treat employees fairly, and ensure that the work environment facilitates productive work to take place to reciprocate employees' investment of time and effort in their work (Lim, 2002).

Despite the link to workplace deviance, other work in the academic literature points to possible positive effects of cyberloafing. Employees may use social media to distract themselves from a stressful event, task, or stream of thought (Davis et al., 2002). Blanchard and Henle (2008) propose that employees do not see minor cyberloafing as deviant behavior at work. Instead, employees may see minor cyberloafing as similar to making and taking personal telephone calls at work. Although previous studies largely examined the negative impact of cyberloafing, Lim (2002) found that using social media for nonwork purposes has a positive impact on employee affect. Viewing social media was found to have a positive impact on employee emotions. Thus, future research should explore these potential complex effects of cyberloafing on employee engagement.

Disciplinary Action

Emerging social media topics relate to employees spreading negative information about their organization, coworkers, or supervisor (McFarland & Ployhart, 2015). When posting comments about an employer on social media where they can be viewed by an unforeseen number of people, the comments cease to be private and become public. In addition, inadvertent disclosure of an organization's proprietary information is a major concern (Skeels & Grudin, 2009). Using an example of Facebook, employees may relay some work-related information to others at work, but inadvertently relay this potentially confidential information to nonwork acquaintances as well. Employee participation in social media can cause reputational damage, trigger lawsuits, cause humiliation, crush credibility, destroy careers, create electronic business records, and lead to productivity losses (Flynn, 2012).

As such, comments which are threatening or attack the integrity of management can be a valid reason for disciplinary action, even where there is no social media policy in place (Dissel, 2014). In the case *Spanierman v. Hughes* (2008), a Connecticut teacher's firing was upheld for inappropriate social media postings. In another case, a manager was fired for falsely claiming to be on jury duty, but her Facebook status indicated she was on vacation (Slattery, 2010). Beyond losing her job, she was arrested and charged with jury duty summons forgery.

Beyond these cases, it is possible that employers proactively search social media for information about an employee illegal activities, legal activities that harm company reputation, criticisms of the organization, and watching for employee disclosure of confidential company information (Davison et al., 2011). Acting exclusively on information obtained from social media to make disciplinary actions without validation or verification from other sources is problematic. Although job-relevant information may be available, this information should be verified (Davison et al., 2011). Thus, beyond instances of cyberloafing, disciplinary actions are generally related to the use of SNWs (see Table 2). Future research in this emerging area of social media is needed.

DISCUSSION

This chapter sought to investigate the current state of practice and research regarding the impact of social media in human resource management affecting organizations. Although past scholarly research has examined in detail the use of SNWs in employee selection (Kluemper, 2013), this chapter examines a broader range of social media as a relevant to human resource management functions. In doing so, we began with the definition of social media as Web 2.0 applications (Elefant, 2011) and focus on the use of social media in organizations as related to external stakeholders, employment selection, performance enhancement, and workplace deviance. Kaplan and Haenlein's (2010) classification of social media provides a rich framework through which to assess the salience of various types of social media on different aspects of HRM.

In the past, organizations have made use of social media as a tool to market its brand image to its external stakeholders like customers, suppliers, and shareholders. However, more recently organizations are making use of social media to signal pieces of information about its internal culture, career growth opportunities, and compensation structures to prospective job applicants who are one of their key stakeholders. Social media enables organizations to leverage multiple stakeholder engagement through communication-enriching platforms to shape its organizational image and attract both active and passive job seekers. Employers make use of employee referral networks to advertise job postings which enable them to attract applicants in geographically dispersed locations in a faster and efficient manner (McFarland & Ployhart, 2015). Company web sites in particular provide job seekers an opportunity to gauge their P-O fit as social media provides them real-time feedback about their fit with the organization, which further influences their decision about whether or not to pursue recruitment opportunities with the organization (Hu et al., 2007).

The most pervasive research on social media in human resource management has been done in the area of personnel selection. SNWs as important employee selection tools, and the benefits (improved company performance) and risks (e.g., privacy and discrimination) involved with it have been reasonably well discussed (Kluemper et al., 2015), though empirical research remains lacking. Past research has revealed some of the reasons behind an employer's rejection of a job applicant based on the information found on applicant's social networking profile (e.g., inappropriate photos, alcohol/drug abuse content, bad-mouthing a previous employer, or making discriminatory comments). Interestingly, research has found that organizations screen job applicant's social networking profile to find those hidden pieces of information which are not tangible in one's resume. However, use of SNWs as a screening tool comes with its own legal and ethical obstacles (Kluemper, 2013) as job applicants may view it as a breach of privacy, whereas employers may claim that SNWs are a legitimate mean to access public information (Gustafson, 2012). On the other hand, the U.S. Fair Credit Reporting Act (Juffras, 2010), the European Union's Data Privacy Directive (Massey, 2009), and several state laws may limit employers from collecting such applicant information. A possible solution to minimize privacy concerns is to obtain informed consent from job applicants before conducting searches of SNWs (Kaslow et al., 2011).

Another problem that may arise based with regard to social media screening is the possibility of discrimination based on one's protected class status information (like age, sex, race, sexual orientation, and physical disability status) which may be easily available in an applicant's social media profile. Social media screening might also adversely impact the hiring of minorities or older job applicants who may not have access to or utilize social media. However, if proper background investigation (social media screening) is not conducted, at least in some industries, it may lead to negligent hiring and create legal liability for the company in the future. Given the associated risks, if social network screening is to become a defensible selection approach, several forms of validity pertaining to SNW screening should be investigated (Kluemper, 2013), such as criterion-related validity with important organizational outcomes (Smith & Kidder, 2010) such as job performance, organizational citizenship behavior, workplace deviance, lateness, absenteeism, or turnover (Roth et al., 2016). Another possible concern with regards to social media screening is the reliability of potential measures. For example, behavioral changes in an applicant across different phases of life might adversely affect test-retest reliability (Slovensky & Ross, 2012). The issue of generalizability becomes a concern when multiple SNWs (e.g., Facebook vs. LinkedIn) are compared, with each having its own divergent purposes, target audience, ability to restrict access, and volume of information (Kluemper, 2013). Similarly, SNW screening may only be relevant for certain kinds of industries such as banking, private security firms, or military suppliers (Slovensky & Ross, 2012).

A growing concern with the potential use of SNW screening is that applicants may engage in impression management by manipulating certain content on their SNW profiles to present a more favorable image of themselves to recruiters (Kluemper et al., 2012). However according to Qualman (2012), maintaining multiple identities in social media to protect one's personal, social, and professional image is challenging. Another issue is that job applicants may have negative reactions to SNW screening. Some may find it to be unethical or a breach of privacy while others may consider it to be violation of informational, distributive, and procedural injustice (Slovensky & Ross, 2012). However, Gustafson (2012) claims that these negative reactions may be reduced if permission is provided in advance by applicants to access their SNW profiles.

This chapter also highlights the different job-relevant constructs that may be measured from applicant SNW profiles including personality traits, KSAOs like network ability (Davison et al., 2012) and communication and interpersonal skills (Roth et al., 2016). Similarly, biographical data available in applicant profiles may shed light on applicants' past behavior, beliefs, and value system which may help in predicting applicants' future behavior. Recruiters may also use social media screening in an attempt to gauge applicants P-O fit or perhaps seek to reveal potential disqualifying information about the applicant like past drug or alcohol abuse or affiliation with hate groups.

Moreover, different applications of social media in human resource management beyond SNWs were also discussed. We detail the importance for organizations to adopt social media policies to maintain organizational, regulatory, and legal compliance (Altimeter, 2011; Flynn, 2012) and to leverage employee productivity and engagement. Interestingly, past research has explored the impact of social media use by employees during office hours on reduced productivity due to information overload (Al-Busaidi, 2014) and multitasking (Turkle, 2011). However, research has also revealed the positive impacts of social media use on increased job satisfaction and organizational commitment (Moqbel et al., 2013) and improved work-life balance (Leidner et al., 2010).

It may be that social media can be a boon as well as a bane. If planned strategically, organizations can use social media to leverage employee engagement by enabling employees to network with other employees and create a collaborative work environment (Nov et al., 2010). This will help organizations to reap benefits by fostering strong interpersonal workplace relationships and improved team performance. It can be helpful to connect employees working in virtual teams, to spread across different geographic locations or across different cross-functional domains, to share resources and collaborate with each other on different work projects.

Social media can be also used to design interactive training platforms which can improve employees' team-working and social skills (Minocha, 2009). Social media can also promote knowledge sharing and knowledge creation through user content generation, peer to peer communication, networking, multimedia orientation, and user-friendly interfaces (Hakami et al., 2014). There can be numerous ways to create information (through YouTube, employee resource groups, etc.), debated and influenced (through blogs), disseminated (by social networks like Facebook, LinkedIn, and Twitter), as well as preserved as social capital (through Wikipedia) (Sigala & Chalkiti, 2015). Social media also enables employees to shift knowledge sharing from centralized to decentralized processes (Kane & Fichman, 2009) or from an intermittent to a continuous workflow (Ellison & Boyd, 2013). Organizations can also create virtual communities

of interests, which empower employees in information sharing and knowledge transfer, thereby amplifying productivity levels (Zhang, 2012).

Furthermore, social media helps employees to build strong networking
based workplace relationships, thus expanding their social capital. Through
these networks, employees can build new contacts as well as reconnect with
their previous colleagues, thus gaining access to a larger professional community. Social media can also be used by organizations to signal its internal
organizational culture and workplace climate to its external stakeholders.
Organizations can inform prospective employees about their corporate
social responsibility initiatives, or inclusive workplace policies through
company web sites or its official pages on SNWs like Facebook and
LinkedIn. Thus, social media serves as an important platform to reduce
information asymmetry between organizations and its multiple stakeholders. This movement can be specifically driven by company top management teams or the CEO. Leaders can make use of online forums to address
stakeholder grievances and resolve their queries and get valuable feedback
from them. This helps develop effective communication channels between
employers and employees.

As a form of workplace deviance, prevalent use of SNWs by employees
also has several negative implications in the workplace. For example,
employees can bad-mouth their employees on these platforms or disclose
organizational proprietary information (Skeels & Grudin, 2009) leading to
corporate reputation damage, expensive lawsuits, loss of competitive
advantage, and market credibility (Flynn, 2012). Another major concern
for employers is to prevent its employees from engaging in cyberloafing
activities in the workplace which are counterproductive workplace behaviors (like online chatting, gaming, dating, and random Internet browsing)
that reduce employee productivity and engagement. Thus it becomes essential for organizations to better understand employee intentions to cyberloaf
and to take proactive actions to mitigate such forms of deviant behavior.

We thus arrive at the conclusion that social media is an important
asset to organizations, which if handled strategically, can benefit them by
simplifying and augmenting several critical human resource management
functions and processes encompassing personnel selection, employee
engagement, teambuilding, employee productivity, and organizational
image. At the same time, social media also serves as a potential liability for
organizations, which likewise needs to be managed effectively. As such, we
believe that social media is in the early stages of what is likely to be a conti-
nually changing dynamic for nearly every aspect of human resource
management. Despite the dynamic and impactful impact of social media on

the organizational environment, more academic study is needed in virtually every area of this nexus between social media and HRM.

REFERENCES

Aberdeen Group. (2008). *Web 2.0, talent management and employee engagement.* Retrieved from http://www.Aberdeen.com

Akinbode, J. O., Opayemi, R., & Sokefun, E. (2013). Impact of online social networking on employees' commitment to duties in selected organizations in Lagos State, Nigeria. *International Journal of Business and Economic Development, 1*(1), 94–100.

Al-Busaidi, K. A. (2014). SWOT of social networking sites for group work in government organizations: An exploratory Delphi study from IT managers' perspective. *The Journal of Information and Knowledge Management Systems, 44*(1), 121–139.

Alberghini, E., Cricelli, L., & Grimaldi, M. (2014). A methodology to manage and monitor social media inside a company: A case study. *Journal of Knowledge Management, 18*(2), 255–277.

Allan, D. G., Mahto, R. V., & Otondo, R. F. (2007). Web-based recruitment: Effects of information, organizational brand, and attitudes toward a web site on applicant attraction. *Journal of Applied Psychology, 92*, 1696–1708.

Altimeter. (2011). *Social business readiness: How advanced companies prepare internally.* Retrieved from www.slideshare.net/jeremiah_owyang/social-readiness-how-advanced-companies-prepare

APCI & McDonald, G. (2012). Retrieved from http://www.apcoworldwide.com

Askew, K., Buckner, J. E., Taing, M. U., Ilie, A., Bauer, J. A., & Coovert, M. D. (2014). Explaining cyberloafing: The role of the theory of planned behavior. *Computers in Human Behavior, 36*, 510–519.

Askew, K., Coovert, M. D., Taing, M. U., Ilie, A., & Bauer, J. (2012). Work environment factors and cyberloafing: A follow-up to askew. Poster presented at SIOP, San Diego, CA.

Askew, K., Coovert, M. D., Vandello, J. A., Taing, M. U., & Bauer, J. A. (2011). Work environment factors predict cyberloafing. Poster presented at the Annual Meeting of the Association for Psychological Science. Washington, DC.

Back, M. D., Stopfer, J. M., Vazire, S., Gaddis, S., Schuukle, S. C., Egloff, B., & Gosling, S. D. (2010). Facebook profiles reflect actual personality, not self-idealization. *Psychological Science, 21*, 372–374.

Baker, J., & Phillips, J. (2007). E-mail, decisional styles, and rest breaks. *CyberPsychology & Behavior, 10*(5), 705–708.

Bangerter, A., Roulin, N., & König, C. J. (2012). Personnel selection as a signaling game. *Journal of Applied Psychology, 97*, 719–738.

Barber, A. E. (1998). *Recruiting employees: Individual and organizational perspectives.* Thousand Oaks, CA: Sage Publications.

Behringer, N., & Sassenberg, K. (2015). Introducing social media for knowledge management: Determinants of employees' intentions to adopt new tools. *Computers in Human Behavior, 48*, 290–296.

Bell, B. S., & Kozlowski, S. W. J. (2002). A typology of virtual teams: Implications for effective leadership. Cornell University, School of Industrial and Labor Relations site. Retrieved from http://digitalcommons.ilr.cornell.edu/hrpubs/8/

Bingham, T., & Conner, M. L. (2010). *The new social learning: A guide to transforming organizations through social media*. Alexandria, VA: ASTD Press.

Black, S. L., Johnson, A. F., Takach, S. E., & Stone, D. L. (2012). Factors affecting applicant's reactions to the collection of data in social network websites. Presented at the Academy of Management Annual Conference, Philadelphia, PA.

Blanchard, A. L., & Henle, C. A. (2008). Correlates of different forms of cyberloafing: The role of norms and external locus of control. *Computers in Human Behavior, 24*, 1067–1084.

Blau, G., Yang, Y., & Ward-Cook, K. (2006). Testing a measure of cyberloafing. *Journal of Allied Health, 35*(1), 9–17.

Boehle, S. (2000). Online recruiting gets sneaky. *Training, 37*(5), 66–74.

Bohnert, D., & Ross, W. H. (2010). The influence of social networking websites on the evaluation of job candidates. *Cyberpsychology, Behavior, and Social Networking, 13*, 341–347.

Boyd, D. M., & Ellison, N. M. (2007). Social network sites: Definition, history, and scholarship. *Journal of Computer-Mediated Communication, 13*(1), 210–230.

Bozarth, J. (2010). *Social media for trainers: Techniques for enhancing and extending learning*. San Francisco, CA: Pfeiffer.

Braddy, P. W., Meade, A. W., & Kroustalis, C. M. (2008). Online recruiting: The effects of organizational familiarity, website usability, and website attractiveness on viewers' impressions of organizations. *Computers in Human Behavior, 24*, 2992–3001.

Brandenburg, C. (2008). The newest way to screen job applicants: A social networking nightmare. *Federal Communications Law Journal, 60*, 598–614.

Brodkin, J. (2008). One in four firms block Facebook. *Network World, 25*, 20.

Brown, K. G. (2001). Using computers to deliver training: Which employees learn and why? *Personnel Psychology, 54*(2), 271–296.

Brown, V. R., & Vaughn, E. D. (2011). The writing on the (Facebook) wall: The use of social networking sites in hiring decisions. *Journal of Business and Psychology, 26*, 219–225.

Cable, D. M., & Yu, K. Y. T. (2006). Managing job seekers' organizational image beliefs: The role of media richness and media credibility. *Journal of Applied Psychology, 91*(4), 828–840.

Capelli, P. (2001). Making the most of online recruiting. *Harvard Business Review, 79*, 139–146.

Caplan, S. (2007). Relations among loneliness, social anxiety, and problematic internet use. *CyberPsychology & Behavior, 10*(2), 234–242.

Cho, H., Chen, M. H., & Chung, S. (2010). Testing an integrative theoretical model of knowledge sharing behavior in the context of Wikipedia. *Journal of the American Society for Information Science and Technology, 61*, 1198–1212.

Clark, R. E. (1983). Reconsidering research on learning from media. *Review of Educational Research, 53*, 445–459.

Cober, R. T., Brown, D. J., Blumental, A. J., Doverspike, D., & Levy, P. (2000). The quest for the qualified job surfer: It's time the public sector catches the wave. *Public Personnel Management, 29*, 479–494.

Cober, R. T., Brown, D. J., Keeping, L. M., & Levy, P. E. (2004). Recruitment on the net: How do organizational web site characteristics influence applicant attraction? *Journal of Management, 30*, 623–646.

Constantinides, E., & Fountain, S. (2008). Web 2.0: Conceptual foundations and marketing issues. *Journal of Direct, Data, and Digital Marketing Practice, 9*, 231–244.

Cross-Tab Marketing Services. (2010). *Online reputation in a connected world.* Retrieved from http://www.job-hunt.org/guides/DPD_Online-Reputation-Research_overview.pdf

D'Abate, C. P., & Eddy, E. R. (2007). Engaging in personal business on the job: Extending the presenteeism construct. *Human Resource Development Quarterly, 18,* 361–383.

Daft, R. L., & Lengel, R. H. (1986). Organizational information requirements, media richness and structural design. *Management Science, 32*(5), 554–571.

Davis, R. A., Flett, G. L., & Besser, A. (2002). Validation of a new scale for measuring problematic internet use: Implications for pre-employment screening. *Cyberpsychology & Behavior, 5*(4), 331–345.

Davison, H. K., Bing, M. N., Kluemper, D. H., & Roth, P. (in press). Social media as a personal selection and hiring resource: Reservations and recommendations. In R. N. Landers & G. Schmidt (Eds.), *Using social media in employee selection: Theory, practice, and future research.* Springer.

Davison, H. K., Bing, M. N., Kluemper, D. H., & Roth, P. (in press). Social media as a personal selection and hiring resource: Reservations and recommendations. In R. N. Landers & G. Schmidt (Eds.), *Using social media in employee selection: Theory, practice, and future research.* New York, NY: Springer.

Davison, H. K., Maraist, C., & Bing, M. N. (2011). Friend or foe? The promise and pitfalls of using social networking sites for HR decisions. *Journal of Business and Psychology, 26,* 153–159.

Davison, H. K., Maraist, C. C., Hamilton, R. H., & Bing, M. N. (2012). To screen or not to screen? Using the internet for selection decisions. *Employee Responsibility and Rights Journal, 24,* 1–21.

Dineen, B. R., Ash, S. R., & Noe, R. A. (2002). A web of applicant attraction: Person organization fit in the context of web-based recruitment. Journal of Applied Psychology, 87(4), 723–734.

Dissel, B. M. P. v. (2014). Social media and the employee's right to privacy in Australia. *International Data Privacy Law, 4*(3), 222–236.

Dreher, S. (2014). Social media and the world of work a strategic approach to employees' participation in social media. *Corporate Communications: An International Journal, 19*(4), 344–356.

Elefant, C. (2011). The "Power" of social media: Legal issues & best practices for utilities engaging social media. *Energy Law Journal, 32*(1), 1–55.

Ellison, N. B., & Boyd, D. (2013). Sociality through social network sites. In W. H. Dutton (Ed.), *The oxford handbook of internet studies* (pp. 151–172). Oxford: Oxford University Press.

Ellison, N. B., Steinfield, C., & Lampe, C. (2007). The benefits of Facebook "friends": Social capital and college students use of online social network sites. *Journal of Computer-Mediated Communication, 12,* 1143–1168.

Epstein, D. (2008). Have I been googled? Character and fitness in the age of Google, Facebook, and YouTube. *The Georgetown Journal of Legal Ethics, 21,* 715–727.

Filipczak, B. (1995). Putting the learning into distance learning. *Training, 32*(10), 111–118.

Flynn, N. (2012). *The social media handbook: Policies and best practices to effectively manage your organization's social media presence, posts, and potential risks.* San Francisco, CA: Pfeiffer.

Forty-five percent of employers use social networking sites to research job candidates. (2009). CareerBuilder survey finds: Career expert provides dos and don'ts for job seekers on social networking. Press Releases. Retrieved from http://www.careerbuilder.com/share/aboutus/pressreleasesdetail.aspx?id= pr519&sd = 8/19/2009&ed = 12/31/2009

Frampton, B. D., & Child, J. T. (2013). Friend or not to friend: Coworker Facebook friend requests as an application of communication privacy management theory. *Computers in Human Behavior, 29,* 2257–2264.

Goffman, E. (1959). *The presentation of self in everyday life.* New York, NY: Doubleday Anchor Books.

Gossett, L. M. (2006). My job sucks examining counterinstitutional web sites as locations for organizational member voice, dissent, and resistance. *Management Communication Quarterly, 23*(1), 63–90.

Gustafson, D. A. (2012). *Perceived fairness in the use of Facebook in the selection process.* Unpublished master's thesis. University of Texas at Arlington.

Hakami, Y., Tam, S., Busalim, A. H., & Husin, A. R. C. (2014). A review of factors affecting the sharing of knowledge in social media. *Science International, 26*(2), 679–688.

Hannon, J. M. (1997). Leveraging HRM to enrich competitive intelligence. *Human Resource Management, 36,* 409–422.

Henle, C. A., Kohut, G., & Booth, R. (2009). Designing electronic use policies to enhance employee perceptions of fairness and to reduce cyberloafing. *Computers in Human Behavior, 25*(4), 902–910.

Hill, A. (2008). *BT enterprise 2.0: Social media tools as an aid to learning and collaboration in the workplace, for the digital-generation and beyond. Case study from the career innovation group.* Retrieved from http://richarddennison.files.wordpress.com/2008/09/ci-digital-generation-bt.pdf

Hoch, J. E., & Kozlowski, S. W. J. (2014). Leading virtual teams: Hierarchical leadership, structural supports, and shared team leadership. *Journal of Applied Psychology, 99*(3), 390–403.

Hoffmann, C. P., & Lutz, C. (2015). The impact of online media on stakeholder engagement and the governance of corporations. *Journal of Public Affairs, 15*(2), 163–174.

Hu, C., Su, H.-S., & Chen, C.-I. B. (2007). The effect of person–organization fit feedback via recruitment web sites on applicant attraction. *Computers in Human Behavior, 23,* 2509–2523.

Huy, Q., & Shipilov, A. (2012). The key to social media success within organizations. *MIT Sloan Management Review, 54*(1), 73–81.

Ipe, M. (2003). Knowledge sharing in organizations: A conceptual framework. *Human Resource Development Review, 2,* 337–359.

Jarrahi, M. H., & Sawyer, S. (2013). Social technologies, informal knowledge practices, and the enterprise. *Journal of Organizational Computing and Electronic Commerce, 23*(1) (Special Issue on Knowledge Management and Social Media: The Challenges, Edited by R. Mason and D. Ford).

Johnson, P. R., & Indvik, J. (2004). The organizational benefits of reducing cyberslacking in the workplace. *Journal of Organizational Culture, Communications, and Conflict, 8*(2), 55–62.

Johnston, J. (2015). Loose tweets sink fleets' and other sage advice: Social media governance, policies and guidelines. *Journal of Public Affairs, 15*(2), 175–187.

Jonassen, D. H. (2000). *Computers as mindtools for schools: Engaging critical thinking.* Upper Saddle River, NJ: Merrill/Prentice Hall.

J. S., v. Bethlehem Area Sch. Dist. 757 A.2d 412. (Pa. Commw. Ct. 2000).

Juffras, D. (2010). Using the internet to conduct background checks on applicants for employment. *University of North Carolina School of Government Public Employment Law Bulletin, 38*, 1–22.

Kane, G. C., & Fichman, R. G. (2009). The shoemaker's children: Using wikis to improve is research, teaching, and publication. *MIS Quarterly, 33*(1), 1–22.

Kane, G. C., Fichman, R. G., Gallaugher, J., & Glaser, J. (2009). Community relations 2.0. *Harvard Business Review, 87*(11), 45–51.

Kaplan, A. M., & Haenlein, M. (2010). Users of the world, unite! The challenges and opportunities of social media. *Business Horizons, 53*, 59–68. doi:10.1016/j.bushor.2009.09.003

Karl, K., Peluchette, J., & Schlaegel, C. (2010). Who's posting Facebook faux pas? A cross-cultural examination of personality differences. *International Journal of Selection and Assessment, 18*, 174–186.

Kaslow, F. W., Patterson, T., & Gottlieb, M. (2011). Ethical dilemmas in psychologists accessing internet data: Is it justified? *Professional Psychology, Research & Practice, 42*, 105–112.

Kluemper, D. H. (2013). Social network screening: Pitfalls, possibilities, and parallels in employment selection. In T. Bondarouk & M. Olivas-Lujan (Eds.), *Social media in human resource management* (Vol. 12). Advanced Series in Management. Bingley, UK: Emerald Group Publishing Limited.

Kluemper, D. H., Davison, H. K., Cao, A., & Wu, B. (2015). Social networking websites and personnel selection: A call for academic research. In I. Nikolaou & J. Oostrom (Eds.), *Current issues in work and organizational psychology: Employee recruitment, selection, and assessment.* Hove: Psychology Press.

Kluemper, D. H. (in press). Social media in selection. In S. Rogelberg (Ed.), *Encyclopedia of industrial/organizational psychology* (2nd ed.). Thousand Oaks, CA: Sage.

Kluemper, D. H., McLarty, B., & Rosen, P. (2013). What can LinkedIn tell us about potential job applicants? Exploring the relationship between individual characteristics and LinkedIn use. Presented at the Society for Industrial and Organizational Psychology meeting, April 2013, Houston, TX.

Kluemper, D. H., & Rosen, P. (2009). Future employment selection methods: Evaluating social networking websites. *Journal of Managerial Psychology, 24*, 567–580.

Kluemper, D. H., Rosen, P., & Mossholder, K. (2012). Social networking websites, personality ratings, and the organizational context: More than meets the eye? *Journal of Applied Social Psychology, 42*, 1143–1172.

Knight, J., & Weedon, A. (2014). Identity and social media. Convergence: The international. *Journal of Research into New Media Technologies, 20*(3), 257–258.

Lebrecque, L. I., Markos, E., & Milne, G. R. (2011). Online personal branding: Processes, challenges, and implications. *Journal of Interactive Marketing, 25*, 37–50.

Lee, C. S., & Ma, L. (2011). News sharing in social media: The effect of gratifications and prior experience. *Computers in Human Behavior, 28*, 331–339.

Leidner, D., Koch, H., & Gonzalez, E. (2010). Assimilating generation Y IT new hires into USAA's workforce: the role of an enterprise 2.0 system. *MIS Quarterly Executive, 9*, 229–242.

Levashina, J., & Campion, M. (2009). Expected practices in background checking: Review of the human resource management literature. *Employee Responsibilities & Rights Journal, 21*, 231–249.

Liberman, B., Gwendolyn, S., McKenna, K. Y. A., & Buffardi, L. E. (2011). Employee job attitudes and organizational characteristics as predictors of cyberloafing. *Computers in Human Behavior, 27*, 2192–2199.

Lievens, F., & Harris, M. M. (2003). Research on internet recruiting and testing: Current status and future directions. In C. L. Cooper & I. T. Robertson (Eds.), *International review of industrial and organizational psychology* (Vol. 16, pp. 131–165). Chicester: Wiley.

Lim, V. K. G. (2002). The IT way of loafing on the job: Cyberloafing, neutralizing and organizational justice. *Journal of Organizational Behavior, 23*(5), 675–694.

Lin, N. (2001). Guanxi: A conceptual analysis. *Contributions in Sociology, 133,* 153–166.

Liu, X., Magjuka, R. J., Bonk, C. J., & Seung-Jee, L. (2007). Does sense of community matter? An examination of participants' perceptions of building learning communities in online courses. *Quarterly Review of Distance Education, 8*(1), 9–24.

Locyker, L., Patterson, J., & Harper, B. (2001). ICT in higher education: Evaluating outcomes for health education. *Journal of Computer Assisted Learning, 17,* 275–283.

Lynch, C. G. (2008). *Lockheed Martin shows off internal social software platform.* Retrieved from http://www.cio.com/article/393264/Lockheed_Martin_Shows_Off_Internal_Social_Software_Platform

Mangla, I. S. (2009). Fired for Facebook: Don't let it happen to you. *CNN.* Retrieved from http://moremoney.blogs.money.cnn.com/2009/04/21/fired-for-facebook-dont-let-it-happen-to-you/. Accessed on April 17, 2011.

Markus, M. L. (1994). Electronic mail as the medium of managerial choice. *Organization Science, 5,* 502–527.

Massey, R. (2009). Privacy and social networks: A European opinion. *Journal of Internet Law, 13,* 1–17.

Mastrangelo, P., Everton, W., & Jolton, J. (2006). Personal use of work computers: Distraction versus destruction. *CyberPsychology & Behavior, 9*(6), 730–741.

Maznevski, M. S., & Chudoba, K. M. (2000). Bridging space over time: Global virtual team dynamics and effectiveness. *Organizational Science, 11*(5), 473–492.

McFarland, L. A., & Ployhart, R. E. (2015). Social media: A contextual framework to guide research and practice. *Journal of Applied Psychology, 100*(6), 1653–1677. doi:http://dx.doi.org/10.1037/a0039244

McLarty, B., Kluemper, D. H., & Rosen, P. (2013). Social networking websites and organizational relevance: Exploring relationships with LinkedIn adoption and use. Presented at the Southern Management Association Conference, October, 2013. New Orleans, LA.

Mills, J., Hu, B., Beldona, S., & Clay, J. (2001). Cyberslacking! A liability issue for wired workplaces. *Cornell Hotel and Restaurant Administration Quarterly, 42,* 34–47.

Minocha, S. (2009). An empirically-grounded study on the effective use of social software in education. *Education & Training, 51,* 381–394.

Moqbel, M., Nevo, S., & Kock, N. (2013). Organizational members' use of social networking sites and job performance: An exploratory study. *Information Technology & People, 26*(3), 240–264.

Mumford, M. D., Costanza, D. P., Connelly, M. S., & Johnson, J. F. (1996). Item generation procedures and background data scales. Implications for construct and criterion-related validity. *Personnel Psychology, 49,* 360–398.

Murphy, G., & Salomone, S. (2013). Using social media to facilitate knowledge transfer in complex engineering environments: A primer for educators. *European Journal of Engineering Education, 38,* 70–84.

Murphy, G. D. (2010). Using web 2.0 tools to facilitate knowledge transfer in complex Organizational environments: A primer. In *ICOMS, asset management conference (ICOMS 2010),* June 21–25, University of Adelaide, South Australia.

Myors, B., Lievens, F., Schollaert, E., Cronshaw, S. F., Mladinic, A., Rodriguez, V., & Sackett, P. R. (2008). International perspectives on the legal environment for selection. *Industrial and Organizational Psychology: Perspectives on Science and Practice, 1*, 206–246.

Nov, O., Naaman, M., & Ye, C. (2010). Analysis of participation in an online photo sharing community: A multidimensional perspective. *Journal of the American Society for Information Science and Technology, 61*, 555–566.

Orzano, A. J., McInerney, C. R., Scharf, D., Tallia, A. F., & Crabtree, B. F. (2008). A knowledge management model: Implications for enhancing quality in health care. *Journal of the American Society for Information Science and Technology, 59*(3), 489–505.

Parry, E., & Solidoro, A. (2013). Social media as a mechanism for engagement? In T. Bondarouk & M. Olivas-Lujan (Eds.), *Social media in human resources management* (Vol. 12, pp. 121–141). Advanced Series in Management. Bingley, UK: Emerald Group Publishing Limited.

Paus, V. (2013). New media and leadership: Social media and open organizational communication. *Manager, 17*, 73–78.

Pietrylo v. Hillstone Restaurant Group. 2008. WL 6085437 (D.N.J. 2008).

Pike, J. C. (2011). *The impact of boundary-blurring social networking websites: Self-presentation, impression formation, and publicness.* Unpublished doctoral dissertation. University of Pittsburg.

Puijenbroek, T. V., Poell, R. F., Kroon, B., & Timmerman, V. (2014). The effect of social media use on work-related learning. *Journal of Computer Assisted Learning, 30*(2), 159–172.

Qualman, E. (2012). *Socialnomics: How social media transforms the way we live and do business.* London: Wiley Press.

Rambling Tech. (2008). *Unity – Lockheed-Martin's implementation of a social computing platform.* Retrieved from http://chuckjohnson.wordpress.com/2008/06/28/unity-lockheed-martin%E2%80%99s-implementation-of-asocial-computing-platform/

Reeve, C. L., & Schultz, L. (2004). Job-seeker reactions to selection process information in job ads. *International Journal of Selection and Assessment, 12*, 343–355.

Resnick, P. (2002). Beyond bowling together: Sociotechnical capital. In J. M. Carroll (Ed.), *Human-computer interaction in the new millennium* (pp. 247–272). Reading, MA: Addison-Wesley.

Robinson, S. L., & Bennett, R. J. (1995). A typology of deviant workplace behavior: A multidimensional scaling study. *Academy of Management Journal, 38*(2), 555–572.

Roth, P. L., Bobko, P., Van Iddekinge, C. H., & Thatcher, J. B. (2016). Social media in employee selection-related decisions: A research agenda for uncharted territory. *Journal of Management, 42*, 269–298.

Rynes, S. L., Bretz, R. D. J., & Gerhart, B. (1991). The importance of recruitment in job choice: A different way of looking. *Personnel Psychology, 44*, 487–521.

Rynes, S. L., & Cable, D. M. (2003). Recruitment research in the twenty-first century. In W. C. Borman, D. R. Ilgen, & R. J. Klimoski (Eds.), *Comprehensive handbook of psychology: Industrial and organizational psychology* (Vol. 12, pp. 55–76). New York, NY: Wiley.

Sanchez, R. J., Roberts, K., Freeman, M., & Clayton, A. C. (2012). Do they care? Applicant reactions to on-line social networking presence checks. Paper presented at the Academy of Management Annual Conference, Boston, MA.

Scheufele, D. A., & Shah, D. V. (2000). Personality strength and social capital: The role of dispositional and informational variables in the production of civic participation. *Communication Research, 27*, 107–131.

Schneckenberg, D. (2009). Web 2.0 and the empowerment of the knowledge worker. *Journal of Knowledge Management, 13*(6), 509–520.

Schwartz, R., & Halegoua, G. R. (2015). The spatial self: Location-based identity performance on social media. *New, Media & Society, 17*, 1643–1660.

Sharma, S. K., & Gupta, J. N. D. (2003). Improving workers' productivity and reducing internet abuse. *Journal of Computer Information Systems, 44*, 74–78.

Sheikh, A., Atashgah, M. S. A., & Adibzadegan, M. (2015). The antecedents of cyberloafing: A case study in an Iranian copper industry. *Computers in Human Behavior, 51*, 172–179.

Shiller, K. (2010). Getting a grip on reputation. *Information Today, 27*, 1–44.

Short, J., Williams, E., & Christie, B. (1976). *The social psychology of telecommunications.* London: Wiley.

SHRM. (2011). *SHRM survey findings: The use of social networking websites and online search engines in screening job candidates.* Retrieved from http://www.shrm.org/research/surveyfindings/articles/pages/theuseofsocialnetworkingwebsitesandonlinesearchenginesinscreeningjobcandidates.aspx

Siebert, S., Downes, P. E., & Chrostopher, J. (2012). Applicant reactions to online background checks: Welcome to a brave new world. Paper presented at the Academy of Management Annual Conference, Boston, MA.

Sigala, M., & Chalkiti, K. (2015). Knowledge management, social media and employee creativity. *International Journal of Hospitality Management, 45*, 44–58.

Simmons, C. (2010). GOP ramps up attacks on SEC over porn surfing. *USA Today*. Retrieved from http://www.usatoday.com/money/companies/regulation/2010-04-22-secemployees-%20porn_N.htm?POE = click-refer

Sivertzen, A. M., Nilsen, E. R., & Olafsen, A. H. (2013). Employer branding: Employer attractiveness and the use of social media. *Journal of Product & Brand Management, 22*(7), 473–483.

Skeels, M., & Grudin, J. (2009). Social networks cross boundaries: A case study of workplace use of Facebook and LinkedIn. GROUP' *09*, pp. 95–104.

Slattery, J. (2010). S.I. woman allegedly faked jury duty to take vacation. *CBS New York.* Retrieved from http://newyork.cbslocal.com/2010/10/28/s-i-woman-allegedly-faked-jury-duty-to-take-vacation/

Slovensky, R., & Ross, W. H. (2012). Should human resource managers use social media to screen job applicants? Managerial and legal issues in the USA. *Info, 14*, 55–69.

Smith, W. P., & Kidder, D. L. (2010). You've been tagged! (Then again, maybe not): Employers and Facebook. *Business Horizons, 53*, 491–499.

Spanierman v. Hughes. (2008). U.S. Dist. LEXIS 69569 (D. Conn. Sept. 16, 2008).

Timimi, F. K. (2013). The shape of digital engagement health care and social media. *The Journal of Ambulatory Care Management, 36*(3), 187–192.

Turkle, S. (2011). *Alone together: Why we expect more from technology and less from each other.* New York, NY: Basic Books.

Ugrin, J. C., & Pearson, J. M. (2013). The effects of sanctions and stigmas on cyberloafing. *Computers in Human Behavior, 29*, 812–820.

Ullrich, C., Kerstin, B., Heng, L., Xiaohong, T., Liping, S., & Ruimin, S. (2008). Why web 2.0 is good for learning and for research: principles and prototypes. In *Proceedings of the 17th International World Wide Web Conference*, Beijing, China, 21–25.

Valkenburg, P. M., Peter, J., & Schouten, A. P. (2006). Friend networking sites and their relationship to adolescents' well-being and social self-esteem. *CyberPsychology & Behavior*, *9*, 584–590.

Van Hoye, G., & Lievens, F. (2007). Investigating web-based recruitment sources: Employee testimonials vs. word-of-mouse. *International Journal of Selection and Assessment*, *15*, 372–382.

Van Iddekinge, C. H., Lanivich, S. E., Roth, P. L., & Junco, E. (2013). Social media for selection? Validity and adverse impact potential of a Facebook-based assessment. *Journal of Management*. Advance online publication. doi:10.1177/0149206313515524.

Vega, T. (2010). *Tools to help companies manage their social media*. *N.Y. TIMES*. Retrieved from http://www.nytimes.com/2010/11/15/business/media/15social.html

von Krogh, G. (2012). How does social software change knowledge management? Toward a strategic research agenda. *The Journal of Strategic Information Systems*, *21*, 154–164.

Vuori, V., & Okkonen, J. (2012). Knowledge sharing motivational factors of using an intra-organizational social media platform. *Journal of Knowledge Management*, *16*(4), 592–603.

Wallace, J. C., Page, E. E., & Lippstreu, M. (2006). Applicant reactions to pre-employment application blanks: A legal and procedural justice perspective. *Journal of Business and Psychology*, *20*, 467–488.

Walters, R. D., Burnett, E., Lamm, A., & Lucas, J. (2009). Engaging stakeholders through social networking: How nonprofit organizations are using Facebook. *Public Relations Review*, *35*(2), 102–106. doi:10.1016/j.pubrev.2009.01.006

Weatherbee, T. G. (2010). Counterproductive use of technology at work: Information & communications technologies and cyberdeviancy. *Human Resource Management Review*, *20*, 35–44.

Weatherbee, T. G., & Kelloway, E. K. (2006). A case of cyberdeviancy: CyberAggression in the workplace. In E. K. Kelloway, J. Barling, & J. J. Hurrell (Eds.), *Handbook of workplace violence* (pp. 445–487). Thousand Oaks, CA: Sage.

Weber, J. (2015). Investigating and assessing the quality of employee ethics training programs among US-based global organizations. *Journal of Business Ethics*, *129*, 27–42.

Willey, L., White, B. J., Domagalski, T., & Ford, J. C. (2012). Candidate-screening, information technology and the law: Social media considerations. *Issues in Information Systems*, *13*, 300–309.

Williams, D. (2006). On and off the 'net: Scales for social capital in an online era. *Journal of Computer-Mediated Communication*, *11*, 593–628.

Woska, W. J. (2007). Legal issues for HR professionals: Reference checking/background investigations. *Public Personnel Management*, *36*, 79–89.

Yan, J. (2011). Social media in branding: Fulfilling a need. *Journal of Brand Management*, *18*, 688–696.

Yang, S. C., & Lin, C. H. (2011). The effect of online training on employee's performance. *Journal of Computers*, *6*, 458–465.

Yates, D., & Paquette, S. (2011). Emergency knowledge management and social media technologies: A case study of the 2010 Haitian earthquake. *International Journal of Information Management*, *31*, 6–13.

Zhang, Z. J. (2012). A social software strategy for knowledge management and organization culture. *OR Insight*, *25*, 60–79.

THE CALL OF DUTY: A DUTY DEVELOPMENT MODEL OF ORGANIZATIONAL COMMITMENT

Charn P. McAllister and Gerald R. Ferris

ABSTRACT

Although the concept of duty has a historic and philosophical foundations dating back to Aristotle, there is very little theory and research in this area of scientific inquiry. In an effort to address this lack of scholarship, a theoretical foundation and a model are presented that clearly delineate the construct of duty, and the nature of its development within an individual-organization relationship. Using social exchange theory and the three-component model of organizational commitment as the conceptual foundations, the proposed duty development model explains the individual-level antecedents and the phases of commitment that individuals may progress through during their tenure in an organization. The various types of exchanges and transactions inherent in the social exchange theory provide the basis for each phase of commitment individuals experience. It is proposed that certain antecedents make individuals more likely to form a sense of duty toward an organization, but the development of this type of relationship requires an organization to focus on commitment building efforts, such as perceived organizational support and organizational culture. Contributions to theory and

Research in Personnel and Human Resources Management, Volume 34, 209–244
Copyright © 2016 by Emerald Group Publishing Limited
ISSN: 0742-7301/doi:10.1108/S0742-730120160000034012

research, organizational implications, and directions for future research are discussed.

Keywords: Moral duty; commitment; loyalty; performance

Organizations today are facing the challenges of attracting, selecting, and retaining one of the most mobile generations the workplace has ever witnessed (Sujansky & Ferri-Reed, 2009). Developing a workforce of committed employees is a daunting task for any organization, but it is especially true for those interested in retaining the new generation of employees often referred to as Millennials. This segment of the population is both highly mobile and keenly focused on maintaining a successful work-life balance, which leads them to constantly seek out new opportunities (Twenge, 2010).

As such, one of the major problems of today's businesses is the loss of human and social capital due to high voluntary turnover rates (Dess & Shaw, 2001; Hancock, Allen, Bosco, McDaniel, & Pierce, 2013; Pencavel, 1972). As the dynamics of organizational commitment continue to change, there can be no doubt that organizations need to adapt to this new environment or fall behind those that do. For this reason, organizations' focus on the development of duty in its members is critical to their ability to maximize resources through retention and commitment.

Typically, duty is defined as an internalization of the highest commitment to an entity (e.g., organization) or a course of action, and it is a term often reserved for the military, police forces, or for purely philosophical conversations. As such, duty is a term not often heard in the workplace, but it is nonetheless present implicitly in the everyday exchanges between employees and their employers. Just as the military cannot expect its personnel to internalize automatically a sense of duty, business organizations cannot expect the highest level of commitment out of their employees. The military continuously strives to instill a sense of duty within their ranks, and if other organizations seek to ensure a similar outcome, they need to dedicate resources toward the achievement of those ends.

The purpose of this chapter is to establish a model of duty development in organizations, predicated on Meyer and Allen's (1991) widely accepted and popular three-component model (TCM) of organizational commitment. This model specifically allows for a careful analysis of the source of individuals' commitment toward a target in the form of normative, affective, and continuance commitments. Other constructs pertinent to this analysis include organizational climate (Noordin, Omar, Sehan, & Idrus, 2010), organizational culture and identity (Ashforth, Rogers, & Corley, 2011), and perceived organizational support (Eisenberger, Armeli, Rexwinkel, Lynch, & Rhoades, 2001), and they all have been linked theoretically and/or empirically to organizational commitment. Despite the extensive nature of the commitment literature, built over three decades of work, the research on organizational commitment is ostensibly lacking in the analysis of the highest form of commitment – duty.

Social exchange theory is used as the primary theoretical driver to explain why individuals enter into, and continue to build upon, the psychological contract of commitment with an organization. The proposed model takes into account the individual-level antecedents that "push" an employee in the direction of developing a sense of duty. From the organizational perspective, it also examines how organizations can "pull" individuals through the model in the process of cultivating a sense of duty.

This chapter also extends the forward thinking work of Meyer and Parfyonova (2010), who proposed that moral duty stems from a commitment profile of high normative and affective commitment. Specifically, they defined moral duty as "mindset that carries with it a strong sense of desire to pursue a course of action of benefit to a target because it is the right and moral thing to do" (Meyer & Parfyonova, 2010, p. 287). Although their work on moral duty has provided an invaluable contribution to the understanding of organizational commitment, by their own admission, it left room for further theoretical grounding and development of the duty construct upon which this chapter is based.

This analysis begins with a brief review of the theoretical underpinnings of duty. Next, a conceptual model of duty is proposed that focuses on individual and organizational antecedents, psychological processes, and the eventual outcomes of duty. A detailed review of the four phases of the model comprises the majority of the analysis. Special attention is devoted to the final phase (i.e., the Duty Phase), in order to effectively delineate the construct domain of duty, and establish its theoretical significance for both organizational commitment and other outcomes. Lastly, the chapter concludes with some implications and suggestions for future research.

BACKGROUND THEORY AND RESEARCH

Organizational Commitment

There have been well over three decades of important contributions to the organizational commitment literature. Beginning with Becker's (1960) side-bet theory, scholars have continuously attempted to accurately conceptualize the nature of commitment. These efforts have led to numerous contributions, such as the discovery of links between commitment and turnover (O'Reilly & Chatman, 1986), the attitudinal approach (Mowday, Steers, & Porter, 1979; Porter, Steers, Mowday, & Boulian, 1974), and several multi-dimensional approaches (Meyer & Allen, 1984; Meyer & Herscovitch, 2001). Although there are still several conceptualizations of commitment, it is Meyer and Allen's (1991) TCM of organizational commitment that dominated this field of research (Cohen, 2007).

Despite the fact that our knowledge and understanding of commitment has grown over the past three decades, there has been extremely limited theory and research in the area of duty, notwithstanding its recognized importance (Meyer & Parfyonova, 2010). This is a unique anomaly considering that duty, or some variation on the term (e.g., loyalty), has been mentioned in numerous articles for many years (Allen & Meyer, 1990; Hirschman, 1970; Wiener & Vardi, 1980). Unfortunately, even though there have been efforts by key scholars in this area to articulate the sub-dimension of duty, it was not until recently that Meyer and Parfyonova (2010) provided an initial conceptualization of moral duty. Until now, duty has represented a critical gap in the literature. We consistently have acknowledged its existence, both in academic and practical conversation, yet we have failed to fully explain its similarities and differences when compared with its parent construct: organizational commitment. Therefore, for both theoretical and practical reasons, the development of a more informed understanding of the duty construct represents a critically important need for the organizational sciences.

Social Exchange Theory

At the most basic level, the establishment of duty involves some type of exchange between two entities. Blau (1964, p. 6) believed social exchanges to be "limited to actions that are contingent on rewarding reactions from others and cease when these expected reactions are not forthcoming."

Typically, it is not comprised of only a single exchange, but rather it involves a series of exchanges that become progressively more demanding of each entity. During the course of these interactions, a set of rules or guidelines becomes established, which help members of the exchange better delineate their roles and responsibilities within the relationship (Emerson, 1976). Once these rules and norms of exchange have been established, it becomes possible to qualify the nature of the relationships.

Social exchanges rely heavily upon two specific rule sets: reciprocity rules and negotiated rules. Reciprocity rules are self-evident in that they insist on both entities repaying each other in kind for the other's actions. Gouldner (1960) distinguished between three types of reciprocity, which included interdependent exchanges, folk beliefs, and moral norms. Interdependent exchanges are the most basic form of reciprocity and suggest that the actions of one entity require an in kind response by another (Cropanzano & Mitchell, 2005; Gergen, 1969). However, folk beliefs and moral norms are based more on individuals' perceptions and ideals. Rather than base their actions on actual exchanges, their reciprocity is guided by personally held beliefs (e.g., spiritual, philosophical) regarding fairness and the treatment of others. Negotiated rules are marked by the offer of one quantity in return for another; these exchanges in particular are ever-present in daily life, with basic employment contracts (e.g., money in exchange for time) being the most ubiquitous example. Both of these exchange rule sets, and the accompanying types of reciprocity, represent critical components in the formation of a sense of duty between two members in a relationship and are discussed further in our duty development model.

Moral Duty

Duty is a construct so well-known in society that it immediately conjures up lay definitions, thereby making it difficult to fully capture the entirety of this construct in a scholarly fashion. For example, recent research by Hannah, Jennings, Bluhm, Peng, and Schaubroeck (2014, p. 220) defined individuals with a *duty orientation* as their "volitional orientation to loyally serve and faithfully support other members of the group, to strive and sacrifice to accomplish the tasks and missions of the group, and to honor its codes and principles." Although we agree with the tenets of this definition, outside of the volitional orientation element, these appear to constitute the outcomes of duty rather than a definition of the construct itself.

Perhaps this is because, logically, a feeling or sense of moral duty must precede the duty *orientation* outlined by Hannah and Colleagues (2014).

As an iteration on, and an evolution of, normative commitment, moral duty was borne from the organizational commitment literature. Just as organizations attempt to develop a sense of commitment in their employees, so must organizations strive to instill a sense of duty. The goal in this developmental process is to take the "I *should* do this" mentality that characterizes individuals high in normative commitment to an extreme. Throughout this chapter, we adopt Meyer and Parfyonova's (2010, p. 287) definition of moral duty, which states that duty is a "mindset that carries with it a strong sense of desire to pursue a course of action (e.g., OCB) of benefit to a target (e.g., organization) because it is the right and moral thing to do." This definition specifically outlines the beliefs espoused by individuals who feel a sense of obligation (or duty) to others or organizations. As such, it follows that individuals who feel this sense of obligation will manifest their beliefs in, for example, supporting group members and obeying codes and principles (i.e., take the form of a duty orientation). The definition offered by Meyer and Parfyonova (2010) also is closely in line with the work of Immanuel Kant who wrote extensively on the subject of duty, its method of developing commitment between individuals, and its relationship with morality.

At its very foundation, duty stems from a commitment that can be either legal or ethical, and results in the need or desire to fulfill an obligation. Kant (1994a) noted that the basis for this type of commitment could initially develop from basic human interactions. He believed that gratitude was a moral duty, such that individuals are obliged to acknowledge the beneficence of others (Kant, 1994a). Likewise, when individuals are in the position of the benevolent, they have a duty to spare their target any loss of self-respect by treating their "beneficence either as a mere debt that is owed him, or as a small favor" (Kant, 1994a, p. 113). What is embedded in each of these examples is the notion of exchange. Duty is formed through an exchange between individuals or agents. It is a response to an exchange that causes at least one of the parties involved to make the ends of the other their own (Kant, 1994a).

In the words of Immanuel Kant, duty and moral law have "by way of reason alone an influence on the human heart so much more powerful than all other incentives" (Kant, 1994b, p. 22). The two critical pieces of this statement are the incredible influence a feeling of duty can have upon individuals, and the inextricable link between duty and morality. We feel that both of these pieces are captured within Meyer and Parfyonova's (2010) definition, and that this definition provides a starting point for understanding how duty can be cultivated between agents through repeated exchanges.

DEVELOPMENTAL MODEL OF DUTY AND PROPOSITIONS

We present a developmental model of duty that utilizes social exchange theory to explain how individuals progress from left to right through the four different phases stemming from the TCM of commitment (see Fig. 1). This is not a typical box and arrow model. Duty development does not lend itself to an easy linear progression, but through this graphical depiction we show just how this process operates. Individual-level antecedents represent the first element of the model, and they illustrate that certain individuals are simply more dispositionally and culturally inclined to demonstrate a sense of duty. The four phases of the model are the Exchange, Development, Commitment, and Duty Phase, and each phase has at least one theoretical driver explaining the processes by which it achieves its intended purpose.

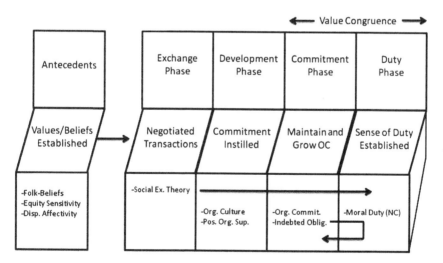

Fig. 1. The Duty Development Model of Individual Organizational Commitment.

For example, the purpose of the Development Phase is to provide a positive organizational culture and positive organizational support in order to instill a sense of commitment in employees. The model also indicates that the effects of social exchange theory are at work in every phase of the model. Essentially, this model illustrates how individuals enter into an organization with different backgrounds, how organizations seek to instill commitment in individuals, and ultimately, how such employees form or develop a sense of duty toward their organizations.

Antecedents of Duty

Each individual enters into an organization or employment contract with a unique disposition and background. There are many factors that can influence the ways individuals commit themselves to organizations, such as their natural dispositional affectivity. Also, individuals' backgrounds, particularly their upbringing, are of great importance in determining the possibility of cultivating a sense of duty. Of particular importance to this process are the exchange rules instilled in individuals leading up to their relationship with organizations. The following is an explanation of the three key antecedents of duty: folk beliefs, equity sensitivity, and dispositional affectivity.

The folk beliefs form of reciprocity is based upon the idea that individuals fully expect to receive what they deserve (Gouldner, 1960). A review of folk beliefs by Malinowski (1932) was reviewed by Cropanzano and Mitchell (2005), in which they explained that these beliefs could be summed up as "(a) a sense that over time all exchanges reach a fair equilibrium, (b) those who are unhelpful will be punished, and (c) those who are helpful will receive help in the future" (Cropanzano & Mitchell, 2005, p. 876). In many ways, this is the primary exchange antecedent that must be present or "believed in" by individuals who eventually are to develop a sense of duty. Without this basic notion being internalized and embraced by individuals, it is impossible to enter into the process that eventually results in duty.

Individuals also must be willing to "buy into" the concept of duty, consciously or unconsciously, if they are ever to develop a sense of duty. Before we can even discuss organizational commitment and its normative subcomponent, it is critical to first understand that some people are likely to be more receptive to embodying a sense of duty than are others. As alluded to above, duty is here conceptualized as a state of mind characterized by intentional action intended to benefit some entity driven or motivated by moral thought (Meyer & Parfyonova, 2010). Thus, it is natural that the development of duty begins with the mindset itself.

The folk beliefs of reciprocity also can be viewed as the "life lessons" that many people pass down to their children. The first is a sense that all exchanges eventually reach a fair equilibrium, and it is little different than telling a child that "you should always do the right thing, even if your friends do not." Why? Simply because everything works out in the end, and one day they will help you. This belief is supported strongly in what is known as the Protestant Work Ethic (PWE), essentially reflecting the belief that the only good things in life come from hard work. Of course, this idea is not exclusive to any one set of ideals or beliefs. Instead, raising individuals to believe in this set of reciprocity norms tills the soil that eventually will allow the seeds of duty to be planted.

Proposition 1. Individuals raised in a family or environment that espoused "folk beliefs" reciprocity norms will be more likely to develop a sense of duty toward a target organization than those who were not.

The second form of reciprocity inherent in social exchange theory is that of reciprocity as a moral norm. At its foundation, this type of reciprocity is based on the idea that there are rules dictating how one *should* or *ought* to behave, which is also the easiest way of differentiating it from folk beliefs. It has been argued that this type of reciprocity is a universal principle that helps guide all action (Gouldner, 1960; Wang, Tsui, Zhang, & Ma, 2003). However, even if we hold that to be true, from personal experience we know that there can be little debate that this norm varies in strength across individuals, cultural beliefs, and norms (Cropanzano & Mitchell, 2005; Shore & Coyle-Shapiro, 2003).

At a young age, individuals begin to learn the basic principles of reciprocity espoused by society. Through experience, their view on how they fit into this relationship becomes ingrained in their view of the world (Allen & Meyer, 1990). Essentially, this world view is akin to the concept of equity sensitivity. Equity theory posits that individuals analyze their relationships with others by assessing their outcomes versus their inputs compared to a referent other in a particular relationship (Miles, Hatfield, & Huseman, 1989). The three types of equity sensitives include entitleds, benevolents, and equity sensitives. Entitleds expect to receive more from a relationship than they are willing to give, benevolents prefer to give more than they receive in a relationship, and equity sensitives aim for an overall level of equality. Empirical research by King, Miles, and Day (1993) has shown that benevolents generally report high levels of job satisfaction even in the absence of rewards. Similarly, benevolents also tend to place a higher level of importance on their work, whereas entitleds tend to focus on their compensation (King et al., 1993).

Psychological research has demonstrated that there is a difference in the degree to which individuals endorse reciprocity (Clark & Mills, 1979), which can be viewed as a key antecedent in the development of duty. Again, duty is framed as a mindset that desires to pursue a course of action of benefit to a target. By definition, an act that is beneficial to a target is a benevolent action. The dutiful individual is not looking for something in exchange, but rather is performing an action for the sake of the referent other. Being a benevolent is not the same as embracing a sense of duty, but rather it is a critical antecedent (e.g., folk beliefs) that can help prepare individuals to espouse the beliefs inherent in duty. As such, the following proposition is formulated:

Proposition 2. Individuals classified as benevolents will be more likely than both equity sensitives and entitleds to develop a sense of duty toward a target organization.

It is just as likely that individuals' ratings on positive affectivity (PA) and negative affectivity (NA) will influence their ability to form a dutiful relationship. Despite the seemingly obverse relationship between these constructs, they are not opposites of each other, and each exists on its own continuum (Perrewé & Spector, 2002). Usually, individuals are rated along the continuum as either high or low, although they can fall anywhere along the spectrum.

We predict that individuals high on PA and low on NA are the most likely to develop a sense of duty. This is supported by previous work on affectivity indicating that individuals high on PA can be seen as "active, self-efficacious, and pleasurably engaged both *interpersonally* and in terms of achievement [emphasis added]" (George, 1992, p. 188). Similarly, those low on NA generally are seen as individuals who retain a sense of calm and are less prone to negative emotions (Cropanzano, Weiss, Hale, & Reb, 2003).

The first statement that high PA is helpful to the development of duty simply is a logically sound argument in that individuals who are more likely to engage in interpersonal relationships also are more likely to eventually strengthen those relationships. The argument is that low NA is also an individual-level antecedent, but it is not as obvious. No matter how hard organizations or individuals work to gain the commitment of others, there will be inevitable set-backs that can cause stress and second-guessing. Those low in NA are more likely to allow such setbacks to wash over them and continue with the relationship, as compared to those high in NA, who have a highly negative view of the world.

Proposition 3. Individuals rated high on PA and low on NA will be the most likely to develop a sense of duty than those in any other affectivity profile.

Proposition 4. Individuals rated high on NA and low on PA will be the least likely to develop a sense of duty.

Exchange Phase

When individuals enter an organization, generally they begin their relationship at what Fig. 1 refers to as the Exchange Phase. Social exchange theory suggests this is a phase characterized by negotiated rules as opposed to reciprocal relationships, where both parties engage in these negotiations so as to ensure that the agreement is mutually beneficial (Cook, Emerson, Gillmore, & Yamagishi, 1983). The arrangements that occur within this phase usually are very explicit, and sometimes can be legally binding (e.g., as seen with employment contracts). However, in most cases, these negotiated rules set the boundary conditions within which both parties agree to operate. There is no requirement to operate outside of these lines whatsoever. If employees are asked to work 40 hours a week, they are expected to work 40 hours a week. If the organization asks its employees to work longer than is contracted, some sort of additional compensation is required. Essentially, everything that is transacted between individuals and organizations is quid pro quo (Cropanzano & Mitchell, 2005).

The nature of these transactions (i.e., being predicated upon a quid pro quo relationship) has a tendency to produce relationships of lower quality between actors when compared to reciprocal exchanges (Molm, 2000, 2003). Particularly, relationships founded on negotiated transactions are characterized by lower levels of trust and commitment, greater uses of power, and a reduced level of equality (Molm, 1997; Molm, Peterson, & Takahashi, 1999; Molm, Takahashi, & Peterson, 2000). These are the types of relationships we expect to see between employees who are either new to an organization, unhappy with the organization, or simply working for a paycheck. There is not a desire to perform organizational citizenship behaviors or attempt to exceed the minimum standard without some form of compensation. For all intents and purposes, this represents the initial phase of almost any relationship, but particularly those of an economic or business nature.

Proposition 5. Individuals who consider themselves to be in a purely exchange-based relationship will express lower levels of trust and satisfaction in that relationship as compared to those who consider themselves in a relationship marked by reciprocal exchange rules.

Because the Exchange Phase of a relationship represents the most basic of exchanges, it is possible to state that everyone engaging in an employee-employer type relationship is capable of operating in this stage. More succinctly, all employment relationships initially must start at this phase, but it is possible for this phase to be bypassed by employees with the right mixture of antecedents, or by those who already have some allegiance to the organizations they are joining. An example of individuals who potentially could bypass this phase include those who begin working at a family business. In this instance, the relationship most likely would move directly into the later phases of the model because the employee (i.e., a family member) already may feel a sense of commitment to the organization (i.e., family owned). A second example is that of military service, where many individuals join the armed forces with a sense of moral obligation that leads them to feel a sense of commitment prior to the actual assumption of their day-to-day responsibilities.

Proposition 6. Individuals who place value in the duty-related antecedents of folk beliefs, moral norms, and reciprocity norms will indicate they spend less time in, or completely bypass, the Exchange Phase of duty development model.

Likewise, some people can remain in the Exchange Phase forever. These individuals could be those who choose their place of employment to meet a specific need, or who view their time in the organization as strictly temporary. Other people may be unable to develop a sense of duty due to an incongruence between their value set and that of the organization, or by choosing not to follow reciprocation norms. These individuals may be characterized as entitleds, who expect significantly lopsided returns on their investments of time and energy from their respective organizations (Miles et al., 1989). Recent research has witnessed a renewed interest in entitlement largely due to both academia and the mainstream media's use of this word to describe the millennial generation

(Fisk, 2010; Hochwarter, Summers, Thompson, Perrewé & Ferris, 2010; Twenge, 2007). Thus, it is possible that some individuals will either choose, or simply not be able, to move beyond this initial phase of their relationship.

Proposition 7. Individuals who do not place value in, or believe in, the duty-related antecedents of folk beliefs, moral norms, and reciprocity norms will have a higher rate of stagnation in the Exchange Phase.

Nonetheless, the onus for establishing commitment toward an organization rests not solely with individuals but also with the organizations themselves. Organizations intent on creating loyal and dutiful employees are required to help stimulate the growth of those psychosocial attachments within their members. Duty is not a construct that is encountered merely by chance, but rather something that is carefully cultivated over time. Some organizations may choose not to pursue any further type of relationship than negotiated transactions, for economic reasons or due to the nature of their employee population (e.g., high rates of turnover).

However, if organizations wish to move beyond relationships that involve only negotiated transactions, they need to work on building an organizational culture that expresses this belief. They need to clearly establish their own set of values that they then ask their employees to espouse. In doing so, organizations help generate a desire for reciprocal transactions among their employees, which tends to move these employees into the Development Phase.

Development Phase

Duty is a belief or concept that needs to be cultivated within individuals. As stated earlier, certain antecedents help render individuals more likely to become committed to organizations, but the responsibility for creating a sense of commitment generally rests with the referent other. For example, organizations go to great lengths to establish work programs and to construct workplaces that reinforce their identity and inspire commitment (Ashforth et al., 2011; Hatch & Schultz, 1997).

In a demonstration of commitment to employees, *Facebook* offered up to $3,000 for child-care expenses and an adoption assistance package worth up to $5,000 (Goodman, 2012). Increasingly, organizations are beginning to adopt practices that demonstrate commitment to their employees, such as providing on-site child-care and exercise facilities. Although it would be nice to believe that these represent altruistic acts of good will indicative of a progressive society, the reality is that they reflect purposeful actions aimed at facilitating a sense of commitment within their employee base. The logic behind these organizational actions relies heavily upon the norms of reciprocity.

The Development Phase is based upon the idea of a referent other (e.g., an organization) leveraging the rules of reciprocity and the nature of equity sensitivity to their overall benefit. As demonstrated in a later section of this chapter, duty transcends the rules of reciprocity, but also it has many of its foundations in this phase of development. Just as most people do not propose marriage on a second date, individuals must first establish a relationship before committing themselves completely to an organization. It is during this phase that organizations display themselves (i.e., their core identity and values) to their members. This is the phase in which organizational culture and perceived organizational support come to the forefront of the exchange relationship, thus allowing individuals to decide whether or not to become more engrossed in the relationship.

Organizational culture began with research from anthropologists and folklorists on the study of work customs and traditions (Hatch, 1993). The field of management adopted the study of organizational culture in the 1980s by creating a conceptual framework for not only understanding culture but also for cultural interventions to bring about change (Schein, 1981, 1983, 1984). This framework was developed by Schein, and it envisioned three particular levels of organizational culture: surface (artifacts), below which are underlying values, and at the core are basic assumptions, which represent the taken-for-granted beliefs about reality and human nature. The underlying assumption of Schein's model was that in order to understand the assumptions inherent in organizations, you first need to determine the linkages between their artifacts and values.

Schein's (1985) model was updated by Hatch (1993) so as to represent culture in a more dynamic fashion. Whereas Schein's (1985) model focused on the aforementioned three elements of culture (i.e., artifacts, values, and assumptions), this updated model was more concerned with the reciprocal processes (i.e., manifestation, realization, interpretation, and symbolization) that occurred between these elements (e.g., the manifestation of values leads to assumptions). This model demonstrates that an organization's assumptions and values can lead not only to each other through the process of manifestation but also to symbols and artifacts through the processes of realization and interpretation. In essence, the dynamism of this model asks how each of these elements combine to ultimately represent the organization's culture. As such, Hatch's (1993) cultural dynamics model is used to explain how organizations facilitate the instillation of duty during the Development Phase of duty formation.

In order to fully understand an organization's culture, an observer must have access to both the organization itself and its members. If job applicants had access only to organizations and not its members, they could view its artifacts but not make sense of them. Rather, observers would need access to the organization's members to help reveal the espoused values that the artifacts represent (Schein, 1990). Likewise, the processes at work between the elements of culture usually are not visible to outsiders. Therefore, it is through the process of manifestation that organizations produce artifacts that are representative of their assumptions and values. Hatch put this more succinctly as follows:

> In terms of the cultural dynamics framework, manifestation permits cultural assumptions to reveal themselves in the perceptions, cognitions, and emotions of organizational members. That is, manifestation contributes to the constitution of organizational culture by translating intangible assumptions into recognizable values. This constitution occurs through the advantage that manifestation gives to certain ways of seeing, feeling, and knowing within the organization. (1993, p. 662)

So, the members of the organizations are able to see not only the values but also the underlying assumptions that provide organizational guidance through this process of manifestation. For example, if organizations' underlying assumption is that employees generally feel a sense of duty to perform their jobs to the best of their ability, the organizations themselves will perceive acts of loyalty or duty more readily from their employees. More importantly, though, as indicated in the cultural dynamics model, this process also works in the opposite direction. Thus, individuals whose underlying assumptions include those factors that serve as antecedents of the establishment of duty (i.e., moral norms, folk beliefs, equity sensitivity, dispositional affectivity) will be more likely to perceive the acts of organizations as rewarding their behavior.

Ultimately, this is very similar to the idea of creating autonomy-supportive work climates (Gagne & Deci, 2005) as explained by self-determination theory (SDT; Ryan & Deci, 2000). The goal of the organization, in outwardly expressing its values and supporting its employees, is to facilitate a movement from external regulation (e.g., working because it is contractual) to a more autonomous regulation. Intrinsically motivated individuals, those who are not necessarily spurred forward by external forces, are characterized as internalizing the organizations' values and, subsequently, behaving accordingly without the need to regulate their behavior (Meyer, Becker, & Vandenberghe, 2004). In our model, we acknowledge the parallel to SDT, but focus more on the actions of the organization which facilitate the development of an autonomy supportive climate.

In the Exchange Phase, individuals are merely transacting with organizations that they perceive to be little more than blank slates. Although this may seem to be mere rhetoric, we must recognize that some employees (e.g., college students) may not be concerned with the culture of their current organizations. The blank slate may be a product of employees' choice to not partake in the culture, or it may be the result of organizations who expect high turnover, and therefore, are not interested in expending resources to create a particular culture (i.e., which could be considered a culture in and of itself).

The Development Phase is one step beyond the Exchange Phase, in that organizations now are assumed to be making an effort to present a coherent and very intentional organizational culture to their employees. This emphasis on individual-organizational value congruency was referred to by Wiener (1982) as organizational socialization. The artifacts and symbols of organizations are positioned such that employees are routinely exposed to them, trained in them, and expected to embody them. Through this use of value representation, the actual assumptions and values become known to employees who are subsequently retained, promoted, and evaluated on their adherence to them. At this point, when employees are expected to not only embrace a set of values but also outwardly embody them, an important decision point is reached on their path to developing duty.

Proposition 8. Organizations that dedicate resources to the development and promotion of a positive organizational culture while presenting a high level of organizational support will have more employees that characterize their employment relationship as reciprocally based rather than negotiated.

At this point, when organizations openly have exposed their culture and value set to their employees, a choice must be made as to whether the employees want to adopt a similar set of values. It is quite possible for employees to continue in an organization without adopting the values of the organization, but this situation is unlikely to lead to duty, and more likely to increase intention to turnover. On the other hand, if employees decide that the values *expressed* through the culture are congruent with their personal set of values, it can be expected that such individuals will form a sense of commitment to the organization. Essentially, this is

the difference between conformity to a set of values versus the internalization of a set of value. Whereas the former implies employees are following
external rules, the latter implies employees are controlling their own behavior because the values have become part of them.

This formation of commitment, which leads to reduced turnover, is at
the heart of how cultures perpetuate themselves, that is, through socialization, internalization, and retention. Organizations retain those members
who share the same set of "assumptions, beliefs, and values" (Schein, 1990,
p. 115). This perpetuation of culture continues to surround employees with
like-minded individuals, which can deepen their beliefs about how they fit
into the organization, and subsequently increase their level of commitment.

Commitment Phase

The Development Phase of the relationship between individuals and organizations denotes the move toward interdependence, which is the last of the
three reciprocity norms of social exchange theory. Interdependence is the
antithesis of both independence and dependence. Thus, interdependence
can be viewed as a state in which all parties involved rely upon some form
of mutual exchange, and where each transaction is bidirectional (Molm,
1994). This relationship now can be viewed in two ways. One is under the
lens of power dynamics, which shows that the dependence of actors on
the organization is equivalent to the dependence of the organization on the
actors (Emerson, 1962).

In another way, it could be said that the two entities involved in a relationship are now sacrificing their independence of each other. By continuing the development of the relationship, they are building trust and forging
a stronger reliance upon each other (Molm, 2000). Likewise, as they eschew
independence, they begin to embrace a certain level of dependence. This is
not just dependence on the other, but rather a realization that the referent
other is now just as dependent on the individual. These transactions
of independence and dependence are brought upon and explained best
through the construct of organizational commitment.

Historically, the study of organizational commitment has been divided
into two separate approaches: behavioral and attitudinal (Meyer & Allen,
1991; Mowday, Porter, & Steers, 1982; Reichers, 1985). Mowday et al.
(1982, p. 26) described behavioral commitment as relating "to the process
by which individuals become locked into a certain organization and
how they deal with this problem." The attitudinal approach embodies

the relationship individuals form or develop with organizations, to include the extent to which their values compare to those of the organizations, as well as their feelings of desire or obligation toward continued organizational membership (Meyer & Allen, 1991). Clearly, duty is a component of attitudinal commitment.

The attitudinal approach is the most well-established stream of research on organizational commitment, and it helps explain the initial transactions leading to the development of duty. Originally conceptualized in the 1960s by Howard Becker's *side-bet* theory, it was posited that commitment meant individuals remained with organizations because of the personal costs that leaving would incur (Becker, 1960). This theory was expanded by Porter and colleagues who viewed commitment as a form of psychological attachment to organizations. Specifically, commitment was defined as "... the relative strength of an individual's identification with and involvement in a particular organization" (Mowday et al., 1979).

The next major updates to the commitment literature occurred in the 1980s, with two multi-dimensional models proposed. Ultimately, it was Meyer and Allen's (1984) conceptualization of commitment as two-dimensional, including affective and continuance commitment, that was adopted by most of the field (Cohen, 2007). Eventually, this multi-dimensional model became the TCM when it was expanded to include normative commitment (Meyer & Allen, 1991, 1997).

The intent of the TCM is to accurately conceptualize the psychological states of attitudinal commitment experienced by individuals (Allen & Meyer, 1990). This model was first developed to explain the multi-dimensional nature of commitment experienced by employees in the workplace, but more recently it has been applied to workplace commitments as a whole (Meyer & Herscovitch, 2001). An attitudinal approach to organizational commitment assumes that some set of conditions serve as antecedents to individuals' commitment, which then results in some behavior being elicited. This is in contrast to the behavioral approach that views individuals' behavior as occurring first and then affecting their psychological state, which subsequently either reinforces or attempts to change future behaviors (O'Reilly & Chatman, 1986). Thus, a pre-requisite to commitment is a set of antecedent conditions that lead to the psychological state of commitment.

Foundationally, the TCM is predicated on the idea that all literature regarding attitudinal commitment addresses three key themes: affective attachment, perceived costs, and obligation (Meyer & Allen, 1991). Generally, affective attachment is what is commonly thought of when the term commitment is used in conversation. An early definition by Mowday et al. described commitment as "the relative strength of an individual's identification with and involvement in a particular organization" (1979, p. 226). Perceived costs refer to Becker's (1960) side-bet theory, and also refers to what individuals would lose if they were to sever ties with an organization. Obligation is self-explanatory in that it describes those individuals who feel that it is morally right to remain with an organization for reasons of loyalty or other personal attachments.

The three forms of commitment (i.e., affective, continuance, and normative) align closely with the aforementioned key themes embodied in the TCM. Affective commitment stems from individuals' emotional attachment to organizations, and in its basic form, explains that people remain in their organizations by choice. On the other hand, continuance commitment refers to individuals who feel the need to remain with organizations, which could be for financial stability or other exogenous reasons. Normative commitment is the basic building block for duty, and it refers to a sense of commitment individuals feel because they "ought to remain" with an organization (Meyer & Allen, 1991, p. 67). It is this last form of commitment that is of greatest concern when analyzing duty.

The very nature of normative commitment (i.e., that individuals feel they should remain with an organization) already sounds very similar to most conceptions of duty. Normative commitment has been described by others as being "characterized by a *mindset of obligation* (e.g., obligation to remain with the organization or support a change initiative)" (Meyer & Parfyonova, 2010, p. 283). As such, it is then natural to use this type of commitment as the primary building block of duty. Although normative commitment is the primary form of commitment necessary for establishing duty, Meyer and Parfyonova (2010) posited that both affective and continuance commitments are critical in establishing a difference between moral duty and indebtedness.

The two distinct organizational commitment "formulas" proposed by Meyer and Parfyonova (2010) use normative commitment as the base. One formula, moral duty, posits an affective and normative commitment (AC/NC) combination, whereas the other, indebtedness, posits a continuance and normative commitment (CC/NC) mixture. In many ways, these combinations are similar in nature to the commitment profiles proposed and tested by Meyer and Herscovitch (2001) and Herscovitch and Meyer (2002). It is not that individuals with an AC/NC profile are devoid of continuance commitment, but rather it is that they score more highly on the other two forms of commitment. Individuals' commitment profiles simply represent measures of how they score on each form of commitment, generally broken down into high or low on each. In the case of indebtedness, it can be said that individuals who feel this type of obligation are high on both continuance and normative commitment. It is not that they do not experience feelings of affective commitment, but rather that it is simply not as salient as the others.

Understanding the basis of commitment profiles allows for a further explanation of the distinction between the two profiles: indebted obligation and moral duty. Because it is proposed in our model that only a sense of indebted obligation can exist in this phase (i.e., the Commitment Phase), we begin with an overview of the same. Meyer and Parfyonova (2010, p. 287) described the indebted obligation mindset as reflecting "a sense of having to pursue a course of action of benefit to a target to avoid the social costs of failing to do so." As such, they also proposed that individuals with a CC/NC-dominant profile would demonstrate less positive beliefs and affect toward the target of their commitment. Feelings of guilt and frustration should be expected to be keen motivators of indebted obligation, because these individuals are not impelled forward by a moral calling, but rather by the need to fulfill a perceived debt. This supports the idea that the social exchange theory is still at work in this phase, just as in the first two. The exception is that although this indebted obligation mindset closely resembles the idea of reciprocation, it is actually more a product of interdependence than mutual exchange.

Whereas reciprocation clearly is a quid pro quo process, exemplified in the Exchange and Development Phases, indebted obligation has its roots in an understanding of the need for interdependence between individuals and organizations. At this point of the relationship, the psychological contract between the individual and the organization is well and deeply set. It is likely that if individuals feel they are not contributing to the organization at an adequate level, and thereby breaching this contract, they will experience negative feelings such as guilt (Rousseau, 1995). This belief stems from the recognition that organizations require individuals' efforts in order to be successful and to sustain themselves. Likewise, in the same vein as continuance commitment, individuals also recognize that their future well-being is tied to the success of their organization (Cohen, 2007). This sense of interdependence helps cultivate the sense of commitment between individuals and organizations.

Individuals are no longer *reciprocating* because they have to, but rather because they feel guilty for not doing so. It is no longer about performing a job in return for compensation, but rather for a sense of indebted obligation to the organization as a whole — the abstract manifestation, the supervisors, the subordinates, the peers, the customers, etc. (Meyer & Parfyonova, 2010). It is likely that most individuals will never move beyond the phase of indebted obligation. This should not be surprising as it is most likely that we have all experienced this emotion at one point or another toward an organization, whether it be the workplace or a hobby/volunteer based group with which we are involved. When we say the words − "I really *should* do this because of all they do for me and my family" − we may be expressing a sense of indebted obligation. Apart from staying in the Commitment Phase, there are two other possibilities. Individuals can move on to the Duty Phase, or they can make a temporary excursion into the Duty Phase, only to return back to where they started.

As depicted in Fig. 1, a hooked arrow extends from the Commitment Phase into the Duty Phase, and then returns back to the Commitment Phase. This is representative of the fact that individuals experiencing a sense of indebted obligation are prone to temporarily enter into the final Duty Phase in order to fulfill obligations. However, once the obligation is fulfilled, they are apt to return to the Commitment Phase. It is unlikely that individuals moving into the Duty Phase temporarily actually adopt the duty mindset (i.e., an actual AC/NC profile), but rather simply engages in behaviors similar to that of someone who is in the actual Duty Phase. Thus, although the behaviors are similar, the mindsets/motives behind those behaviors are very different. This aligns with Meyer and Parfyonova's (2010, p. 287) definition of indebted obligation as "something that must be done to avoid social costs." We also add to this definition that indebted obligations also cause individuals to attempt actions that will rebalance the perception that they are in debt.

Although this seems very much like another form of reciprocation, it is quite different in that the employees who are experiencing a sense of indebted obligation are not necessarily reciprocating any particular action by the organization. Here, individuals feel indebted to organizations for more abstract quantities that might include their individual treatment, quality of life, overall value congruence, or even their relationship with their supervisors and subordinates.

Proposition 9. Individuals with a sense of indebted obligation temporarily will demonstrate duty-like behaviors after they perceive some sort of imbalance in their relationship with their organization in which they feel they owe some sort of debt.

An apt, but unfortunately clichéd, example of indebted obligation is that of the character in a novel or movie that saves the life of another. Until they are able to "repay the debt," they remain forever in that person's debt.

Essentially, the indebted individuals now experience a temporary sense of duty that is finite in the sense that it will end when they perceive the debt has been repaid. Although this example may be somewhat extreme, it is not difficult to conjure up similar examples that occur in the workplace. Of course, it is possible that individuals who enter the final phase (i.e., the Duty Phase) will remain there indefinitely. It may have begun simply as a sense of indebted obligation, or it may have been a product of other antecedents and commitment forces, but this final phase marks not only the boundary of social exchange theory but also the highest form of commitment possible between actors and their targets.

Duty Phase

The Duty Phase is the final phase of commitment that individuals can reach, and it frames the focal construct of this chapter. Entrance into this phase specifically is marked by the notion that many of the principles of social exchange theory no longer are applicable. No longer is the relationship between individuals and organizations marked by negotiated transactions, reciprocal interactions, or even a sense of interdependence. These actions and feelings are replaced almost wholly by a sense of dependence. Very much like in the Commitment Phase, where individuals recognize that an organization is dependent on their performance, this phase is marked by a sacrifice of independence by individuals that signifies the understanding that the individuals are responsible for the dependent target. This is a complex interaction of dependencies that is unpacked in the following analysis.

First, it is necessary to note that, at this point in the duty development model of organizational commitment, only a small number of individuals remain. Whereas we could expect a vast majority of the population to enter into the initial Exchange Phase, and a smaller although still large portion of individuals to enter subsequent phases, the Duty Phase witnesses the entrance of only a small number of individuals. This is a product of two processes (i.e., individual antecedents and organizational characteristics), both of which have been extensively covered up to this point, and thus are not belabored further. The point is that individuals are most likely to feel a sense of duty if both they (i.e., through individual-level antecedents), and the organization (i.e., through organizational programs) interact together.

Proposition 10. Individuals who self-report themselves to have entered the Duty Phase also will be more likely to self-report that the antecedents of duty accurately describe themselves, and that their organization invests in duty-related organizational programs.

Proposition 11. Individuals who self-report themselves to have entered the Duty Phase also will be more likely to self-report that they feel their organization supports their beliefs.

Next, a moral duty mindset is born out of a commitment profile that is highest on both affective and normative commitment. Normative commitment can be defined as "the belief by an individual that one has a moral obligation to engage in a mode of conduct reflecting loyalty and duty in all social situations in which one has a significant personal involvement" (Cohen, 2007). The key part of this definition is "moral obligation." In this form of commitment, individuals are drawn not by the threat of material loss, guilt, frustration, or the allure of material gain, but rather by an intrinsic and imperceptible force to do the right thing. Again, much like in SDT, this is very similar to the difference between introjected and identified regulation (Gagne & Deci, 2005).

Meyer and Parfyonova (2010, p. 288) went further and described the moral duty mindset as being "associated with positive beliefs (e.g., inherent goodness, meaningfulness) and affect (e.g., optimism, inspiration) with regard to the target and behavioral implications of the commitment." It is here that the differences between moral duty and indebted obligation become clearly illuminated. The drivers of moral duty are internal, whereas indebted obligation essentially is an externally driven concept. In a similar vein, moral duty is inspired in someone, whereas indebted obligation is born out of guilt.

Understanding the actual make-up of moral duty allows further explanation of the aforementioned dependency dynamics. The key to understanding this relationship is twofold. First, the reader must recognize that duty transcends the rules of social exchange theory, and second, that actors do not always behave rationally (Shafir & LeBoeuf, 2002). Instead, we must look to the less researched, but no less fertile, area of interpersonal exchanges. Even though Fiske (1991) found that little research has been accomplished on this area in management, the fields of anthropology and sociology have developed several models of interpersonal exchange.

A total of six rule sets that help guide action under the umbrella of social exchange theory were posited by Meeker (1971), and it is the interpersonal exchange rule of altruism that helps explain duty. A basic definition of altruism can be considered as "a rule whereby we seek to benefit another person even at an absolute cost to ourselves" (Cropanzano & Mitchell, 2005, p. 879). Essentially, the definition itself seems to defy the use of the term "exchange." In many ways, an "absolute cost" indicates a one way transaction that negates the possibility of a transaction or exchange. Not surprisingly, the inclusion of altruism within social exchange theory has drawn criticism by those who claim this type of relationship is not possible (for a review of this debate, see Batson, 1995).

The claim that altruism cannot be possible is understandable. Perhaps the best evidence of the divisiveness of this issue is its prevalence in the writings of Aristotle, St. Thomas Aquinas, Thomas Hobbes, Nietzsche, Freud, and many others. More recently, authors such as Batson (1991) and Batson and Shaw (1991) have forwarded empirical and theoretical arguments in support of altruism. Generally, the counterarguments to altruism have focused on the ideas of egoism and selfishness (Avolio & Locke, 2002). Within these arguments, it is posited that people will help only as much as they will be helped, or rewarded, in return (Batson & Shaw, 1991).

In many ways, this is an argument that revolves around the notion of the rational man – that all individuals are motivated and driven to make rational decisions within allowable bounds. Nonetheless, we must recognize that people do not always act rationally (Meeker, 1971). The idea of individuals being driven only by rationality has endured great criticism as common sense tells us that there are other motivating factors. Ghoshal (2005) explained the emergence of altruistic behaviors even in situations designed specifically to eliminate them:

> It is not only in behaviors such as mothers taking care of their children, people leaving a tip after a meal in restaurants they are unlikely to visit again, or Peace Corps volunteers toiling amid the depravations of impoverished countries that the limitations of the self-interest model become clear-they become manifest even in careful experiments devised by economists to test their theories under controlled conditions in which "aberrations," such as altruism or love are strictly excluded. (Ghoshal, 2005, p. 83)

Although moral duty is brought about quite rationally, it can result in irrational behavior. What is the rational explanation for employees who work 65 hours a week even though they are only paid for 40? Is it the prestige associated with being the one who "turns out the lights every night?" What if such individuals work from home and there is no one watching their behavior? Is there an intrinsic benefit to being the one who produces the most during a supposed "40" hour time frame? This is a muddy part of duty in that it can be quantified only by the individual in question. As an internal construct, the fine line between acting for some external reward and acting because one feels a sense of duty to an organization only can be elucidated by the individual. If we assume that there are individuals who act altruistically (i.e., at *absolute* cost to themselves), then we must also concede that there is some sense of irrationality present.

It is pertinent to first discuss an extreme example of this irrationality as a form of evidence in support of altruism's existence, and then to present a milder example that facilitates further generalizability. There are countless incidents of individuals who give their lives in order to save the life of another. This act of altruism can occur anywhere, but the proposed perspective suggests that it is most likely to occur in instances in which individuals have a sense of commitment to a target (e.g., actor or organization). As an example, throughout history, soldiers have literally "jumped on grenades" in order to save the lives of their comrades. Such actions, which will result in certain death for the individual, represent the most extreme form of absolute cost. There can be no selfishness in this act.

In a series of correspondences with Bruce Avolio, Edwin Locke argued that it is a "misconception that self-sacrifice or altruism is synonymous with helping others," and that "helping others is not necessarily self-sacrificial ... it can be done for selfish motives" (Avolio & Locke, 2002, p. 170). This statement cannot be refuted outright, as it is clear that many people engage in helping behaviors in order to gain some benefit themselves (e.g., credit, good favor). What is in question here is not a form of impression management, but rather an authentic attempt to help others without benefit to oneself; an attempt that, by definition, should be considered irrational.

The military relies heavily on duty because they require young men and women to take leadership roles early in their careers and consequently, at a fairly young age. Recognizing that these individuals will need to perform without extensive supervision means that instilling a sense of duty is a way to ensure people do "the right thing, even when no one is looking." The benefit of duty is that it instills an internal mechanism in individuals to actively pursue actions that are of benefit to the organization as a whole. Individuals are not simply acting out of a sense of guilt, but rather out of an intrinsic belief that what they are doing is necessary and required of them.

Proposition 12. Organizations that design, implement, and support organizational systems that support the development of affective and normative commitment (organizational culture, positive organizational support, etc. ...) will be more likely to produce dutiful organizational members.

This is a switch from an emphasis on individual gain to group gain. Altruistic motives include the intention to benefit the group as opposed to just oneself, which hearkens back to the equity sensitivity construct. Individuals may put forth a significant amount of input even if the personal return prospect is very small, especially if the overall output/return is large for the group. These examples abound in everyday society, from the volunteers who work at food banks to the police officers who put in extra hours during disaster recovery in order to keep the community safe. In an organizational context, simply volunteering to stay late in order to restock a shelf is an example of altruism. An altruistic act can be small, but it is still made of the same basic stuff inherent in greater levels of sacrifice.

When discussing concepts that lie in the extremes, such as altruism, it is convenient to discuss similarly extreme examples. Obviously, the above example of the soldier is one such extreme. However, it is not likely that this will be applicable to the workplace. Thus, it is imperative to remember that altruism can be operational in even the most basic of actions. Examples might include the following: children that, without being told, hand a stranger a toy truck to play with, adults riding the subway who offer a piece of gum to a complete stranger, and employees who miss one of their children's soccer games to help a coworker finish a project, full well knowing they will receive no credit or reward for their actions. These examples are not meant to trivialize the notion of altruism, but to exemplify that its presence can be felt in day-to-day interactions between people and in organizations.

The examples of duty on the organization level are no less murky than the individual level. Just as the deciding factor as to whether an action is considered altruistic on the individual level is intent, so it is on the organization level as well. The greater difficulty arises because now the possibly altruistic acts are subject to greater levels of external biases and pressures. One possible example is that of Costco and its founder, Jim Sinegal. The employees of Costco are paid up to 40% more than the rivals in their sector (Ranft, Ferris, & Perryman, 2007). Arguments could be made that Sinegal's policy is motivated by selfishness in that he pays more in order to increase profits by reducing turnover, lowering training costs, and developing a committed team. However, if we take him at his word (i.e., he is in the business of "building an organization" not the "business of making money"), we may be able to see his decision as altruistic.

The labor market for employees to work at Costco or Wal-Mart is vast, and the training required for new employees is presumably low. Thus, many of the incentives that Sinegal uses to retain employees actually may be costly for the organization. In fact, Costco's labor costs account for roughly 70% of the their operating costs — a staggering 40% more than Wal-Mart (Cascio, 2006). This action, paired with the potential for its outcome not leading to increased revenue, is inherently irrational. The most rational choice would be to match the wages of his rivals so as to increase overall profits. Instead, in order to demonstrate his *commitment*, or sense of duty, to his employees, Sinegal engages his employees in an altruistic (i.e., though not at a level requiring absolute cost) manner. In his own words, Sinegal claimed that his practices are "not just altruism, it's good business" (Frey, 2004, p. 2).

Furthermore, facilitating "good business" is the underlying reason that many organizations attempt to instill a sense of duty in their employees. Although, duty formation is certainly not a requirement for the success of an organization, it can be viewed as a resource that aids in sustainable performance. Employees of Costco who feel a sense of duty to the organization may reciprocate their higher wages and better working conditions by not missing working, showing more care for the customer, and even remaining in the organization for their entire career.

CONTRIBUTIONS

This chapter makes four important contributions to the commitment literature by building upon Meyer and Allen's (1991) TCM to help solidify the theoretical underpinnings of moral duty. First, the duty development model clearly addresses the lack of scholarship at the highest end of organizational commitment research. Following the charge led by Meyer and Parfyonova (2010), this chapter helps bridge the gap that existed before the formal conceptualization of duty. By providing a strong theoretical framework within which duty and its development can be housed, a greatly needed gap in the organizational commitment literature has been filled. This highest level of commitment, duty, is no longer a construct whose existence only can be acknowledged, but now can be explained, understood, and empirically investigated.

Second, this chapter presents a model of duty development that can be used by both scholars and organizations to better understand the processes through which duty is cultivated. This model provides a double-sided view of commitment as it explicitly requires the reader to recognize that actions by both individuals and organizations are required during these process dynamics. By beginning with individual-level antecedents of duty development, a more refined understanding of duty, and the idea that not everyone is "prone" to experiencing this level of commitment, is possible.

The notion that not all individuals are capable of entering the Duty Phase may be one reason that organizations are often reluctant to expend resources toward developing commitment in their employees. The possibility of these individuals abusing the system is ever-present, but organizations that focus on selecting individuals prone to developing a sense of duty should be able to spend resources on their employees' development with more confidence. Practitioners in organizations willing to undertake the development of duty should find the model easy to understand, with the basic principles being easily extracted for future use. Academics will find the model to be theoretically grounded and ready for empirical testing.

Third, the duty development model of organizational commitment provides the initial framework for further study through empirical testing. The model is built upon well-established theories and constructs drawn from the organizational science literature, which will make future testing possible and beneficial. Along with the model, several key propositions are presented as launching points from which to begin this research. These propositions are by no means exhaustive, but rather what can be construed as the most salient and impactful questions that need to be answered. Further review of the model will yield other important propositions that also will be able to eventually contribute to the field.

Lastly, this study builds upon the social exchange theory literature, particularly altruism, and on the more recent work of Meyer and Parfyonova (2010). Social exchange is one of the most well-established theories in our field and in general, thus in need of little further testing. However, the more nuanced exchange relationships first proposed by Meeker (1971) have not received much attention. Altruism is one of these exchange relationships, and it is a keystone to my argument on duty development. The explanation of altruism in this chapter, along with its use in the individual-organization exchange in the Duty Phase, helps advance this aspect of social exchange theory by both enriching the literature and providing practical examples of its presence in the real world. Lastly, this work is indebted to Meyer and Parfyonova (2010), who first posited that moral duty was comprised of a commitment profile of high normative and affective commitments. Hopefully, by providing a nomological net composed of social exchange theory, the proposed conceptualization is viewed as building upon the initial foundation they laid for this construct.

IMPLICATIONS

The concept of duty, and its development, has several practical implications that can be brought to bear by organizations looking to focus on increasing employee commitment, and eventually instilling a sense of duty in their employees. The antecedents outlined in the model are readily measureable or detectable through regularly used selection processes. A simple employment interview could be used to discover an employee's background in reciprocity norms or folk beliefs, with an administration of the five factor personality model providing a picture of their dispositional qualities. Using this information can lead employers to select those individuals who are most likely to contribute to their organizations over the long term.

At the same time, organizations themselves also are responsible for cultivating a sense of duty by motivating its employees. As outlined in the model, organizations' efforts to embrace and support a positive organizational culture, positive organizational support, and foster a sense of organizational commitment all support the development of a sense of moral duty within individuals. Clearly, this concept is at work in organizations (e.g., military and Costco) that expend a significant amount of resources in an effort to instill a sense of duty in its members. Because duty is pursued by both of these organizations, they are more likely to generate dutiful employees by helping them advance through the phases of commitment.

FUTURE RESEARCH

This initial conceptualization of the construct represents only an initial starting point for research on duty within the study of organizational commitment. Many future research opportunities can be found in the provided propositions. These avenues of research are ready for empirical testing and further explication. The model itself also contains several other areas that can be empirically examined. It is also encouraged that scholars look for other factors that may affect duty development. It is probable that generational and cultural differences, personality characteristics (e.g., conscientiousness), or other individual differences (e.g., grit, Duckworth & Quinn, 2009) will affect individuals' progress through the phases of duty development.

The perspective taken in this chapter is most likely a Western-centric view of duty based on the individualistic culture found in this region of the world. Although we do not expect duty to be exclusive to individualistic societies, it is likely that variations on the presented duty development model will appear in collectivist cultures. Foundationally, there is empirical evidence that individualists are more likely to comply with requests if they have done so in the past; whereas complying to requests in collectivist cultures is based more upon social proof principles (e.g., my peers complied) (Cialdini, Wosinska, Barrett, Butner, & Gornik-Durose, 1999). We presented duty as a steadily building set of increasing commitments made between the individual and the organization. It may be that employees in collectivist cultures develop a sense of duty as a group, or that the actual cycle of duty development is expedited by group norms.

Grit, defined as "maintaining effort and interest over years despite failure, adversity, and plateaus in progress" provides a particularly interesting intersection with duty development (Duckworth, Peterson, Matthews, & Kelly, 2007, p. 1087). Individuals with grit may be able to weather more of the inevitable storms that face an organization, thus leading to their spending a longer duration of time within the duty development model. Using the phases of commitment that lead up to duty will be another viable research tool to help our field expand and further develop organizational commitment research as a whole. The clear delineation of these phases and the processes contained within will lend themselves to helping provide a better understanding of how organizations can instill not just commitment, but duty, in their employees. These phases also may help us understand how, when, and if commitment profiles can change throughout an individual's tenure in an organization.

Creating a measure of duty will be of great importance to future research. Hannah et al. (2014) produced a measure of duty orientation that shows some promise in capturing duty within individuals. Nonetheless, their definition of duty *orientation* does not fully capture the commitment aspect of duty, instead choosing to rely heavily upon the actions of a dutiful individual. Their measure is beneficial, but a greater focus on the aspects of duty related to organizational commitment will be required to adequately measure duty. A new measure of duty not only will need to be able to determine if an individual is dutiful, but also it should help researchers understand where along the duty development continuum they currently reside.

Although the proposed perspective attempted to provide a view of duty from both the individual's and the organization's perspective, there is much room for further research on how organizations develop a sense of duty toward their employees, and how duty development occurs on different organizational levels. For example, instead of perceived organizational support, we may find that ideas like vision statements and identity formation are responsible for shaping organizations and their leaders' sense of duty toward the employee. Similarly, how did Costco come to embrace such a dutiful vision? It is likely that the model is very similar to the one proposed in this chapter, except that instead of individual antecedents, we may see founder's antecedents. Obviously, this is a very complex issue, but it is imperative that we understand duty from this perspective as well. If organizations expect dutiful employees, then employees will expect dutiful organizations.

Additionally, further research on both the benefits and drawbacks of duty is necessary. The intent of this chapter was to focus on the development of duty while also explaining the construct itself. It is likely that the benefits of duty extend beyond retention and work performance. There are other possible benefits that may stem from lower supervisory costs, high levels of value congruence, and many other areas. Despite the benefits, it is likely that there is a possible nonlinear relationship between duty and work outcomes. Thus, although there may be an optimal level of duty, it is possible that exceeding that point could have negative effects on individuals. Duty could be taken to an extreme that may lead to workaholism or just a poor work/life balance. Ultimately, this could lead to negative consequences for organizations, so it is important to conduct further research into the possibility of a nonlinear relationship between duty and work outcomes.

Individuals may become so fiercely loyal to organizations that they cover up wrongdoing on behalf of the organizations. Events such as this may lead to cognitive dissonance brought upon by conflicting "sets" of duty. It is likely that organizations who are prone to dutiful relationships involve themselves in more than one. As such, individuals may feel a duty to their organization, their spouse, their faith, or any other number of areas. If this is the case, it is possible that acting dutifully in one area may lead to a "lapse" in others. A detailed analysis of whether or not individuals can have sets of "competing" duties, and how they interact, is certainly in order.

CONCLUSION

Although organizational commitment has been an active area of scientific inquiry for three decades, there has been little to no dedicated research on its highest incarnation despite its recognized importance, that is, the concept of duty. Despite its rich history in philosophy and numerous mentions throughout the commitment literature, only recently has it begun to be fully developed. Properly harnessed, duty has the potential to help organizations learn to retain individuals in today's highly mobile society. Hopefully, the proposed conceptualization of duty development will stimulate further research and discussion on how our field's understanding of duty can help today's organizations.

ACKNOWLEDGMENTS

The authors would like to thank Dr. John Meyer for his insightful comments on an earlier version of this manuscript. The authors would like to thank Dr. John Meyer for his insightful comments on an earlier version of this manuscript.

REFERENCES

Allen, N. J., & Meyer, J. P. (1990). The measurement and antecedents of affective, continuance and normative commitment to the organization. *Journal of Occupational Psychology*, *63*(1), 1–18.

Ashforth, B. E., Rogers, K. M., & Corley, K. G. (2011). Identity in organizations: Exploring cross-level dynamics. *Organization Science*, *22*(5), 1144–1156.

Avolio, B. J., & Locke, E. E. (2002). Contrasting different philosophies of leader motivation: Altruism versus egoism. *The Leadership Quarterly*, *13*(2), 169–191.

Batson, C. D. (1991). *The altruism question: Toward a social psychological answer*. Hillsdale, NJ: Lawrence Erlbaum.

Batson, C. D. (1995). Prosocial motivation: Why do we help others? In A. Tesser (Ed.), *Advanced social psychology* (pp. 333–381). Boston, MA: McGraw-Hill.

Batson, C. D., & Shaw, L. L. (1991). Evidence for altruism: Toward a pluralism of prosocial motives. *Psychological Inquiry*, *2*(2), 107–122.

Becker, H. S. (1960). Notes on the concept of commitment. *American Journal of Sociology*, *66*(1), 32–40.

Blau, P. M. (1964). *Exchange and power in social life*. New Brunswick, NJ: Wiley.

Cascio, W. F. (2006). Decency means more than "always low prices": A comparison of Costco to Wal-Mart's Sam's Club. *Academy of Management Perspectives*, *20*(3), 26–37.

Cialdini, R. B., Wosinska, W., Barrett, D. W., Butner, J., & Gornik-Durose, M. (1999). Compliance with a request in two cultures: The differential influence of social proof and commitment/consistency on collectivists and individualists. *Personality and Social Psychology Bulletin*, *25*, 1242–1253.

Clark, M. S., & Mills, J. (1979). Interpersonal attraction in exchange and communal relationships. *Journal of Personality and Social Psychology*, *37*(1), 12–24.

Cohen, A. (2007). Commitment before and after: An evaluation and reconceptualization of organizational commitment. *Human Resource Management Review, 17*(3), 336–354.

Cook, K. S., Emerson, R. M., Gillmore, M. R., & Yamagishi, T. (1983). The distribution of power in exchange networks: Theory and experimental results. *American Journal of Sociology, 89*(2), 275–305.

Cropanzano, R., & Mitchell, M. S. (2005). Social exchange theory: An interdisciplinary review. *Journal of Management, 31*(6), 874–900.

Cropanzano, R., Weiss, H. M., Hale, J. M. S., & Reb, J. (2003). The structure of affect: Reconsidering the relationship between negative and positive affectivity. *Journal of Management, 29*(6), 831–857.

Dess, G. G., & Shaw, J. D. (2001). Voluntary turnover, social capital, and organizational performance. *Academy of Management Review, 26*(3), 446–456.

Duckworth, A. L., Peterson, C., Matthews, M. D., & Kelly, D. R. (2007). Grit: Perseverance and passion for long-term goals. *Journal of Personality and Social Psychology, 92*(6), 1087–1101.

Duckworth, A. L., & Quinn, P. D. (2009). Development and validation of the short grit scale. *Journal of Personality Assessment, 91*(2), 166–174.

Eisenberger, R., Armeli, S., Rexwinkel, B., Lynch, P. D., & Rhoades, L. (2001). Reciprocation of perceived organizational support. *Journal of Applied Psychology, 86*(1), 42–51.

Emerson, R. M. (1962). Power-dependence relations. *American Sociological Review, 27*(1), 31–41.

Emerson, R. M. (1976). Social exchange theory. *Annual Review of Sociology, 2*, 335–362.

Fisk, G. (2010). "I want it all and I want it now!" An examination of the etiology, expression, and escalation of excessive employee entitlement. *Human Resources Management Review, 20*, 102–114.

Fiske, A. P. (1991). *Structures of social life*. New York, NY: Free Press.

Frey, C. (2004). Costco's love of labor: Employees' well-being key to its success. Seattle Post Intelligencer, March 29. Retrieved from www.seattlepi.nwsource.com. Accessed on December 12, 2014.

Gagne, M., & Deci, E. L. (2005). Self-determination theory and work motivation. *Journal of Organizational Behavior, 26*, 331–362.

George, J. M. (1992). The role of personality in organizational life: Issues and evidence. *Journal of Management, 18*(2), 185–213.

Gergen, K. J. (1969). *The psychology of behavioral exchange*. Reading, MA: Addison-Wesley.

Ghoshal, S. (2005). Bad management theories are destroying good management practices. *Academy of Management Learning & Education, 4*(1), 75–91.

Goodman, J. (2012). Silicon Valley employers go wild with lavish employee benefits. *Forbes*. Retrieved from http://www.forbes.com/sites/johngoodman/2012/10/30/silicon-valley-employers-go-wild-with-lavish-employee-benefits/. Accessed on April 11, 2013.

Gouldner, A. W. (1960). The norm of reciprocity: A preliminary statement. *American Sociological Review, 25*(2), 161–178.

Hancock, J. I., Allen, D. G., Bosco, F. A., McDaniel, K. R., & Pierce, C. A. (2013). Meta-analytic review of employee turnover as a predictor of firm performance. *Journal of Management, 39*(3), 573–603.

Hannah, S. T., Jennings, P. L., Bluhm, D., Peng, A. C., & Schaubroeck, J. M. (2014). Duty orientation: Theoretical development and preliminary construct testing. *Organizational Behavior and Human Decision Processes, 123*, 220–238.

Hatch, M. J. (1993). The dynamics of organizational culture. *Academy of Management Review*, *18*(4), 657–693.

Hatch, M. J., & Schultz, M. (1997). Relations between organizational culture, identity and image. *European Journal of Marketing*, *31*(5–6), 356–365.

Herscovitch, L., & Meyer, J. P. (2002). Commitment to organizational change: Extension of a three-component model. *Journal of Applied Psychology*, *87*(3), 474–487.

Hirschman, A. O. (1970). *Exit, voice and loyalty: Responses to decline in firms, organizations, and states*. Cambridge, MA: Harvard University Press.

Hochwarter, W. A., Summers, J. K., Thompson, K. W., Perrewé, P. L., & Ferris, G. R. (2010). Strain reactions to perceived entitlement behavior by others as a contextual stressor: Moderating role of political skill in three samples. *Journal of Occupational Health Psychology*, *15*(4), 388–398.

Kant, I. (1994a). Grounding for the metaphysics of morals. In J. W. Ellington (Trans.), *Ethical philosophy*. Hackett: Cambridge.

Kant, I. (1994b). Metaphysical principles of virtue. In J. W. Ellington (Ed.), *Ethical philosophy*. Hackett: Cambridge.

King, W. C., Miles, E. W., & Day, D. D. (1993). A test and refinement of the equity sensitivity construct. *Journal of Organizational Behavior*, *14*(4), 301–317.

Malinowski, B. (1932). *Crime and custom in savage society*. London: Paul, Trench, Tubner.

Meeker, B. F. (1971). Decisions and exchange. *American Sociological Review*, *36*(3), 485–495.

Meyer, J. P., & Allen, N. J. (1984). Testing the "side-bet theory" of organizational commitment: Some methodological considerations. *Journal of Applied Psychology*, *69*(3), 372–378.

Meyer, J. P., & Allen, N. J. (1991). A three-component conceptualization of organizational commitment. *Human Resource Management Review*, *1*(1), 61–89.

Meyer, J. P., & Allen, N. J. (1997). *Commitment in the workplace: Theory, research, and application*. London: Sage.

Meyer, J. P., Becker, T. E., & Vandenberghe, C. (2004). Employee commitment and motivation: A conceptual analysis and integrative model. *Journal of Applied Psychology*, *89*, 991–1007.

Meyer, J. P., & Herscovitch, L. (2001). Commitment in the workplace: Toward a general model. *Human Resource Management Review*, *11*(3), 299–326.

Meyer, J. P., & Parfyonova, N. M. (2010). Normative commitment in the workplace: A theoretical analysis and re-conceptualization. *Human Resource Management Review*, *20*(4), 283–294.

Miles, E. W., Hatfield, J. D., & Huseman, R. C. (1989). The equity sensitivity construct: Potential implications for worker performance. *Journal of Management*, *15*(4), 581.

Molm, L. D. (1994). Dependence and risk: Transforming the structure of social exchange. *Social Psychology Quarterly*, *57*(3), 163–176.

Molm, L. D. (1997). *Coercive power in social exchange*. New York, NY: Cambridge University Press.

Molm, L. D. (2000). Theories of social exchange and exchange networks. In G. Ritzer & B. Smart (Eds.), *Handbook of social theory* (pp. 260–272). Thousand Oaks, CA: Sage.

Molm, L. D. (2003). Theoretical comparisons of forms of exchange. *Sociological Theory*, *21*(1), 1–17.

Molm, L. D., Peterson, G., & Takahashi, N. (1999). Power in negotiated and reciprocal exchange. *American Sociological Review*, *64*(6), 876–890.

Molm, L. D., Takahashi, N., & Peterson, G. (2000). Risk and trust in social exchange: An experimental test of a classical proposition. *American Journal of Sociology, 105*(5), 1396–1427.

Mowday, R. T., Porter, L. W., & Steers, R. M. (1982). *Employee-organization linkages: The psychology of employee commitment, absenteeism, and turnover.* New York, NY: Academic Press.

Mowday, R. T., Steers, R. M., & Porter, L. W. (1979). The measurement of organizational commitment. *Journal of Vocational Behavior, 14*(2), 224–247.

Noordin, F., Omar, S., Sehan, S., & Idrus, S. (2010). Organizational climate and its influence on organizational commitment. *The International Business & Economics Research Journal, 9*(2), 1–9.

O'Reilly, C. A., & Chatman, J. (1986). Organizational commitment and psychological attachment: The effects of compliance, identification, and internalization on prosocial behavior. *Journal of Applied Psychology, 71*(3), 492–499.

Pencavel, J. H. (1972). Wages, specific training, and labor turnover in U.S. manufacturing industries. *International Economic Review, 13*(1), 53–64.

Perrewé, P. L., & Spector, P. E. (2002). Personality research in the organizational sciences. In G. R. Ferris & J. J. Martocchio (Eds.), *Research in personnel and human resources management* (Vol. 21, pp. 1–63). Oxford: JAI Press.

Porter, L. W., Steers, R. M., Mowday, R. T., & Boulian, P. V. (1974). Organizational commitment, job satisfaction, and turnover among psychiatric technicians. *Journal of Applied Psychology, 59*(5), 603–609.

Ranft, A. L., Ferris, G. R., & Perryman, A. A. (2007). Dealing with celebrity and accountability in the top job. *Human Resource Management, 46*(4), 671–682.

Reichers, A. E. (1985). A review and reconceptualization of organizational commitment. *Academy of Management Review, 10*(3), 465.

Rousseau, D. (1995). *Psychological contracts in organizations: Understanding written and unwritten agreements.* Thousand Oaks, CA: Sage.

Ryan, R. M., & Deci, E. L. (2000). Self-determination theory and the facilitation of intrinsic motivation, social development, and well-being. *American Psychologist, 55*, 68–78.

Schein, E. H. (1981). Does Japanese management style have a message for American managers? *Sloan Management Review (Pre-1986), 23*(1), 55.

Schein, E. H. (1983). The role of the founder in creating organizational culture. *Organizational Dynamics, 12*(1), 13.

Schein, E. H. (1984). Coming to a new awareness of organizational culture. *Sloan Management Review, 25*(2), 3.

Schein, E. H. (1985). *Organizational culture and leadership.* San Francisco, CA: Jossey-Bass.

Schein, E. H. (1990). Organizational culture. *American Psychologist, 45*(2), 109–119.

Shafir, E., & LeBoeuf, R. A. (2002). Rationality. *Annual Review of Psychology, 53*(1), 491–517.

Shore, L. M., & Coyle-Shapiro, J. A. (2003). New developments in the employee–organization relationship. *Journal of Organizational Behavior, 24*(5), 443–450.

Sujansky, J., & Ferri-Reed, J. (2009). *Keeping the millennials: Why companies are losing billions in turnover to this generation- and what to do about it.* Hoboken, NJ: Wiley.

Twenge, J. M. (2007). *Generation me: Why today's young Americans are more confident, assertive, entitled – and more miserable than ever before.* New York, NY: Free Press.

Twenge, J. M. (2010). A review of the empirical evidence on generational differences in work attitudes. *Journal of Business and Psychology, 25*(2), 201–210.

Wang, D., Tsui, A. S., Zhang, Y., & Ma, L. (2003). Employment relationships and firm performance: Evidence from an emerging economy. *Journal of Organizational Behavior*,
24(5), 511–535.

Wiener, Y. (1982). Commitment in organizations: A normative view. *Academy of Management
Review*, *7*, 418–428.

Wiener, Y., & Vardi, Y. (1980). Relationships between job, organization, and career commitments and work outcomes—An integrative approach. *Organizational Behavior and
Human Performance*, *26*(1), 81–96.

DARK TRIAD TRAITS AND THE ENTREPRENEURIAL PROCESS: A PERSON-ENTREPRENEURSHIP PERSPECTIVE

Reginald L. Tucker, Graham H. Lowman and Louis D. Marino

ABSTRACT

Machiavellian, narcissistic, and psychopathic traits are often viewed as negative or undesirable personality traits. However, recent research demonstrates that individuals with these traits possess qualities that may be personally beneficial within the business contexts. In this chapter, we conceptualize a balanced perspective of these traits throughout the entrepreneurial process (opportunity recognition, opportunity evaluation, and opportunity exploitation) and discuss human resources management strategies that can be employed to enhance the benefits, or minimize the challenges, associated with Machiavellian, narcissistic, and psychopathic traits. Specifically, we propose that Machiavellian qualities are most beneficial in the evaluation stage of entrepreneurship, and Machiavellian,

Research in Personnel and Human Resources Management, Volume 34, 245–290
Copyright © 2016 by Emerald Group Publishing Limited
All rights of reproduction in any form reserved
ISSN: 0742-7301/doi:10.1108/S0742-730120160000034013

narcissistic, and psychopathic qualities are beneficial in the exploitation stage of entrepreneurship.

Keywords: Dark triad; entrepreneurial process; entrepreneurial personality

The impact of an individual's personality on the entrepreneurship process has been a central area of interest in the management literature for over a century (Knight, 1921). While the popularity of this fundamental research topic has waxed and waned, the core question of why some individuals are more likely to engage and succeed in entrepreneurial ventures has remained of interest to both entrepreneurship scholars and practitioners.

In the most basic conceptualization, the entrepreneurial process consists of stages in which an individual, or a group of individuals, discovers or creates opportunities, evaluates opportunities, and then exploits these opportunities (Shane & Venkataraman, 2000). Pioneering and seminal works in entrepreneurship emphasized the importance of the individual in the entrepreneurial process. Knight (1921) described entrepreneurs as a risk-takers embracing uncertainty, while Schumpeter (1942/2014) considered entrepreneurs to be innovative, achievement oriented, and dominant. Other personality traits such as risk taking, need for achievement, and a willingness to embrace uncertainty also characterize entrepreneurs (Baum, Frese, & Baron, 2007). An extensive body of research indicates that the presence of these personality traits strongly affects how entrepreneurs engage and respond to the entrepreneurial process (Arora, Haynie, & Laurence, 2013; Foo, 2011; Markman, Balkin, & Baron, 2002; Murnieks, Mosakowski, & Cardon, 2014). Exploring this relationship between personality and entrepreneurship has recently reemerged as a phenomenon of interest to management and psychology scholars (DeNisi, 2015; Klotz & Neubaum, 2016; Miller, 2015). However, very few studies have examined the role of an entrepreneur's personality within the context of human resources management.

Current research in entrepreneurial psychology emphasizes the role of an individual's personality, such as a willingness to take on risk and over-confidence, on entrepreneurial behavior (Cardon & Kirk, 2015; Navis & Ozbek, 2016; Raffiee & Feng, 2014). Specifically, these personality traits influence how an individual approaches entrepreneurial entry, challenges associated with starting a venture, and capitalizing on opportunities. Given the benefits generally associated with overconfidence and risk taking in entrepreneurship, it is not surprising that there is anecdotal evidence that other personality traits such as Machiavellianism, narcissism, and psychopathy, referred to as dark triad personality traits (Klotz & Neubaum, 2016), can be beneficial in the entrepreneurial process. However, the anecdotal evidence often fails to consider the impact these personality traits might have on other individuals working alongside, or under, an entrepreneur. It also fails to acknowledge the context in which an entrepreneur is operating.

To address this gap in the literature, this chapter examines how entrepreneurs with dark triad personalities might function within the different stages and contexts of the entrepreneurial process. It also examines how an entrepreneur with dark triad personality traits will likely engage with others involved in the venture. Exploring these relationships provides some clarity to the currently chaotic entrepreneurial personality literature (DeNisi, 2015; Klotz & Neubaum, 2016; Miller, 2015). Additionally, this chapter provides a unique perspective on the entrepreneurial process by examining how and why an entrepreneur's dark triad personality traits might influence human resources management.

Investigating how an entrepreneur's personality relates to the entrepreneurial process is important, as the relationship can provide insight into which personality characteristics promote beneficial, or detrimental, activities and behaviors at each stage of the entrepreneurial process. Consequently, this research seeks to provide insight into which dark triad personality characteristics are optimal and promote productive human resource management practices at each stage in the entrepreneurial process. To accomplish this, the chapter identifies and evaluates the impact of dark triad personality traits on human resources management in three entrepreneurial stages: opportunity discovery, evaluation, and exploitation (Shane & Venkataraman, 2000).

The dark triad traits include Machiavellianism, narcissism, and psychopathy, and share a common theme of violating social norms to acquire personal gain through social interaction (O'Boyle, Forsyth, Banks, & McDaniel, 2012). Personal gain can manifest itself in the form of something physical, such as sexual favors, or something less tangible such as affect (Cleckley, 1950/2015). An individual with strong Machiavellian tendencies has the desire and ability to manipulate for personal gain (Haynes, Hitt, & Campbell, 2015). Narcissists exhibit a grandiose view of one's self with a desire for self-enhancement and a need for praise and admiration from others (Grijalva & Harms, 2014). Psychopathy is associated with being antisocial, a lack of restraint manifested in a disregard for social conventions, and impulsivity (Boddy, 2014). These dark triad traits are generally viewed in a pejorative manner. However, extant research suggests that there can be productive outcomes associated with dark triad personality traits. For example, Akhtar, Ahmetoglu, and Chamorro-Premuzik (2013) found that individuals with higher levels of psychopathy had higher levels of entrepreneurial intentions than those who did not. Thus, our goal is to examine the contradictory outcomes of the dark triad personalities by analyzing how these traits influence individuals at different stages of the entrepreneurial process and how they impact human capital management.

We employ the person-entrepreneurship framework (Markman & Baron, 2003) to analyze these relationships. Within the context of entrepreneurship, Markman and Baron (2003) argue that some people are "better suited to exploit commercial opportunities or create new companies than others" (p. 286). Consistent with this argument, seminal works in the entrepreneurship literature emphasize innovation (Schumpeter, 1942/2014), opportunity perception (Kirzner, 1979), and handling uncertainty (Knight, 1921) as the defining characteristics of entrepreneurs. For each of these traits, Markman and Baron (2003) argued that higher individual scores will enhance the person-entrepreneurship fit (Markman & Baron, 2003). We extend this work by leveraging the person-entrepreneurship fit framework to investigate how entrepreneurs exhibiting dark triad behaviors and characteristics can lead to beneficial or detrimental outcomes in each of the entrepreneurial stages and how those behaviors might influence human resource management.

We begin with a brief review of the person-entrepreneurship fit framework and the dark triad literature. We then employ a simplified three-stage version of the entrepreneurship process that includes opportunity recognition, opportunity evaluation, and opportunity exploitation to examine how dark triad traits can present challenges and benefits to the individual throughout the entrepreneurial process. Specifically, we propose that entrepreneurs with high Machiavellian traits are likely to benefit in the opportunity evaluation and opportunity exploitation stages, those with narcissistic traits in the opportunity exploitation stage, and those with psychopathic traits in the opportunity exploitation stages. To conclude, we propose that societal misfits might find a fit with entrepreneurship.

PERSON-ENTREPRENEURSHIP FIT

The person-entrepreneurship fit paradigm is a derivative of the person-environment fit literature (Markman & Baron, 2003). The person-environment fit literature emphasizes the roles of individual, organizational, and environmental factors in determining career decisions and outcomes (Oh et al., 2014). The person-environment fit conceptual framework draws on principles of interactional psychology, asserting that neither personal nor environmental factors alone are able to explain individual behavior (Lewin, 1951). The underlying premise is evaluating congruence between people and their environment. For example, *person-organization* fit may refer to the congruence of personal and organizational values, while *person-job fit* may refer to congruence between the skills and/or knowledge of an employee and the job requirements (Cable & DeRue, 2002). As a derivative of this literature, the person-entrepreneurship fit conceptual framework offers insight into the congruence between an individual and their engagement in entrepreneurial activity.

Person-entrepreneurship fit refers to the congruence between an individual's personality (i.e., values) and entrepreneurship. Shane and Venkataraman (2000) define entrepreneurship as a "scholarly examination of how, by whom, and with what effects opportunities to create future goods and services are discovered, evaluated, and exploited" (p. 218). Markman and Baron (2003) identified several individual characteristics conducive to entrepreneurship, suggesting certain individuals are a better fit for entrepreneurship than others. These characteristics include professional autonomy and a sense of personal control (Hamilton, 2000), personal goals (Locke & Latham, 1991), high levels of risk taking (Knight, 1921), high reliance on heuristics (Bird, 1988), and the capacity to adapt to and tolerate ambiguity (Bhidé, 2000).

Previous research has generally ignored the existence of dark triad traits or viewed these traits as incongruent with success in the entrepreneurial process. Therefore, our examination of the relationship between dark triad traits and the entrepreneurial process is a departure from previous literature. Within the body of research examining the entrepreneurial process, opportunity recognition is the most studied stage (Shepherd, Williams, & Patzelt, 2015), perhaps because it is most recognizable (Shane & Venkataraman, 2000) and what most distinguishes entrepreneurship from the broader literature (Baron, 2006). To expand this research domain, we include other phases of the entrepreneurial process in addition to opportunity recognition. To this end, we conceptualize the entrepreneurial process as encompassing three phases: opportunity recognition, opportunity evaluation, and opportunity exploitation. We offer a review of each stage of the entrepreneurial process before analyzing each personality trait's influence at that stage.

While several studies have considered the psychological factors important to entrepreneurship (Miller, 2015) and others equally have considered different stages in the entrepreneurial process (DeNisi, 2015), there has been little research that examines the impact of specific psychological factors on human resource management, and interaction with human resource management systems to influence firm success or failure. We seek to expand the literature by examining how the dark triad personality traits impact human resource management and their interaction on firm success throughout the entrepreneurial process.

DARK TRIAD

Among the personality traits that present problems for society in general and for the corporate world in particular are *Machiavellianism, narcissism,* and *psychopathy* (including its less severe variant, *subclinical psychopathy*), often collectively referred to as the dark triad (Babiak & Hare, 2006; Paulhus & Williams, 2002). Research on the dark triad has increased significantly over the last decade (Jonason & Webster, 2010). The dark triad traits are characterized by manipulation and cynicism (i.e., Machiavellianism), vanity and self-centeredness (i.e., narcissism), and callous social attitudes and impulsivity (i.e., psychopathy). Although traditionally studied as pathologies and undesirable traits (Campbell & Miller, 2011), more recent work tries to take a fair and balanced approach by examining these traits in relation to other aspects of personality that are not necessarily pathological or undesirable in subclinical populations.

While these traits were originally investigated as negative attributes within society, recent research has considered whether these traits might be beneficial for an individual, particularly in the short term (Jonason, Webster, Schmitt, Li, & Crysel, 2012). For example, psychopaths are viewed as willing to make tough, although sometimes ethically questionable, decisions that can enhance their success in the workplace (Stevens, Deuling, & Armenakis, 2012). Indeed, studies in the management literature concerning dark triad traits typically focus on the upper echelons of the organization because that is where you are more likely to find individuals with these traits (Babiak & Hare, 2006; Stevens et al., 2012).

Machiavellianism

Five hundred years ago in *The Prince* (Machiavelli, 1513/1981), Italian diplomat Niccolo Machiavelli outlined strategies that a new prince could use to establish and maintain political power. The strategies, highly pragmatic and devoid of traditional social virtues, eventually became associated with an opportunistic and deceptive "Machiavellian" personality. Machiavellianism has received significant attention in the management literature (Calhoon, 1969; Dahling, Whitaker, & Levy, 2008; Gemmill & Heisler, 1972; Greenbaum, Hill, Mawritz, & Quade, in press). Machiavellianism differs from narcissism and psychopathy in various ways. Whereas narcissism involves excessive self-aggrandizement and psychopathy involves an antisocial nature lacking in empathic concern, high levels of Machiavellianism are characterized by a manipulative and self-serving social strategy. Individuals with high levels of Machiavellianism are also characterized by a cynical worldview, a lack of morality, manipulative behavior, and active use of planning, coalition forming, and reputation building (Jones & Paulhus, 2014; see, review by Fehr, Samsom, & Paulhus, 1992).

Christie and Geis (1970) developed scales to differentiate between "low Machs," those with low levels of Machiavellianism, and "high Machs," those with high levels of Machiavellianism. For example, high Machs use exploitative tactics more frequently than low Machs (Vecchio & Sussmann, 1991). In trust games, those scoring high on Machiavellianism are more likely to follow rational strategies maximizing self-interest than those scoring low on Machiavellianism. High Machs also prioritize competition and winning at all costs (Ryckman, Thornton, & Butler, 1994).

High Machiavellianism is negatively correlated with agreeableness and conscientiousness (Paulhus & Williams, 2002), and positively correlated with self-monitoring (Snyder, 1974) and with a strong sense of personal control (Fehr et al., 1992). High Machs tend to use persuasion, self-disclosure (Liu, 2008), and ingratiation to get their way (Fehr et al., 1992), and may be more willing to betray others when retaliation is unlikely (Gunnthorsdottir, McCabe, & Smith, 2002), subscribe to lower ethical standards (Singhapakdi & Vitell, 1991), or self-report being more inclined to behave unethically (Jones & Kavanagh, 1996). For example, high Machs tell more lies (Ghose & Crain, 1995; Kashy & DePaulo, 1996) than low Machs.

Although conceptualized as a form of social intelligence, Machiavellianism has generally not been found to significantly correlate with measures of intelligence (Paulhus & Williams, 2002) and has been found to be negatively related with emotional intelligence (Ali, Amorim, & Chamorro-Premuzik, 2009). While not necessarily related to intelligence, the economic success of Machiavellian behavior is influenced by an individual's education level. Turner and Martinez (1977) found a positive correlation between

Machiavellian traits and income, but only for highly educated men; the correlation was negative among uneducated men.

More generally, high Machs tend to do well in unstructured working environments where there is less managerial supervision and more autonomy (Shultz, 1993). Machiavellianism may have evolved as an exploitative short-term oriented social strategy. Such a strategy works as long as there are non-Machiavellian individuals to exploit (Mealey, 1995) and the same individuals are not repeatedly encountered (Figueredo, Sefcek, & Jones, 2006).

While psychopaths act impulsively, abandon friends and family, and pay little attention to their reputations (Hare & Neumann, 2008), high Machs plan, build alliances, and try to maintain a positive reputation. Research has found that high Machs are strategic rather than impulsive (Jones & Paulhus, 2014), avoid manipulating family members (Barber, 1998), and avoid any other behavioral tactics that might harm their reputation, for example, feigning weakness (Shepperd & Socherman, 1997). In sum, the key elements of Machiavellianism appear to be (a) manipulation and (b) a strategic-calculating orientation.

Narcissism

The term "narcissism" is derived from the myth of Narcissus, who, according to legend, fell in love with his own image in a reflecting pool. So moved was Narcissus by his own reflection that he did not eat, drink, or sleep, resulting in his demise. Today, narcissism is comprised of grandiosity, entitlement, and a need for praise and admiration from others (Jonason et al., 2012). Narcissists are self-aggrandizing and self-absorbed, yet easily threatened and overly sensitive to feedback from others (Patel & Cooper, 2014). This fragility drives narcissists to seek continuous external self-affirmation from interpersonal relationships (O'Boyle et al., 2012). Yet, because narcissists are characteristically insensitive to others' concerns and social constraints, and often take an adversarial view of others, their self-construction attempts often misfire (Morf & Rhodewalt, 2001). Thus, although narcissistic strategic efforts generally help maintain self-esteem and affect short-term goals, they negatively influence their interpersonal relationships and in the long run ironically undermine the self they are trying to build (Grijalva & Harms, 2014).

Narcissists demand attention and admiration but respond to threats to their ego with rage, defiance, shame, and humiliation (Morf & Rhodewalt,

2001). Narcissistic grandiosity also promotes a sense of entitlement (Bushman, Bonacci, Van Dijk, & Baumeister, 2003), even aggression, if that grandiosity is threatened (Bushman & Baumeister, 1998; Jones & Paulhus, 2010). Additionally, grandiosity leads narcissistic individuals on a never-ending quest for ego-reinforcement (Morf & Rhodewalt, 2001), often resulting in self-destructive behaviors (Vazire & Funder, 2006). Rather than deliberate, the cognitive processes of narcissists are self-deceptive; they seem to believe their boasts even when an outsider can verify that they exaggerate their competence (Paulhus & Williams, 2002).

Narcissism's unique contribution to the dark triad lies in people's sense of entitlement and superiority to others (Jonason et al., 2012). Narcissists do not just feel good about themselves – they feel that they are inherently better and more deserving of the respect and admiration of those around them. Recently, researchers have pioneered different types of narcissism, such as *grandiose* narcissism (i.e., individuals who like to show off and draw attention to themselves) and *vulnerable* or *fragile* narcissism (i.e., individuals whose self-image is tied to external feedback; e.g., Schoenleber, Roche, Wetzel, Pincus, & Roberts, 2015). Additionally, narcissism may be a milder trait, whereas the other two dark triad traits are correlated with more antisocial outcomes. It is the grandiose variance of narcissism that is represented in the dark triad. Whereas ego-reinforcement is the all-consuming motive behind narcissistic behavior, high Machs and psychopaths are more motivated by instrumental or material gain.

Psychopathy

Psychologists define psychopathy as a particular constellation of antisocial behaviors and emotions, including shallow affect, low remorse, low fear, low empathy, egocentrism, impulsivity, aggression, and criminality (Babiak & Hare, 2006; Cleckley, 1950/2015). Seminal researchers (Cleckley, 1950/2015; Hare, 1970; Lykken, 1995) have pointed to two key elements of psychopathy – deficits in affect (i.e., callousness) and self-control (i.e., impulsivity). The self-control deficit has remained central to criminal (Hare & Neumann, 2008) as well as noncriminal conceptions of psychopathy (Babiak & Hare, 2006). Consequently, psychopaths manifest their callousness in a short-term fashion (Jones & Paulhus, 2014). For example, they lie for immediate rewards, even if those lies compromise long-term interests (Cleckley, 1950/2015). A lack of empathy for others and a desire for thrill-seeking activities converge to form a bold and disinhibited behavior (Hare & Neumann, 2008).

Generally, researchers believe there are two factors of psychopathy. The first factor is *primary* psychopathy. Shallow affect, low empathy, and interpersonal coldness are the core elements of primary psychopathy. Individuals with profound levels of these traits are referred to as "emotionally stable" psychopaths (Jonason et al., 2012). *Secondary* psychopathy is composed of the socially manipulative and deviant facets of psychopathy and is referred to as aggressive, impulsive, and neurotic psychopathy (Jonason et al., 2012). Primary psychopathy concerns the psychopath's cognition whereas secondary psychopathy concerns the psychopath's behavioral outcomes.

Psychopathy has demonstrated several important interpersonal and intrapersonal correlates. Psychopaths tend to score relatively low on agreeableness, conscientiousness, and neuroticism. Psychopathy is also associated with romantic relationship functioning, including positive correlations with sexual assault, intimate partner violence, infidelity, and mate-poaching (Brown & Forth, 1997).

Psychopathy is strikingly different from other dark triad traits in terms of the degree to which men and women differ on the trait. Whereas Machiavellianism and narcissism display small to negligible sex differences in most studies (Jonason, Li, Webster, & Schmitt, 2009; Jonason & Webster, 2010), sex differences in psychopathy are nearly universal and are moderate to large in size (Cale & Lilienfeld, 2002). For example, men tend to be more sensitive to environmental cues involving antisociality (Mealey, 1995).

The motivations of the different dark triad member traits sometimes align, thereby precipitating similar behavior. The reason is that they share a common callousness that encourages interpersonal manipulation (O'Boyle et al., 2012). Thus, similar instances of callous manipulation would be evident in all three dark triad traits. In other cases, the three traits exhibit unique behavior. For example, high Machiavellianism best predicts strategic orientation outcomes, narcissism best predicts ego-promoting outcomes, and outcomes invoking reckless antisocial behavior are best predicted by psychopathy. Additionally, the element of impulsivity is key in distinguishing psychopathy from Machiavellianism. In sum, Jones and Paulhus (2011) concluded the following: (a) ego-identity goals drive narcissistic behavior, whereas instrumental goals drive Machiavellian and psychopathic behavior, (b) Machiavellianism differs from psychopathy with respect to temporal focus, and (c) all three have a callous core that encourages interpersonal manipulation.

DARK TRIAD FIT AND ENTREPRENEURSHIP

Entrepreneurship is an iterative process wherein individuals recognize, evaluate, and exploit opportunities (Pryor, Webb, Ireland, & Ketchen, 2016). The entrepreneurial process presents various difficulties for a number of reasons. Complications within the entrepreneurial process can be dependent upon several factors such as current financial resources, socio-economic background (Koellinger, Minniti, & Schade, 2007), or individual cognition (Baron & Ensley, 2006; Shepherd et al., 2015). Personality characteristics also contribute to the individual's ability to recognize, evaluate, and exploit opportunities (Hisrich, Langan-Fox, & Grant, 2007). Dark triad personality traits influence everyday decision-making and can be expected to influence the decision-making of entrepreneurs in the entrepreneurial process.

Recent conversations within the entrepreneurial personality literature highlight how important dark personalities are to entrepreneurship (DeNisi, 2015; Klotz & Neubaum, 2016; Miller, 2015, 2016). For example, "the act of creating a firm may be indicative of narcissistic tendencies" (Grijalva & Harms, 2014, p. 121). Some scholars have gone so far as to argue that many entrepreneurs are motivated by narcissistic tendencies (de Vries, 1996). Alternatively, Akhtar and colleagues (2013) found that psychopathy increased entrepreneurial intentions. While these papers offer a new avenue with which to explore personality traits and entrepreneurship, they largely ignore the fact that successful new ventures are not created by individuals. In this chapter, we propose that while dark traits might offer benefits to individuals throughout the entrepreneurial process, these benefits occur because of the strategic use of human capital. At their core, dark triad traits are interpersonal traits, suggesting that they manifest in relation to other individuals. Therefore, entrepreneurs with dark triad personalities utilize and manipulate individuals involved in the venture, which can lead to negative or positive outcomes throughout the entrepreneurial process. For example, high Machs need someone to manipulate in order to acquire personal gain. Narcissists require the praise and admiration of others. Psychopaths achieve their goals by callously working with and through others.

The first stage in the entrepreneurial process is opportunity recognition. In the following section, we discussion how these dark triad traits are beneficial when recognizing opportunities. In subsequent sections, we examine the role of these traits in evaluating and exploiting opportunities. This is followed by examining the impact dark triad entrepreneurs have on human capital management.

OPPORTUNITY RECOGNITION

Opportunities are the fundamental component in the first stage of the entrepreneurship process (Shepherd et al., 2015). Opportunities are defined as "a perceived means of generating economic value (i.e., profit) that previously has not been exploited and is not currently being exploited by others" (Baron, 2006, p. 107). However, it is the recognition of opportunities that can separate entrepreneurs from non-entrepreneurs (Baron & Ensley, 2006). Opportunity recognition is conceptualized as the process in which individuals are able to recognize patterns and ideas that are subsequently profitable opportunities (Baron, 2006). Scholars theorize that the ability to recognize opportunities is a critical distinction between entrepreneurs and non-entrepreneurs (Davidsson, 2015).

The discovery perspective is the primary perspective that entrepreneurship scholars have used when analyzing opportunity recognition (Alvarez & Barney, 2007). The discovery perspective takes the approach that opportunities exist, independent of entrepreneurs and that the decision-making context is risky (Alvarez & Barney, 2007). The discovery perspective prescribes that individuals come upon opportunities that already exist and are observable (Eckhardt & Shane, 2003). Since all opportunities are observable by individuals, entrepreneurs have a unique ability to discover and exploit the opportunities (Alvarez & Barney, 2007). However, there is risk involved in discovering opportunities (Knight, 1921). Discovered opportunities are risky because others might also have found them and the entrepreneur may invest in an opportunity that can be better exploited by another party who previously discovered it (Krueger & Dickson, 1994). Additionally, the pursuit of an opportunity implies that other discovered opportunities cannot be pursued, risking one opportunity over another (Janney & Dess, 2006).

Opportunity Discovery

Machiavellianism
High Machs are likely to invest significant resources in building networks of human capital and use human capital to recognize opportunities. According to the discovery perspective, opportunities exist independent of the entrepreneur and can be discovered by anyone. Since high Machs strategically use others for personal gain, it is likely they will utilize this tactic in hopes of discovering profitable opportunities (Ferris & Judge, 1991).

The strategic and calculating nature of Machiavellians suggest that high Machs are likely to discover opportunities through the strategic use of others' human capital (O'Boyle et al., 2012). First, they will likely know who to work with and where to look because of their ability to manipulate others for personal gain (Touhey, 1973). In the realm of entrepreneurship, discovering an exploitable opportunity is equivalent to personal gain (Baron, 2006). Since opportunities exist independent of the entrepreneur under the opportunity discovery paradigm, a high Mach, through social skill and intellect, can manipulate others to persuade them to share information otherwise not privy to the Mach.

As a strategist, a high Mach will find it useful to talk to those in the know at the right place and the right time (Christie & Geis, 1970). In contrast to those who frivolously try to network, a high Mach is more likely to approach networking from a utilitarian perspective and strategically choose who he or she talks to (O'Boyle et al., 2012). The purpose of networking for a Mach is to discover and acquire what others know that is exploitable and profitable (Ferris & Judge, 1991). The cold and calculating nature of a high Mach will facilitate his or her movement within the inner circles of those who often or have discovered successful opportunities in the past.

Overall, the Machiavellian trait can be beneficial for entrepreneurs in the opportunity discovery process. High Machs, by nature, attempt to discover and exploit opportunities that will bring them personal gain (Paulhus & Williams, 2002). It is likely to be the most beneficial dark triad trait in the opportunity discovery phase of the entrepreneurial process.

High Machs are likely to use human capital in a calculating manner to aid them in identifying opportunities because they are characteristically suited to use others for personal gain. They are likely to cultivate broad networks of high quality human capital both inside and outside of their organization to discover valuable opportunities. In the earliest stages of a new venture when the entrepreneur may be working alone, this could take the form of an informal advisory group. In a more established entrepreneurial venture, this may take the form of board of directors, or of partners of employees. To help discover promising opportunities, high Machs are likely to encourage the traditionally espoused entrepreneurial culture – "one in which new ideas and creativity are expected, risk taking is encouraged, failure is tolerated, learning is promoted, product, process and administrative innovations are championed, and continuous change is viewed as a conveyor of opportunities" (Ireland, Hitt, & Sirmon, 2003, p. 970). In these cultures, high Machs can encourage creativity and ideation while also appropriating the ideas of others.

By utilizing human capital in this manner, high Machs are able to mitigate the risk associated with opportunity discovery by relying on the knowledge, skills, and abilities of other informed individuals or teams. Whether through manipulation, deception, or guile, a high Machiavellian will most likely garner the trust of others so that valuable information regarding new ideas and opportunities will flow freely to the Mach.

Proposition 1. High Machs will strategically use the human capital of others in order to discover opportunities.

Narcissism
Unlike Machiavellianism, the self-enhancing nature of narcissists is likely to be detrimental to an entrepreneur in the opportunity discovery process (Grijalva & Harms, 2014). For the narcissists to discover an opportunity, the primary motivation is to be seen, not only as competent and entrepreneurial by others, but the most competent and entrepreneurial by others (Chatterjee & Hambrick, 2007). The opportunity discovery process will be self-serving and unashamedly ego-enhancing. With a reliance on their ego as a guide for everything, narcissists are likely to miss opportunities unless their discovery is validated by others or they think it will be validated by others.

The concern for self as well as praise and admiration from others indicates that the narcissist is likely to poorly use the human capital of those around him or her (Galvin, Lange, & Ashforth, 2015). There are several reasons for this. First, the narcissist is not concerned with the voice of others and is likely to only hear what he or she wants to hear (Grijalva & Harms, 2014). This is problematic in the opportunity recognition stage because opportunities are rarely discovered by lone individuals (Lumpkin & Lichtenstein, 2005), and even less so by individuals who are unwilling to hear the voice of others (Kirzner, 1973). Additionally, the narcissistic entrepreneur is less likely to focus on the quality of the input an individual can provide, as opposed to whether the individual will provide feedback that is consistent with the entrepreneur's perceptions. Indeed, any criticism directed at the narcissist or the opportunity discovered will not be received kindly, but will result in dismissal of criticism (grandiose narcissism) or a retaliation (vulnerable narcissism) (Dickinson & Pincus, 2003). This is problematic for the narcissist because criticism that might refine the opportunity into something better is likely to be rejected and the highest quality human capital might not be accessed.

Another concern for individuals with narcissistic tendencies when recognizing opportunities is that they are likely to overshare that they have recognized an opportunity in order to attract attention. While the narcissist is attempting to exude competence in order to receive glory, it is more likely that others will focus on the potential of the opportunity. This is problematic that as the narcissist shares information regarding the opportunity in search of validation, the opportunity may be appropriated by others.

Proposition 2. Narcissists are less likely to effectively utilize the human capital of others in order to recognize opportunities.

Psychopathy

Psychopaths, similar in nature to Machs, are likely to discover opportunities because of their desire to get ahead rather than get along (O'Boyle et al., 2012). Extant research suggests that psychopaths often have higher levels of education than the general population (Stevens et al., 2012). Additionally, in business settings, psychopaths are usually found in executive suites, on boards, and positions of power (Babiak & Hare, 2006). The impulsive nature of psychopaths is likely a positive rather than a negative in opportunity discovery because psychopaths will act upon their impulsivities with knowledge and information that others usually do not have. This array of information suggest that psychopaths are prone to discover opportunities that others cannot because of their education, impulsivity, and propensity for risky decisions (O'Boyle et al., 2012). However, psychopaths are likely to be less rational when recognizing opportunities. This is important because there is an inherent risk of irrational decision-making when an individual believes he or she has discovered an opportunity (Miller, 2007). Opportunity recognition requires foresight and attention to alternative states, as well as performance implications (Baron, 2006). For this reason, it is less likely that the psychopathy will successfully recognize opportunities without the aid of others. Psychopaths are beset by impulsive behavior and irrational decision-making (O'Boyle et al., 2012). They are less likely to have foresight regarding opportunities, if at all, and are prone to take action before considering the outcomes (Babiak & Hare, 2006). The use of human capital provides an interesting context which can help to mitigate, or can further harm, the psychopath's recognition of opportunities.

Impulsivity will likely influence the psychopathic individual to consider nearly every idea an opportunity, particularly if the opportunity is wrapped in thrill and adventure-seeking (Babiak & Hare, 2006). A reliance on rationale individuals reduces the chances that the psychopath will waste time and effort pursuing an unprofitable opportunity. Anecdotal evidence suggests that psychopaths, like narcissists, keep a small circle, however, for different reasons. While those in narcissists' circle fulfill a role fulfilling the narcissist's vain desires, the psychopath's circle provides valuable input (Cleckley, 1950/2015). The psychopath still stands to benefit from these relationships like the narcissists, but the relationship is not arms-length like those of the narcissist (Paulhus & Williams, 2002). Because of the willingness of the psychopath to form closer relationships, capable and respected individuals can play an influential role in the psychopath's entrepreneurial decision-making, particularly in the early stages.

The potentially detrimental aspect of the psychopathic personality in the opportunity discovery process stems from the psychopath's inability to hear the voice of others who might have attempted the exploit the same opportunity earlier. Additionally, the psychopath might be reluctant to share information with others outside of their close circle who could validate, or refute, the value of an opportunity.

Interpersonally, psychopaths are unlikely to share with others that they have discovered an opportunity. This will give them extra time to evaluate the opportunity by closely guarding the discovery of its existence thus increasing the possibility that they have discovered something exploitable and profitable. This too, is likely a benefit for the psychopath, for they are able to discover opportunities through calculated moves, but unlike the high Mach, the potential for betrayal having the idea appropriated due to information sharing is greatly reduced. Put simply, psychopaths are likely to discover opportunities because they are more motivated to actively search for discoverable opportunities.

Proposition 3. Psychopaths will use others' human capital to mitigate the risk associated with opportunity recognition.

OPPORTUNITY EVALUATION

Most entrepreneurs find it relatively easy to generate ideas, as there are numerous sources of ideas of what they can sell, but *evaluation* is the key to differentiating an idea from a promising opportunity (Keh, Foo, & Lim, 2002). Opportunity evaluation is an intensive cognitive process, during which information describing a person's external environment guides and updates his/her emergent cognitive representations (Autio, Dahlander, & Frederiksen, 2013). Deciding whether an idea is an opportunity involves judgments made under conditions of risk, uncertainty, and complexity (Alvarez & Barney, 2007). Perceived risk is a significant aspect of how entrepreneurs evaluate available ideas (Keh et al., 2002). Opportunity evaluation is predicated upon risk, which is the probability that an entrepreneur is able to successfully turn an idea into an opportunity (Shepherd et al., 2015). Opportunities associated with lower levels of risk receive more favorable valuations and are more likely to be pursued (Ardichvili, Cardozo, & Ray, 2003). Opportunity evaluation is composed of having a desired course of action and determining whether the defined course of action is feasible and desirable (Autio et al., 2013). Put simply, entrepreneurs who believe that they are able to predict how well the business will do, and perceive a low probability of failure, will view the idea to be an opportunity that is feasible and worth considering (Townsend, Busenitz, & Arthurs, 2010). Opportunity evaluation decision policies are constructed as future-oriented, cognitive representations of "what will be" assuming one were to exploit the opportunity under evaluation (Haynie, Shepherd, & McMullen, 2009).

Machiavellianism

Due to the high level of uncertainty in the opportunity evaluation stage, the risks involved in entrepreneurship are perhaps the most evident in this stage (Autio et al., 2013). Therefore, the calculative and strategic nature of high Machs is likely to be especially beneficial in this stage. Entrepreneurs with high Machiavellian personality characteristics will use every resource at their disposal to make the best choices concerning recognized opportunities and to reduce the uncertainty. Unlike the psychopath, high Machs are willingly to see time as beneficial when evaluating an opportunity and are more likely to perform a methodical evaluation of the opportunity. High Machs are more likely to focus on the feasibility rather than the desirability of the opportunity. If the narcissist miscalculates the feasibility of an opportunity and failure results, this will lead to a loss of reputation for the entrepreneur. The calculating and charming nature of high Machs is eviscerated if there is harm or loss to a Mach's reputation due to a failed venture (Christie & Geis, 1970). For this reason, we argue that high Machs will value feasibility more than desirability. Since high Machiavellians value time more than the narcissist or psychopath, he or she is likely to be rational when evaluating an opportunity. While the narcissist will evaluate the opportunity and its subsequent interpersonal rewards and the psychopath will be influenced by thrill-seeking, a high Mach's traits fit with the opportunity evaluation stage. At their core, they evaluate in order to take strategic action.

We propose that they will do this through the knowledge, skills and abilities of others. High Machs are master communicators (Ferris & Judge, 1991). Originally, Nicollo Machiavelli conceived this persona as a political figure who, through guile and ambition, would successfully govern state affairs. Machiavelli believed that in order to determine the intelligence of a man, you should start with those around him (Machiavelli, 1513/1981). Much more than the narcissist or psychopath, the individual with high Machiavellian traits is likely to be aware of his or her limitations, particularly in entrepreneurship. Because of this self-awareness, high Machs will employ the talents of others to reevaluate or revalidate already opportunities (Belschak, Hartog, & Kalshoven, 2013). Therefore, entrepreneurs with high Machiavellian characteristics are more likely to rely on the strategic use of human resources than are entrepreneurs with narcissistic or psychopathic tendencies. These entrepreneurs will rely not only on identifying and acquiring human capital that will help them achieve their goals but also on designing incentive systems to make sure that the goals of their employees, and others associated with the firm, will be aligned with the entrepreneur.

Proposition 4. Individuals with high Machiavellian traits use others in order to evaluate opportunities.

Narcissism

While high Machs and psychopaths seek personal gains, narcissists are likely to evaluate opportunities using criteria beyond the desirability and feasibility factors. A narcissist will evaluate the opportunity according to the possible interpersonal rewards that he or she may gain from undertaking a venture. For example, while desirability and feasibility of the opportunity are still important to the narcissist, the praise and admiration that might be gained from attempting to pursue the opportunity is more important. Evaluation of the praise and admiration to be garnered for undertaking such a venture is what will most concern a narcissist (Chatterjee & Hambrick, 2007; Patel & Cooper, 2014; Wales, Patel, & Lumpkin, 2013).

Narcissists are likely to pursue opportunities that offer praise and admiration even when the narcissist is aware that ultimately the opportunity will fail or has a high likelihood of becoming a failure (Navis & Ozbek, 2016). Narcissists are likely to evaluate opportunities that they have noticed are desirable to others because this affords them the knowledge that there is some reward attached to it (Campbell, Goodie, & Foster, 2004). In this respect, narcissists will want to be in the circles of those whose praise and admiration they are seeking to gain, and subsequently understand what opportunities those individuals find extraordinary. It is not a requirement that these individuals themselves are able to pursue these opportunities or even know how. Narcissists are only concerned with the praise and admiration they will receive. Additionally, a narcissist is likely to hone in on opportunities known only to a selected few, but highly important individuals are aware.

Narcissists will find opportunities that do not provide for praise and admiration to be the riskiest. Thus, a narcissist will attempt to be strategic and calculate what opportunities offer these interpersonal rewards and those that do not (Chatterjee & Hambrick, 2007). On average, opportunities that pose less risk are often more favorable in entrepreneurship (Keh et al., 2002). However, a narcissist will consider opportunities that offer more rewards in terms of praise and administration as the least risky (Patel & Cooper, 2014).

The human capital function serves a unique purpose for the narcissist when evaluating opportunities. Narcissists are concerned with the opportunity evaluations of others to the extent that they will afford them personal gain such as attention and admiration. A favorable opportunity in this case is one that allows a narcissist to self-enhance (O'Boyle et al., 2012). This can be detrimental for several reasons. First, narcissists are likely to positively evaluate an opportunity if it is favorably evaluated by others who may or may not have the requisite knowledge, skills, and abilities to evaluate profitable opportunities. Thus, they are likely to act on the assumption that if others deem the opportunity profitable, bold, risky, or daring, he or she will receive accolades for evaluating the opportunity in a similar fashion. The approval of others is a powerful motivator in a narcissist's life. From a human resources perspective, a narcissistic entrepreneur is more likely than entrepreneurs with high Machiavellian or psychopathic tendencies to acquire human capital in the form of employees, advisors, and partners that are cognitively similar to the entrepreneur and that will provide affirmation to the entrepreneur's perceptions. This need is perpetual, suggesting that a narcissist is likely to create a culture in which challenging the entrepreneur's direction will result in ostracism from the "in" group and possibly being let go from the firm. The resulting lack of cognitive diversity will likely eventually lead to a pattern of unsuccessfully evaluating profitable opportunities. Thus, a narcissist's irrational desires are likely to prevent thoughtful decision-making and analysis in this stage.

Proposition 5. Narcissists will use others' human capital to their detriment when evaluating opportunities.

Psychopathy

The impulsive nature of psychopaths is a detriment in the opportunity evaluation stage. Certainly, psychopaths can be right, and more right than wrong, but the heuristic decision-making process of psychopaths does not take into account long-term outcomes associated with decision-making (Babiak & Hare, 2006). Psychopaths are concerned with the here and now and are more likely to evaluate opportunities based on short-term gains rather than long-term rewards (Akhtar et al., 2013).

Desirability is the tenet of opportunity evaluation that psychopaths will focus on. A recognized opportunity will capture the attention of a psychopath, prompting him or her to concentrate all effort and attention on the new opportunity. While this appears to be positive, it is a negative because a psychopath, prone to impulsivity and thrill-seeking, will likely find every recognized opportunity desirable (O'Boyle et al., 2012). The impulsive and thrill-seeking nature of a psychopath prevents him or her from turning down opportunities that the high Mach or narcissist, in contrast, might reject.

Psychopaths and their ventures are also likely to suffer regarding the feasibility of opportunities. Their concern to get ahead rather than get along can impeded a rational and systematic evaluation of a venture opportunity. Rather, a psychopath is likely to exhibit overconfidence concerning the feasibility of an opportunity (Hayward, Shepherd, & Griffin, 2006). The entrepreneur with psychopathic tendencies can mitigate deficiencies in the evaluation stage by leveraging the human capital of others. However, psychopaths, on average, are not well equipped at team building and are likely to intimidate others into having congruent opinions (Babiak, 1995). Similar to the narcissist, research finds that psychopaths are willing to listen to the opinions of others when the opinion is similar to that of a psychopath. Obviously, this can be positive or negative. However, unlike the high Mach or narcissists, the risk associated with opportunity evaluation will most likely attract the psychopath and compel him or her to ignore the voices of more rational decision-makers (Stevens et al., 2012). Therefore, similar to entrepreneurs with high Machiavellian tendencies, entrepreneurs with psychopathic tendencies are likely to value the strategic use of human resources in building a team with valuable human capital.

However, similar to the entrepreneur with narcissistic tendencies, they are unlikely to be able to garner the benefit of human capital to which they have access.

Proposition 6. Psychopaths' tendencies to embrace risk and uncertainty, particularly when evaluating opportunities, suggest that psychopaths will ignore the knowledge, skills, and abilities of others.

In sum, high levels of Machiavellianism are beneficial during the opportunity evaluation stage. High Machs are strategic and calculating, keen to evaluate circumstances before taking action, and will rely on others who they consider more competent to evaluate opportunities. On the other hand, narcissists are driven to satisfy their need for self-enhancement and will likely evaluate opportunities in light of the praise and admiration they may offer. Further, their evaluations will be distorted by their irrationality of personal gain. They will rely on others, but only with hopes that this reliance will allow for some form of self-enhancement. Psychopaths are disinhibited thrill-seekers with a propensity toward risk while devaluing feasibility. Their preference for adventure suggest that they will consider the voices of those who are willing to go along for the ride but are likely to ultimately rely on their own judgment. This is detrimental to a psychopath because it not only suggests that a psychopathy will hazardously evaluate opportunities but also damage relationships with equity investors who evaluate opportunities with a more systematic, pragmatic, and thoughtful process.

OPPORTUNITY EXPLOITATION

Opportunity exploitation is comprised of strategic planning (Shepherd et al., 2015) and feasibility analysis (Hmieleski & Baron, 2008). How an entrepreneur determines the most effective or most desirable approach to planning and strategy is influenced by his or her knowledge, experience, motivation, and personality (Baum, Locke, & Smith, 2001; Shepherd et al., 2015). Other factors that impact venture growth are network activity, number of partners, internal locus of control, need for achievement (Lee & Tsang, 2001), achievement motivation (Collins, Hanges, & Locke, 2004), and self-efficacy (Baum & Locke, 2004). Strategic entrepreneurship scholars posit that individual's knowledge, skills, abilities, along with their motivation and passion to perform, are important for a firm to exploit an opportunity and achieve a competitive advantage for long-term success (Hitt, Ireland, Sirmon, & Trahms, 2011).

The advantages commonly associated with formal planning in the entrepreneurial process are not universally accepted and have been the focus of considerable debate (Brinkmann, Grichnik, & Kapsa, 2010; Shepherd et al., 2015). For example, Honig and Samuelsson (2012) found that neither formal planning nor modifications to the business plan to adjust for environmental changes had a significant influence on venture performance. In contrast, Chwolka and Raith (2012) proposed that entre-preneurs benefit from utilizing a multi-stage decision process based on the rational decision model. Based on this process, an entrepreneur evaluates the cost of planning against the value of the information obtained from planning (Shepherd et al., 2015). An entrepreneur then determines if plan-ning is an effective means for improving venture performance (Delmar & Shane, 2003). As the venture grows and develops, an entrepreneur can revise and reapply information gained in early stages to assist in making new decisions about planning (Chwolka & Raith, 2012). The result is planning that provides a greater return as the entrepreneur acquires infor-mation from past experiences as the venture matures leading to more effective planning (Brinkmann et al., 2010). An entrepreneur must also determine the amount of time spent planning (Matthews & Scott, 1995). This is done by comparing the value of time spent planning against the value of time spent on other activities that might improve venture performance.

The success of this approach is linked to an entrepreneur's ability to evaluate the two opposing options (to plan or not to plan). If used effec-tively, an entrepreneur can determine if the cost of planning is useful in a given situation. When planning is used, it can lead to sound decisions and allows an entrepreneur to create clear operational steps to achieve goals (Delmar & Shane, 2003). The use of planning also helps prevent the venture from disbanding and facilitates product-development and organizational-forming activities (Delmar & Shane, 2003). Therefore, making decisions on the appropriate use of planning is critical to opportunity exploitation (Hmieleski & Baron, 2008).

However, as Chwolka and Raith (2012) note, entrepreneurs often use heuristics to make decisions and have limited information to determine the cost-benefit of planning. Therefore, the personal characteristics of an entrepreneur might result in a deviation from the optimal choice between planning and not planning (Chwolka & Raith, 2012). Additionally, planning is only as useful as the opportunity recognized and evaluated

(Chwolka & Raith, 2012). If failure is imminent, or the plan employed is ineffective, the use of planning will not be beneficial.

Competitive strategy also plays a critical role in the exploitation stage due to its direct link to venture growth (Baum et al., 2001). Traditionally, there are three forms of competitive strategy: focus, low cost, and differentiation (Porter, 1980). The focus strategy targets specific customers, markets, or products, while the low cost strategy uses cost-effectiveness and efficiency to sell products or services at a lower price than the competition (Porter, 1980). The differentiation strategy is based on creating a unique service or product sold at a higher price (Porter, 1980). The environment often determines the success of each particular strategy, assuming the strategy is implemented properly (Dess & Davis, 1984; Porter, 1980). However, regardless of the environment, the selection of one of these options is critical for a business to be successful (Dess & Davis, 1984; Porter, 1980). When lacking a definitive strategy, businesses are left directionless and often fail as they attempt to pursue multiple strategies simultaneously (Baum et al., 2001; Dess & Davis, 1984).

The decision of whether to use or not use a distinctive competitive strategy can be costly for an entrepreneur, as the lack of a clear strategy can hamper the growth of the venture (Baum et al., 2001; Dess & Davis, 1984). According to Baum et al. (2001), the use of a competitive strategy can be linked to personal characteristics. These include the individual's predisposition, motivation, and self-efficacy (Bandura, 1986; Hollenbeck & Whitener, 1988). Another factor that influences strategic decisions is the individual's personal networks, as the networks provide opportunities to acquire additional resources (Ostgaard & Birley, 1994). This is a critical component in the exploitation stage as the strategy-growth relationship only exists when an entrepreneur has the resources and capabilities needed to support the strategy being implemented (Chandler & Hanks, 1994).

Machiavellianism

High Machs' natural tendency toward planning, alliance building, and networking (Jones & Paulhus, 2014) positions them well for the exploitation stage. When working through the multi-stage decision process (Chwolka & Raith, 2012), high Machs are the most likely of the three dark triad personalities to utilize planning. High Machs are rational planners and strategists (Jones & Paulhus, 2011). This should result in a high Mach developing high-quality plans that are both efficient and effective. Because of the quality of planning produced by a high Mach, the value of planning increases. This will lead to the benefits of planning outweighing the benefits of not planning and provides a justification for them to invest time in planning that could be spent elsewhere (Chwolka & Raith, 2012). Additionally, they are rarely impulsive (Jones & Paulhus, 2011) and would likely be apprehensive moving a venture forward without some sort of strategic plan.

High Machs' reliance on planning will likely benefit their venture as it leads to clear organizational goals and helps prevent the venture from disbanding (Delmar & Shane, 2003). However, in some cases planning can be detrimental to the growth of the venture. This could occur if the cost of planning, such as the time, effort, or money required to plan effectively outweighs the value of the information obtained from planning (Chwolka & Raith, 2012). When the information used to generate the plan is invalid or incomplete, the value of planning can also decrease. In these two situations, excessive cost and incomplete information, a high Mach's propensity to plan could result in missed opportunities or wasted resources.

Developing competitive strategies is another area where individuals with high levels of Machiavellian traits are likely to provide benefits. They have a predisposition toward utilizing strategy to accomplish goals (Jones & Paulhus, 2014). This predisposition, paired with their competitive and win at all costs nature, will likely drive them to select the competitive strategy that best undermines their competitors (Ryckman et al., 1994). High Machs are also likely to have the strongest personal network out of the three dark triad personalities due to their tendency toward alliance and coalition building (Jones & Paulhus, 2014). This provides additional avenues for them to exploit as he or she attempts to acquire resources. This can result in two significant benefits for a high Mach. First, it allows them a wider range of options when choosing a competitive strategy, as he or she will have access to resources that might not be available internally (Ostgaard & Birley, 1994). Second, once the strategy is in place, access to outside resources will help maintain the venture's resources capabilities, which will aid in implementing and maintaining the competitive strategy (Chandler & Hanks, 1994). The modus operandi for high Machs is to strategically exploit opportunities. Given this propensity, we propose that opportunity exploitation will come natural to the high Machiavellians.

Proposition 7. High Machs will exploit opportunities by employing others who have the knowledge, skills, and abilities to exploit opportunities competently.

Narcissism

Similar to high Mach traits, narcissism will be beneficial to the entrepreneur when exploiting opportunities. In working through the multi-stage decision process, a narcissist is likely to follow a similar route as a high Mach. However, a narcissist's tendency toward overconfidence (Campbell et al., 2004) and feelings of superiority (Jonason et al., 2012) might reduce the value of information obtained through the planning process. Additionally, overconfidence could result in a narcissist ignoring the planning process and instead relying on his or her instincts to make decisions. This, paired with feelings of superiority, could cause a narcissist to believe any action will be successful; therefore, they may believe that time should not be wasted on planning, but instead be used for action.

Despite this overconfidence, there are some driving forces that could result in narcissists participation in the planning process. Narcissists are often consumed by thoughts of power and success (Morf & Rhodewalt, 2001). The planning process might be appealing to a narcissist as a means to project visions of grandeur and set goals that draw the attention of others. This could provide a significant benefit to venture growth as they provide an inspiration to those involved to achieve lofty goals in pursuing the entrepreneur's vision of grandeur. It also aligns with Maccoby's (2000) perspective of productive narcissists as visionary leaders. In this setting, the visionary leader is an entrepreneur inspiring those around him or her to advance the growth of the venture. However, boasting of future grandeur and creating elaborate plans to achieve growth could also be a method of masking challenges faced by an entrepreneur. This could be particularly true if the venture is not performing well. For example, a narcissist might rely on continual planning and boast of future performance instead of acknowledging the actual state of the failing venture (Wales et al., 2013). In this circumstance, planning would be a method to delay the acceptance of failure. This would allow a narcissist to maintain an air of superiority and achievement, despite the poor performance of the venture.

An additional area of concern in the opportunity exploitation stage is a narcissist's reluctance to heed the advice of others, their sensitivity to critical feedback, and their general resistance toward being mentored (Maccoby, 2000). These characteristics could prove problematic if a narcissist lacks quality information and needs to acquire outside information to plan successfully. If this information is not obtained, it could result in their plans being based on faulty information and ultimately being ineffective in improving the growth of the venture. This is in stark contrast to high

Machs, who collect information from personal networks to maximize the value of the planning process.

Where a narcissist might struggle in utilizing the multi-stage decision process, he or she makes up in the use of a competitive strategy. Unlike a high Mach who benefits from a predisposition toward strategy, a narcissist benefits from his or her self-aggrandizing motivation and self-efficacy. The need for admiration and the quest for power fuels a narcissist's competitive spirit, resulting in a constant pursuit to outperform the competition (Maccoby, 2000). To accomplish this, they will likely utilize a competitive strategy that undermines the strategies used by competitors. If the strategy is successful, a narcissist will impede the competitor's performance, while also improving the performance and facilitating the growth of his or her own venture. A successful strategy will also appeal to a narcissist's need for admiration, as venture growth is a clear demonstration of business success (Lee & Tsang, 2001).

Given these outcomes, the utilization of a competitive strategy provides a narcissist an excellent opportunity for self-enhancement. According to Wallace and Baumeister (2002), this situational factor moderates the relationship between narcissism and performance. When accomplishing a task leads to admiration from others, a narcissist puts forth maximum effort to reach a high level of performance (Wallace & Baumeister, 2002). Based on this finding, narcissists are likely to put forth a considerable amount of effort and energy to identify and execute a successful competitive strategy.

Self-efficacy also plays a role in the use of a competitive strategy (Baum et al., 2001) and directly effects venture growth (Baum & Locke, 2004). Narcissism has been found to be significantly positively correlated to self-efficacy (Mathieu & St-Jean, 2013). This relationship is not surprising as a narcissist has a tendency to be overconfident (Campbell et al., 2004). However, where overconfidence can be detrimental to the perceived value of planning, self-efficacy can be beneficial in believing a successful strategy is identifiable and that the execution of that strategy is possible (Baum et al., 2001). In a similar manner, Baum et al. (2001) proposed that tenacity and proactivity also influence the ability to select a successful competitive strategy. Given the competitive nature of narcissists when attempting to garner praise and admiration (Maccoby, 2000), these two traits might also be characteristic of the entrepreneurial narcissist as they utilize a competitive strategy to undermine their competition.

Another beneficial link between self-efficacy and the use of a competitive strategy relates to growth-oriented intentions. Douglas (2013) found that entrepreneurial self-efficacy has a significant positive correlation to growth-oriented intentions. Individuals with growth-oriented intentions seek to expand the profitability of their venture overtime (Douglas, 2013). This is opposed to independence-oriented intentions, which occur when the entrepreneur is primarily concerned with self-employment and providing income for other activities (Douglas, 2013). The narcissist's quest for power (Morf & Rhodewalt, 2001) and positive correlation to self-efficacy (Mathieu & St-Jean, 2013) could result in the development of growth-oriented intentions. The drive to accomplish growth will likely lead a narcissist to utilize a competitive strategy.

Two other factors that might influence venture growth for a narcissist are the need for achievement and extraversion. According to Lee and Tsang (2001), the need for achievement has a significant positive impact on venture performance. This could be driven by a fear of failure, as venture performance is often used to evaluate an entrepreneur's ability to achieve business success (Lee & Tsang, 2001). A narcissist's continual pursuit of affirmation from achievements will likely be a strong motivator for developing and maintaining a high performing venture. Extraversion, which significantly positively correlates with narcissism (Paulhus & Williams, 2002), might also provide advantageous for venture growth. Lee and Tsang (2001) found that extraversion influences the development of personal networks and therefore has an indirect effect on venture growth. Based on these two factors, along with motivational factors and self-efficacy, narcissism is beneficial when exploiting opportunities.

> **Proposition 8.** Narcissists are likely to exploit opportunities by taking bold and daring actions without relying on the competence of others around them.

Psychopathy

The entrepreneur with psychopathic tendencies is likely to be the least suited to exploit opportunities. This is due to a psychopath's often erratic, impulsive, and callous nature (Williams, Paulhus, & Hare, 2007). Chwolka and Raith (2012) state there are two factors that determine the value of planning: quality of the idea and quality of the planning, with the quality of the planning directly linked to the quality of the information used to develop the plan. Given that psychopaths are often well educated (O'Boyle et al., 2012), the quality of the idea is unlikely to devalue the use of planning. However, a number of characteristics common to psychopaths might negatively influence the quality of the planning. The first of these is a psychopath's erratic tendencies (Williams et al., 2007). This will likely result in a psychopath making use of planning in some situations while ignoring the option for planning in others. The sporadic use of planning prevents a psychopath from developing an effective system for planning. This could result in a considerable amount of time being wasted when a psychopath does decide to utilize planning, which effectively decreases the efficiency and quality of planning. The waste of time due to an ineffective system also increases the opportunity costs associated with planning, as the time wasted could be used for other activities critical to the success of the venture.

In a similar manner, a psychopath's impulsive nature (Williams et al., 2007) could also be detrimental to the quality of planning. The seemingly erratic use of planning by a psychopath is likely driven by impulse instead of a strategic evaluation of the utility of planning. As Jones and Paulhus (2011) note, this type of impulsivity common to psychopaths is generally dysfunctional. Therefore, a psychopath's impulse driven decisions regarding the evaluation and use of planning might be inaccurate. The result is a negative influence on the quality of planning as the decision is based on impulse instead of quality information.

Callousness toward others (Williams et al., 2007) is another characteristic that might decrease the quality of planning. Despite the potential use of charm (Babiak, Neumann, & Hare, 2010) and other methods of manipulation, the general callousness of psychopaths is likely to prevent the development of strong work relationships. As a result, the information available to a psychopath will likely be limited to what he or she already knows and what he or she is able to extract from others using manipulation. This could decrease the quality of planning, especially if the quality of information obtained through manipulation is poor. Similar to the lack of an effective system for planning, this method of collecting information could also waste a considerable amount of time, which decreases the value of planning by increasing the costs associated with wasting time.

The erratic, impulsive, and callous tendencies of a psychopath also influence one of the key benefits of planning: the development of operational goals and the actions needed to achieve those goals (Delmar & Shane, 2003). When planning is used, a psychopath's erratic and impulsive actions will likely confuse others involved in the venture. The goals and actions identified in the planning process could change without notice as a psychopath follows erratic impulses. A general lack of diligence and reluctance to set definitive deadlines (O'Boyle et al., 2012) will encourage these kinds of sporadic changes. This will result in uncertainty and a lack of direction for the venture, which essentially neutralizes one of the primary advantages of planning.

An erratic, impulsive, and callous nature can influence a firm's use of a competitive strategy in a number of ways. First, a psychopath's tendency towards erratic behavior (Williams et al., 2007) and lack of diligence (O'Boyle et al., 2012) will likely prevent a psychopath from sustaining a consistent competitive strategy. This could have a negative impact on the venture, as lacking a definitive strategy is detrimental to a venture's growth and performance (Baum et al., 2001; Dess & Davis, 1984). Second, making a dysfunctional impulsive decision leading to the use of an ineffective competitive strategy could be costly to the success of the venture. This is due to a psychopath failing to evaluate alternative competitive strategies that might be more effective or appropriate for the venture.

Finally, callousness can play a role in the use of a competitive strategy. Psychopaths' lack of respect toward others and their willingness to hurt others to get ahead (Williams et al., 2007) could lead a psychopath to adopt a very aggressive competitive strategy. It could also lead a psychopath to use unethical behavior in attempts to undermine the competition. As criminal tendencies are not far removed from subclinical psychopathy (Williams et al., 2007), the decision to use unethical practices would not be unexpected. Utilizing this approach to strategy could lead to the acquisition of additional resources and an improvement in the venture's performance and growth in the short term. However, if the unethical behavior is discovered, it could lead to negative legal outcomes and potentially the ultimate ruination for both a psychopath and the venture.

However, a psychopath's callousness could provide beneficial when making difficult decisions that improve the venture's chances of success. For example, a psychopath will not hesitate to fire or relocate employees if doing so opens the door for a competitive advantage. A psychopath is also likely to exploit employees, in terms of working conditions or pay, if doing so will allow the venture to become more competitive. Similar to the use of unethical behavior, these decisions have the potential to improve short-term outcomes, but will likely prove detrimental to the psychopath's venture overtime (Table 1).

Proposition 9. A psychopath's success at exploiting opportunities will be enhanced by his or her desire to get ahead rather than get along. However, the psychopath's callousness and propensity to be antisocial will ultimately lead to negative decision-making, harming the firm's successful exploitation of business opportunities.

Table 1. Analysis of Dark Triad Traits and the Entrepreneurial Process.

	Machiavellianism Cold and calculating; manipulative; socially astute; opportunistic; self-centered; deceptive	Narcissism Self-aggrandizement; egoistic; lovers of self; perpetual need for praise and admiration from others	Psychopathy Callous; emotionally distant; impulsive; thrill-seeking; lack of empathy
Opportunity recognition	Machiavellians' reliance on others will present an obstacle when attempting to recognize opportunities. Others are likely to notice before the Machiavellian and subsequently be a first mover over the Machiavellian.	Concern for praise and admiration influences the narcissist to pay more attention to opportunities that appear to result in praise and admiration rather than profit. Self-aggrandizing needs are likely to influence the narcissist to not notice profitable opportunities or a significant number of unprofitable opportunities.	The desire to get ahead rather than get along influences the psychopath to be more alert to opportunities than the Machiavellian or narcissist. Additionally, the thrill-seeking nature of psychopaths suggest that they are continually on the look-out for opportunities.
Opportunity evaluation	Strategic and calculating are positive attributes when evaluating opportunities. Machiavellian traits are most positive in this stage.	Narcissists are likely to evaluate opportunities based off of personal reputation gain as opposed to a viable business opportunity. Their concern for self-esteem needs influences them to irrationally positively evaluate large and daring opportunities.	Thrill-seeking and impulsivity make for irrational decision-making when evaluating opportunities. Accurate evaluations are more likely the result of luck as opposed to any opportunity evaluation skill.
Opportunity exploitation	Machiavellians are able to exploit opportunities because of strategic thinking and opportunistic orientations. They know when to act and when not to act.	Narcissists can positively exploit opportunities because they are willing to take audacious risks when others are not willing or are afraid to do so. As valiant and decisive risk-takers, narcissists are likely to flourish when exploiting opportunities.	Psychopathic traits are most positive in this stage. Already given to exploiting others, the psychopath naturally exploits opportunities that come before them.

Post Exploitation

The entrepreneurial process is an iterative process that can be interpreted as an unstructured environment (Sarason, Dean, & Dillard, 2006). New ventures consist of little, if any, organizational structure (Vinnell & Hamilton, 1999). Research finds that the dynamic environment of entrepreneurship is characterized by major and rapid changes in consumer preferences and producers' offerings (Wijbenga & van Witteloostuijn, 2007). These environments are less stable, less predictable, more uncertain, and move at a rapid speed compared to that of stable environments (Miller, 1988). Individuals working in these environments are likely to experience high levels of stress and anxiety (Waldman, Ramirez, House, & Puranam, 2001). Dynamic environments are attractive to those who embrace risk and are undeterred by uncertainty (Wijbenga & van Witteloostuijn, 2007) particularly entrepreneurs who believe their innovative and bold actions can result in successful outcomes (Miller, de Vries, & Toulouse, 1982; Miller & Toulouse, 1986). Additionally, management scholars theorize that successful outcomes in dynamic environments depend on chance (Wijbenga & van Witteloostuijn, 2007). Entrepreneurs might revise the opportunity several times, use different measures to evaluate the same opportunity, or pivot after unsuccessfully exploiting an opportunity (Ensley, Pearce, & Hmieleski, 2006). Thus, unstructured environments are a promising venue for individuals with dark traits. On average, individuals with dark traits are also likely to thrive in unstructured environments because they are able to violate social norms without any organizational structure or accountability. Further, while on average, unstructured and rapid changing environments can cause stress for individuals on average, individuals with dark traits are less likely to experience stress. As leaders of their ventures, entrepreneurs, particularly with dark traits, are likely to have a significant impact on the human resource function (Ensley et al., 2006).

Entrepreneurs with dark triad personalities can have a considerable impact on human resources management and the venture's human capital. These impacts may be beneficial in the early stages of the entrepreneurial process (e.g., opportunity exploitation). However, as the firm grows and the entrepreneur's tenure with the venture increases, it is likely that others involved in the venture will view the entrepreneur's dark triad personality in a negative light. We propose that negative outcomes, such as poor venture performance and deficient human resource management practices, are also likely to ensue. This progression into negative outcomes and poor long-term relationships is common for each of the dark triad personalities (Jonason et al., 2009).

Boddy (2014) found support for the potential negative reactions to dark triad personalities, specifically for psychopaths in the corporate setting. Results indicated that the presence of corporate psychopaths can lead to increased conflict in the workplace and a decline in employee well-being (Boddy, 2014). The existence of psychopathic traits in management has also been linked to psychological distress in employees and decreased job satisfaction (Mathieu, Neumann, Hare, & Babiak, 2014). We propose these findings are also applicable for high Machiavellians and narcissists in the workplace. Additionally, we believe the effects are likely magnified when an entrepreneur has a dark triad personality given the prominent role an entrepreneur occupies in the venture. These findings by Boddy (2014) and Mathieu et al. (2014) highlight the potential for poor human resources management by dark triad entrepreneurs as they facilitate conflict, diminish employee well-being, and decrease employee job satisfaction. This could also result in a decrease in available human capital as conflict and/or low job satisfaction impedes the employee's ability to complete work responsibilities.

We also propose that dark triad entrepreneurs are unlikely to implement commitment-based HR systems, which prioritize long-term relationships with employees (Arthur, 1992, 1994). The practices implemented by commitment-based HR systems include employee involvement in decision-making and training (Arthur, 1992, 1994). These practices run counter to the general disposition and tendencies of dark triad personalities, as granting autonomy and providing training to employees encourage a dispersion of power and a focus on long-term relationships. Instead, we propose that overtime dark triad entrepreneurs will foster a corrupt and aggressive culture that values short-term gains (Cohen, 2016). The culture will be fueled by the lack of respect and mistreatment of others exhibited by the dark triad entrepreneur, which will become apparent to those involved in the venture overtime. Mistreatment will contribute to decrease employee well-being (Lim & Cortina, 2005) and will decrease job satisfaction (Penney & Spector, 2005). According to Pearson and Porath (2005), this will ultimately have a negative impact on organizational resources.

Trust is another area where dark triad entrepreneurs have the potential to create discord in their ventures and to devalue the human capital of their employees. According to Mayer, Davis, and Schoorman (1995), trust entails belief in the other party's ability, benevolence, and integrity. We propose that overtime dark triad entrepreneurs will begin to lose the trust of those around them. The smokescreen of narcissists continual boasting and ego-inflation will eventually clear, and those involved in the venture will lose belief in the entrepreneur's abilities. Likely sooner than later, individuals will call into question the benevolence of a psychopathic entrepreneur as he or she exhibits complete disregard for the feelings of others. Finally, a high Machiavellian's integrity will be compromised as schemes and social manipulations are untangled and exposed. We propose a psychopathic entrepreneur will be the first out of the dark triad personalities to garner distrust, while the high Machiavellian entrepreneur will maintain trust among key constituencies the longest among the three dark triad traits.

The lack of trust in an organization or venture can have significant consequences on human resources management and human capital. For example, the presence of trust has been identified as a critical component for establishing effective work relationships (Colquitt, Scott, & LePine, 2007). Additionally, Collins and Smith (2006) proposed that distrust restricts the flow of information between individuals, which results in a decrease in firm performance. Further, a culture of distrust prevents the venture from capitalizing on the numerous benefits (e.g., increased revenue, sales growth, and individual performance) of a trusting culture (Collins & Smith, 2006).

In sum, these outcomes have the potential to derail an entrepreneur's venture and relationships with others involved. We propose the potential for negative outcomes increases as a dark triad entrepreneur's tenure increases. These negative outcomes have implications for human resources management and human capital. Entrepreneurs that exhibit dark triad tendencies are likely to influence the behavior of their employees, as explained by social learning theory (Bandura, 1971). This could hamper employee development and foster a mentality of counterproductive work behavior (Boddy, 2014). Secondly, the violation of trust and conflict that follows dark triad personalities could inhibit effective working relationships (Colquitt et al., 2007), therefore, preventing the venture from developing and utilizing the human capital of those involved.

DISCUSSION

Extant literature within the entrepreneurship domain demonstrates that personality traits influence entrepreneurship (Akhtar et al., 2013; Miller, 2015) and entrepreneurial decision-making (Shepherd et al., 2015). Previous literature has largely focused on the role of positive personality characteristics such as self-efficacy. However, in a departure from the previous literature, we examine how dark personality traits influence entrepreneurs in their decision-making at each stage of the entrepreneurial process and propose that there is a congruence between dark triad traits and entrepreneurship. We have identified this congruence as a fit between these traits and the entrepreneurship process. We extend the person-environment framework to the person-entrepreneurship fit domain (Markman & Baron, 2003) to highlight both the positives and negatives of these traits throughout the entrepreneurship process. Further, we analyze how these traits employ others' human capital throughout these stages. This analysis helps to shed more light on the interdisciplinary nature of entrepreneurship. First, we identify that entrepreneurship is a constellation of personality, fit, and the management of interpersonal relationships. However, just as the stars do not always align, there is not always a fit between these elements of entrepreneurship. One must discover an opportunity, rationally evaluate it, and successfully exploit it. Yet, contrary to the popular press, entrepreneurial success is rarely accomplished by the sole efforts of a single individual (Lechler, 2001; Watson, Ponthieu, & Critelli, 1995). We began by analyzing how each trait would operate within each stage in the entrepreneurial process, and then proposed how each trait would impact human capital within the organization within each stage.

We propose that, generally, high Machs, as compared to narcissists and psychopaths, are likely to be the most successful in entrepreneurship. The calculating and strategic nature of high Machs allows them to make rational decisions that narcissists may be to self-absorbed to see and psychopaths to impatient to follow. This is perhaps why Nicolo Machiavelli's *The Prince* has stood the test of time regarding politics and political action. A high Mach personality's end goal is personal gain without reputation loss (Christie & Geis, 1970). While a psychopath desires gain at any cost, even at the cost of losing relationships (Cleckley, 1950/2015), a high Mach operates from a place of trust (Christie & Geis, 1970). In contrast to a self-absorbed narcissist, a high Mach uses his or her relationships in order to recognize opportunities, evaluate them, and then exploit them (Jonason & Webster, 2010). In spite of the billionaire entrepreneurs that grace magazine covers, there is general acceptance that successful entrepreneurship results from the efforts of a team rather than those of a single individual (Eisenhardt, 2013). Among the three personality traits analyzed in this chapter, Machs are the most likely to assemble teams in pursuit of a goal, even if the ultimate goal is to benefit the Mach.

While we propose that high Machs will achieve greater success at each stage of the entrepreneurial process, we also propose that the narcissist-entrepreneurship fit exists. First, de Vries (1985) hypothesized decades ago that entrepreneurs exhibit narcissistic traits. However, a narcissist is less concerned with entrepreneurship as much as he or she is concerned with the fame, fortune, and accolades associated with entrepreneurship (Navis & Ozbek, 2016). The desire for praise and admiration from others can certainly motivate an individual to look for opportunities, successfully evaluate them, and profitably use them, it is more likely that these desires will overpower an individual's rational decision-making, subsequently causing harm, loss, or both at some stage in the entrepreneurial process.

Psychopaths are the *misfits* in society and by definition are not concerned with others or with what others have to say (Babiak & Hare, 2006). While this might appear to be a challenge to non-psychopathic individuals, it is the modus operandi for individuals with psychopathic traits. A psychopath's self-reliance and bent toward unconventional methods can be a positive when recognizing opportunities, evaluating them, and exploiting them. However, these characteristics can just as easily result in negative outcomes. Similar to a high Mach, a psychopath desires to get ahead. However, a psychopath is a thrill-seeker and is more likely to forego long-term gains for short-term pleasure. This is not only problematic in entrepreneurship (Hisrich et al., 2007), but life as well (Babiak & Hare, 2006). Self-reliance and thrill-seeking are characteristics that appear to be antithetical to a successful entrepreneur.

Given that research finds a fit between dark traits and entrepreneurship (Akhtar et al., 2013; Mathieu & St-Jean, 2013), we not only wanted to extend the conversation to the entrepreneurial process, but to also examine how these traits might impact others in the firm and the entrepreneur's ability to secure and cultivate human capital. Our arguments were predicated upon the notion that the founder's personality would have an impact, either positive or negative, on others in the firm. Specifically, we analyzed the influence of the entrepreneurs' dark traits on others' human capital as either mitigating or aggravating factors throughout the entrepreneurial process.

Throughout each stage, we proposed that high Machs would successfully utilize the knowledge, skills, and abilities of others. High Machs are characterized as strategic and calculating, suggesting that they not only look for opportunities to evaluate and exploit, but they are both crafty and rational when doing so (O'Boyle et al., 2012). Regardless of their education or experience, they are the most likely among the dark triad, to rely on others in order to obtain personal gain (Ferris & Judge, 1991). One of the most significant differences between high Machs and the other two traits is that high Machs are less likely to be irrational or impulsive (Paulhus & Williams, 2002). For this reason, high Machs are likely to strategically seek and establish connections with others more easily, even if they are just as superficial connections. Further, high Machs have a natural proclivity for manipulating others (Dahling et al., 2008), indicating that they have the ability to make use of others' knowledge, skills, and abilities to recognize, evaluate, and exploit opportunities. This leads them to be likely to be the most active and strategic in their use of human resources programs to acquire, cultivate, and leverage human capital.

In contrast, narcissists rely on superficial relationships with others in order to garner sustained praise and admiration (Navis & Ozbek, 2016). A narcissist maintains these types of relationships because of threats to ego and self-esteem (Grijalva & Harms, 2014). Since others are kept at a distance, they usually are not able to see the less salutary attitudes and behaviors of a narcissist (Miller, 2015). We proposed that superficial relationships may allow for a measure of success in recognizing opportunities, but less so when evaluating and exploiting opportunities. For this reason, we acknowledge that there is a narcissist-entrepreneurship fit, but most likely only in the opportunity recognition stage. In the other stages, a narcissist will likely need the assistance of other managers, especially in the selection, development, and compensation of employees. These managers can build a human resources program that shields a narcissistic entrepreneur from their own weaknesses. Specifically, these individuals can help develop programs to make sure that employees are hired, compensated, and promoted based on their merits, knowledge, skills, and abilities rather than their penchant for agreeing with the entrepreneur.

While evidence exists of the psychopath-entrepreneurship relationship (Akhtar et al., 2013), there is a paucity of evidence regarding how psychopathic traits impact others in the entrepreneurship context. Recent literature has suggested that psychological disorders can be beneficial in entrepreneurship (Verheul et al., 2015). However, by ignoring the impact of dark traits on others in the enterprise, their picture of these relationships is incomplete. This is particularly true of psychopathy as psychopaths are often highly educated and experienced, suggesting a propensity for opportunity recognition (Stevens et al., 2012). However, the antisocial tendencies of the psychopath, taken together with impulsive behaviors and an inclination for thrill-seeking, suggest that psychopaths are irrational decision makers (Cleckley, 1950/2015). Moreover, because psychopaths are less likely to rely on the voice of others, there is little chance that erroneous evaluations or failed attempts to exploit opportunities will be corrected. In sum, psychopaths are the least likely of all the dark triad personalities to effectively leverage the knowledge, skills, and abilities of others. Due to the personality traits of psychopaths, interpersonal relationships are likely to suffer and firm performance may suffer as well. To help mitigate these challenges, self-aware psychopaths can hire individuals skilled in human resources to manage and develop employees, effectively acting as a buffer between himself or herself and employees.

In addition to the dark triad, there are other personality traits and psychological disorders that might influence entrepreneurship. For example, Thiel and Masters (2014) suggest that Asperger's syndrome has a positive influence on entrepreneurial entry and outcomes. The current conversation concerning personality and entrepreneurship (DeNisi, 2015; Klotz & Neubaum, 2016; Miller, 2015) indicates that there is a wide variety of personality traits and characteristics that are often overlooked and should be considered in the entrepreneurship process. Building on these observations, future researchers have a fertile ground to empirically test the relationships developed here and to expand the research stream to include additional psychological disorders.

Methodologically, researchers should employ a longitudinal design to understand how individuals with these traits recognize, evaluate, and explore opportunities. A temporal focus can illuminate whether, or alternatively, how these traits influence entrepreneurial decision-making. For example, time will tell how thrill-seeking or impulsivity is a negative when evaluating opportunities. Additionally, researchers in the area of strategic human resources could examine the extent to which the development and adoption of a formal HR system can help mitigate potential challenges, and enhance potential benefits, associated with entrepreneurs who have dark triad traits. Another potentially fruitful area of research is derived from the relatively low base rate of entrepreneurs with dark triad traits. For example, a qualitative study is likely to yield valuable results for theory building (Eisenhardt, 1989) in areas such as life history theory (Jonason et al., 2012) or role congruity theory (Eagly & Karau, 2002). Finally, the high levels of entrepreneurial failure warrant further study of not only firm characteristics but also the role entrepreneurial personality in these failures. Multilevel studies investigating dark triad traits and entrepreneurial failure may help to explain the difference between those who try and do not make it in entrepreneurship and the antiheroes celebrated in the business world (Jonason et al., 2012).

CONCLUSION

Individuals exhibiting any of the dark triad traits are often considered a problem in society. These individuals are often viewed as misfits who cause harm to others, and often eventually to themselves. However, within the context of entrepreneurship, dark triad personality traits might offer certain advantages, particularly at various stages of the entrepreneurial process. It is important, however, to consider that success in entrepreneurship is rarely accomplished by one individual (Eisenhardt, 2013). Entrepreneurs work with others, often relying on their subordinates' knowledge, skills, and abilities for entrepreneurial success. Thus, there must not only be a fit between the individual's personality and entrepreneurship but also how they employ others' human capital in the entrepreneurship context.

REFERENCES

Akhtar, R., Ahmetoglu, G., & Chamorro-Premuzik, T. (2013). Greed is good? Assessing the relationship between entrepreneurship and subclinical psychopathy. *Personality and Individual Differences, 54*(3), 420−425.

Ali, F., Amorim, I. S., & Chamorro-Premuzik, T. (2009). Empathy deficits and trait emotional intelligence in psychopathy and Machiavellianism. *Personality and Individual Differences, 47*(7), 758−762.

Alvarez, S. A., & Barney, J. B. (2007). Discovery and creation: Alternative theories of entrepreneurial action. *Strategic Entrepreneurship Journal, 1*(1−2), 11−26.

Ardichvili, A., Cardozo, R., & Ray, S. (2003). A theory of entrepreneurial opportunity identification and development. *Journal of Business Venturing, 18*(1), 105−123.

Arora, P., Haynie, J. M., & Laurence, G. A. (2013). Counterfactual thinking and entrepreneurial self-efficacy: The moderating role of self-esteem and dispositional affect. *Entrepreneurship Theory and Practice, 37*(2), 359−385.

Arthur, J. B. (1992). The link between business strategy and industrial relations systems in American steel minimills. *Industrial & Labor Relations Review, 45*(3), 488−506.

Arthur, J. B. (1994). Effects of human resource systems on manufacturing performance and turnover. *Academy of Management Journal, 37*(3), 670−687.

Autio, E., Dahlander, L., & Frederiksen, L. (2013). Information exposure, opportunity evaluation, and entrepreneurial action: An investigation of an online user community. *Academy of Management Journal, 56*(5), 1348−1371.

Babiak, P. (1995). When psychopaths go to work: A case study of an industrial psychopath. *Applied Psychology, 44*(2), 171−188.

Babiak, P., & Hare, R. D. (2006). *Snakes in suits: When psychopaths go to work*. New York, NY: Regan Books.

Babiak, P., Neumann, C. S., & Hare, R. D. (2010). Corporate psychopathy: Talking the walk. *Behavioral Sciences & the Law, 28*(2), 174−193.

Bandura, A. (1971). *Social learning theory*. New York, NY: General Learning Press.

Bandura, A. (1986). *Social foundations of thought and action: A social cognitive theory.* Englewood Cliffs, NJ: Prentice-Hall.

Barber, N. (1998). Sex differences in disposition towards kin, security of adult attachment, and sociosexuality as a function of parental divorce. *Evolution and Human Behavior, 19*(2), 125–132.

Baron, R. A. (2006). Opportunity recognition as pattern recognition: How entrepreneurs "connect the dots" to identify new business opportunities. *Academy of Management Perspectives, 20*(1), 104–119.

Baron, R. A., & Ensley, M. D. (2006). Opportunity recognition as the detection of meaningful patterns: Evidence from comparisons of novice and experienced entrepreneurs. *Management Science, 52*(9), 1331–1344.

Baum, J. R., Frese, M., & Baron, R. A. (2007). Entrepreneurship as an area of psychology study: An introduction. In J. R. Baum, M. Frese, & R. A. Baron (Eds.), The *psychology of entrepreneurship* (pp. 1–18). New York, NY: Lawrence Erlbaum Associates, Inc.

Baum, J. R., & Locke, E. A. (2004). The relationship of entrepreneurial traits, skill, and motivation to subsequent venture growth. *Journal of Applied Psychology, 89*(4), 587.

Baum, J. R., Locke, E. A., & Smith, K. G. (2001). A multidimensional model of venture growth. *Academy of Management Journal, 44*(2), 292–303.

Belschak, F. D., Hartog, D. N. D., & Kalshoven, K. (2013). Leading Machiavellians: How to translate Machiavellians' selfishness into pro-organizational behavior. *Journal of Management, 41*(7), 1934–1956.

Bhidé, A. V. (2000). *The origin and evolution of new business.* New York, NY: Oxford University Press.

Bird, B. J. (1988). Implementing entrepreneurial ideas: The case for intention. *Academy of Management Review, 13*(3), 442–453.

Boddy, C. R. (2014). Corporate psychopaths, conflict, employee affective well-being and counterproductive work behaviour. *Journal of Business Ethics, 121*(1), 107–121.

Brinkmann, J., Grichnik, D., & Kapsa, D. (2010). Should entrepreneurs plan or just storm the castle? A meta-analysis on contextual factors impacting the business planning–performance relationship in small firms. *Journal of Business Venturing, 25*(1), 24–40.

Brown, S. L., & Forth, A. E. (1997). Psychopathy and sexual assault: Static risk factors, emotional precursors, and rapist subtypes. *Journal of Consulting and Clinical Psychology, 65*(5), 848–857.

Bushman, B. J., & Baumeister, R. F. (1998). Threatened egotism, narcissism, self-esteem, and direct and displaced aggression: Does self-love or self-hate lead to violence? *Journal of Personality and Social Psychology, 75*(1), 219–229.

Bushman, B. J., Bonacci, A. M., Van Dijk, M., & Baumeister, R. F. (2003). Narcissism, sexual refusal, and aggression: Testing a narcissistic reactance model of sexual coercion. *Journal of Personality and Social Psychology, 84*(5), 1027.

Cable, D. M., & DeRue, D. S. (2002). The convergent and discriminant validity of subjective fit perceptions. *Journal of Applied Psychology, 87*(5), 875–884.

Cale, E. M., & Lilienfeld, S. O. (2002). Sex differences in psychopathy and antisocial personality disorder: A review and integration. *Clinical Psychology Review, 22*(8), 1179–1207.

Calhoon, R. P. (1969). Niccolo Machiavelli and the twentieth century administrator. *Academy of Management Journal, 12*(2), 205–212.

Campbell, W., Goodie, A. S., & Foster, J. D. (2004). Narcissism, confidence, and risk attitude. *Journal of Behavioral Decision Making, 17*(4), 297–311.

Campbell, W. K., & Miller, J. D. (2011). Narcissism and narcissistic personality disorder: Six suggestions for unifying the field. In W. K. Campbell & J. D. Miller (Eds.), *The hand-book of narcissism and narcissistic personality disorder: Theoretical approaches, empirical findings, and treatments* (pp. 485–488). Hoboken, NJ: Wiley.

Cardon, M. S., & Kirk, C. P. (2015). Entrepreneurial passion as mediator of the self-efficacy to persistence relationship. *Entrepreneurship Theory and Practice, 39*(5), 1027–1050.

Chandler, G. N., & Hanks, S. H. (1994). Market attractiveness, resource-based capabilities, venture strategies, and venture performance. *Journal of Business Venturing, 9*(4), 331–349.

Chatterjee, A., & Hambrick, D. C. (2007). It's all about me: Narcissistic chief executive officers and their effects on company strategy and performance. *Administrative Science Quarterly, 52*(3), 351–386.

Christie, R., & Geis, F. L. (1970). *Studies in Machiavellianism*. New York, NY: Academic Press.

Chwolka, A., & Raith, M. G. (2012). The value of business planning before start-up—A decision-theoretical perspective. *Journal of Business Venturing, 27*(3), 385–399.

Cleckley, H. (1950/2015). *The mask of insanity: An attempt to clarify some issues about so-called psychopathic personality*. Mansfield Centre, CT: Martino Publishing.

Cohen, A. (2016). Are they among us? A conceptual framework of the relationship between the dark triad personality and counterproductive work behaviors (CWBs). *Human Resource Management Review, 26*(1), 69–85.

Collins, C. J., Hanges, P. J., & Locke, E. A. (2004). The relationship of achievement motivation to entrepreneurial behavior: A meta-analysis. *Human Performance, 17*(1), 95–117.

Collins, C. J., & Smith, K. G. (2006). Knowledge exchange and combination: The role of human resource practices in the performance of high-technology firms. *Academy of Management Journal, 49*(3), 544–560.

Colquitt, J. A., Scott, B. A., & LePine, J. A. (2007). Trust, trustworthiness, and trust propensity: A meta-analytic test of their unique relationships with risk taking and job performance. *Journal of Applied Psychology, 92*(4), 909–927.

Dahling, J. J., Whitaker, B. G., & Levy, P. E. (2008). The development and validation of a new Machiavellianism scale. *Journal of Management, 35*(2), 219–257.

Davidsson, P. (2015). Entrepreneurial opportunities and the entrepreneurship nexus: A re-conceptualization. *Journal of Business Venturing, 30*(5), 674–695.

de Vries, M. F. K. (1985). The dark side of entrepreneurship. *Harvard Business Review, 63*(6), 160–167.

de Vries, M. F. K. (1996). The anatomy of the entrepreneur: Clinical observations. *Human Relations, 49*(7), 853–883.

Delmar, F., & Shane, S. (2003). Does business planning facilitate the development of new ventures? *Strategic Management Journal, 24*(12), 1165–1185.

DeNisi, A. S. (2015). Some further thoughts on the entrepreneurial personality. *Entrepreneurship Theory and Practice, 39*(5), 997–1003.

Dess, G. G., & Davis, P. S. (1984). Porter's (1980) generic strategies as determinants of strategic group membership and organizational performance. *Academy of Management Journal, 27*(3), 467–488.

Dickinson, K. A., & Pincus, A. L. (2003). Interpersonal analysis of grandiose and vulnerable narcissism. *Journal of Personality Disorders, 17*(3), 188–207.

Douglas, E. J. (2013). Reconstructing entrepreneurial intentions to identify predisposition for growth. *Journal of Business Venturing, 28*(5), 633–651.

Eagly, A. H., & Karau, S. J. (2002). Role congruity theory of prejudice toward female leaders. *Psychological Review, 109*, 573–598.

Eckhardt, J. T., & Shane, S. A. (2003). Opportunities and entrepreneurship. *Journal of Management, 29*(3), 333–349.

Eisenhardt, K. M. (1989). Building theories from case study research. *Academy of Management Review, 14*(4), 532–550.

Eisenhardt, K. M. (2013). Top management teams and the performance of entrepreneurial firms. *Small Business Economics, 40*(4), 805–816.

Ensley, M. D., Pearce, C. L., & Hmieleski, K. M. (2006). The moderating effect of environmental dynamism on the relationship between entrepreneur leadership behavior and new venture performance. *Journal of Business Venturing, 21*(2), 243–263.

Fehr, B., Samsom, D., & Paulhus, D. L. (1992). The construct of Machiavellianism: Twenty years later. In C. D. Spielberger & J. N. Butcher (Eds.), *Advances in personality assessment* (pp. 77–116). Hillsdale, NJ: Erlbaum.

Ferris, G. R., & Judge, T. A. (1991). Personnel/human resources management: A political influence perspective. *Journal of Management, 17*(2), 447–488.

Figueredo, A. J., Sefcek, J. A., & Jones, D. N. (2006). The ideal romantic partner personality. *Personality and Individual Differences, 41*(3), 431–441.

Foo, M. D. (2011). Emotions and entrepreneurial opportunity evaluation. *Entrepreneurship Theory and Practice, 35*(2), 375–393.

Galvin, B. M., Lange, D., & Ashforth, B. E. (2015). Narcissistic organizational identification: Seeing oneself as central to the organization's identity. *Academy of Management Review, 40*(2), 163–181.

Gemmill, G. R., & Heisler, W. J. (1972). Machiavellianism as a factor in managerial job strain, job satisfaction, and upward mobility. *Academy of Management Journal, 15*(1), 51–62.

Ghose, D., & Crain, T. L. (1995). Ethical standards, attitudes toward risk, and intentional noncompliance: An experimental investigation. *Journal of Business Ethics, 14*(5), 353–365.

Greenbaum, R. L., Hill, A., Mawritz, M. B., & Quade, M. J. (in press). Employee Machiavellianism to unethical behavior: The role of abusive supervision as a trait activator. *Journal of Management*, doi:10.1177/0149206314535434

Grijalva, E., & Harms, P. D. (2014). Narcissism: An integrative synthesis and dominance complementary model. *Academy of Management Perspectives, 28*(2), 108–127.

Gunnthorsdottir, A., McCabe, K., & Smith, V. (2002). Using the Machiavellianism instrument to predict trustworthiness in a bargaining game. *Journal of Economic Psychology, 23*(1), 49–66.

Hamilton, B. H. (2000). Does entrepreneurship pay? An empirical analysis of the returns to self-employment. *Journal of Political Economy, 108*(3), 604–631.

Hare, R. D. (1970). *Psychopathy: Theory and practice*. New York, NY: Wiley.

Hare, R. D., & Neumann, C. S. (2008). Psychopathy as a clinical and empirical construct. *Annual Review of Clinical Psychology, 4*, 217–246.

Haynes, K. T., Hitt, M. A., & Campbell, J. T. (2015). The dark side of leadership: Towards a mid-range theory of hubris and greed in entrepreneurial context. *Journal of Management Studies, 52*(4), 479–505.

Haynie, J. M., Shepherd, D. A., & McMullen, J. S. (2009). An opportunity for me? The role of resources in opportunity evaluation decisions. *Journal of Management Studies, 46*(3), 337–361.

Hayward, M. L., Shepherd, D. A., & Griffin, D. (2006). A hubris theory of entrepreneurship. *Management Science, 52*(2), 160–172.

Hisrich, R., Langan-Fox, J., & Grant, S. (2007). Entrepreneurship research and practice: A call to action for psychology. *American Psychologist, 62*(6), 575–589.

Hitt, M. A., Ireland, R. D., Sirmon, D. G., & Trahms, C. A. (2011). Strategic entrepreneurship: Creating value for individuals, organizations, and society. *The Academy of Management Perspectives, 25*(2), 57–75.

Hmieleski, K. M., & Baron, R. A. (2008). When does entrepreneurial self-efficacy enhance versus reduce firm performance? *Strategic Entrepreneurship Journal, 2*(1), 57–72.

Hollenbeck, J., & Whitener, E. (1988). Reclaiming personality traits for personnel selection. *Journal of Management, 14*(1), 81–91.

Honig, B., & Samuelsson, M. (2012). Planning and the entrepreneur: A longitudinal examination of nascent entrepreneurs in Sweden. *Journal of Small Business Management, 50*(3), 365–388.

Ireland, R. D., Hitt, M. A., & Sirmon, D. G. (2003). Strategic entrepreneurship: The construct and its dimensions. *Journal of Management, 29*(6), 963–989.

Janney, J. J., & Dess, G. G. (2006). The risk concept for entrepreneurs reconsidered: New challenges to the conventional wisdom. *Journal of Business Venturing, 21*(3), 385–400.

Jonason, P. K., Li, N. P., Webster, D. G., & Schmitt, D. P. (2009). The dark triad: Facilitating a short-term mating strategy in men. *European Journal of Personality, 23*(1), 5–18.

Jonason, P. K., & Webster, G. D. (2010). The dirty dozen: A concise measure of the dark triad. *Psychological Assessment, 22*(2), 420–432.

Jonason, P. K., Webster, G. D., Schmitt, D. P., Li, N. P., & Crysel, L. (2012). The antihero in popular culture: Life history theory and the dark triad personality traits. *Review of General Psychology, 16*(2), 192–199.

Jones, D. N., & Paulhus, D. L. (2010). Different provocations trigger aggression in narcissists and psychopaths. *Social Psychological and Personality Science, 1*(1), 12–18.

Jones, D. N., & Paulhus, D. L. (2011). The role of impulsivity in the dark triad of personality. *Personality and Individual Differences, 51*(5), 679–682.

Jones, D. N., & Paulhus, D. L. (2014). Introducing the short dark triad (SD3): A brief measure of dark personality traits. *Assessment, 21*(1), 28–41.

Jones, G. E., & Kavanagh, M. J. (1996). An experimental examination of the effects of individual and situational factors on unethical behavior intentions in the workplace. *Journal of Business Ethics, 15*(5), 511–523.

Kashy, D. A., & DePaulo, B. M. (1996). Who lies? *Journal of Personality and Social Psychology, 70*(5), 979–995.

Keh, H. T., Foo, M. D., & Lim, B. C. (2002). Opportunity evaluation under risky conditions: The cognitive processes of entrepreneurs. *Entrepreneurship Theory and Practice, 27*(2), 125–148.

Kirzner, I. M. (1973). *Competition and entrepreneurship.* Chicago, IL: University of Chicago Press.

Kirzner, I. M. (1979). *Perception, opportunity, and profit.* Chicago, IL: University of Chicago Press.

Klotz, A. C., & Neubaum, D. O. (2016). Research on the dark side of personality traits in entrepreneurship: Observations from an organizational behavior perspective. *Entrepreneurship Theory and Practice, 40*(1), 7–17.

Knight, F. H. (1921). *Risk, uncertainty and profit*. New York, NY: Hart, Schaffner, & Marx.

Koellinger, P., Minniti, M., & Schade, C. (2007). "I think I can, I think I can": Overconfidence and entrepreneurial behavior. *Journal of Economic Psychology, 28*(4), 502−527.

Krueger, N., & Dickson, P. R. (1994). How believing in ourselves increases risk taking: Perceived self-efficacy and opportunity recognition. *Decision Sciences, 25*(3), 385−400.

Lechler, T. (2001). Social interaction: A determinant of entrepreneurial team venture success. *Small Business Economics, 16*(4), 263−278.

Lee, D. Y., & Tsang, E. W. (2001). The effects of entrepreneurial personality, background and network activities on venture growth. *Journal of Management Studies, 38*(4), 583−602.

Lewin, K. (1951). *Field theory in social science*. New York, NY: Harper & Row.

Lim, S., & Cortina, L. M. (2005). Interpersonal mistreatment in the workplace: The interface and impact of general incivility and sexual harassment. *Journal of Applied Psychology, 90*(3), 483−496.

Liu, C. C. (2008). The relationship between Machiavellianism and knowledge sharing willingness. *Journal of Business and Psychology, 22*(3), 233−240.

Locke, E. A., & Latham, G. (1991). *A theory of goal setting and task performance*. Englewood Cliffs, NJ: Prentice-Hall.

Lumpkin, G. T., & Lichtenstein, B. B. (2005). The role of organizational learning in the opportunity-recognition process. *Entrepreneurship Theory and Practice, 29*(4), 451−472.

Lykken, D. T. (1995). *The antisocial personalities*. Hillsdale, NJ: Lawrence Erlbaum Associates.

Maccoby, M. (2000). Narcissistic leaders: The incredible pros, the inevitable cons. *Harvard Business Review, 78*(1), 68−78.

Machiavelli, N. (1513/1981). *The prince*. New York, NY: Bantam Books.

Markman, G. D., Balkin, D. B., & Baron, R. A. (2002). Inventors and new venture creation: The effects of general self-efficacy and regretful thinking. *Entrepreneurship Theory and Practice, 27*(2), 149−165.

Markman, G. D., & Baron, R. A. (2003). Person-entrepreneurship fit: Why some people are more successful as entrepreneurs than others. *Human Resource Management Review, 13*(2), 281−301.

Mathieu, C., Neumann, C. S., Hare, R. D., & Babiak, P. (2014). A dark side of leadership: Corporate psychopathy and its influence on employee well-being and job satisfaction. *Personality and Individual Differences, 59*, 83−88.

Mathieu, C., & St-Jean, É. (2013). Entrepreneurial personality: The role of narcissism. *Personality and Individual Differences, 55*(5), 527−531.

Matthews, C. H., & Scott, S. G. (1995). Uncertainty and planning in small and entrepreneurial firms: An empirical assessment. *Journal of Small Business Management, 33*(4), 34−52.

Mayer, R. C., Davis, R. H., & Schoorman, F. D. (1995). An integrative model of organizational trust. *Academy of Management Review, 20*(3), 709−734.

Mealey, L. (1995). The sociobiology of sociopathy: An integrated evolutionary model. *Behavioral and Brain Sciences, 18*(3), 523−541.

Miller, D. (1988). Relating Porter's business strategies to environment and structure: Analysis and performance implications. *Academy of Management Journal, 31*, 280−308.

Miller, D. (2015). A downside to the entrepreneurial personality. *Entrepreneurship Theory and Practice, 39*(1), 1−8.

Miller, D. (2016). Response to "Research on the dark side of personality traits in entrepreneurship: Observations from an organizational behavior perspective". *Entrepreneurship Theory and Practice, 40*(1), 19−24.

Miller, D., de Vries, M. R. K., & Toulouse, J. M. (1982). Top executive locus of control and its relationship to strategy-making, structure, and environment. *Academy of Management Journal, 25*, 237–253.

Miller, D., & Toulouse, J. M. (1986). Chief executive personality and corporate strategy and structure in small firms. *Management Science, 32*(11), 1389–1409.

Miller, K. D. (2007). Risk and rationality in entrepreneurial processes. Strategic *Entrepreneurship Journal, 1*(1–2), 57–74.

Morf, C. C., & Rhodewalt, F. (2001). Unraveling the paradoxes of narcissism: A dynamic self-regulatory processing model. *Psychological Inquiry, 12*(4), 177–196.

Murnieks, C. Y., Mosakowski, E., & Cardon, M. S. (2014). Pathways of passion: Identity centrality, passion, and behavior among entrepreneurs. *Journal of Management, 40*(6), 1583–1606.

Navis, C., & Ozbek, O. V. (2016). The right people in the wrong places: The paradox of entrepreneurial entry and successful opportunity realization. *Academy of Management Review, 41*(1), 109–129.

O'Boyle, E. H., Jr., Forsyth, D. R., Banks, G. C., & McDaniel, M. A. (2012). A meta-analysis of the dark triad and work behavior: A social exchange perspective. *Journal of Applied Psychology, 97*(3), 557–579.

Oh, I. S., Guay, R. P., Kim, K., Harold, C. M., Lee, J. H., Heo, C. G., & Shin, K. H. (2014). Fit happens globally: A meta-analytic comparison of the relationships of person-environment fit dimensions with work attitudes and performance across East Asia, Europe, and North America. *Personnel Psychology, 67*(1), 99–152.

Ostgaard, T. A., & Birley, S. (1994). Personal networks and firm competitive strategy—A strategic or coincidental match? *Journal of Business Venturing, 9*(4), 281–305.

Patel, P. C., & Cooper, D. (2014). The harder they fall, the faster they rise: Approach and avoidance focus in narcissistic CEOs. *Strategic Management Journal, 35*(10), 1528–1540.

Paulhus, D. L., & Williams, K. M. (2002). The dark triad personality: Narcissism, Machiavellianism, and psychopathy. *Journal of Research in Personality, 36*(6), 556–563.

Pearson, C. M., & Porath, C. L. (2005). On the nature, consequences and remedies of work incivility: No time for "nice"? Think again. *Academy of Management Executive, 19*(1), 7–18.

Penney, L. M., & Spector, P. E. (2005). Job stress, incivility, and counterproductive work behavior (CWB): The moderating role of negative affectivity. *Journal of Organizational Behavior, 26*(7), 777–796.

Porter, M. E. (1980). *Competitive strategy: Techniques for analyzing industries and competition* (p. 300). New York, NY: Free Press.

Pryor, C., Webb, J. W., Ireland, R. D., & Ketchen, D. J., Jr. (2016). Toward an integration of the behavioral and cognitive influences on the entrepreneurship process. *Strategic Entrepreneurship Journal, 10*(1), 21–42.

Raffiee, J., & Feng, J. (2014). Should I quit my day job? A hybrid path to entrepreneurship. *Academy of Management Journal, 57*(4), 936–963.

Ryckman, R. M., Thornton, B., & Butler, J. C. (1994). Personality correlates of the hypercompetitive attitude scale: Validity tests of Horney's theory of neurosis. *Journal of Personality Assessment, 62*(1), 84–94.

Sarason, Y., Dean, T., & Dillard, J. F. (2006). Entrepreneurship as the nexus of individual and opportunity: A structuration view. *Journal of Business Venturing, 21*(3), 286–305.

Schoenleber, M., Roche, M. J., Wetzel, E., Pincus, A. L., & Roberts, B. W. (2015). Development of a brief version of the pathological narcissism inventory. *Psychological Assessment, 27*(4), 1520–1526.

Schumpeter, J. A. (1942/2014). *Capitalism, socialism, and democracy.* Floyd, VA: Impact Books.

Shane, S., & Venkataraman, S. (2000). The promise of entrepreneurship as a field of research. *Academy of Management Review, 25*(1), 217–226.

Shepherd, D. A., Williams, T. A., & Patzelt, H. (2015). Thinking about entrepreneurial decision making: Review and research agenda. *Journal of Management, 41*(1), 11–46.

Shepperd, J. A., & Socherman, R. E. (1997). On the manipulative behavior of low Machiavellians, feigning incompetence to "sandbag" an opponent. *Journal of Personality and Social Psychology, 72*(6), 1448–1459.

Shultz, C. J. (1993). Situational and dispositional predictors of performance: A test of the hypothesized Machiavellianism structure interaction among sales persons. *Journal of Applied Social Psychology, 23*(6), 478–498.

Singhapakdi, A., & Vitell, S. J. (1991). Analyzing the ethical decision making of sales professionals. *Journal of Personal Selling & Sales Management, 11*(4), 1–12.

Snyder, M. (1974). Self-monitoring of expressive behavior. *Journal of Personality and Social Psychology, 30*(4), 526–537.

Stevens, G. W., Deuling, J. K., & Armenakis, A. A. (2012). Successful psychopaths: Are they unethical decision-makers and why? *Journal of Business Ethics, 105*(2), 139–149.

Thiel, P., & Masters, B. (2014). *Zero to one: Notes on startups, or how to build the future.* New York, NY: Crown Business.

Touhey, J. (1973). Intelligence, Machiavellianism, and social mobility. *British Journal of Social and Clinical Psychology, 12,* 34–37.

Townsend, D. M., Busenitz, L. W., & Arthurs, J. D. (2010). To start or not start: Outcome and ability expectations in the decision to start a new venture. *Journal of Business Venturing, 25*(2), 192–202.

Turner, C. F., & Martinez, D. C. (1977). Socioeconomic achievement and the Machiavellian personality. *Sociometry, 40*(4), 325–336.

Vazire, S., & Funder, D. C. (2006). Impulsivity and the self-defeating behavior of narcissists. *Personality and Social Psychology Review, 10*(2), 154–165.

Vecchio, R. P., & Sussmann, M. (1991). Choice of influence tactics: Individual and organizational determinants. *Journal of Organizational Behavior, 12*(1), 73–80.

Verheul, I., Block, J., Burmeister-Lamp, K., Thurik, R., Tiemeier, H., & Turturea, R. (2015). ADHD-like behavior and entrepreneurial intentions. *Small Business Economics, 45*(1), 85–101.

Vinnell, R., & Hamilton, R. (1999). A historical perspective on small firm development. *Entrepreneurship Theory and Practice, 23*(4), 5–18.

Waldman, D. A., Ramirez, G. G., House, R. J., & Puranam, P. (2001). Does leadership matter? CEO leadership attributes and profitability under conditions of perceived environmental uncertainty. *Academy of Management Journal, 44*(1), 134–143.

Wales, W. J., Patel, P. C., & Lumpkin, G. T. (2013). In pursuit of greatness: CEO narcissism, entrepreneurial orientation, and firm performance variance. *Journal of Management Studies, 50*(6), 1041–1069.

Wallace, H. M., & Baumeister, R. F. (2002). The performance of narcissists rises and falls with perceived opportunity for glory. *Journal of Personality and Social Psychology, 82*(5), 819–834.

Watson, W. E., Ponthieu, L. D., & Critelli, J. W. (1995). Team interpersonal process effectiveness in venture partnerships and its connection to perceived success. *Journal of Business Venturing, 10*(5), 393–411.

Wijbenga, F. H., & van Witteloostuijn, A. (2007). Entrepreneurial locus of control and competitive strategies – The moderating effect of environmental dynamism. *Journal of Economic Psychology, 28*(5), 566–589.

Williams, K. M., Paulhus, D. L., & Hare, R. D. (2007). Capturing the four-factor structure of psychopathy in college students via self-report. *Journal of Personality Assessment, 88*(2), 205–219.

ABOUT THE AUTHORS

P. Matthijs Bal is Reader at the School of Management, University of Bath, United Kingdom. He obtained his PhD from VU University Amsterdam, the Netherlands, and also worked for Erasmus University Rotterdam. His research interests concern flexibility in the workplace, individualization at work, workplace dignity, and the role of fictional narrative at work. Recently, he published two edited books, one on aging workers in the contemporary workplace and another on idiosyncratic deals between employees and organization. He currently works on a theory of workplace dignity. More information about his work can be found on his website www.matthijsbal.com.

Ho Kwan Cheung is doctoral student of Industrial-Organizational Psychology at George Mason University after receiving her B.A. in Psychology and Spanish from Penn State University in 2014. Her research focuses on: (1) manifestations of discrimination in the workplace, with a special focus in gender, (2) consequences of discrimination in the workplace, particularly in the form of barriers to work-life balance, and (3) remediation strategies to ensure a diverse, inclusive workplace.

Gerald R. Ferris is Francis Eppes Professor of Management, Professor of Psychology, and Professor of Sport Management at Florida State University. He received a Ph.D. in Business Administration from the University of Illinois at Urbana-Champaign. He has research interests in the areas of social influence processes in human resources systems. Ferris is the author of numerous articles published in such journals as the *Journal of Applied Psychology*, *Organizational Behavior and Human Decision Processes*, *Personnel Psychology*, *Academy of Management Journal*, and *Academy of Management Review*. He served as editor of the annual series, *Research in Personnel and Human Resources Management*, from 1981 to 2003. Ferris has been the recipient of a number of distinctions and honors. In 2001, he was the recipient of the Heneman Career Achievement Award, and in 2010, he received the Thomas A. Mahoney Mentoring Award, both from the Human Resources Division of the Academy of Management.

Paul G. W. Jansen is Professor of Industrial Psychology, Faculty of Economics and Business Administration, VU University Amsterdam, The Netherlands. He has published over 60 scholarly articles and chapters, and (co)edited 18 books. Paul Jansen graduated, cum laude, in 1979, with specialization in Mathematical Psychology at the University of Nijmegen; PhD in social sciences in 1983. Paul Jansen is one of the founders, and current board member of the 'HRM Network NL'. His research interests are in management development, careers, assessment (e.g. assessment centers, 360-graden feedback) and performance management. Publications in, for example, *Applied Psychology: An international Review*, *Psychometrika*, *Applied Psychological Measurement*, *Journal of Organizational and Occupational Psychology*, *Journal of Applied Psychology*, *Journal of Organizational Behavior*, *Journal of Vocational Behavior*, and *Journal of Management Studies*. For his scientific work he was awarded the Dutch HRM Network award 2013 at the 8th International Biannual Conference "*'H' versus 'R' in HRM*" in Leuven, Belgium.

Molly Kilcullen is master's student of Industrial-Organizational Psychology at George Mason University. Her research interests include employee selection, adaptive leadership, teamwork under stress, and cross-cultural competency. In addition to being a student, she also works as a Research Fellow at the Army Research Institute at Fort Belvoir.

Eden King joined the faculty of the Industrial-Organizational Psychology program at George Mason University after earning her Ph.D. from Rice University in 2006. Dr. King is pursuing a program of research that seeks to guide the effective management of diverse organizations. Her research integrates organizational and social psychological theories in conceptualizing social stigma and the work-life interface. This research addresses three primary themes: (1) current manifestations of discrimination and barriers to work-life balance in organizations, (2) consequences of such challenges for its targets and their workplaces, and (3) individual and organizational strategies for reducing discrimination and increasing support for families. In addition to her academic positions, Dr. King has consulted on applied projects related to climate initiatives, selection systems, and diversity training programs, and she has worked as a trial consultant. She is currently an Associate Editor for the *Journal of Management* and the *Journal of Business and Psychology*.

Donald H. Kluemper is Assistant Professor of Management at the University of Illinois at Chicago (UIC) and Director of UICs Institute for Leadership Excellence and Development (iLEAD). His research interests are centered on personality, workplace mistreatment, and leadership. Donald has published in outlets such as the *Journal of Applied Psychology*, *Personnel Psychology, Organizational Behavior and Human Decision Processes*, the *Leadership Quarterly*, and the *Journal of Management* and is lead author of a manuscript entitled "Social networking websites, personality ratings, and the organizational context: More than meets the eye?" published in the *Journal of Applied Social Psychology* in 2012 that appeared in over 1,500 combined media outlets.

Alex Lindsey is a fifth year doctoral student of Industrial-Organizational Psychology at George Mason University. He received his Bachelor of Science in Psychology from Indiana University − Purdue University Indianapolis (IUPUI) in 2011, where he will be returning as an Assistant Professor starting in the fall of 2016! Alex's research interests include diversity, inclusion, and the general well-being of employees in the workplace, with a focus on prejudice and discrimination reduction strategies. Alex's dissertation focuses on the affective and motivational drivers of diversity training effectiveness in addition to the organizational and individual difference boundary conditions of these effects.

Graham H. Lowman is doctoral student in management at the University of Alabama. He obtained a Bachelor's of Science in Accounting from the University of Alabama and a Master's of Science in Industrial-Organizational Psychology from the University of Tennessee at Chattanooga. His research interests include cross-cultural recruitment and selection, the dark triad personality traits, and person-environment fit.

Louis D. Marino is Professor of Entrepreneurship and Strategic Management at The University of Alabama. He earned his PhD in Management with a specialization in Strategic Management from Indiana University in 1998. Professor Marino's research focuses on how entrepreneurs and entrepreneurial firm's respond to environmental uncertainty, and how entrepreneur's characteristics and a firm's entrepreneurial orientation impacts the nature and efficacy of their response. His research has been published in leading journals such as the *Academy of Management Journal*, the *Journal of Business Venturing*, the *Journal of International Business Studies*, and *Entrepreneurship Theory and Practice*. His research has been recognized with best paper awards at both the Academy of Management and at the Babson College Entrepreneurship Research Conference.

Hannah M. Markell is doctoral student of Industrial-Organizational Psychology at George Mason University. She received a B.A. from Washington University in St. Louis in Philosophy-Neuroscience-Psychology, with minors in Public Health and Psychology. Hannah conducts research related to examining different forms of discrimination in marginalized populations, such as ex-convicts, LGBT individuals, racial minorities, and older employees. She blends this interest with her desire to focus on improving statistical methodology as it is employed in the organizational sciences.

Charn P. McAllister is doctoral student in Organizational Behavior and Human Resources at Florida State University. His primary research interests include social influence, stress, and self-regulation. He has published his work in outlets including the *Journal of Management, Journal of Organizational Behavior, Group and Organization Management*, and *Military Psychology*.

Ashley Membere is doctoral student in the Industrial-Organizational Psychology program at George Mason University. She received her Bachelor of Arts in Psychology from Rice University in 2013. Her research interests include diversity, inclusion, discrimination, and well-being in the workplace. Her main focus is on how individuals' multiple identities can influence their experiences of discrimination in the workplace and how interventions can be tailored to account for these multiple identities.

Arjun Mitra is doctoral student of Business Administration at the University of Illinois at Chicago with a concentration in Organizational Behavior/Human Resources Management. He holds a Master of Business Administration degree from Xavier University, India in Human Resources Management. He conducts research related to strategic human resources management and workforce diversity, with a specific emphasis on use of social media in HRM, executive compensation, gender diversity, and LGBT diversity.

Eddy S. Ng is Professor of Organizational Behaviour and the F.C. Manning Chair in Economics and Business at Dalhousie University. His research focuses on managing diversity for organizational competitiveness, the changing nature of work and organizations, and managing the millennial workforce. He is an Associate Editor for *Personnel Review* and a Book Review Editor for *Equality, Diversity and Inclusion*. He also sits on the Editorial Boards of *Management Communication Quarterly, Public Personnel Management, Employee Relations*, and *Cross-cultural and Strategic Management*. Eddy co-edited the *Handbook of International and Comparative Perspectives on Diversity Management* (2016), *International Handbook on Diversity Management at Work: Country Perspectives on*

Diversity and Equal Treatment (2014) and *Managing the New Workforce: International Perspectives on the Millennial Generation* (2012).

Emma Parry is Professor of Human Resource Management (HRM) at Cranfield School of Management, UK. Emma received her doctorate in Applied Psychology from Cranfield University in 2001. Her primary research interests are related to the impact of the changing context on managing people, in particular the influence of age demographics, technological advancement, and national context on HRM and careers. She has published widely on these topics in journals such as *Journal of International Business Studies* and *Human Resource Management Journal*. Emma is the Senior Associate Editor of the *International Journal of Human Resource Management* and is an Academic Fellow of the Chartered Institute for Personnel and Development (CIPD).

Reginald L. Tucker is doctoral student of Management at the University of Alabama with a concentration in Entrepreneurship. He received a B.A. in English, M.B.A., and J.D. from Louisiana State University. He conducts research related to psychology and entrepreneurship, with a specific emphasis on the dark triad and psychological disorders.

Siting Wang is doctoral student of Department of Managerial Studies at the University of Illinois at Chicago with a concentration in Organizational Behavior and Human Resource Management. She received a B.A. from the University of Nebraska at Lincoln in Psychology with a minor in Business. Her current research includes leadership (e.g., leader-member exchange), work group effectiveness, and the influence of emotions in the workplace.